Ralph G. Martin

CISSY

SIMON AND SCHUSTER · NEW YORK

DESIGNED BY EVE METZ
MANUFACTURED IN THE UNITED STATES OF AMERICA

1 2 3 4 5 6 7 8 9 10

LIBRARY OF CONGRESS CATALOGING IN PUBLICATION DATA

MARTIN, RALPH G. DATE.
CISSY.
BIBLIOGRAPHY: P.
INCLUDES INDEX.
1. PATTERSON, ELEANOR MEDILL, 1881–1948.
2. UNITED STATES—BIOGRAPHY.   I. TITLE.
CT275.P42M37   070'.92'4 [B]   79–10752

ISBN 0-671-22557-X

For Murray Krim, whose friendship dates back to third grade.

And for some dear friends who have left the scene but have not left my life: George Baker, Pat Coffey, Bill Estoff, Robert Hind, Milt Lehman, Mack Morriss, Nellie Myers, Bob Neville, Irma Remsen, Mark Senigo, Harry Sions, Harry Sloan, Colonel Egbert White, and Don Wolfe.

Prologue

She had just returned from Chicago where she had buried her mother's ashes in the family plot, and now she had come to spend the night in her mother's bed in her mother's house in Maryland.

Dower House sits alone on a high, wooded point, past a lake, at the end of a long, winding road where only the birds and wind break the silence. The house has a history of ghosts, including that of a young, lovely woman walking during the witching hours, wailing and wringing her hands for the lost lover who had gone to sea a hundred years before.

That night, there was a new ghost.

The woman who had buried the ashes of her mother—for whom she had shed no tears—slept the deep sleep of emotional exhaustion.

"Suddenly, I woke up," she said, "and I heard the voice of my mother saying, 'Leave my things alone and get out of here!'

"I sat up in her bed and said out loud, as cooly as I could, 'I'm sorry, Mother, but you're gone, and I'm doing the best I can. This is my card game now.' And I went right back to sleep."

It would be just like Cissy to come back from the grave to tell her daughter what to do.

In a world where most people are gray, Cissy was very black and very white. Her faults could be overwhelming, but her gifts were glorious. What she had more than anything else was courage and a sense of adventure. Put her life between a frame of two phrases, and they would be "Why not?" and "What the hell!"

Alice Roosevelt Longworth, the daughter of a President, who lived her own life with unique flair, said of her friend and enemy, "Cissy's life was so much richer than mine. I said a lot of things, but Cissy *did* them!"

1

To understand Cissy you must understand her childhood, because that is when the pattern is shaped, and the pattern sticks.
—Dr. Alvan Barach, her friend and analyst

"Over all this terrible scene was a sullen roar, much like that one hears when close to Niagara Falls, but mixed with crackling sounds and constant reverberations, loud as thunder, from falling walls and explosions, and I could see the great brick buildings tumbling and masses of flame thrown high in the air. It was an awful sight . . . a whirling square mile of sparks and high rolling volumes of smoke and flame. . . .

"Our faces were black. Our clothes had been on fire scores of times. Our hair and beards were singed. Our faces and hands were scorched and blistered. Even our shoes were burned from stamping on the spots of fire on the hot roof. . . . In some of the rooms, the heat was so great that the glass in the windows was cracked in all directions and the varnish on the furniture smoked. The men ran around knocking over chairs, desks and tables and throwing water on them and applying wet cloths. . . . A pressman told me that they had attempted to go to press but the basement was so hot that the rollers had melted into a mass and nothing could be done with them, that there was so much smoke that men could not live."

The man who wrote that story was the tall, beetle-browed, black-eyed editor of the Chicago *Tribune,* Joseph Medill, working to save his building from the Great Fire of 1871. While his friends were burying their family heirlooms and grand pianos or sitting on chairs in Lake Michigan with only their heads above water, he fought the blaze. A sign on a burned-out house read: "Everything Gone But Wife Children and Energy"—a sentiment with which Medill would have whole-heartedly agreed. The forcefulness of this stubborn red-haired man who became a giant of American journalism was passed on to his stubborn, red-haired granddaughter.

Cissy Patterson had not only her grandfather's intelligence, drive, and temper, but also his shrewd intuitions, hot streak of impulsiveness and impatience, and terse, vigorous writing style, which conveyed his meaning clearly if not always gracefully. Grandfather Medill transformed the Chicago *Tribune* from the sickly newspaper of a Swedenborgian minister into one of the country's most powerful editorial voices—powerful enough to reshape the Republican party and help elect a rural lawyer named Abraham Lincoln to the Presidency. When Medill proposed that Lincoln run for President rather than Vice President, Lincoln protested, "See here . . . you've got me up a peg too high." But Medill was sure his choice was right and helped swing Ohio's crucial vote for Lincoln at the Republican national convention. Lincoln would later write about his "debt of gratitude which I fear I shall never be able to repay." Such was his "peculiar intimacy" with Lincoln that Medill could say, "Get your damn feet off my desk, Abe."

Medill often remarked how he himself was constitutionally barred from becoming President of the United States because he had been born in Canada. He was born near St. John in New Brunswick in 1823, when that area was still considered part of the United States—it was later ceded to Canada. His Scotch-

Irish Presbyterian parents had migrated there in 1819 from Northern Ireland. Medill early ancestors were Huguenots who had fled religious persecution in France in 1685 to go to Scotland. Medille is still a French name.

The Medills moved again in 1832, heading for St. Louis. Detoured by a cholera epidemic, they settled in Massillon, Ohio. Joseph Medill was nine then. He worked on his father's farm and taught himself at home from borrowed books with an occasional teacher "to help me out on the hard places." Medill eventually became a lawyer and teacher, fell in love with one of his pupils, and married her. Her name was Catherine Patrick, and she was a pretty girl with a passion for chicken dinners. She was a great reader and a good talker, but her most extraordinary quality was her graceful manner.

Catherine's father, James Patrick, the son of William and Rachel Patrick, was not pleased with the marriage. He had been schooled in Belfast, where "sons of gentlemen went." James was particularly proud that his uncle was a professor at the University of Dublin. Patrick later became an Indian agent, a judge, a Presbyterian elder, and the publisher of the *Tuscarawas Advocate,* the second newspaper in eastern Ohio. A short, slender man, and a fiery orator, Patrick wore a fur-collared cape, had his oysters in the shell brought over the mountains in saddlebags, and liked to breed fine horses—as well as children. It was said that when he lived in New Philadelphia, Ohio, a remarkable number of children in town looked like him.

Joseph Medill worked for Patrick as compositor, reporter, city editor, managing editor, commercial editor, job printer, solicitor, pressman, advertising man and even the boy who inks the rollers. "The smell of printer's ink once inoculated into the human system, possesses its victim until death," said Medill's hero, Benjamin Franklin.

Medill bought his own newspaper, the Coshocton (Ohio) *Republican,* in 1849, and made it plain that he intended to run it so that people would swear *by* it while they swore *at* it. He soon bought another, in Cleveland, and at the age of thirty-two became part owner of the Chicago *Tribune.*

He declared his credo in 1869 to a convention of editors: "Preserve your independence of all demagogues . . . and never submit to their dictation; write boldly and tell the truth fearlessly; criticize whatever is wrong and denounce whatever is rotten in the administration of local and state affairs, no matter how much it may offend the guilty or wound the would-be leaders of your party. Never willingly deceive the people or trifle with their confidence."

But for all his high principles about newspapers, Medill had mean ones for some people. Here was his solution for vagrancy: "To put a little strychnine or arsenic in the meat and other supplies furnished the tramps," he wrote in the *Tribune* in 1887, "produces death within a comparative short period of time . . . [and is] a warning to other tramps to keep out of the neighborhood, puts the coroner in good humor, and saves one's chickens and other portable property from constant depradation."

Medill felt that the Republican party, which he is often credited with naming, should be run by "native" Americans and that the city's immigrants, largely Democrats, were "a scaly crew." They, in turn, charged him with being "a tool of the haters of foreigners." But Joseph Medill was nobody's tool: his prejudices, like his principles, were his own. "We go our way, at our own time, in our own manner, in company of our own choosing, knowing as we do that vindication will be sure to follow."

Cissy acquired this inner sense of righteousness from him. It was almost regal. When Medill wrote on an editorial memo, "MUST. J.M.," there was no discussion, no argument. Even when told that an article he wanted to run had been previously printed, he roared, "Print it anyway!" Two generations later the tone and words were the same, but the voice was Cissy's. Marshall Field marched in one day in a fury, demanding a reporter be fired for an article that had displeased Field. Field was not only the *Tribune's* biggest advertiser, but he was also the man who had loaned Medill the money to buy full control of the paper in 1874. In Field's presence, Medill called in the reporter and questioned him about the story. Then he told

Field that although he had the right to protest, the newspaper stood behind its reporter. "From that day on," said the reporter, Frank Vanderlip, "I think that for the *Tribune* under Medill, I would have hidden bodies."

Not everyone shared this loyalty. Medill could be as starchy as his boiled shirt, as stiff as his celluloid collar. When Chicago elected him mayor in 1871 on the Union-Fireproof ticket, he not only shut down all the bordellos but also ordered the city's 3,000 saloons closed on Sunday, recommending that people drink "water instead of whiskey." These edicts did not last long, and neither did Mayor Medill. A German-language newspaper called him "Dictator Joseph I." He resigned shortly before his term was to end. Years later, when he was asked to run for the U.S. Senate, he refused, saying, "Politics and office seeking are pretty good things to let alone for a man who has intellect and individuality."

Embittered by his mayoral experience, Medill took his wife and three daughters abroad for a year in 1873. Their youngest daughter, Josephine, died in Paris. The other two, Elinor (eighteen) and Catherine (twenty) were called Nellie and Kate; either could have played the feminine lead in *The Taming of the Shrew*. "Is it my fault that I'm the father of the worst two she-devils in all Chicago?" Medill once asked.

For all his maxims and morals, Medill had raised his daughters to expect all their oysters to have pearls. Each resembled the Edith Wharton character who "had everything she wanted . . . but still felt, at times, there were other things she might want, if she knew about them." Their indulgent father was occupied with his work, and their mother was caught up in Chicago's active social life. The two naturally combative and competitive sisters became arrogant, conceited, and jealous of each other.

"Kate the Curst," as many called her, was the brighter, more vicious, and wittier of the sisters, but both were ambitious and domineering. Their greatest frustration, often expressed, was that they had not been born men. With their father's base of money and power, and with their own drive, they could have cut a broad swath. Their tragedy was that their father had given them everything they wanted except peace of mind and a sense of humor about themselves.

Of the two sisters, Nellie was the beauty. She knew this and spent an inordinate amount of time and money to enhance and maintain her appearance. She bloomed early, a fact she never let her daughter Cissy forget. Nellie paid special regard to the trappings that indicated social status. Carriages had to be custom-made with broadcloth upholstery, cream-fringed silk shades, and a cut-glass vase for flowers. The horses were high-stepping chestnut trotters or Morgan Reds, and the harness, of course, was silver.

"Money is power," the prominent Reverend Russell H. Conwell once told some of Chicago's 200 millionaires. "You ought to be reasonably ambitious to have it. You ought, because you can do more good with it than you could do without it." Nellie believed this and drummed it into Cissy.

Nellie married the tall, square-jawed, and handsome Robert Patterson, a man who shared few of her traits. He was gentle, thoughtful, meditative, philosophic, and scrupulous in his dealings with his fellowmen. A graduate of Williams College, Patterson had deserted the law for the newspaper business. He proved himself on the Chicago *Tribune* as night city editor, drama critic, and literary editor, but by marrying the boss's daughter, he opened his future and destroyed his life.

"If Chicago was the Rome of the Presbyterian Church, then the Second Presbyterian Church was its St. Peter's." Patterson's father, the classical scholar Reverend Robert Wilson Patterson, was the founding minister of the Second Presbyterian Church, and his public voice was as eminent as Medill's. From Londonderry, Ireland, Patterson ancestors had migrated to South Carolina, east Tennessee, and then Chicago.

The wedding in 1878 that united two such important Chicago families was surprisingly small. No more than fifty guests attended the simple ceremony and modest reception. But a reporter did write that "people actually enjoyed themselves."

Nellie regarded her husband as "a hopeless drag on her in Society." He was not much of a "go-getter"; he didn't push himself, as she did. It was not that he was weak. He had principles and could stand up to his father-in-law. He once resigned because Medill overruled him, and it was Medill who backed down. Like Medill, Patterson had strong views: he opposed union labor and government regulation of business, and he preferred to see Republican party power in the hands of native Americans of proper social standing. Like Medill, Patterson was "neutral in nothing" but felt strongly and surely that the *Tribune* should present the news rather than his own views. He even resigned from the Chicago Club because "Everybody I meet there wants to get something into the paper, or keep something out."

His personal tragedy was that he was a reed in his wife's storm. While he could stand up to Medill or his peers or the world, he could not face the fury of his wife. "After all, the money was all mine," she later said. "Always was mine." She could hurt him easily, because he was tenderhearted, affectionate, a "sweet, sensitive man." Nellie drove her husband to drink, then to his club, and finally to a breakdown.

This ill-matched couple had a son, Joseph Medill Patterson, in 1879; a daughter, Elinor Josephine Patterson, was born two years later. She later changed the spelling of her first name to "Eleanor" and also changed her birth date several times. When her friend Rose Crabtree asked her age, she said, "God, Rose, I don't know. I've lied about it so much, I'm not sure anymore." Her birth certificate states that she was born on November 7, 1881, and gives her father's age as thirty-one and her mother's as twenty-six.

In 1881 the Boers were fighting the British in South Africa, Japan established political parties, the French granted freedom of the press, and the British military finally abolished flogging. In the United States, trolley cars had started to replace those pulled by horses, electric lights had appeared in scattered homes, and the telephone system had begun to grow. On the day of Cissy's birth the newspapers reported that the U.S. Cavalry had killed four hostile Apaches in Arizona. Disraeli and Dostoevski died that year, and Picasso was born. Franklin D. Roosevelt would be born a year later. The last federal troops occupying the American South had been withdrawn four years before, and the bitterness of the Civil War was beginning to ebb. The mood of the country was complacent and prosperous until four months before Cissy was born. On July 2, 1881, a disappointed office seeker had shot President James Garfield in the Washington, D.C., railroad station. Garfield died of his wounds on September 19.

Nobody expected much of Garfield's successor, Chester Arthur, a tall, well-rounded, fashionably dressed man with full side-whiskers who liked to sleep late and linger several hours at dinner. Among his first acts was the installation of modern plumbing in the White House. And he held a rummage sale—Mrs. Grant's bird cage and Abraham Lincoln's trousers were among the articles from the White House which were sold. Arthur had been a minor cog in the New York political machine, but as President, he surprised everyone. He instituted a commendable civil service merit system, acquired Pearl Harbor for a naval base, built a new steel Navy, and vetoed a huge political pork-barrel bill.

On the November day Cissy was born, the winds in Chicago were warm; the Indian summer made the day seem "as green as September." But the weather would break sharply and soon, bringing snowdrifts high enough to interrupt railroad traffic. The big local news that fall was the opening of the Fourth Annual Fat-Stock Show. From the city's beginning, cattle had walked on wooden blocks in the stockyards and had drunk pure artesian well water, while citizens moved in mud and drank the filthy water of the lake. This was because "people could not be processed, smoked, barrelled and shipped out at great profit." Every thirty seconds a pig's throat was cut, its carcass scraped, disemboweled, and hung by its heels to cool.

Chicago, at Cissy's birth, was a city of brass and impudence, "the wickedest city on earth . . . the town of fast horses, faster men, falling houses and fallen women." The city's prosperity came from being the country's railroad crossroads with a superb location at the southern tip of Lake Michigan. The Queen City of the Lakes covered fifty square miles of level land, its streets making an immense checkerboard pattern.

"Our city is the biggest thing on the planet," claimed the Reverend Samuel Manning. "We had the biggest fire. We lifted the city five feet out of the mud. We made a river run up hill. . . . And it's the only city on earth every inch of which is covered three inches deep in mortgages." H. L. Mencken later added: "I give you Chicago. It is not London-and-Harvard. It is not Paris-and-buttermilk. It is American in every chitling and sparerib, and it is alive from snout to tail."

Chicagoans liked to think of themselves as more kindly and polite than New Yorkers ("We'll kill you with kindness if you let us"), more broad-minded than Bostonians or Philadelphians. "New York has the money, Boston the brains, but *we* start the big ideas, and carry them out with eastern money." It took centuries to produce an aristocracy in Europe and three generations—the pioneers, the builders, and the inheritors—in the eastern United States. But in Chicago, the three generations were compressed into one, and the founders enjoyed the ripe fruits of success.

The city's spirit had its impact on Cissy. An incident that occurred on the day of her birth would have amused her: a mule shed was built on Michigan Boulevard to the great annoyance of the members of the adjacent Racquet Club.

Chicago's mayor, through much of Cissy's youth, was Carter Harrison. The stout, bearded, black-eyed former Kentucky planter loved to gallop down the Chicago streets on a white horse, his hat at a rakish angle, stopping frequently to listen to the citizens' troubles. Even his enemies grudgingly admitted his honesty. He was reelected five times, mostly by the 78 percent of the city's population who were either foreign-born or children of immigrants. Unlike Medill, he kept the saloons open on Sunday. And his manners were far more polished than those of Long John Wentworth, Medill's predecessor as mayor. (Wentworth was famous for his introduction of the Prince of Wales to a Chicago gathering: "Boys, *this* is the Prince of Wales! He's come to see the city, and I'm going to show him around. Prince, *these* are the boys!")

In 1886 a bomb was set off during a mass meeting in Chicago's Haymarket Square. The police fired in all directions.

Clubs broke skulls. Seven policemen and four others were killed. More than one hundred were injured. The bomb thrower was never identified, but four anarchists were hanged. A delegation of distinguished citizens called on Mayor Harrison and urged him to suppress free speech, stating, "We represent great interests in Chicago. . . ." The Mayor interrupted, saying, "Any poor man owning a simple small cottage as his sole possession has the same interests in Chicago as its richest citizen."

Cissy was only five years old, so she didn't remember the Haymarket Riot and its aftermath, but her cousin Bertie did. He remembered shouting at the widow of one of the executed anarchists who lived nearby. He also remembered seeing her dog in the street and riding over it on his high bicycle, "but fortunately did not kill it."

Cousin Bertie was Robert Rutherford McCormick, the second son of Nellie's sister Kate. Aunt Kate had married Robert S. McCormick in 1876. Robert's Uncle Cyrus had patented the main wheel operating the gears in the reaper and had made millions. The *Tribune* intimated that Cyrus had stolen the reaper idea, fought him bitterly when he unsuccessfully ran for political office, and mocked his suggestion that "he negotiate a cease fire" in the Civil War. McCormick, in turn, called the *Tribune* "a dirty sheet." The wonder was that the McCormicks and Pattersons and Medills were united by marriage.

Aunt Kate's first son, Joseph Medill, was four years older than Cissy, Bertie only a year older. Bertie had almost been named Katrina II, after his sister who had died. Aunt Kate had compromised, called him "Roberta," and dressed him in pink girl's clothes until he was seven.

"Cissy" was her brother Joe's nickname for Eleanor, and it stuck. She never made any effort to discourage its use. Her mother could not consider it "too common," since Cissy was Potter Palmer's pet name for his celebrated wife, and the Palmers were the paragons of Chicago society.

Potter Palmer had coupled his imagination with his millions to drain the marshes along the lake shore and convert this stretch into a Gold Coast of wealthy homes. He had married the beautiful Bertha Honoré, a Kentucky girl half his age who later traced her heritage to Charlemagne. She was intelligent, tenacious, self-disciplined, and independent and had "the gracious bearing of a Marquise of old France." A friend said she had romantic eyes but added that "she was less romantic than anyone I ever knew." Envious contemporaries called her "Big Bertha," because of her majesty and social power, and they said that like Edith Wharton's Mrs. Bly, she "kept on being queenly in her own room, with the door shut." But Bertha was a very down-to-earth monarch indeed. She wrote to her mother from a Belgian castle: "Dear Ma, I thought you might like to hear from me when I'm visiting the Queen."

Her husband built her a Gold Coast palace, liver-colored and rococo, resembling the kind of castle found in goldfish bowls. He gave her diamonds as big as Tokay grapes and a seven-strand dog collar with seven diamonds and 2,068 pearls. He bought her homes in Florida, Newport, and London. He also left her all his millions. When his lawyer reminded him at the signing of his will that these millions would go to Cissy's future husband, Palmer said, "He'll need the money."

Cissy Palmer was Cissy Patterson's model. She was the queen of Chicago society, and the young Cissy could think of no higher ambition. When the elder Cissy patted the head of the younger Cissy and spoke some affectionate words to her, it became a cherished memory.

Cissy was reaching out for a model because her mother had only minimal interest in her. Fashionable mothers usually slept in the morning while their children were in the park, ate lunch while their children studied, and when children were free, mothers were making social calls. Her mother's world was a world of calling cards where North Side ladies were "at home" on Monday, South Side ladies on Tuesday, and the right-hand corners of calling cards were turned down to indicate a personal call. The usual calling hours were from two to five in the afternoon, and "The Chicago Society Directory and Ladies' Visiting and Shopping Guide" noted, "In the immediate neighborhood, first calls among social equals are due from the oldest resident." One of the ladies proudly noted in her journal: "Tuesday I had nearly forty calls!"

Piano duets before dinner, a day with the dressmakers and milliners, a lunch party with whist afterward, a Shakespeare class, a lecture on Love and Theology, afternoon tea with English biscuits served on Royal Worcester—this was Nellie Patterson's world. She and her husband usually dined after the children were in bed. Two weeks might go by without their seeing the children.

Cissy grew up in a house that held little love. Her parents' marriage had degenerated very quickly into the thinnest, coldest politeness. For almost forty years, her mother and father called each other "Mr. Patterson" and "Mrs. Patterson." Her father was warm and affectionate by nature, and he loved Cissy. Cissy made plain her preference for him, cuddling in his lap whenever she could. This was one of the few weapons Cissy had to hurt her mother. Nellie's bitter tongue was too much of a whip for her husband, and Cissy's father grew increasingly estranged from his family. His newspaper was his final refuge: it became his home, his spouse, and his family.

Even as a little girl, Cissy was "already fierce." Walking near St. James Episcopal Church on a warm Sunday afternoon, wearing her white straw hat with the blue ribbon, the ten-year-old was suddenly inspired to climb to the top of the church steeple. The janitor brought her down, and her mother boxed her ears.

Still defiant, she set up a lemonade stand in front of her home. She sold lemonade she had made herself; she poured from a large white pitcher, fishing out flies with her finger. Arriving in her victoria, her mother again boxed her ears, complaining, "I don't know why you want to make a mick out of yourself when I try so hard to make you into a lady."

Cissy took lessons in diction, but she countered these with the hours she passed with the Irish servant girls in the kitchen. In the quiet, palatial house, she loved the coziness of the kitchen, with its warmth, laughter, giggles, and cookies.

"I'll tell you what I'll do," proposed her mother. "I'll give you a cent every time you say 'cawn't' and 'shawn't,' and fine you a cent every time you say 'cayn't' and 'shayn't.' "

Cissy saucily answered, "You cayn't remember half the time yourself."

Dancing lessons were also mandatory. Cissy spent every Wednesday afternoon with the pallid, strict teachers at the school run by the white-haired Eugene Bournique. The boys in their high collars and patent pumps and the girls in their starched dresses and satin bows moved together in a one-step or a two-step or a polka around the floor, while some mothers watched critically from a platform at the end of the room. Cissy learned to stand up very straight. "You would, too," she observed, "if your mother made you walk with a book on your head."

Her mother was away during the day more and more often, and Cissy found herself more frequently on her own. There were the many watchful servants, but Cissy, not yet in her teens, was a girl with mercurial quickness. Cissy and her friends at first played in the yards and the streets "and sometimes we had our own gang warfare in the back alleys."

The older she got, the farther away she ventured. The Gold Coast architecture was a mixture of "picturesque Gothic cottages" with bizarre Oriental pagodas scattered among Italian villas. At Emma Schmidt's Emporium, the clerks paid special attention to her; she might get a piece of real maple sugar at Gunther's candy store on State Street, or go up to the second floor and inspect all the ancient armor. The Palmer House barber shop had real silver dollars imbedded in the floor.

Cissy's contact with the "common people"—as her mother put it—was the nickel ride she took on the Clark Street trolley car to the end of the line. The new car had a coal stove in the center, unlike the Rush Street horse-drawn cars, which still had straw on the floor for warmth. Clark Street's skid row fascinated Cissy. For her its "low, disorderly frame buildings [were] redolent of something forbidden and secret; of something hideous and alluring, something which hoarsely whispered, even to the clean little ears of nice little girls, of lawlessness and vice." It was an area of saloons, pawnshops, pool halls, dirty pavements, and cigar stores with wooden Indians. Her favorite shop for chocolate ice-cream sodas had smeared windows and greasy floors. "She gazed at her reflection in the big, fly-specked mirror and admired the gestures of her slender little hand as it manipulated the long spoon. She crooked her little finger. [Her mother] always said it was common to curl her little finger. But [she] knew lots of ladies who did just the same."

Outside, she once saw a drunken woman "screaming, or rather howling at the top of her voice, hatless, hair hanging, the waist of her dress unbuttoned down the front." She saw a dead dog "horribly still and forlorn, left in some back alley." And there was a poster advertising a dime museum, showing a mermaid, naked to the waist. She heard the city's slang: "Sock 'em in the snoot," "Twenty-three skidoo," "Baloney," and "Freeze your teeth and give your tongue a sleigh-ride."

The wandering Cissy loved the unpredictability of Chicago's weather, the east wind making it clear and raw, the west wind sharp and dry, and the wild northeasters whipping the waves of Lake Michigan and sending plumes of spray over her.

Her house was full of private places—corners of attics, enormous closets, secret spaces under oversized tables—but she never found pleasure there. Cissy's great refuge was Grandfather Medill. He was her grown-up confidant, her substitute father. He listened to her and loved her, and his love was her anchor. He saw her extraordinary qualities, even in her early years. It was not simply that she was his only granddaughter, or that little boys do not sit still on a grandfather's lap; it was more that he saw in her so many of the traits that were his own but that his daughters did not have. His daughters had his energy, but they were noisy and superficial. This granddaughter also had his force, but she was quiet and deep. And when he talked to her about history and animals and newspapers, he could feel how hard she was listening, how much she was absorbing. In her large brown eyes, he saw her sensitivity, warmth, and potential—and he would write to her about these qualities when she was away at school. He felt she was brighter than her brother and his other grandsons, and he knew she needed his love and understanding more than anyone else in the family. He gave it to her fully and without reservation.

Grandfather Medill offered Cissy something even more—the fun of a farm in Wheaton just west of Chicago where she could ride horses and walk in the woods and the silent meadow. "My hens, my pup, and my pony leave me hardly no time to go to bed," she wrote. Her grandfather indulged her with perfect freedom and peace. Cissy's paternal grandfather, the Reverend Patterson, had founded Lake Forest as a Presbyterian refuge—just as nearby Evanston was a Methodist haven. Lake Forest was a beautifully wooded region of high bluffs intersected by ravines and the windings of four rivers. The village itself had no streetlights or paved roads or fences, and cows often wandered across the lawns. Most people came here to escape from "the loose living" of Chicago. An inebriated cyclist here might find himself confronted by a man jumping from behind a bush, yelling, "Sign a pledge and be a blessing!" The church was the village social and moral focus. Cissy also loved it here.

The overwhelming love of Cissy's young life was her brother, Joe. She adored him. He was two years older, daring and intelligent, and she trusted him absolutely. There is something tender about two children, close in age, a protective brother and a younger sister, living in a house where there is no love, two children growing into each other because their mutual need for affection is overwhelming.

Joe was not as reticent as Cissy. She had had little of her brother's early freedom, and she had been hurt more deeply by her uncaring mother. Her emotions were buried deep within her. Very few of her friends would ever see her cry. Even as a child, she was a stoic, and her defenses were almost always up. Joe listened to her, understood her, loved her, and defended her. He had his own friends, though, and they did not like adoring little sisters trailing after them. Boys have more escapes from loneliness. They can roam and run and hide and feel the freedom of climbing on top of a pile of wood in a lumberyard, or they can simply stretch out and stare at the sky. But a small girl has fewer options in a city.

Besides Joe, Cissy had her cousins Medill and Bertie. Bertie admired Cissy but was somewhat afraid of her. She called him "Bertie the Swipe" and made him nervous enough to stammer. But Medill was a slim, brilliant, turbulent boy, as willful as Cissy. They were alike in many ways—their high spirits, their sense of adventure, their love of animals. For as long as she could remember, she had a crush on him.

Nellie and Kate took their broods to Newport for the summers of 1891 and 1892. The two sisters were bored with their husbands, bored with their lives, and searching for excitement; they were determined to storm this posh society resort on the Rhode Island shore.

Newport was not an easy place to storm. Newport status was set with an ingrained snobbery. The massive seventy-room marble mansions on Bellevue Avenue's oceanfront, complete with forty-foot ceilings and twelve chimneys and ballrooms and stables, were called "cottages." In one cottage each room had been done by a different decorator. Luncheons were served on gold plate; baby lobsters bathed in butter; a footman behind each chair; centerpieces of orchids. Everything was a monument to money—too many Persian rugs, too many priceless tapestries. When the Vanderbilts had a dinner dance, it might feature a series of quadrilles where guests in different costumes danced as Russians, gypsies, Persians, or The Seasons.

Nellie and Kate rented large houses and managed to join some clubs and to be invited to some parties. But they always felt like midwestern primitives running the gauntlet of snubs and sneers. Despite their open checkbooks, they never quite made the inner circle.

In their frenzied drive for social position, Nellie and Kate had little time for their children. For ten-year-old Cissy and for her brother and cousins, Newport meant pleasure and freedom with swimming and sailing off the long stretch of Bailey's Beach. Cissy was exhilarated when her handsome cousin Medill called her "*la princesse*."

Frustrated by their Newport failure, in 1893 Nellie and Kate took their children to vacation in Thomasville, Georgia, with their family friends, the Hannas.

Marcus Alonzo Hanna, whom Cissy called "Uncle Mark," was

often cartooned as an obese moneybag or as a coarse, insolent-looking man lugging a hurdy-gurdy with William McKinley as the dejected monkey hitched to his master's wrist. It was true that Hanna was a millionaire, and it was also true that Hanna, a power in the Republican party, was determined to make McKinley President of the United States. However, behind his ever-present cigar was an encyclopedic mind, a dynamic force, as well as wit, directness, and intelligence. Cissy sat through long discussions at the Hanna supper table where McKinley asked most of the questions and Hanna had most of the answers.

Cissy was twelve, a gangly girl with a blotchy face. She enviously watched the sixteen-year-old Medill being entranced by thirteen-year-old Ruth Hanna, "a peach of a girl." Ruth wore wide bloomers when she galloped through the pine woods, her thick braid of hair flapping between her shoulders. How it grieved and embarrassed Cissy to be seated at the children's table with Bertie, while Medill and Joe and Ruth ate with the grown-ups.

That was the year of the World's Columbian Exposition in Chicago, which entertained some seventeen million people in the celebration of the 400th anniversary of the discovery of America by Columbus. It was a youngster's paradise: Buffalo Bill's Wild West Show, "untamed savages" from the South Seas living in native huts, a Ferris wheel 264 feet high, moving sidewalks, Russian cossack dancers and Venetian glassblowers (as well as Venetian gondolas), Little Egypt with a "hootchy-kootchy dancer" (who turned out to be a native of Chicago), a telephone line to New York City, and a delicious new dessert called an ice-cream sundae.

Even when its population had passed a million and it had replaced Philadelphia as the nation's second largest city, Chicago was still influenced by the East; everything eastern was admired and copied. Since "all the little girls of the best families in the East have governesses," Cissy's mother decided that Cissy would have one.

In *Fall Flight*, her autobiographical novel, Cissy often presents conversations that surely come from her life. The

27

heroine and her mother quarrel about the need for a governess.

"You are getting terribly slouchy and round-shouldered and sulky all the time. I'm ashamed of you when there's company. It's just one continual fight. And I'm not sure I'll let you walk around the streets alone anymore. . . . All the nice little girls in New York . . . you see them walking around with their governesses."

"I won't have a governess. I want to go to school with the other girls. I don't see why you can't let me alone—I don't want to be different. . . . I just want to be like other girls. I won't have a governess and walk arm in arm and have everyone laugh at me. I won't . . . I won't." And then she fell into wild weeping.

Cissy escaped the governess for a time, but not the cold morning tub. "Every decent well-brought-up child in England takes a bath every single day," her mother insisted. Happily for Cissy, her mother never tested the water, and so it was never too cold.

Nellie was often painfully candid in her comments to her growing daughter: "Your teeth aren't as good as mine, but they're even and white. Now you know your mouth is a little full. Try sucking it in at the corners." Nellie admitted that Cissy had a lovely, low forehead but pointed out that it was "broken out. Nobody likes to look at little girls with bad complexions. People don't want them around." Then she continued callously, "You're very underdeveloped. Why, when I was your age I was almost like I am now. . . . I was so handsome, Mama wouldn't let me walk down Main Street alone, men stared so. My bust was developed like I was twenty-five."

Cissy scrubbed her skin until it was almost translucent. She tried cutting out all sweets but then would gorge on a big bag of coconut creams. "Bitterly she envied the girls . . . earlier matured than she . . . who wore a corset already and shields under their arms and got telegrams and violets during the holidays and whispered secrets apart to each other about their beaux."

Ultimately, the governesses arrived, a scattered string of them, to imprint on Cissy some smattering of education. She learned more from her own reading. The awkward, lonely young Cissy wrote sad and romantic poems based on the sad and romantic novels she read, stories of lives she so much wanted to live. She devoured *Wuthering Heights, Nana, Madame Bovary,* the tales of De Maupassant, *The Three Musketeers, Vanity Fair.* Her mother disapproved of such books, and so Cissy stuffed underwear at the bottom of her door to hide the light when she read. Her adolescent life was drab, and she escaped to the make-believe world of books. She sketched her self-portrait at thirteen—a girl sitting alone in the fog.

Steeped in fantasy, she found it easy to lie to her mother to get what she wanted. When that failed, she tried tantrums. And when those didn't work, she forced herself to get sick; she once threw up all over her mother's favorite coat, a yellow one from Paris.

Joseph Medill had built a ninety-one room mansion in 1892 on Chicago's Gold Coast for his daughter Nellie and her family. Designed by Stanford White, it had foot-thick walls, agate doorknobs, and marble bathrooms, some of which had silver fittings. Its iron-grilled gate was a thing of grandeur, but Cissy saw it as the door of a plush prison. And for all its size, the house was not big enough to house Nellie's growing social aspirations.

Nellie Patterson took Cissy on a trip to England and France for two months in the summer of 1894 in the hope of exposing her to culture. Cissy described that sailing on the liner *Paris* as "a crush of humanity the like of which has never been seen before." During the voyage the three theatrical companies on board fairly howled with joy and had a very merry time, dancing, drinking, and laughing. The romantic Cissy delighted in the easy spirit of theatrical people. But when she reached Europe, she despised being strictly controlled by governesses in confined hotel rooms in London and Paris. Nellie Patterson did not want her social life hampered by a child. When Nellie suggested that Cissy accompany her to Europe again several years later, Cissy pleaded, "Oh, don't take me, Mama—please don't take me. I hate Europe."

Cissy gradually started growing out of her gawkiness by

1895, when she was fourteen. The only compliment she remembered receiving from her mother at that time was: "Your shoulders have a pretty line to them . . . you could stand the dress off your shoulders."

These were the days of gas lamps, hourglass figures, family albums, top hats, and gold-headed canes. A prominent bride's stockings were cataloged for opera, carriage, reception, morning, and evening, and her corset was white satin made to order with a hundred whalebones in it. Men wore celluloid collars. They were not only easy to clean but could also be used to open doors guarded by spring locks. Mrs. Marshall Field gave a party for her two teenage children, converting her mansion into a Japanese garden for five hundred Japanese-costumed guests. The party cost $75,000 at a time when sirloin steaks were fifteen cents a pound and milk cost a penny a quart. Mrs. Field's husband later fell in love with his best friend's wife. (She was astonishingly full-breasted, and a foreign diplomat who had been seated next to her at dinner later remarked that he had found it difficult to maneuver to eat when she faced him.) Cissy heard rumors of an underground tunnel connecting the houses of the two lovers.

Edith Rockefeller McCormick—remotely related by marriage—intrigued Cissy even more. Mrs. McCormick learned to play the violincello, studied psychiatry in Switzerland with Carl Jung, and helped subsidize a writer in Paris named James Joyce. In Chicago, she had a corps of liveried servants in knee breeches, and her daily menus were written in French. When Cissy saw her, she had an ermine wrap of 275 skins spread like a tent about her and rode in a plum-colored Rolls-Royce driven by a chauffeur in a plum-colored uniform. Mrs. McCormick had the intense conviction that she was the reincarnation of the child wife of Tutankhamen.

The daughter of John D. Rockefeller, she had married Harold McCormick, whose hobby was whistling. This changed, however, after he had had the Steinach gland-rejuvenation operation to restore sexual vigor; he then fell in love with a Polish opera singer. Cissy's teenage circles paraphrased Longfellow:

Under the spreading chestnut tree
The village smithy stands;
The smith, a gloomy man is he;
McCormick has his glands.

Cissy knew all these stories because Chicago society was too small for secrets. Cissy and her friends also giggled about the Everleigh Club, "the most celebrated banging shop in the world," run by two Kentucky girls, Aida and Minna. It had solid-gold spittoons and a gilt piano in the Gold Room; a Rose Room and a Chinese Room were among the thirty other boudoirs.

Although Cissy knew all about the people on Prairie Avenue, "The Sunny Street That Held The Gifted Few . . . the very mecca of Mammon," she knew little about the soup kitchens. One of her good friends was the niece of George M. Pullman, the developer of the sleeping car named for him. He had a stone mansion with a private park on Prairie, with a ballroom big enough to hold a theater. At the time of the bloody Pullman Strike in 1894, when thirty strikers died, Eugene Debs was invited to the Presbyterian Church in Lake Forest to present labor's case. He described the "model" industrial town Pullman had built for the workers at his railway car factory. Debs told the congregation that Pullman had cut wages 40 percent without lowering rents. He accused Pullman of overcharging the town's residents—they even had to pay rent for the church. When Pullman took all his deductions from the workers' wages, some were left with only seven cents in cash. If Cissy was not moved by Debs's oratory, her brother was. Joe Patterson later became a campaign manager for Debs when he ran for President on the Socialist party ticket.

The Pattersons were very much interested in their son's direction but were relatively unconcerned about Cissy's future. She was, after all, only a girl. Cissy would be considered educated if she knew some arithmetic, geography, and the structure of the English sentence. Daughters of the upper classes also learned good manners, how to dance, a bit about music and art. "Chicago girls are not mere butterflies of fashion; they have souls and brains," stated *Elite Magazine* at the time. But "souls" meant the qualities of goodness and charity and charm, and "brains" meant the ability to cope with an occasional lecture on an esoteric subject. They were not expected to know anything about politics, money, or current news. Men still took their brandy and cigars together after dinner, while the ladies discussed children, recipes, and clothes.

Girls were not supposed to have ambitions; they were supposed to grow up and get married. If Cissy had a view on any issue, nobody was interested. If Cissy had a secret love of learning, it was quickly dampened. If Cissy had any ambition to go to college, it would have been absolutely discouraged.

A few of her friends had entered convents, some had moved away, but most of them were going to finishing schools. And now, in 1896, it was Cissy's turn.

Miss Hersey's was generally regarded as the best girl's school in Boston. Heloise Hersey had taught English at Smith, lectured on Shakespeare, and edited a book of poems by Robert Browning. She believed in strict social rules and an easy marking system. All of proper Boston knew "Miss Hersey's girls."

Miss Hersey's girls were more ripened than finished. Cissy was fifteen years old. As if by magic, her pimples disappeared, and her figure developed curves. The gawky girl became a lovely young woman, with a camellia-like complexion, large, dark, velvety eyes, and long red hair. Along with this came a gradually growing self-confidence, though sophistication would come only much later.

Her first beau was Blair Fairchild, a Harvard man, almost twenty years old. She had no shame in pursuing him:

My dear Miss Patterson,
   Did you think me rude on Friday? Or will you believe me when I assure you that I wanted very much to come to your tea but I was tutored all that day . . . for an important exam."

But then he added that he was delighted that he would be lunching with her that Sunday. And, in another note:

It will give me the greatest pleasure to avail myself of the opportunity of calling—but when? Shall I be very rude if I say I can't read the word. . . . But I hasten to add, *that* is the only one."

Darkly handsome, Blair Fairchild was right out of her romantic novels. He was a Groton graduate, and she could talk about Groton—her brother had gone there. His dream was to live in Paris and write music, and she had been to Paris, so they could talk about that, too. The United States had a new President, William McKinley, and Cissy could mention, softly and sweetly, that she had had dinner with the President in Thomasville, Georgia, where they had mutual friends.

Bicycles were the new craze, and they could go riding—some citizens even played hockey on bicycles. The lucky ones could corral a car for a short run. The country's first automobile had had a trial run in Kokomo, Indiana, two years before and had traveled at the rate of eight miles an hour. Ultimately, however, it had to be towed out of town by a horse. Chicago held a fifty-three-mile endurance race that year and two automobiles managed to finish, the winning car averaging almost five miles an hour.

When Fairchild departed, there were soon others. The younger boys at Groton were even more available, and Cissy's classmates were most impressed that she had a cousin there, as well as another cousin and a brother at Yale, all of them tall and handsome. Ninety percent of the Reverend Endicott Peabody's students at Groton were in the Social Register, among them one of Bertie's younger schoolmates, Franklin Delano Roosevelt. When Bertie told his father how he had been hazed by older students, his father said, "Tell them they are descendants of Boston tradesmen and you are descended from Virginia gentlemen."

Growing up for the boys meant Joe's trip to New Mexico, where he tried to act like a cowboy; Bertie's exploration of Hudson Bay; and Medill's horseback journey across Haiti.

Growing up for Cissy meant a Groton dance and a Harvard beau and also a feeling of freedom. Her allowance from her indulgent father gave her all the money she needed. Boston had just completed its subway that year, thanks mainly to the Irish immigrants who made up half of its population, and the subway made all of the city an area of adventure for Cissy. For the three years of Hersey's "finishing," Cissy was in a high, exultant mood—despite the school's "inedible" food. During all this, her most faithful correspondent was Grandfather Medill, who had retired from the *Tribune* in 1893.

Grandfather Medill had lost much of his hearing; he used an ear trumpet and dramatically put it aside when he wanted to end an argument. His major disagreements were with his two daughters. In 1895 he had had an offer of $6 million for the *Tribune* and he had wanted to accept it. But Nellie and Kate had come to him with tears of fury. Nellie wanted the paper in the family so her husband could remain editor; Kate wanted it to provide leverage for another diplomatic appointment for her husband. Joseph Medill had wavered and surrendered.

Even after putting Cissy's father in charge, Medill still insisted, however, that Robert Patterson report to him daily on his news decisions. The world had changed, but not Medill. He still had his hot opinions. "The people demand war!" he said during the crisis with Spain over Cuba. "Spain is the yellow dog of nations . . . entitled to the same treatment that all snapping, biting curs receive."

He was still an incessant reader, spoke almost in monologues, smoked a cigar a week, and had kept his gift of remaining calm in a room of panic. Most of all, he maintained contact with his grandchildren, encouraging them, helping them articulate their goals. "I would wager money in matching the four grandchildren against the production of any family," he wrote Cissy proudly. He signed his letter "Doting Grandpa."

She wrote him exuberantly, telling him how much she enjoyed reading and writing, and he complimented her on the "freedom and swing in the sentences." He was impressed that she was the youngest girl at her school, as well as the tallest. "Yankee-land is noted for tall, slim girls, but you do not look very tall, as you carry it off with a light step and an erect figure." He then became more grandfatherly and pulled out his maxims: "I am glad that your school and teachers please you. I look for more rapid progress in your studies and a fine polish on your manners, because, like rosewood and sugar maple, you have a grain that is susceptible of taking on an elegant tone. Those little domestic habits being taught will always be useful to you. Such as promptness; dressing quickly; rising at an early hour; coming to meals on time; learning to do a little sewing. 'A stitch in time saves nine.' There is nothing better than order and punctuality in all things. It is said that is nature's first law."

Cissy graduated from Miss Hersey's in 1899; now a young woman of seventeen. Boston had been good to her, and she hated to leave. She posed for a picture at that time with her grandfather, brother, and cousins Medill and Bertie. Grandfather Medill saw it as a summing up of his posterity. His grandchildren all had the same bright look of eagerness, mixed with a strong stamp of arrogance. It was as if they were all saying to themselves, "We are young and rich and we are Medills."

"Yes, I'm a snob," Cissy's mother once had told her. "And what's more, I intend to be a snob. And what's more, I'd like to know where you'd be today if your mother and father hadn't been snobs, and your grandparents before them."

Perhaps to polish up that snobbism, to make Cissy more of an image of herself, Nellie Patterson sent her for further finishing to Miss Porter's School in Farmington, Connecticut, one of the country's most exclusive girls' schools. Nellie herself had gone there. At the school, uniformed chambermaids served the girls, and the educational emphasis was on social graces. The dining room featured a portrait of the Duchess of Lancaster.

The colonial quaintness of Farmington had none of the excitement of Boston's Beacon Street. There was too much sewing and hymn singing for Cissy. Hot water was turned on only from six to six-fifteen in the mornings. Bicycles were not permitted. Upon arrival, a new student wrote: "Miss Porter is little and old and very nice. . . . I felt as though we were going to a funeral." The rules were strict for the school's hundred girls: "Waving of handkerchiefs, making or returning any signals to young men or boys is an offense THAT WILL

DEMAND DISMISSAL FROM SCHOOL." New Girls were supposed to speak only when spoken to, offer Old Girls their seats, and step off the boardwalk to let them pass.

Cissy appealed to her grandfather. "You speak of being homesick," he answered. "I remember that is what your mother said in her letters from Farmington, a quarter of a century ago. . . . But she got reconciled and liked it better before she left there. So will you."

What Cissy liked best at Miss Porter's were the horses and the beautiful, quiet riding trails. Ruth Hanna was there, too, as an Old Girl, and this eased the transition.

It was in her first year at Farmington that Cissy had the first great shock of her life—the news of her grandfather's death. She had thought of him as her unfailing anchor in time of trouble, the one person on whom she could always depend for love. He had kept her on keel, shared with her his vast learning, planted in her so many seeds: the importance of words, the excitement of a newspaper, a feeling for history. He died on a ranch in San Antonio, Texas, in 1899, and his last words (to Bertie) were "What's the news?"

2

Give crowns and pounds and guineas
But not your heart away . . .
                                    —A. E. Housman

Cissy was nineteen at the turn of the century. She was done with finishing schools. She had left Miss Porter's prematurely after the second year because she had had spells of dizziness and fainting and palpitations. Long before, she had learned to use feigned sickness as a weapon against her mother's anger, and perhaps now she employed it to escape from her stultifying cloister. Apart from manners, morals, hymns, and social graces, she had learned little at finishing school. Her intellectual curiosity had been stimulated in only the most gentle manner. If she thought about anything much then, she thought about romance and adventure. War was adventure. Nothing was more exciting than her brother Joe's taking a year off from Yale to write about the Boxer Rebellion in China for Hearst. The New York *Evening Journal's* new editor, Arthur Brisbane, had given Joe the assignment. Brisbane, who also later helped give Cissy her start in journalism, was much aware that Joe's father was editor of the Chicago *Tribune*. For Joe, it was another way to revolt. He had shown an earlier sign of independence when he escorted his mother to the Chicago opera wearing tan shoes, unpressed trousers, a cap, and a sweater.

Mildly alarmed by the undiagnosed illness that had ended Cissy's career at Miss Porter's, her mother sent her to the Hannas in Thomasville, Georgia, for the summer of 1900. She was accompanied by a nurse, a French mademoiselle, and a cook; her mother stayed in Washington, D.C., to oversee the construction of their new house on Dupont Circle.

Cissy could not have been more delighted, nor her complete cure more miraculous. This was her first experience of full freedom as an adult. The French mademoiselle was supposed to be a chaperon, but she *was* French. As a child, Cissy had told Mrs. Hanna, "Oh, I wish, I wish, I wish you were my real mother." "Uncle Mark" might have seemed forbidding to the world—the President maker "who advertised McKinley as if he were a patent medicine," and now the President's chief advisor, the distributor of federal jobs, and the Republican party leader in the U.S. Senate—but to Cissy, he was warm and wonderful and kindly. His daughter Ruth had become one of Cissy's closest friends. She had been her guide and protector at Miss Porter's, and the two shared a common feeling for Cissy's cousin Medill. If Cissy was jealous of the slightly older Ruth, she kept her feelings hidden. The two young women were both tall and straight, lithe and supple, their hands long and capable, their brown eyes a little too large for their faces, their gazes steady and direct. Cissy was slimmer and more sensual but was self-conscious about her pug nose. Mocking herself in a later novel, Cissy writes of a character: "Her nose turns up so much, I fear she suffers when it rains." And Cissy herself, when a partner became seriously attentive at a dance, laughed and said, "You must love me for my long, Grecian nose."

The Thomasville life was a combination of the highly rustic and the highly social. Summer was a season of parties and dances and fox hunts. Cissy and Ruth both loved the horse and the hunt, the challenge of the high fence, and the reward of the fox tail for being first at the kill. Cissy prepared for dances as if she were anointing herself for a special ritual: the hard scrubbing of every inch of her body, the careful perfuming and powdering, then sitting cross-legged on the floor, like her mother, concentrating intensely on manicuring her toenails. Unlike her mother, however, she refused to submit to the practice of "all proper southern ladies" of drenching her face with sour cream.

Fashionable dress included a wide-brimmed hat that caught the breeze, a high satin collar, a flaring skirt so long that its heavy "brush binding" had to be replaced every few weeks. Almost everything else fitted snugly—tight kid gloves, narrow shoes, and a corset pulled so tight that the waist could be "easily clasped with both hands."

Cissy and Ruth both shared an urge for fun, and neither was demure. The young men who clustered around them considered them provocative, witty, and gay. Cissy already felt grown up. Her long red hair and her whirlwind manner made her a magnet for the young men. Ruth had more than men on her mind. She had caught from her father an incurable infection called politics. Cissy had been exposed to political history by her grandfather, but Ruth presented it to her as something living and now. She had traveled with her father in his special train during the Presidential campaign of 1896, and its frenzy had caught her. She remembered what her father had said of a Democratic candidate hesitating to accept the nomination. "Hesitate? Does a dog hesitate for a marriage license?" And she confided that her father had opposed the nomination of Theodore Roosevelt for the Vice Presidency so strongly that he had said, "Don't you understand that there is just one life between this crazy man and the Presidency?"

Cissy was pulled in by the aura of power, and she listened more intently now when "Uncle Mark" talked at the dinner table. Something he said had impact on her: "Life is a matter of competition. . . . Things don't happen; they are brought about."

That summer she flourished and flowered. "I've never been happy before," she said. "I'll never be happy again."

Her mother was waiting to take over Washington. Nellie Patterson, rich and handsome, was not a stupid woman. She might have been narrow and snobbish, but she was sufficiently intelligent to count Henry James among her friends. She had reached an age when all her frustrations seemed to converge on her. Her life was directed into the thin channel of upper-class social life because she believed she had no other options. Women did not have careers. The overweening dream of her life was to become Washington's preeminent social hostess. As the setting for this conquest, she was building a marble palace of a home designed by none other than Stanford White, who had designed her house in Chicago. Much of her planned rise in Washington society had been contingent on her husband's becoming a United States senator. But he had given up his own dream of a happy home and a happy marriage and had drowned himself in drink. Illinois political leaders had eliminated him from their lists of possible candidates.

Nellie Patterson had to revise her plans. She now looked at Cissy with fresh interest and new hope. Buttressed by a new palazzo, an unlimited checkbook, and new and powerful acquaintances, perhaps she could use her daughter to create her own social immortality. The first step would be an important marriage for Cissy. Nellie could then bask in the glow of that match, enjoying the same kind of satisfaction that Mrs. Potter Palmer had when she married her sister to President Grant's son and her niece to a Russian prince.

Cissy had a candidate of her own in a tall, dark-haired, virile polo player named Freddie McLaughlin. Freddie could be aggressive, arrogant, and hot-tempered. Like Cissy, though, he had the saving graces of wit and the ability to laugh at himself. Back in Chicago, they rode their horses through the countryside down to Lake Michigan. If the horses were hot, they were allowed to lie down in the water and cool off. Cissy's mother was usually waiting for her when she came in at night. Cissy would then go to her room and turn off the light. Soon afterward, she would slip out, and she and Freddie would ride their horses along the beach in the moonlight. They were always quarreling and making up. Cissy would often leave him in a rage, slamming a door behind her. But the storms passed quickly.

The romance worried Nellie Patterson. Freddie was pleasant, but Nellie did not consider him a serious suitor. She could not forget that Freddie's father had delivered coffee to their house in a horse and wagon. She was not impressed that this same man was now the Coffee King of Chicago or that Freddie was a Harvard graduate. Nellie had set her sights higher. She wanted somebody socially startling, and the best was none too good. She could not dissuade Cissy from seeing Freddie, so she concentrated on making them uncomfortable. She broke in on them unexpectedly, and she hid Cissy's riding clothes.

In those Victorian days a kiss was exchanged after a formal engagement—never before. It was acceptable for a couple to dance together—"if he intends to marry her." Typical of the times was a cartoon showing a father and daughter:

> "Are all men bad, Papa?" asked the daughter.
> "No, no, my child; you will always be safe with your grandpa and me."

Cissy's upbringing had been strict. So when Freddie McLaughlin kissed her through her heavy riding veil, she was so shocked that she temporarily broke off their relationship. Cissy told this story to illustrate the morality of the times. It is difficult to believe, however, that she would have been so startled by a kiss. In any event, Cissy was soon caught up in preparations for her coming-out party. Queen Victoria had died and President McKinley had been assassinated—and Theodore Roosevelt was now President of the United States— but surely neither event was of greater moment to Cissy than her debut in the winter of 1901.

What mattered was the delicate pink chiffon Worth gown from Paris and the jewels from Cartier that she wore. On the night of her party she felt like a bird of paradise flying high and free as she glided into the ballroom, her red hair piled on her head. Her freedom was perhaps more symbolic than real because her mother still criticized her escorts, checked her arrivals and departures, rifled through her private papers, and even opened her mail. In defense and defiance, Cissy began to mimic her mother, and Nellie was often driven from Cissy's room, enraged by her daughter's barbed imitation.

Cissy's chance for escape came unexpectedly. Her Aunt Kate had posed as the Chicago *Tribune*'s principal stockholder (which she was not) and reminded President McKinley—shortly before he was killed—that he owed the paper a political debt for its support. She plainly pointed out that her husband would like to be an ambassador. The President appointed him envoy extraordinary and minister plenipotentiary of the United States to the Court of Francis Joseph, emperor of Austria and king of Hungary.

The *Tribune*'s editor, Robert Patterson, was furious. He felt that his paper had been compromised. Aunt Kate was not one to care about Patterson's feelings, nor was she overly concerned about her sister's pique. However, she genuinely liked Cissy, perhaps seeing her as the daughter she had lost. In any event, she invited Cissy to join them in Vienna.

Cissy was entranced by thoughts of court balls, a real emperor, counts, and princes, and handsome officers in splendid uniforms. And she would enjoy the social coup of a court presentation. This last persuaded Nellie to give her consent to the journey.

This voyage to Europe was different from Cissy's earlier crossings. She was no longer a little girl in the way; she felt herself the most shining creature on the dance floor. Her most persistent admirers were two brothers, titled Englishmen, who tried to monopolize her. On their last night at sea, the younger brother stuttered a proposal, "Will you m-m-marry me? I'm awfully fond of you." Her first marriage proposal made her feel "like those merry-hearted, flouncing, round-breasted little girls" whom she had once envied so bitterly.

Vienna was a city of music, lilacs, stately grace, and whipped cream, "an earthly paradise without fig leaves, serpent, or tree of knowledge." Nowhere else were holidays so numerous, work so eagerly neglected, and good living so prized. The favorite word of the Viennese was *Gesellschaft*, which meant a party of any kind. They had them everywhere—in their homes, in the open air, and especially in the cafes. "If I stay here," a visitor wrote, "I shall have to give up wit, liberalism and Havana cigars, none of which are to be found here. But after a few weeks . . . you cease to feel the lack of anything."

"Vienna is the prettiest, gayest, most frivolous place one could imagine," Cissy wrote home.

Aristocrats ruled Austria. Asked by a train passenger if she would object to his smoking a cigar, Princess Metternich answered. "I don't know. Nobody has ever dared to smoke in my presence." Prince Lichtenstein could get into any cab and say, "Take me home," and be sure that the driver would recognize him and know where to go.

While admiring their ease of manner, Cissy felt that the Viennese were more educated than intelligent. She would have agreed with the comment of another visitor: "It was, I thought, a pity that they could express their thoughts in so many different languages when they had so few thoughts to express."

A once-great power, the Austro-Hungarian empire was in the twilight of its existence. Emperor Francis Joseph, who had ruled since 1848, was a rosy-cheeked seventy-two; trim and straight, he was bald but had long snow-white whiskers. Everybody called him "the old gentleman," and everyone knew he slept on a simple, narrow camp bed in a whitewashed room without a carpet. Franz Joseph had had much sorrow in his life. His brother Maximilian, the emperor of Mexico, had been shot and killed there in 1867. His wife Elizabeth, who had gone mad after the death of their only son in 1889, was assassinated in Geneva in 1898. The old Emperor remarked to a friend, "Nothing has been spared me in this world."

This world of lonely kings, mad queens, and doomed princes had a romantic fascination for Cissy. After learning the soft-sounding Viennese patois, Cissy heard many scandalous stories at the *contessen soirées,* the evening parties attended only by young unmarried women. Cissy sensed that the guests' virgin blood was boiling at a fever pitch; they were "pawing the ground like impatient racehorses at the starting line, ready to race off with all their passions and desires, delights and disappointments, as soon as the thin rope was cut." Cissy had her own thin rope to cut. The men, she wrote home, were so handsome, "but *Tiens!* these men are so constrained in female company!"

This constraint was as much a part of their heritage as hand kissing and heel clicking. A young woman of good family could be flirted with, kissed, and courted, but no more. A married woman was fair game, but only after her husband had fathered their first child. Cuckolded husbands were the most enjoyable subject of gossip.

Cissy said the young countesses were like "a herd of sheep." Their social circle was so small and so set that they saw each other constantly—at church, at court, at festivals, at parties. The young women followed careful rules when they were with their young men. The safe subjects of conversation with their beaux were music, theater, literature, and society. The goal was to become kissing close, without being intimate. Every young woman's behavior was closely watched. If a girl danced twice with a man, it was quickly remarked by the older women in the ballroom. Cissy commented that a European woman married because there wasn't anything else for her to do.

The young unmarried women, so proper in their own conduct, delighted in stories of others' improprieties. A stream of gossip came directly to them from the German governesses who taught the children of the several hundred noble families. Cissy soon learned how the pretty young Duchess of Cumberland—fifteen years younger than her ugly husband— often went to dances alone. She was Princess Thyra, the youngest daughter of Denmark's King Christian IX; one of her sisters would be Queen Alexandra of England, and the other sister, Dagmar, married the Czar of Russia and became the mother of Czar Nicholas II. The Archduke Otto had abandoned his wife and drank to excess; he once stopped a funeral in the street so that he could win a bet by jumping his horse over the hearse. As for the eccentric Princess Metternich, she could do anything she wanted—wearing only green or yellow dresses, and painting her mouth brilliant red. People forgave her much because of her wit and ready laugh.

Cissy observed that the Viennese men looked like finely bred greyhounds "with their long, lean bodies and small heads." This sameness of physique was a visible result of frequent intermarriage over many generations. Bred into them, too, was a *noblesse oblige,* a paternalism toward the peasants on their estates, an agreeable unpretentiousness among themselves. They spent much time together riding horses, climbing mountains, and going on long shooting trips. If they lacked ambition, perhaps it was because they had been born at the top of society.

This small aristocratic circle impatiently waited all year for Vienna to come alive. They were like a cast of frozen characters in a Swiss clock waiting for someone to wind the key. The "someone" was the Emperor, and the Season was the six weeks before Easter.

It began with the first Court Ball. Only those aristocrats could attend who had sixteen quarterings, four full generations of noble birth. Foreigners were, of course, exempt from this requirement, and Cissy was invited because she was the niece of the American ambassador.

On the night of the ball, Cissy was swept away by waves of new experiences. The slow-moving line of carriages at the great palace doors; the last quick look in the hall mirror and then the long, high staircase; the slow climb past the line of guards on the stairs; the white and gold ballroom of the palace with its brilliant brocade walls lit by thousands of candles; the men in full dress uniform complete with gold braid and heavy medals; the women's diamonds and diadems and heavy curls and delicate faces; the sudden silence, then three raps on the floor announcing the Emperor's arrival; the nervous remembrance that the guest must reply to him in the language he chose to speak; the procession, the curtsy, the Emperor's quick approving look, his warm smile, a few words of greeting in English. Strauss waltzes enveloped the guests, and the dancers whirled without stop until supper was served. Everyone ate quickly because plates were whisked away when the Emperor was done, and the Emperor ate little.

The heroine of Cissy's autobiographical novel is described as "slim, slim, yielding slim, but not a bone showed anywhere . . . graceful as a fawn . . . she had even dimples in her back, and her dark eyes looked out from a casque of honey-colored hair. She was not pretty, if you looked at her unkindly, for her nose turned up, and her mouth, though small, was coarse at the corners. But every man who watched her standing there in the doorway stirred to her presence."

Countess May Wurmbrand, who met Cissy in Vienna, said that she was "very chic and very bright. I liked her. I liked her very much. Cissy was new to our parties, a fresh face and a fresh figure and the young men all crowded around her, and she loved it. And why not?"

The Countess's mother was Austrian, her father Greek. "Not many young Viennese spoke English very well, but I did because my grandmother was English and my father made me read English newspapers and discuss them in English." Her family had an estate in Moravia, two hours away, where they had an annual party in June, a special train bringing fifty friends from Vienna. They set up giant tents on the lawn, one for dinner and the party, the other for the auction of fifty yearlings sired by their great stallions. The Countess arranged to have Cissy attend one of these parties.

"I asked my father to invite Cissy and I think it was at that party that she met Count Gizycki. The Count was very tall and dark, with a mustache. . . . He was handsome, well-built, very intelligent. He was a very literate man, fluent and widely read in many languages. I always felt he could be anything he wanted to be—even Prime Minister—if he hadn't been so lazy. He liked to sleep late. He liked good food. He was an expert on wine, especially burgundy. He would teach his various women the different tastes of different vintages and years.

"But most of all, he was sexual. I think it was the main interest of his life—the pleasuring of women in a physical way. He loved to gamble, and he did have some men friends, but he was easily bored by them. Women fascinated him and challenged him. And he fascinated women. He was amoral and cynical, but he was a marvelous lover."

Cissy first saw him across the room, "his lean, ivory-pale face, with its long black brows, showing anything but humor, but evidently he was exceedingly amusing to the primitive-minded little group around him . . . the attentive attitude of the four or five young officers appeared somehow deferential. They were laughing as if to please him, as loudly as decorum permitted."

Cissy was wearing a white tulle dress by Worth of Paris. The skirt was frosted with a tracery of iridescent morning glories, and an embroidered spray of these flowers trailed lightly over one shoulder down to the tiny blue and mauve satin girdle. Gizycki was wearing a dark-green uniform coat, smartly cut, and British-made patent leather top boots. She watched him make his way through the crowd: as he passed two young girls, he clicked his heels and bowed. She was afraid to believe he was really coming for her. And when he came close to her, she caught her breath and felt that she gave herself away "by the intense expression of her dark eyes."

And then, suddenly, he was in front of her. He bowed and, without a word, offered his arm. She saw now his intense black eyes, "the long nose and cruel nostrils; the lean jaws sloping down to the narrow chin, and the jet black hair springing with odd vitality from the pale fine skin of the forehead." When she took his arm, "she felt her fingertips turn icy cold," and her heart "began to beat in heavy sickening thuds."

As they danced, she felt his silver shoulder strap against her chin, and she was caught in a storm of emotions. Compared with him, the young men she had met before were all boys, handsome, eager, but still boys. This Count Gizycki seemed so absolutely sure of himself, as if there were nothing he could not do. He held her firmly, and there was no question about who was leading. She could not put him off with the usual small talk. She could not play coy with him as she had learned to do, because he was so forceful, so direct. She had never felt weak before. With her father, she had been in command; even with her mother she had learned how to stand up and fight back. With this man, she felt powerless. She felt he could do what he wanted with her, and this prospect was unexpectedly exciting.

When the dance ended, she felt distressed and bewildered "as if she had been rudely awakened from a delicious dream." She knew the French phrase for what she felt, a *coup de foudre*—a flash of instantaneous and irresistible attraction.

Intensifying her feelings was his notoriety. The young countesses warned her that Gizycki was "one of the most dangerous men in the empire." Pictures of women he had loved were displayed on his piano and throughout his rooms. The countesses said that his sexual prowess was prodigious, that his knowledge of sexual arts was encyclopedic. But despite these qualities, he seemed more interested in the courtship than in the actual physical conquest. The more a woman reacted, the more he was interested. If he wanted a particular woman, he never gave up. He would call on her at all hours, barrage her with flowers, and flatter her by saying, "You will be the first. Call me when you want me, and I will make myself available, no matter who else I am supposed to be with."

On a whim, Gizycki had once made love to a plain unmarried countess. She fell deeply in love, a love he did not return. She knew that she would never have a suitor to match him, and this realization almost drove her mad. On another occasion, he had arranged a rendezvous with the unhappily married grand-daughter of the Emperor. They were to meet in her private railroad car. When he entered and saw the pink sheets of the bed turned down and ready, he turned and left. He spent the night with a young woman he met in the third-class coach. The princess had offended him by being too sure of him.

If these stories were supposed to frighten Cissy, they only titillated her. Cissy watched him at dinner, leaning back as he told a story, "and, as if to exasperate the eager attention of his audience, paused to blow long, slow spirals of cigarette smoke in the air."

He was saying that while American women were extraordinarily charming, American husbands were the most obnoxious in the world. "I do not feel tender to the American husband, because he bores me to tears, running tears." He made a comic puckered face, like a child about to cry. Several girls at the table giggled shyly.

Cissy felt herself laughing but heard herself answer, "I don't think American men are bores."

She saw him put aside his champagne glass and pick up a

cut-glass decanter of burgundy, holding it to his nostrils to inhale the aroma. Behind the pose she felt his magnetism, his charm, his sweeping charm, "the charm of the devil himself."

His friends saw him as "an absolute gentleman, very popular, and respected for his impulsive kindness." Like many of his aristocratic peers, he was lighthearted, bad-tempered, and undirected. He obviously enjoyed life to the hilt, said what he wanted to say, did what he wanted to do.

Thirty-five-year-old Count Josef Gizycki had all the aristocratic quarterings he needed. His family could be traced back to the fifteenth century, and the Gizyckis had long served as judges and officers and counselors to kings. Although his title was Austrian, his family owned vast estates in the eastern part of Poland, then belonging to Russia. His father, however, had dissipated much of his inheritance and had died unexpectedly when Josef was twenty-nine. His mother was the lovely Countess Ludmilla Zamoyska. A member of a prominent Austrian family, she had been a lady-in-waiting to Princess Sophie, mother of the Empress. She was also a superb pianist and had studied under Franz Liszt. She had died shortly after Josef's twenty-first birthday. He had adored her, and the gold cufflinks she had given him for his birthday were his most precious possession. He kept her piano in his apartment, although he himself did not play.

In the Jockey Club Register, Josef gave his address as "Schloss Nowosielica, Post Starokonstantynowbolhynien, Russland." Nowosielica was the village he had inherited in the Ukraine on the Russian-Polish border. But he was seldom there, except to collect rents and hunt; he much preferred his Vienna flat.

Why would such a man want Cissy? It was not simply that she was rich. Vienna was full of wealthy princesses from ancient families who would have been delighted to share his name and bed. Nor was it her beauty and brains. An Austrian husband did not consider intelligence an asset in his wife. And although Cissy had a fine figure and a striking face, there were dozens of young women in Vienna who were more beautiful.

What Gizycki wanted was something he saw when he watched

her dance the spirited mazurka. The other women seemed like shy partridges, peeking, fluttering, with small smiles. This American girl danced without reserve; smiling radiantly, she swayed with a kind of abandon.

At this dance an old aunt had said to him, "Why do you waste your time on these young married women—some of them come to dance before their milk is dry. . . . And your ballet girls with horrible diseases. . . . Why don't you pick out a sweet little wife of your own tonight, and marry and behave yourself for a while?"

The Count's closest friend, Charles Kinsky, had just broken off his fiery affair with Lady Randolph Churchill, the former Jennie Jerome of New York. He had done this because of family pressure to marry and produce an heir. Gizycki understood Kinsky's decision. His also was an ancient heritage that needed an heir. Gizycki was now in his middle years, all the oats sown, with a need for roots. The blood of those shy, giggly countesses had been thinned by too much inbreeding. He knew enough about horses to know that the foal gets its courage from the mare. He wanted this American filly's spirit, not just for himself, but for a son.

In Vienna, balls and parties and dances followed upon each other in dazzling succession, night after night. The carriages and fiacres crowded the cobblestoned streets, and pedestrians had to flatten themselves against the walls as the carriages rolled by. In the next weeks, Cissy and the Count saw each other often, but not alone. A proper young woman in Vienna never went anywhere without a chaperon, certainly never to a restaurant without a female escort, and never alone with a man. Viennese society would countenance a nobleman's affair with a married woman or with a young singer from the Opera. Madame Sacher's intimate hotel with its winding corridors had private dining rooms for such lovers. But unmarried young women of good family were not the proper objects of illicit passions. Had Gizycki breached this unwritten code, Viennese society would have been closed to him.

This cosmopolitan count, who had been everywhere and done everything, now had to confine his courting to balls and parties. He had a way of talking to Cissy as no man before him had ever had. He talked to her in the same way and on the same subjects as he talked to men—and this American filly could not have been more flattered. She would watch him in the ballroom, his long, calm figure, the single enormous black pearl stud, the exaggerated velvet collar, his brows so intense, his face an implacable mask. And how superb he always looked when he walked slowly across a room "with that theatrical touch to his manner . . . all the young women smiling excitedly, peeking out at him through their lashes. He could have had any of them." When he finally looked at her, blood rushed to her cheeks. "I want Cissy to make a great marriage," Nellie Patterson had told her friends, "but I want her to settle down and be respectable. She has a very physical nature."

Aunt Kate was not taken with Cissy's Prince Charming. "This country is rotten with titles," she told Cissy, trying to keep her on keel. "In England, a title amounts to something; only the eldest child gets it. But here every child has the same title as its parents. Besides," she added, "these Continentals make wretched husbands—the worst in the world." She told of all the American brides who had been greatly disappointed in their European husbands. Only a few marriages had turned out well, among them those of Mary Leiter and the Marquis de Curzon and of Julia Grant and Prince Catacuzene of Russia. Aunt Kate reminded Cissy that Count Gizycki had attended Julia Grant's wedding at Newport, Rhode Island. He drank heavily and caused something of an uproar by showering the musicians with ten-dollar bills when they played an Austrian gavotte that he liked.

Cissy was unmoved by her aunt's warnings. She was not immune to the romantic lure of a title, but she had no driving ambition for one. It was the man who had caught her. She knew many international marriages were unhappy, but she agreed with an article in *Elite Magazine* which said, "There are some unfortunate, miserable international marriages, but does anyone for an instant suppose they outnumber the unhappy ones made upon our own soil?"

Out of naive curiosity, on an impulse, Cissy asked Gizycki

about his apartment. He told her it was not a pretentious place, but it was elegant. It was on the first floor, he said, and on some nights he could hear the music from the nearby Prater. When she pressed him for details, he told her he had a sitting room, study, bedroom, and kitchen. He described his antique furniture and paintings and porcelains. He told her he loved flowers and kept his rooms filled with them. Did he have a grand piano, she asked. Why yes, he said, how had she known?

Gizycki told her the address, 11 Am Schuttel Street. He then took a small gold object from his waistcoat pocket, dropped it on the table, and covered it quickly with two fingers. He bent forward toward her, lowering his voice, smiling slightly as if he were amused with himself. "Here is my key," he said. "You may have it whenever you like."

Cissy felt shocked "in a physical sense, as if someone hidden behind her chair had struck her." She opened her mouth but could think of nothing to say, then swiftly turned her head aside. From the corner of her eye, she saw him pick up the key and pocket it again. How often she would relive this scene in her mind. Again and again she would see the key and the gesture of his muscular hands as he placed it on the table and then covered it.

Word came from home that her brother was getting married that November 1902 and she was to be a bridesmaid. After graduating from Yale in 1901, Joe had gone to work for his father on the Chicago *Tribune* for $15 a week, but he still received an annual allowance of $10,000 from his family. Joe had discussed the hypocrisy of this situation with Cissy but had shown no inclination to renounce his family income. His socialist leanings did not influence his personal financial arrangements and certainly played no role in his choice of a wife. He was to marry Alice Higinbotham, the daughter of Marshall Field's partner.

Cissy looked forward to seeing her brother and her cousins Medill and Bertie. Medill had joined the *Tribune* as a police reporter after his graduation from Yale the year before Joe. Like Joe, Medill had gone to the Orient, and then to the Philippines to report on the American troops fighting the rebels among "our little brown brothers." Medill had written Cissy that he and Ruth Hanna planned to marry soon. Bertie was still a senior at Yale. One of his nicknames there was "Rubberfoot," and he had told Cissy he found the classics "stupid" and planned to study law.

It was a strange homecoming for Cissy, as if she had stepped out of a fairy wonderland into a coarse lusterless reality. Vienna was still so much with her, and the Count, too. Being a bridesmaid made her think all the more of him. Her mother received an unflattering description of the Count from Kate, but Nellie was inclined to discount her sister's criticism. She felt that Kate was jealous because Nellie might become the mother of a countess. Cissy's uncle, Robert McCormick, meanwhile had been transferred to St. Petersburg as ambassador to Russia. When Cissy soon asked to return to Europe, Nellie agreed.

Compared with St. Petersburg, Vienna now seemed a charming museum. St. Petersburg was then celebrating its bicentennial as a city of more than 1.5 million. It was one of Europe's most brilliant capitals. The Czar of Russia could have a dance in the ballroom of his Winter Palace for three thousand guests, then seat them all for supper.

Going to a ball, Cissy was swept through the freezing night along the lifeless Neva, "over the snow-covered wooden pavements to the enormous, brilliantly illuminated Winter Palace." Then the impatient line of carriages and sleighs, the dozens of servants in gorgeous red capes with long staffs in their hands, the vast marble stairway lined with the Emperor's guards, who wore gold helmets, adorned with silver imperial eagles, and snug uniforms of red and blue and gold.

Guests arrived at four different entrances—the military, diplomats, civilians, and the Imperial Family. Cissy followed Aunt Kate "like a bewildered filly running close to its dam." There seemed to be miles of polished floor, and hall after hall, before they reached the great rotunda where bearded cossacks "immense in red kaftans and black astrakhan caps stood guarding the entrance to the Grand Ballroom, the wild savage soul of them glittering through their unwinking eyes."

The Grand Master of Ceremonies soon rapped three times with his staff on the floor, the room hushed, and three thousand guests bowed their heads as Czar Nicholas II and Czarina Alexandra entered through the golden doors.

As Cissy joined the procession to meet "the little father," Aunt Kate whispered—it seemed like a shout to Cissy—"Don't forget to curtsy and smile." Then she nudged her, adding impatiently, "And for God's sake, keep off my train."

Cissy curtsied to the very ground, her pink tulle skirts billowing around her. She was astonished how little the "little father" really was: "a man below middle height, the shortness of his legs accentuated by the blue baggy trousers tucked into high boots . . . just an average kind of man—bearded with slavic cheekbones, a short, inadequate nose and full-lidded, kind and faithful eyes." Cissy liked his beard and mustache.

The Czarina was much taller than he, dressed in white and silver, set off by flashing jewels and a glittering tiara. "She had a classic head, the kind of profile you find on cameos or coins, a beautiful face with abundant blonde hair rolled tightly into a simple bun." But her face was expressionless, frozen. "In her eyes there was a sense of great distance from the viewer, a great distance." She had borne four daughters in eight years but still had not had a son and heir for Russia.

"And do you like St. Petersburg?" she asked Cissy and her aunt. "And is this your first visit here?" As they answered nervously, Cissy noticed the desperate trembling of the long tips of the ostrich feathers in the Czarina's fan. "Gee, she's just as scared as we are," Cissy later whispered to Aunt Kate.

Tradition dictated that the officers wear their spurs while dancing. This meant that their partners' long dresses were soon torn and ragged. After dancing with the thick-tongued but agreeable Grand Duke, Cissy had ducked behind a pink marble column to pin up a tear in her skirt when she saw the Czar and his aides coming directly toward her. As described in *Fall Flight,* she stood petrified, "holding the flounces of her pink tulle skirts in two hands, like some scared creature of the wild, breathless, believing if she made neither sound nor movement, she might escape unseen." He simply smiled, half halted as if to speak, then moved on.

It was almost 30 degrees below zero outside, but inside the dining room there were enormous palm trees, each set in a bed of hyacinths and roses. Strawberries were served on rock crystal dishes mounted on stands of beaten gold. Cissy refused them because, as she told her aunt later, "Strawberries sometimes give me hives." At first taste, she found the iced almond-milk "rather sickish" but soon thought it "blandly refreshing."

Cissy's Uncle Robert, the ambassador, felt awkward during this ball, the first formal party he had attended in Russia. He had been mistaken for a butler because he had worn evening clothes rather than a uniform. "Russia is a country," reported the Westminster *Gazette,* "where uniforms seem to be worn by everyone, except those who sell candles or tea." Indeed, the Court Chamberlain diplomatically suggested that the ambassador should have stayed home and said he was ill. McCormick promptly had himself outfitted with a cocked hat, a blue and gold coat covered with gold braid, knee breeches, and a long sword. "Were he to wear it at a Charity Ball in Chicago," commented the Chicago *American,* "it would create a sensation." As an ambassador, however, McCormick was neither a caricature nor a joke. During the anti-Semitic pogroms in Russia, he negotiated the admittance of visiting American Jews into Russia. He also spoke out in praise of a priest who had led a food march at a time when the mass of Russians lived in wretched poverty. Even Princess Catacuzene confided how distressing it was to her to see her servants showing "sunny faces," while "in their own home villages [they] lived in such a sad, unhealthy way."

Mrs. Potter Palmer's niece, now Princess Catacuzene, acted as an older sister to Cissy, telling her which men were the most dashing and the most dangerous. As in Vienna, Cissy enjoyed a great social success. The Princess reported, "Each cavalry guard regiment had a 'carrousel,' like dancing a quadrille on horseback. The officers invited their girls to ride, and often the Czar came to watch. Cissy was always invited. She was very popular and looked particularly lovely on horseback, wearing a red Hunt Club habit and a tricorn hat over one eye. Very smart, very striking, very pretty. She was always surrounded by beaux."

Cissy's social calendar was always packed, her dance card always full. Each escort seemed more handsome than the last. Then, one day, she received a note from Count Gizycki.

"I hope you will write me your plans. How long do you stay still in St. Petersburg? When are you going to Vienna? Going there you should visit Nowosielica which is only 24 hours from Vienna. I just bought twenty first-class mares, but besides the horses I am sure you will enjoy the place, specially nice in spring. . . . I am very sorry to say I probably shan't be able to appear in St. Petersburg now, although I should like to go there very much."

And then, suddenly, one day he arrived. It was during the afternoon, and she met him in the hall, near the grand stairway, in her house.

She felt "terribly concerned over the strange trembling which had laid hold of her arms and knees," and she wondered if he had noticed it. She knew he wanted to take her in his arms and kiss her, "and she craved with queer sudden anguish to be taken. Her heart beat so she was afraid he would feel its pounding and even through the high crest of her excitement, she felt horribly aware of herself, of him." But, instead of kissing her, he simply stroked her hair, which he loved, and passed a finger down her cheek. Aunt Kate called from the top of the stairs, and Gizycki suggested she go to her room before seeing her aunt if she could. "You have got pale," he told her.

Long afterward, years afterward, she remembered everything about him that day. "The way he adjusted his brown tweed trousers at the knees, and his large well-shaped feet encased in a pair of immaculately polished tan shoes and faun-colored spats. His linen was perhaps conspicuous—dark blue with a brown stripe. He wore plain gold cufflinks. But the head of his walking stick was overly large and made of malachite. His brown soft hat and fawn-colored gloves, which he had placed neatly together on a chair, were of sober English pattern." His appearance was naturally so striking, she added, that "the detail of anything he carried or put on became immediately noticeable."

She had heard that a woman in a passing coach had once tossed her earring at him. And she had seen women wrapped in furs peering at him sideways from their open sleighs, like curious kittens, and pretty girls openly staring at him in the street.

Cissy and the Count went everywhere. Suppers started at some palaces at midnight. Dancing seemed never to stop, night after night, often lasting to the morning coffee. Some of the regimental officers in the party went straight to their regimental drill without any sleep at all. St. Petersburg was a late city, restaurants open into the early morning hours. Many of them had *cabinets particuliers,* small private dining rooms with discreetly veiled windows ensuring complete privacy. In the middle of a party, the host might call for troikas, everyone would bundle up under fur rugs, and soon they would be skimming over the ice and smooth snow, everyone dizzy with the cold and the city's wintry beauty. At a dimly lit gypsy cafe there would be steaming native dishes and champagne and exotic fruits. Then the gypsy singers, mostly women, would perform, and the singing and drinking would go on and on until the early hours of morning.

Cissy and Gizy—as she now called him—might be an hour late for a dinner party, but Gizy would never apologize. The hostesses were so delighted to have him at all that they never seemed to care. Cissy reveled in him—how scintillating he was, how magnetic, how witty, and how passionate. He seemed passionate about everything, whether it was horses or a piece of news about which he was well informed, and he seemed so well informed about everything.

He did not talk about his young years, and she did not probe. She knew he had a brother in South America. His description of Nowosielica made it sound like a small kingdom. The mystery of the man made him more intriguing than ever to Cissy. She thought more and more about marriage. Gizy kept her heart in a turmoil, but he had not yet asked her, and she herself did not yet know what she would answer. However, Aunt Kate was a woman not even Gizy could completely charm. She had a hard head and cold eyes, and she saw him simply as a man who wanted to marry her niece's money. Aunt Kate made it plain she planned to tell Gizy that Cissy didn't have a cent of her own, and never would have, and that this surely would discourage him. Kate being Kate, she probably did tell him; Gizy being Gizy, he probably knew it wasn't true. Cissy never thought much about money, because she didn't have to. Money was simply something used to get what she wanted, and if she wanted something, she usually got it.

Gizy had to return to Vienna. There was still no specific understanding between them, and Cissy's social life continued at the same frenetic pace. A Chicago newspaper reported that she "was having the time of her life in St. Petersburg with dances and dinners, wonderful fancy dress balls, suppers and wondrously brilliant court entertainments at the most sumptuous court in the world. . . . She knows the pleasure of the troika and the delights of skating on the beautiful lake of the Imperial Tauride. She has danced with grand personages and has had opportunities of enjoying life at St. Petersburg such as come to few of her countrywomen."

Medill McCormick joked about her success in a telegram to his father: "We even learn that so distinguished a man as the Grand Duke is charmed by Miss P's red hair." Medill also told of his own plans for a June wedding in 1903 to Ruth Hanna. Cissy learned that her good friend Helen Johnson—George Pullman's niece—was being married in May and wanted her to be a bridesmaid, as did Ruth. After Cissy's dramatic rush home by steamship, Pullman had a private train waiting. A Chicago paper commented: "It really isn't good form to get married unless Eleanor is bridesmaid."

Medill's wedding was a national event, starring President Roosevelt and his daughter Alice.

If Cissy had not then been full of Gizy, Medill's marriage might have been painful for her. To her, he always had been a kind of romantic knight errant. The most important knight in her life, her brother Joe, told her excitedly that he had decided to run for the Illinois State Legislature on an anti-boss ticket. The main thing he wanted to do when elected was to push for municipal ownership of the streetcar lines. He was then twenty-four. Cissy enjoyed his excitement but was preoccupied with her own thoughts. Her mind was still full of weddings when a formal letter to her parents arrived from Count Gizycki. He asked them for Cissy's hand in marriage.

3

Those were the butterfly years. . . .
                                    —*Marguerite Cassini*

Mr. and Mrs. Robert Patterson were not happy about the marriage proposal from the foreign aristocrat. As a careful newspaper editor, Patterson had ordered some serious checking. Count Gizycki's heavy drinking and gambling habits did not disturb Patterson as much as the stories of his women. He was said to have had lovers throughout Europe and was known to have fathered several children. There was the documented story of a married woman, whose husband was impotent, who had asked Gizycki to father her child. He agreed but warned her, "You'll never be the same again." And she never was. This affair was the longest of Gizycki's many liaisons. There were also serious questions about the Count's debts. Patterson told Nellie of his researches, and she sent Gizycki a short, sharp note calling his attentions premature and adding, "Is it true that you have dissipated several fortunes?" She wanted to "show these foreigners that some American girls were not available for the mere asking."

But Gizy had set his mind on Cissy and was determined to marry her. He knew women, and he knew he had captured not only Cissy's heart but also her romantic imagination. He quickly wrote her that he could understand her parents' reluctance to let their daughter marry a foreigner who was a stranger to them, but perhaps they could accompany Cissy to Europe. He would show them then that he had no horns. Cissy answered immediately, saying that she would try to persuade them to come to Europe.

Having a count waiting in the wings, wanting to marry her, gave Cissy an increased éclat among her peers. She found herself in a social whirl when she went to Washington.

Washington, D.C., in 1903 tingled with an excitement that Vienna and St. Petersburg could not match. This excitement had its basis in the political hurly-burly peculiar to the American democracy, but it was heightened by a new jettisoning of hidebound social tradition. Most responsible for the fresh spirit was the blustering energy of the aggressive forty-three-year-old President, Theodore Roosevelt. The President's daughter Alice was a hellcat, a saucy young lady and the first unmarried girl in the White House since Nellie Grant. Everything she did, wore, or ate was news. She was seen smoking, and the nation debated whether or not well-bred women should smoke. When she was photographed at the races, she caused a scandal. If she danced twice with any man, she was said to be in love.

"And when I danced the hootchie-kootchie on Grace Vanderbilt's roof in Newport," she said, "you would have thought the world was coming to an end." One account even had her stripped to her chemise and pirouetting on a tabletop.

"I was a very disagreeable young person," Alice reflected later.

Queried about his frenetic daughter, President Roosevelt replied, "My dear fellow, I can either try to run the country or try to control Alice. I cannot possibly do both."

Cissy and Alice and Marguerite Cassini, the daughter of the Russian ambassador, soon became an inseparable trio tagged by the press as the Three Graces. They might have been more aptly called the Three Furies. If there was something "outlandish" to do, they did it. Bobsledding on Connecticut Avenue below Dupont Circle, and "hooking on" to trolleys; planning the entertainment, flowers, menus, and guest list for an elaborate party given in their honor by an admiring host—and then deciding it would be fun not to go to their own party; arranging a dance with sixteen of their prettiest girl friends, half of them dressed as cavalry officers. They were three young ladies animated by a similar spirit.

Maggie Cassini, who was a countess and hostess for her father at his embassy, was the most glamorous and beautiful of the three. Her father, Arthur Paul Nicholas, the Marquis de Capizzuchi-de-Bologna, the Count of Cassini, let her own and drive one of Washington's first automobiles. (Her father's ancestor was a Maltese knight who remained loyal to the Czar after the Russian fleet defended Malta against the French.)

Alice was the prankster of the trio, "with a smile that curls off in mischief." But she was not beautiful: her hair was an indefinite blond, and her gray-blue eyes were oddly shaped. Cissy with her red hair and white skin and "divine figure" was the lively sparkler who kept things going.

Besides the wild times, there were the supposedly quiet ones: the sleighing parties on double sleighs with a coachman in livery, the taffy pulls, the small picnics. Any of the three could look in the mirrors and say, as Maggie Cassini did, "I am too happy. I have everything; it is not possible to be so happy. I really should be sad at times; it would be more becoming." Maggie tried to adopt a sad expression but could not.

Into their delightful lives fate tossed a dazzling apple of discord—Nicholas Longworth, the young congressman from Ohio. The celebrated Washington hostess Mrs. Richard Townsend introduced him to them, saying, "Be careful, he's dangerous."

Nick played all three women as well as he played his violin—and he was a superb violinist. He had a slashing wit that delighted Alice, a smooth dancing style that captivated Maggie, and a charm that enchanted Cissy. If he liked a woman, and he liked many, he would discover her favorite flower and send her dozens of them. The high-spirited Nick was full of limericks and high jinks and impulse. He was an excellent cook whose specialties included terrapin, Welsh rabbit, and scrambled eggs and small sausages. His "Toothsome Terrapin" was properly done "when the claws became so soft as to pinch into a pulp by a moderate pressure between the thumb and the forefinger." Nick would invite Cissy, Maggie, and Alice to an exclusive bachelor's club called the Alibi, seat them, head for the kitchen, and prepare the dinner. His wines were always of the finest vintage and were served at the right temperatures.

All three of them fell in love with him, in varying degrees. Nick, in turn, courted all of them, often at the same time. Even Cissy felt, in the French phrase, *un petit béguin,* a little love.

The Three Graces abandoned their wide-skirted tulle evening dresses, wearing instead pencil-slim velvet gowns. These dresses had small trains that they flicked up with their heels the way Mrs. Patrick Campbell did on the stage. Evalyn Walsh McLean, five years younger, was awed by the casual way in which the three smoked cigarettes and powdered their faces. Together with Nick, the three had a party for the young actress Ethel Barrymore, and they all competed for Nick with an "excessive display of youthful charms" in daring costumes that ranged from Spanish gypsy to Egyptian queen.

Nick found it hard to choose. Cissy was technically out of the running since she was almost engaged. Alice would often laughingly ask Maggie if Nick had proposed yet. The answer was always no. Alice seemed to have the edge. She was, after all, a national celebrity. A cartoon showed her at the races with the crowd watching her instead of the horses. "Alice blue" became a fashionable color, and a popular song was written about her. The Kaiser's brother gave her a diamond bracelet when he visited Washington, and the press began calling her "Princess Alice." But the only title Alice wanted was that of Mrs. Longworth. Then, one day, Alice again asked Maggie if Nick had proposed, and Maggie said yes. Mischievous Maggie did not add that she had refused Nick. There was no sharp break, but it was the end of the era of the Three Graces. Cissy served as the bridge between the other two, but even that bridge soon broke, and the three went separate ways.

Cissy was caught in her own romantic turmoil. Gizy's letters became more ardent, more impatient. Cissy knew her strongest weapon with her mother: Gizy's family and title. Nellie's favorite column in the Chicago *Tribune,* the only one she read regularly, was the society column written by the Marquise de Fountenoy. Titles mattered a great deal to Nellie, and she was not alone in her snobbism. When the heiress Mae Goelet married the Duke of Roxburgh that November, the newspapers reported that thousands of women "pushed, mauled, surged and fought to get into the church; to get close to the carriage of the frightened bride; to carry off souvenirs; to touch the bridal robes." It took a platoon of police with nightsticks to disperse the crowd, "who fought, scratched and screeched like a parcel of wildcats disputing a quarry."

Nellie understood their urge but berated their breeding. She regarded herself as better bred than her Dupont Circle neighbor Mrs. Joseph Leiter, whose husband was a partner with Marshall Field. When Mrs. Leiter's daughter married a marquise, a friend remarked on the shapeliness of Mary Leiter's arm, and Mrs. Leiter responded, "Oh yes, we're having a bust made of it in Paris."

Cissy found someone to share her romance with Russia right on Dupont Circle. The Wadsworths, a highly respected Washington family, had a half-Russian niece of Cissy's age, Nelka Smyrnof, and the two became close friends. She and Cissy talked continually about St. Petersburg, giving it a heightened romantic aura, and making Cissy more nostalgic than ever. Anything Russian or Polish now appealed to her. She spent more time alone with Maggie and often asked her to sing Russian songs. Another former Chicago neighbor corralled Ignace Paderewski for a piano recital. Carried away by the swelling romantic music, Cissy dreamed of her dashing count.

Despite such dreams, Cissy was still naturally flirtatious.

Maggie Cassini felt that this was Cissy's way of compensating for not being truly beautiful. Maggie believed that Cissy deeply envied any glamorous beauty.

Nellie Patterson no longer had many social fantasies about her daughter. The gulf between them had long ago become too wide to cross. Nellie would have liked her daughter to be a younger version of herself going onward and upward into the social world, but now Nellie simply hoped for a marriage that would somehow settle Cissy. It was probably this concern, more than Cissy's open pleading, that finally persuaded Nellie to go to Paris and meet the Count.

Nellie was an easy and natural conquest for Gizy. She was then in her middle forties, her youthful beauty blurred by age and overweight, and he was a highly sophisticated man less than ten years younger. Had there been no Cissy, and had Gizy been simply a gigolo, Nellie would have been an easy catch. Gizy was everything Nellie had ever wanted her own husband to be. He had *savoir faire,* which she admired more than any other quality—the ability to be amusing, entertaining, and provocative—and breeding that was apparent in every gesture. How she would have reveled in such an elegant companion. Gizycki knew all this, and beyond that, he sensed the awful loneliness in her life, the emptiness of her marriage, the need she had for smiles and sympathy, since her tears were never far away. He had dealt with dozens of women in similar circumstances, and he knew how to soothe and entertain Nellie.

Gizycki did not feel that he had embarked on a campaign of deception. He was simply doing what had to be done to win the woman he wanted. In his own eyes, he was a gentleman and an aristocrat of quality. Into this match, he brought his heritage and title. What more could a woman want?

Nellie was warmed by Gizy's charm and allowed the Count to come courting. She continued, however, to keep a sharp eye on the lovers. When she was engaged elsewhere, her cousin Mary acted as Cissy's chaperon, and Mary was not easily sidetracked.

Paris had a Russian patina. The earlier visit of the Czar and Czarina had set off a craze for Russian clothes, music, and dance. Bearded Russians and Frenchmen embraced each other in the street; the Russian Imperial Guard band seemed to be giving concerts everywhere. Chic Parisians wore Cossack boots, Ukranian hats, and Caucasian blouses.

Gizy basked in this sympathetic atmosphere of acceptance. But he continued to be thwarted in his efforts to see Cissy alone. Finally he was able to maneuver an evening for the two of them without chaperons. He had decided that they would dine together in her hotel suite. He chose the menu, saying, "What does a little filly like you know about ordering a dinner?"

"If I could only always look this way," Cissy murmured as she gazed into the mirror. She was wearing a black chiffon gown, its neck cut into a deep V. This would be the magic night when the ugly duckling turned into a swan, when Cissy would complete the capture of her Prince Charming. All that day she had been filled with a fever of apprehension and impatience. She began to feel that perhaps he was after her money. On the other hand, she desperately wanted him to love her or at least to be intensely attracted to her. She wanted to be loved for herself, but the prime thing was to be loved, for whatever reason. With a whole generation of her romantic peers, she believed that a woman must be loved, that all the sufferings, troubles, hardships of the world were as nothing when the heart was full. She wanted to be loved as a woman, and she wanted to be dominated by her lover. She had set her heart on her handsome, virile, powerful count. And if her money helped get him, what did it matter so long as she had him?

Cissy was still unsure of herself; she was, after all, only twenty-two. Gizycki was a man with whom she could not play games, and so she waited for him, frightened and excited.

He had ordered a small dining table featuring a great bunch of violets, moist and delicious-smelling, resting on her napkin. Their two places were set in front of the sofa, where they would sit side by side. The written menu rested on a porcelain holder.

Cissy waited and grew desolate as Gizy failed to appear. After an hour she heard him at the door; she rushed across the room to a chair near the fireplace, pretending to be reading as he entered. "No one with you," he said, after kissing her hand.

"No old chaperon dragons about?" Then he looked her over quietly. "In that dress, you are really prettier than ever."

His eyes were extraordinarily black, his face as pale as the gardenia in his buttonhole, his voice a light staccato monotone, "each syllable on the same note, but with a deadly intentness."

The maître d'hôtel was waiting at the door for Gizycki's coat and his directions. "We will want one, perhaps two, bottles of Steinberg Cabernet 1878. By the way, how many do you have left? And the usual champagne."

The vodka was not waiting, as he had ordered, and he raged at the waiter. She had admired his simple sense of command, and now she was astonished at his anger. She asked him why he was so furious. "I was an officer in the army for fifteen years," he said. "I believe in discipline." She knew he had a pale-faced valet, and she asked him if he beat his valet. Gizy laughed. "Nearly every day," he said, "that's why he adores me." Would he also beat his wife, she wondered, and what would that be like?

He put his arm through hers. "American ladies are always so beastly late," he said softly. "I thought, of course, you would be late in getting dressed, too. I forgot you are only a little girl."

Two waiters appeared, one with a tray of vodka and small glasses, the other with soup plates and tureens. Gizycki drank three or four glasses of vodka in quick succession. Very seldom had he and Cissy been utterly alone before. Almost always, they had been part of a party. Then the conversation had always been gay and skipping. Now there were uncomfortable silences and stares, an undertone of tension. As the dinner progressed, he did most of the talking, describing his estate in the Ukraine. He told her of the rolling countryside, the woods, the lilacs and nightingales in the summer.

"People won't believe what quantities of nightingales we have," he said. His castle was not the largest or the most handsome in the Ukraine, he said, "but it is quite comfortable. You will see it perhaps one day."

She didn't want any wine, but he insisted. "I ordered it especially for you. You've never tasted anything like this. Maybe you will live all your life and never have the chance to taste anything like it again. Why do you disappoint me?" He beckoned the sommelier to fill her glass, and closing her eyes, she swallowed blindly till the glass was half empty.

"You drink as if you were just thirsty," he said, "as if you had no palate, no tongue, no nose, and you have really a charming nose."

She sensed the slightest tinge of disappointment in his voice when he added, "I find it very difficult to talk to little girls, little snowfields like you."

"You use such funny expressions," she said.

"But why should everyone use the same expressions? I use my own expressions in five different languages."

When he filled her glass again, she refused, but he insisted. "Finish this while I drink my brandy. This is Napoleon brandy, but I will not give you any because little girls do not understand brandy. They only make faces and cough and swallow it the wrong way."

She wanted to open a window, but she couldn't move to do it. She felt dizzy. Suddenly, he was kissing her hair and throat with the same deliberate savoring with which he had earlier tasted his wine. He was making love like a gourmet delighting in tidbits.

She tried to resist, crossing her legs, crossing her arms over her breast, trying to get free. But when he kissed her on the mouth, her lips "opened like the petals of a stubborn flower." One corner of her mind warned her ceaselessly like "the pealing of a bell."

She longed to escape, but she made no move, said no word. When she felt his full weight upon her, she made a final effort to get free, but he held her easily, half supporting her as she slipped to the floor. He placed a pillow from the sofa under her head. She was no longer struggling, but she kept her eyes closed tight, her knees pressed together. It was as if she were proving to herself that she was no longer responsible for whatever might happen.

She suddenly felt him relax and raise himself on his elbow to look at her. He stood up abruptly and turned to a mirror while straightening his waistcoat and smoothing the waves in his hair. "My little snowfield," he said softly, coming back to her, "you know you should not wear thin black dresses like that." Then he smiled, bowed, and left, quietly closing the door behind him.

She jumped to her feet, her heart beating wildly; she ran into the hall and called his name plaintively. He stopped to ask her what she wanted, and her voice was almost a whisper, "I don't know." He bowed again and was gone.

She had surrendered, and he had refused. Had he left because she had had too much to drink. Or because she was socially prominent, and the news of such a seduction might get back to Vienna. In Vienna, one did not seduce the young woman one wanted to marry.

If the evening had been calculated to heighten her desire, it had worked wonderfully well. "I thought of him every hour of every day," she later admitted. "And all night too."

Despite their chaperones, Gizy unwrapped Paris for Cissy like a series of surprises. Ice skating at the Palais de Glace belonged to the young girls in the morning, properly married women in the early afternoons. By five, it was crowded with unattached clubmen and their bejeweled, sabled mistresses in long velvet gowns, sitting in sideline boxes watching young lovers skate. Cissy soon recognized them all: the Spanish dancer La Belle Otero, for love of whom five men had committed suicide; of the last one, who had killed himself on her bed, she had said, "The pig! He has soiled my lace sheets!" There was the celebrated Comtesse de Ségur, the onetime Comédie Française star who wore only diamond belts around the smallest waist in Paris; and Diane de Pougy, whose Rumanian prince always sat at her feet in her open victoria while they drove around Paris.

Gizy was full of entertaining stories about all of them. He seemed to know everyone and every place in Paris. When they managed to outwit or bribe their chaperones, Gizy knew the quiet corners and the romantic bistros and the dramatic views. When he took her to a restaurant, the maitre d'hôtel quickly clicked his heels, bowed, and said his name respectfully.

Wherever they went, Gizy always remained in complete control, masterful, absolutely sure of himself. Cissy watched in wonder.

Nellie Patterson was often insensitive about her daughter, but she was not stupid. She knew it was time to send Cissy and her cousin Mary to Baden-Baden while she kept Gizy behind to talk about marriage. Gizy wrote Cissy:

I just saw Mama. As she told me, the marriage in any case ought to be in two months, and not now, in one month. . . . If there was a real reason for doing so, you know very well, my little filly, I should not only wait one month more but even walk to Siberia and back again, if necessary, but I don't see the reason why. . . . It means one has to wait, each in a separate convent, to have time to think and also get [a] better acquaintance set—study the character of the unfortunate bridegroom etc. There is nothing more idiotic, as it is rather easy to be a charming husband from a far distance—and very hard to study the character of a man 7,000 miles away. Now, of course, as Mama is very sensible, after all, and as I explained her all that (several hours), I had the pleasure to leave her in a rather good mood—only one must keep her in that good mood. Then I rather think it necessary to make the acquaintance of your father—who arrives about Monday. And I will on that purpose rush back from Vienna, especially.

I just came to think of a very charming and commonplace phase of the average wedding: it keeps both the unfortunate bride and bridegroom in a kind of show (it is just like putting a strong oak in a small hut) to "try them" and see if they are "made for each other." Of course the victims being bored to death may perhaps—especially if they are fellow-sufferers—be nice to each other, but generally are beastly to their chaperones, as well as to the guardians and visitors of the menagerie (as, in that kind of zoo, visitors are allowed to tease the animals). . . .

Of course, one says, "Isn't it awful they are not a bit in love." Then the bridegroom—having less control than the bride and generally brought directly from the wilderness of the jungle to the narrow menagerie cage—bites now and again the Keepers.

Oh Lord! The visitors roar with horror; how nasty he is, what a vile nature he must have—imagine how beastly he will be afterwards when he is obnoxious even now—we pity the poor bride etc., etc. . . . .

I did not bite anyone yet, and I am not going to do so as I look forward to you, my little filly, and long for the moment to escape together in the open free jungle! But I really dare try. We ought not to make our menagerie time last long—especially as though I am not going to bite my keepers, I am far from willing to learn anything during my captivity. . . .

This letter revealed much about Gizy. He was an imaginative man. He was a cynic. He was a man of wit with a satirical eye. He was a man impatient for life. Gizy was in a hurry for everything. Now that he had finally made up his mind to marry and have a proper home and children and roots, he was impatient for it all to happen. He had picked his wife; he had no intention of losing her. Gizy did not like to lose in anything—whether it was a bet, a card game, a horse race. When he had been a young officer, he had made his reputation by winning a horse race from Berlin to Vienna. Money was important, and like many of his peers, he had borrowed money to spend on pleasure or prestige. It would be so much more pleasant to have a fortune so great that he could exercise his imagination and his taste, with no thought of the cost involved.

Robert Patterson met Gizy and was not impressed. To him, Gizy was a fortune-hunting rake. Patterson had been unhappy in his marriage, but he cared deeply about his daughter. He could neither understand his socialist-leaning son nor reach him. He agreed with the folk wisdom that "a son is a son till he marries a wife; a daughter's a daughter for all of her life." He did not want to see Cissy hurt and destroyed, as he had been by his marriage. Patterson seldom stood up to his wife, but he did this time. He again brought up the unsavory details of Gizy's womanizing and gambling and debts, the difference in age and religion, the need for the two to have more time to consider. Nellie was again swayed. So many of these international marriages had proved disastrous, their scandalous details spread all over the newspapers. Such a match would make her a laughing stock. As she wavered, Nellie was visited by an old Washington friend, who said firmly, "Don't let your daughter marry a foreigner!"

So the Pattersons decided that a short wait was necessary. Cissy and Gizy did not agree, but the keepers of the menagerie had made their decision.

Had Gizy been one of his peers, he would have shrugged, turned, and looked elsewhere for a wife. Had he been negotiating to auction his title to the highest-bidding bride, he would have quickly turned his attentions elsewhere. For a handsome count with his heritage, there were buyers everywhere. Gizy had only to pick and choose. But this was now a contest, a card game with a big stake; he had decided to have Cissy and he would not lose her.

The Pattersons took their highly emotional, reluctant daughter back to America. To appease her, they said they had agreed to an informal engagement but that there were many arrangements to be made and a short delay was essential. Patterson asked Gizy for further documents on his financial status. He considered Gizy "conceited, overbearing, very susceptible, and devoid of our ideals of manhood." But it was Nellie Patterson who had the money to make the marriage move; it was she who would give the couple an allowance from her private fortune— the decision was hers. She hesitated. She was not concerned about the money. The title was good. How much she was concerned about her daughter's happiness is an open question. But her fear of being made foolish by a swindle, the fear of social embarrassment, was sharp. Because of this wariness, she was prepared to let her husband complete his financial investigation of the Count. In the meanwhile, the memory of Gizy's charm stayed with her. Perhaps she imagined herself in her daughter's romantic place.

January, February, and March of 1904 were whirling months for Cissy. She simply assumed her engagement was set and made no secret of it. She bought clothes, made lists, planned parties. She and her mother traveled to Chicago on the new deluxe train, the Twentieth-Century Limited, which was "select and fastidious, modishly togged, gracefully mannered and delightfully companionable." It traveled nearly a mile a minute for a twenty-eight-dollar fare, the dining as sumptuous as Delmonico's for a dollar a meal.

Waiting for her in Chicago was a letter from Gizy:

My dear little filly . . . the letters take such a beastly long time to come from America, and they seem to arrive here seldom. . . .

Notwithstanding, since I got your perfectly charming wire . . . I am in a splendid mood, and probably much nicer to people. . . . I wrote Mama a few words which she might, I'm afraid, think sarcastic, but tell her that she really saved my life—no influenza till now. . . .

I saw my lawyer here about the last document. . . . I promised to prove that there are no mortgages on Nowosielica except the one mentioned. Now there are awful difficulties to get the document officially, as according to the old routine it proves now that there are several "protests" from very old times—for instance, one about a widow anno 1851 who had about $3500, but the person being dead it is nearly impossible to clear it off officially. . . .

He was making arrangements to have a post office built in Nowosielica; Gizy added: "It will be a great comfort to you, and now Mama can wire easily every day." He said he was planning to get the government help to start a railway that would pass through Nowosielica. "But all that is a *great secret*. Don't speak of it especially to Russian people. . . ."

Using his letter as further evidence of his faithful fulfillment of all requests for financial information, Cissy besieged her parents with tears, threats, promises, love. Nellie was becoming convinced that she should allow the marriage. Her Chicago friends had reacted favorably to the title of count. Mrs. Potter Palmer was pleased by the possibility of another Russian-Chicago connection and had given the match her blessing. An embittered Robert Patterson retreated to his drink, his club, and his newspaper, only occasionally to emerge.

"I must confess I am relieved," Gizy wrote Cissy after

receiving Nellie's wire agreeing to the marriage. "It is all very well to play the smart but sensitive flirt, in cold blood, but this time, all the time since I left you, I wasn't a moment happy or content, though I arranged and managed my little affairs perfectly."

Gizy's best man, Count Ivan von Rubido-Zichy, arrived at the Austrian Embassy. Cissy hurried back to Washington to meet him and promptly took him in tow as her escort to dinners and parties. A newspaper columnist wryly noted that Zichy had "had to pay for only one dinner since his arrival."

One of the first dinner parties they attended was a birthday celebration for Alice at the White House, where Zichy also met Maggie Cassini and Nick Longworth. President Theodore Roosevelt was there, and Cissy felt him stare at her. Alice later told her that her father had said, "Watch the way that girl moves. She moves as *no one* has ever moved before." Alice also confided that Nick was going on a government tour of the Philippines with a group of congressmen, and her father was letting her go along. When they returned, perhaps she would also have an announcement.

Two days later, Cissy had her own party. It was a dinner-dance, the first party in the recently completed ballroom at her mother's Dupont Circle home. Cissy let all her friends know that it was her engagement party even though her parents had not yet made a formal announcement.

Cissy's brother Joe had come in from Chicago, and Maggie Cassini asked to be seated next to him at dinner. The suggestion originally had come to Maggie from her father, the Russian ambassador. The Japanese fleet had made a surprise attack on the Russians at Port Arthur, and the Russians had declared war. Most American newspapers, as well as the State Department, seemed to side with the Japanese, and Maggie's father wanted her to inform Joe about the Russian case— Russia was stopping Japan's expansion toward China. But Joe was no longer working for his father on the Chicago *Tribune*, and Maggie's father credited him with more influence than he had.

In fact, Joe had no influence on his father or on the editorial policy of the *Tribune*. After his election as state representative, Joe had helped pass the legislation establishing municipal ownership of streetcar lines, which the *Tribune* had opposed. In a heated fight on the House floor, Joe had thrown an inkwell at the Speaker. He further alienated his father by supporting a Democrat for mayor of Chicago, a man his father opposed. And Joe had alienated his wife by publicly denouncing her father for "paying sweatshop wages" at his department store. Here at his sister's engagement party, Joe relaxed. He long ago had let his sister know how much he opposed any marriage to a foreign title. But he could see how gloriously happy she was, and he had no wish to cloud her evening. Besides, Maggie Cassini entranced him.

"Joe listened with amusement, but he listened," Maggie said. "After dinner, while the others danced under the crystal chandeliers in the ballroom, I and my reporter sat on the red-carpeted marble stairs. Once in a while, he would get up quietly and bring two glasses of iced champagne."

Maggie had taken particular care that night to bring out what she called *beauté du diable*.

"Our artificially built-out bosoms, fortified with deadly weapons in the way of diamond and emerald set pieces, together with our long cast-iron corsets and gown, made of materials so stiff and rich that the boast was 'They could stand alone,' were all calculated to keep the male at a safe and sound distance," she later wrote. Maggie, however, made sure that the distance was not too safe.

Once he brought back his pockets full of favors: silver bracelets, pencils, frames and what-not and dumped them in my lap. Once while he was gone a few minutes, Cissy drifted over, delighted, "He likes you so much, Maggie! I'm so glad. He's a wonderful person."

Toward four in the morning, whether it was the music, all the champagne, me, or all three, I don't know, but he suddenly said, "All right, you win. I agree. Now, will you marry me?"

Naturally, I was astonished, as he was already married, as I pointed out. "I won't be if you wish," he said. I told him I most emphatically did not wish, and when he pressed, I laughed him off. That was the end of that.

Cissy saw herself that night as a combination of Cinderella and Juliet. Everyone was congratulating her, kissing her, hugging her. The future seemed roses and wine.

Robert Patterson had not fully given up his fight against the marriage. More European reports convinced him that Gizy was a bounder out for a fortune. Once more he managed to stir up doubts and questions in his wife's mind. Once more they told Cissy of their concern, and she poured out all her distress in her letters to Gizy. He answered her with soothing and encouraging words:

> Now my little filly, didn't they do everything possible and impossible since we parted in Paris to poison your mind? If at the present moment we will stick together, it proves that we were born to do so—of course, you have been perfect all the time through, and if I failed perhaps lately in some details, you must forgive me, Cissy, because I am going through the worst crisis of my life—and one is only human.
>
> Now goodnight, Cissy darling, I kiss you ever so nice (have not smoked cigars). . . . I feel rotten without you.

Gizy decided that he had waited long enough; if he did not act at once, they might be separated by more than an ocean. He sailed for the United States immediately to force the issue. Cissy now regarded him as an impatient knight come to rescue her and carry her away, and she loved him in this role. The Pattersons did not invite Gizy to stay at their spacious home in Dupont Circle. Instead, they reserved rooms for him in one of the less desirable sections of the New Willard Hotel. It was a slight he did not forget, and his revenge was soon and sweet.

With her lover at hand, Cissy's impatience intensified. She saw the frank envy of her friends as Gizy escorted her to a series of dinners and parties. He was so handsome, so charming, so witty—and in so many languages. Alice Roosevelt thought he was "absolutely delightful"—and he gave her a gold bracelet as a keepsake. He gave Maggie five hundred dollars for her Russian benefit. She was completely captivated and referred to him admiringly as "a fascinating and rascally Pole." Cissy kept close to his side and basked in the waves of approval from all her women friends.

Gizy wasted no time in asserting full command of Cissy. "Rubido-Zichy and myself are coming to fetch you for a ride at three o'clock *sharp*," he wrote in a note. "Be dressed and have your mare, if possible, ready, so that we can start at once." To soften the tone of the note, he added a postscript: "Won't smoke cigars in the morning."

Unable to force a marriage date out of her parents or even a formal announcement of her engagement, Cissy decided to wait no longer.

"Society was startled when Miss Patterson made a round of visits to her friends and announced her engagement to the Count," reported the New York *World*. "Her parents were keenly annoyed, but hurried to put out a formal announcement."

The announcement caused a fresh flurry of articles about the Count and international marriages.

"He himself says that so much misinformation has been circulated concerning him since he landed here that he has in reality been deprived of his name, his faith and his country— although carrying away a charming maiden," one magazine commented. The same article mentioned that "although he never has been a diplomat, he hopes for an assignment as military attaché in the United States, or at an equally agreeable place." Discussing the failure of so many international marriages, a Washington newspaper added, "The Count, by the way, is one of the best representatives of foreign nobility to be found in Russia. He is an intelligent, clean-cut young chap who has large estates of his own."

Other accounts claimed that the Count's estate was so enormous that one needed a passport from him to enter his domain. Still others said his palace grounds were surrounded by high walls, "the most exalted guests thus becoming prisoners when once within." They also remarked that he owned "the finest horses on the Continent."

That same month of March in 1904 three other Chicago girls married foreign titles—a baron, a viscount, and a prince. A writer also wryly remarked that so many Italian nobles were marrying American wives "that you wonder what the poor Italian women are doing for mates." The press gave considerable publicity to an American girl who turned down a handsome Italian prince for a red Mercedes automobile from her father.

"Eleanor Patterson's Chicago friends are saying it is a pity that such a nice girl should have elected to marry a foreigner when there are so many eligible Americans in love with her," a magazine reported. "The Count's love of horses and his fine stable doubtless counted in his favor, for Miss Patterson is a fine equestrienne, and has little use for a man who cannot follow the hounds."

One newspaper reported that Cissy had hurried to New York to buy the jeweled tiara she would wear as a countess. Another announced that she would buy her trousseau in Paris. The truth was that the marriage date was still not set. It was again Cissy who forced the issue. She hinted to family and friends that she and Gizy might decide to elope. Nellie felt elopement was a social disaster. She swiftly set the wedding date for April 14.

Cissy was overjoyed. Gizy still faced hard issues of religion and money. Since he was a Catholic, he wanted a religious ceremony as well as a civil one. He also insisted that their children must be raised as Catholics. The Pattersons reluctantly agreed. The dowry was not only a matter of cash, but a point of principle. It should reflect the Pattersons' worth, as well as his. After all, as Prince Catacuzene had asked Mrs. Potter Palmer, "How much do you pay your cook?"

As the wedding date drew closer, the dowry sum still had not been fixed. Nellie, however, had agreed to pay $10,000 a year to Cissy, and another ten to Gizy. There was neither time nor inclination in the final rush for a formal financial contract, such as the one signed by Charles Robert Spencer, later the duke of Marlborough, when he married Consuelo Vanderbilt less than ten years before. That arrangement specifically listed the sum of $2.5 million plus 50,000 shares of the Beech Creek Railway Company, out of which an annual income was to be paid to the groom for his lifetime.

Gizy later insisted that there had been no dowry; others placed the sum close to $500,000. There was never any hard evidence to support either side. But there were surely some promises made. Gizy's concern about the dowry and financial arrangements bothered Cissy. She confided to Maggie Cassini, "He does not love me. He loves the money I have and the fact that I'm a virgin."

As the time came close, Cissy set aside her doubts. She was going to marry Gizy and she wanted all the festivity and elegance of a large formal wedding. But such an event would require months of planning, and she sensed the need for speed. Her father always had been against the marriage, and so was Joe, but at the critical points her romantic-minded mother had sided with her. Now, however, her mother was increasingly hesitant and unsure and unhappy about the marriage. Nellie's misgivings burst forth in a moment of panic the night before the wedding. Her husband had pulled out all the stops, picturing a disastrous marriage that would profoundly humiliate their daughter. As a newspaper editor, he had fortified himself with the worst case histories. Nellie was frightened. She knocked on her daughter's door, but Cissy wouldn't let her in. So through the closed door, she yelled, "If you don't marry him, I'll give you my pearls." When Cissy later told the story she added ruefully, "I have the pearls anyway. . . ."

Nellie sent Ruth Hanna McCormick to see her late that same night. Ruth, too, had qualms about this marriage. So did Medill. Ruth pointed out the danger of Gizy's well-known record as a womanizer. Cissy said she knew all that, but she didn't care. She loved him, she said; she loved him.

On the eve of the marriage, with all her doubts, Cissy believed Gizy had real feeling for her. She knew his love was not as strong as hers, she knew his needs in this marriage were not her needs; but she hoped his love would grow and his needs would change.

The Pattersons had decided against a wedding in a Catholic church and instead decorated their Dupont Circle home. If there had to be a wedding, Nellie wanted it worthy of the Pattersons. If it couldn't be a big one, it would be absolutely elegant. The ballroom was a bower of flowers. The ten-foot marble mantel at the end of the room was banked with ferns and covered with roses and spring flowers. At one end of the mantel was a mass of white lilacs. At the other end, as if growing there, was a vine surrounded by long-stemmed white roses.

The wedding was at noon. Cissy wore a white dress of Liberty gauze over chiffon and silk, with a tulle veil, and carried white roses. Her father escorted her to the altar with slow, reluctant steps. The wedding was the climax of a week of emotional storms. Cissy's parents and Ruth and Joe and Aunt Kate and some of her friends had used every argument and plea to dissuade her, but she had resisted them. She had long waited for this day. She was twenty-three years old. She was more than ready, more than willing. No one there, though, was as pleased as Gizy. This wedding once again proved that as a man and a lover he could beat any odds, win any prize.

After the ceremony and the reception, Cissy went upstairs to change into her tan, tailor-made traveling costume and large hat. But when she came down, the groom was gone. Someone said Gizy had gone to his hotel to change. Concern changed into consternation when the delay became noticeable, then interminable. Gizy telephoned and asked that his wife meet him at the station.

"The answer that came from Mr. Joseph Medill Patterson, the Count's only brother-in-law, was frank, as becomes Chicago," a society reporter later revealed. Joe was not only angry, but vituperative. The Count, however, refused to return to the house. Maggie Cassini's escort, Count Rubido-Zichy, was sent to talk to him. "It seemed there had been a small misunderstanding," said Maggie. "Cissy's dowry of a million dollars, or whatever it was, had not been deposited. Gizycki was ready to leave—alone. I always felt that Cissy, who was proud, held it against me that I had been a witness to this humiliating page of her life. Of course, from Gizycki's point of view, a bargain was a bargain: his chateau needed repair; in return he was offering an illustrious and ancient name, and an enviable social position. It was a 50–50 affair. But he had to be sure there was no slip."

Gizy's revenge was sweet. This family had humiliated him for too long; he was not good enough for them. They had probed and questioned and delayed; they had piled indignity on indignity. They had not invited him to stay at their home, and his father-in-law would not shake his hand after the ceremony. Gizy had to show these Americans that he was the husband and he was the master and that his wife must do his bidding.

Alice Roosevelt witnessed the day's "depressing climax." Cissy was wet-eyed but determined. Accompanied by her mother, she rode off in a carriage to the railroad station (Maggie had tied a bunch of orange blossoms with white ribbons to the wheel spokes of the carriage). Just before the carriage arrived at the station, Nellie Patterson told her daughter, "Darling, remember, you can always come home."

4

Marriage is not like crossing a green field.
—*Russian proverb*

Married less than twelve hours, Cissy lay alone and distraught in the hotel suite in New York. She had read so much about the emotional storms, the pulsing intensities, and the constant caresses that marked a wedding night. But Gizy had shown none of the impatient desire she had expected. After a late supper, he had left her, saying, "Now go to bed, little filly; perhaps I will see you later."

He came to her, hours later, pulled the sheet off her naked body, looked at her intently, muttered, "Ugh!" Then he took her roughly and silently "without a word or caress . . . like a panther rutting in the dark" until she cried out in fright and pain. During times of drinking and reminiscence in later years, in retelling the story with wry amusement and a touch of bitterness, Cissy always added: "But he was a *man,* every inch of him!"

On its face Gizy's behavior seems incomprehensible. His great need and pride in life had been the constant proving of himself in the pleasuring of women. But he had long smarted from her family's humiliation of him, and he might have been determined to establish his mastery of this woman at the beginning of their marriage. Whatever the reason for the wedding night brutality, his pleasure of their love soon began. They were both highly sexual, and Cissy, very much in love, was an ardent pupil. Their two-month honeymoon in Paris and Vienna became her warmest memory.

"Cissy was so fresh and eager when she got married," remembered Countess May Wurmbrand, "but she was so unsophisticated, so young in the world. What could they talk about after the passion of physical sex had quieted?"

Gizy had warned Cissy that he found it difficult to talk to "little girls, little snowfields like you." They could not talk about her family, because he disliked almost all her relatives. Nor was he interested in her early life, since he felt she had so little to tell. And Gizy would not discuss his parents. His mother was a sacrosanct subject; he worshiped her as a paragon of beauty and virtue. Hers had been an unhappy marriage, and all her love had been given to her son. Some friends thought his grief over her death had been excessive, that much of the warmth within him had died with her. One friend told Cissy, "I don't believe he has cared in his heart for any other woman." Nor would he tell Cissy anything of his father, who had died insane.

Cissy had been badly educated, and she was not well read. Her world had been a social whirl of parties and flirtations; there had been more chatter than conversation, more sensation than thought.

There was one subject on which they could talk—horses. Cissy's knowledge was naive compared with his, but they shared the same appreciation, the same chords of feeling, the same quickening pulse during a hard ride on a fast horse.

Only in bed was their awkwardness in conversation forgotten and forgiven. These times of loving were for Cissy peaks of wonder, explosions of herself that she had never known possible. Only in bed did she feel that she really possessed him.

Years later she came to realize that the possession had been his, not hers.

In a world of givers and takers, Gizy was a taker. Few had ever challenged his conviction that he was an aristocrat of aristocrats, superior in every way. He had adopted the life-style of his class without question. He had never doubted his right to the lifetime service of his inherited tenants. He had accepted the love of women as his due, and he believed that his wife should bend to his wish and whim. Gizy was not unique in his feelings; he was truly a product of his class and his time.

The Count found it stimulating to teach his fresh, inexperienced wife about food and wine and love. But he was restless, and one woman, one experience, could never hold him. He was a moody, unpredictable man often accustomed to acting on his impulses. Many aristocrats were satisfied by their lives of leisure, their formalized routines. Gizy was more intelligent than most; he was easily bored and thrived on drama and change. While he was not a naturally warm human being, he could be extraordinarily charming and amusing. He was not a callous man: friends testified to his gentleness and generosity. Nor was he crude; but he did break rules, and some thought him eccentric. He was a very private person, always in control of himself, and might have made a skilled diplomat.

He always knew what he wanted to say and what he wanted to do, and said it and did it. His certainty of manner, his glowing self-confidence, drew people to him, and at parties he was always surrounded by eager listeners. What he said was usually direct and not always what people wanted to hear. This candor made him interesting though sometimes brutal.

Cissy soon realized how little she knew the man she had married. Six weeks after their wedding, while they were visiting Vienna, Gizy left Cissy after dinner. He did not tell her where he was going, and he did not return until dawn.

"I was frightened," said Cissy. "I locked the door of my room and he beat on it until I let him in. He told me he had been gambling and lost a very serious sum of money, and then he added, 'Of course I can get some money. I can get it, but it is very difficult. I will have to have it tomorrow morning.'"

"I can lend you some money," Cissy told him. She had money from her family to buy wedding presents in Europe.

"I need eleven thousand dollars. Just give it to me for a few days, and save me time."

She gave it to him and never saw it again.

She was happy and proud to be able to help her husband. She wanted so much to be an anchor for him, rather than just a weight. Cissy disliked his gambling, because it took him away from her and she could not share it. She did not then understand that this was one of the few compulsions that her highly controlled husband could not always contain. To him gambling was not simply a pleasant way to pass an evening; it was an expression of the quintessence of his manhood, and it brought him a sharp pleasure, rivaling that of sexual excitement.

Gizy insisted on the privacy of his bedroom. A telegram arrived for him one morning, and Cissy brought it to his room, knocked, and entered without waiting. What she saw frightened her. There was her husband drinking tea and reading a newspaper, wearing a tight black cap over his hair to help set its long wet waves. A weird appliance of wire and gauze held it with rubber bands so that it passed behind his ears to keep the ends of his mustache fixed in place. The two stared at each other in silence, and his look was black. Never again did she enter his room without waiting for an answer to her knock.

Toward the end of their honeymoon, she told him in the quiet of their bed that she wished she had become his mistress rather than his wife. She explained that if she were his mistress, she would be sure that he really loved her. He spoke sharply, telling her that if she didn't grow up, she would become boring. His remark frightened her. "Boring" was the word she most hated to hear from him. But try as she would, she could not refrain from questioning him about the women he had known.

"Now, my little filly, I am afraid you are getting quite tiresome," he told her. "So I better tell you once and for all, I have been loved the whole of my life; and the sooner you make up your mind to it, the better for all concerned."

She never made up her mind to it.

There had been "great agitation" in Gizy's family when they learned about his American bride, said Mme. Marie de Steiger, Gizy's first cousin. "But then Josef brought us a beautiful and charming young cousin, and I liked Cissy very much."

But this charming young cousin was beginning to sense the profound gulf between the world she had known and the one she had chosen. She knew Vienna and had friends there. But no matter how friendly the parties, she still felt she *was* a foreigner—a gulf she had not been aware of in the earlier busy days there. No matter how good her German, and it was passably good, no matter how quickly she picked up the patois, she still felt herself missing nuances and jokes. She felt that even if she lived there for the rest of her life, she would never truly belong. Cissy was young, saucy, deeply in love, and much afraid.

Cissy's trepidation grew as they prepared to leave Vienna for Nowosielica, a tiny village inside the Russian border, about halfway between Warsaw and Odessa. It was one of several hamlets that had belonged to the Gizycki family for more than 200 years. In a succession of battles and wars, they had been overrun and burned and rebuilt many times. Gizy had inherited Nowosielica at his father's death. One of Poland's ancient heroes, Wacław Rzewuski, had lived nearby and was said to have buried treasure there. Rzewuski's great interest in Arabic and Turkish studies had led to his travels in Arab countries, where he befriended the Bedouins. After his return home, he had become active in Polish resistance to Russian domination and was probably killed in battle, while leading his Polish regiment against Russian troops. In Nowosielica, a tablet on the manor house displayed Gizy's family crest, an inscription referring to Rzewuski, telling of the valiant knight "who boldly fought, and brought his country's foes to nought."

Embroidering on Gizy's shadowy disclosures, Cissy looked forward to a sort of King Arthur's court with an ancestral castle and seventy servants. On the train to her new home, Cissy had moments of excitement and exultation. At Nowosielica she would have him utterly to herself; she would really possess him.

It was five o'clock on a summer morning when the train

stopped at Proskurow station. Gizy's servant got off first, staggering under traveling bags and rugs. Cissy's French maid then stepped off with Cissy's dressing case, which she had had stamped with the gold crown of a princess.

She looked like a princess. She wore a pretty black straw tricorn hat on her coiled hair, a wisp of which trailed along her cheek, a smart tweed jacket in the latest Paris fashion, a frilly blouse of expensive lace. As they had traveled, she had felt swallowed up by the vastness of the country. Every moment and every mile had taken her farther from everything she was and everything she knew. Here at the station, she felt important again. A group of peasants had come to greet their master and new mistress. Two bearded old men held their caps reverently in both hands. A pretty blond peasant girl pressed the hem of Cissy's dress to her lips, then fervently embraced the left sleeve of her jacket. "I thought she was going to bite me," said Cissy.

Cissy noticed a half-dozen children hiding behind their mothers, all of them undernourished. The stationmaster arrived on the dirty wooden platform, cap in hand, smiling broadly, bowing twice. Cissy held tightly on to her gloves, smiled, and hoped hard that Gizy would hurry down and take command.

Gizy paused before stepping down, glancing neither to the left nor to the right, "with the implacable self-sufficiency of an Egyptian idol," and lit a cigarette. Cissy knew how he hated to be touched by anyone, how he avoided touching the arms of a chair when he sat down. She suspected that he washed his hands after touching her—a possibility that infuriated her. She watched him then as he buried his left hand in his pocket, thrust his right elbow forward.

As the crowd surged to surround him, Cissy noted how striking he looked in his English tweeds, a head taller than any of them. Among the first to reach him was the pretty blonde, who succeeded in kissing the back of his wrist. Cissy noticed the young boy at her side—why did he seem oddly familiar to her? Her puzzlement was forgotten as they made their way to the waiting wide-wheeled carriage drawn by four gray horses. To mark the occasion, the coachman wore a peacock feather in his cap. He drove with the dignity of a priest performing a rite, but Cissy noticed a still-lit pipe stuck in his boot. She felt as festive as the coachman. She had slept little but was too excited to be tired. The carriage raced by the dark-green forests and the quiet ponds, and everywhere there were birds and flowers in the sparkling air. A relay of horses waited for them on the main road, and it was dusk before Gizy waved his arm and said, "Our village . . ."

All Cissy could see were mud-and-thatched huts leaning against each other for support, unpaved streets filled with mangy dogs, ragged children with animal eyes, women with babies at their breasts, their faces expressionless. On the hillside was a small Russian church with red, white, and blue walls and golden dome and cross. Cissy kept her shock within her.

A mile beyond the village was the estate, and here the peasants were at their picture-book best. The men wore high boots and sleeveless sheepskin jackets, and the women colorful skirts. A large group stood near the estate's white stucco gate, which had been decorated with flowers. As the carriage drew up, they shouted their greetings. Two old men stepped forward, one carrying a loaf of black bread on a wooden plate, the other a dish of coarse brownish-gray salt—the traditional homecoming greeting to newlyweds. Gizy touched his hat with his forefinger in response, and the crowd cheered.

For a moment, Cissy forgot the mud and poverty of the nearby village. This costumed greeting at the gate was closer to what she had expected, and she was moved by it. For these people, she was the mistress, the "little mother." They would depend on her, and she promised herself she would not fail them. It was one thing to have her luggage stamped with a gold crown, but now she felt really regal.

She felt more so when a young couple came out of the crowd, knelt, and bowed in front of them, their foreheads touching the ground. The girl was ribboned in red, wearing poppies; the young man awkward and embarrassed. They asked Gizy's permission to marry, and he granted it, putting some money in the young man's hand. The girl then kissed the hem of Cissy's coat. It was only later that Cissy learned that Gizy had the *droit de seigneur*—the right to spend the first night after the wedding with the new bride, a right he often exercised—according to Cissy. After that, Cissy noticed how many of the children in the village looked like her husband, and she recalled the boy with the blond woman at the station.

As their carriage passed the long brick stables, Gizy remarked that some of his horses had been turned out in the pastures for the summer, and some had been shipped to the track for racing. He added that he would soon show her the horse that he had bought for her.

As they swept past the fragrant lilacs and down the avenue of poplars, Cissy saw her "castle." She had expected moats and drawbridges, turrets and battlements. Instead she saw a wide white building, two stories high, bare and gaunt, the windows without curtains or shutters. The walls of the entrance hall were lined with portraits of Gizy's ancestors—some in white wigs and lace, a few in armor with drooping Mongolian mustaches, all of them hard-eyed as if they had examined her and found her wanting. The drawing room had a large fireplace, massive mahogany tables, two cracked leather chairs, and several horsehair side chairs. The walls and floors were bare. Gizy explained that his father had never properly furnished this house because he spent so little time here.

Cissy suddenly felt very tired and empty. The castle, where was the castle? She had expected so much.

"But you and I, little filly, we will work here together. It will be for you much more amusing." "You and I"—the phrase almost made this bare house a castle. But while Gizy simply wanted Cissy to give her money, energy, and taste to reshaping and revitalizing his house, Cissy saw them working side by side, planning, enjoying, changing, building, laughing, loving, growing into each other. Gizy saw his estate becoming grand in scale and manner; Cissy saw their marriage working this house into a home.

The servants were waiting: instead of a staff of seventy, there was a fat, bald, very old butler, covered with warts, wearing a grease-spotted morning coat and white cotton gloves, and four bowing houseboys.

She suddenly wished that the house were empty and that Gizy would carry her over the threshold and lay her gently on his bed. Then she might not mind the bare, shabby rooms. Walking through the house, she found herself in Gizy's bedroom. Next to his brass double bed was a wide table covered with photographs. They were all of women, all kinds of women, some in court dresses, some in riding costumes, and some in almost nothing—and every photograph bore a fond dedication. There was also a plaster cast of a small, coquettish, slightly plump woman's foot, on which was written a most affectionate message. She would have liked to close her eyes, but they kept searching and staring. She would have liked to wipe her mind clean, but the pictures were burning bright. She would have liked to scream in anger, but it stayed tightly inside. In Gizy's dressing room, near his English hair lotion and his French mouthwash, lay a long, twisted, woman's buttonhook. Next to it was yet another photograph, larger and more elaborately framed, of a pretty, dark, curly-haired young woman holding a small girl in a frilly dress, signed: "Phyllis and baby Phyllis, 1902."

Should she have been shocked? She had known about these women, even about his illegitimate children. On the night before her wedding she had boasted about this knowledge during her conversation with Ruth Hanna McCormick. She had told Ruth that she knew and she didn't care. Gizy himself had told her he had been loved all his life and she must get used to it.

The shock came from finding these women still in the home that was now hers. The first day! She knew the need to control herself. She must not seem immature, unsophisticated. She did not want to be "boring." She felt about to burst with rage and pain, and she ran from his room. Suddenly, there he was, staring at her quizzically. He chose not to notice her agitation, instead pointing out a circular stairway in his room that led to her bedroom directly above. She hurried up the stairs, and the first thing she saw was the lovely view of the trees from her windows.

She looked out at the peaceful beauty of the place until her heart stopped pounding. A steaming copper kettle had been placed on the simple wooden washstand. Just thinking of washing the dirt from herself felt good. A dressing table trimmed with worn but freshly washed white muslin stood next to the washstand, and as she waited for the water to cool, she idly opened its drawer. There she saw a black wire hairpin, which she touched "with the tip of her finger as if it were a noxious live thing." Her heart was pounding again, her eyes again searching nervously. She saw a blotter on the small writing table, held it to the mirror, and read, "Write soon, Phyllis." She sat down on the wide, sagging bed feeling as if she had been hit hard in the stomach.

She felt sick and frightened. Chicago and Washington were a million light-years away. Except for a silly French maid she was alone, utterly alone. She couldn't even speak the language of her servants. She was married to a man whom she loved but whose remoteness she had not pierced even in the intensity of a loving bed, whose soul she had never penetrated beyond his passion, and whose inscrutable mind she sensed she would never truly know.

She wanted to cry hysterically, to smash the pictures in Gizy's rooms, to scream and hammer her fists on him. But if she did, she knew he would mock her, his "little filly," twenty-three years old and still a little girl. This would crush her. She could pretend she had seen nothing, show him an undisturbed face and be a loving, obedient wife ready to accept her husband completely. He would expect that, and he would like that. Or she could run away. He might even let her.

This was the first real crisis of her adulthood. Her mind was in turmoil, her body tingling with tension. She still sat on the bed, breathing hard. Gradually, she quieted. As her mind cooled and cleared, she decided that she would fight for herself, and for him.

She found him downstairs in his easy chair wearing a wine-colored velvet jacket and shiny black pumps, reading an old copy of the London *Times*. The front page was partly covered with the sticky black ink of the Russian censors who had blocked out the bad news of the war with Japan. As she looked at him even now, "his strange beauty affected her painfully . . . caused her a real and sudden anguish she could not herself explain." He was drinking a glass of vodka. He asked her to drink with him because he found it boring to drink alone. He poured her some brandy, and she drank it down in one swallow. As he began to criticize her for gulping such fine brandy, her temper finally triggered her speech.

"I'll never never sleep in that woman's room. Never as long as I live! I will never put my foot inside it again! How could you do this to me? How could you bring me here? Right where she lived all these years! And never change one thing!"

Gizy seemed neither annoyed nor surprised. He lifted his eyebrows but not his voice. "There are quite a lot of other rooms in the house," he said.

He liked her temper. He liked the challenge of taming it. Her spirit was part of the reason he had wanted her. The breaking of a wild filly gave great satisfaction, as long as the horse's will was controlled rather than crushed. He wanted Cissy's spirit exciting him in bed, sparkling for him and his guests at parties, stimulating him when he was bored. They had a long life to live together, and he did not want a dry stick for a wife.

He could understand her sensitivity about the photographs. Perhaps it had been tactless of him to leave them on display. Still, his life had been a life of freedom and he would not give up that freedom for all the money in America. Gizy wanted everything he had had before he married. He wanted to retain his private memories, his old habits, his life-style; Cissy would have to fit into a corner of his life as best she could. In his world, women stayed home and raised children while men pursued their own interests at leisure. Of course, no matter how he enjoyed himself, or with whom he slept, he would always return to her. She was his wife, and this was their home. Her constant need for reassurance about his love irritated him. She must understand that he had loved her enough to pursue her across continents for three years before she married him.

She must understand that he had loved her enough to give her his name, to promise to live with her the rest of his life, to make her the mother of his children.

"Marriage in itself is an entirely different thing in Europe and America," Cissy later observed. "From one point of view their marriages are more successful than ours. They last. Economics and family pride hold them together. They are not negotiated with any romantic view, in the first place, and consequently the husband, and often the wife, too, find all their romance outside of marriage. The only requirement is that the wife be always a lady in public. The word marriage has an entirely different meaning."

Cissy then neither understood this nor wanted to. If she had, perhaps she would have left him. But she was a woman in love and wanted only to possess her husband completely. While she was strong enough to fight him, she was not yet strong enough to win. But fight she would. "We're a naturally buoyant race, resilient in misfortune," she once said. "You can't keep us down long."

The bedroom she chose for herself was over the dining room, a square half-furnished room with French windows that extended almost from the floor to ceiling. The wallpaper was very old, a faded ivy pattern on a soft, white ground. An immense Empire bed with a lumpy, musty mattress stood on the hardwood floor, which shone like a mirror. There were also four mahogany side chairs, a large mahogany table, an oil lamp with a porcelain shade. It was simple, but Cissy liked it. She did not like being without a connecting stairway to Gizy's room. "Perhaps I will come to see you later in your nice room," he would say to her during the day, and she would dismiss her round-eyed French maid early and wait. He preferred the left side of the bed and did not like to find it rumpled. Her mother had warned her that sleeping with her long hair loose would cause its ends to break, but she always left it loose at night because Gizy loved to run his hands through the length of it, admiring its softness and brightness. She had read an article telling new brides to cultivate an air of mystery, to trail about in clinging gowns and undefined perfumes. "Adopt fads; insist on having your rooms filled with gardenias when they are out of season; faint away at the sight of a certain shade of mauve. Then spring surprises. Be sudden, be extraordinary, be unexpected. Do things!"

She laughed at this advice now. Gizy was the one who liked to maintain the mystery, arrange the unexpected, spring all the surprises. How she waited for his unhurried footsteps, "the dragging slap of his slippers coming down the long, bare corridor." He did not always come, but when he did, she forgot much and forgave everything. On the nights when he didn't come, she would roll over onto his side of the bed, burying her nose in his pillow, savoring the scent of his hair lotion—spice and white carnations. She would often fall asleep with her cheek against the sleeve of one of his old dressing gowns.

Gizy took her to meet some of their neighbors. The closest neighbors were far enough away—a long day's drive—so that one always went for the weekend. One of these neighbors, an attractive married woman, told Cissy she thought that Gizy was "a rather hard man, like my husband. And you are, I believe, quite shy still, seeking self-assurance just as I was at your age. If he does fail you, you may naturally seek for love elsewhere, because at your age, with your temperament, what else besides love would interest you at all? Of course some women take their love affairs like their meals, but I don't think you are like that. But try to remember, darling, your one solution will be in your children. Have lots of them. And take a real interest in your place. And ride all the time. You must ride hard. It's a wonderful antidote." Cissy later learned that this woman had once been Gizy's mistress.

Cissy followed her advice about riding. She rode every morning and sometimes went out again in the afternoon. Gizy had bought her a seal-brown Irish-bred mare. It was almost seventeen hands high, and "her quarters looked as if she might negotiate the moon." Gizy told her, "She knows all there is to know about hunting . . . and she's always got a leg to spare over the ditches and banks, and she goes very well under a side-saddle."

Cissy loved her Irish mare. With this horse, she found she did not need the spur or the whip. Best of all, the horse was tall enough for her. A riding master in Chicago once had told her, "You have a natural seat; you will make a real horsewoman one day; you are made for it." Cissy also knew that to have good hands one must like horses and understand them.

Cissy was a good rider, but Gizy was a perfectionist. John de Rosen tells of his father, a court painter to the Russian Court and a friend of Count Gizycki who visited the Gizyckis. He saw Cissy ride around the ring while the Count stood in the center, cracking his whip at the horse and occasionally flicking Cissy. The Count explained to the artist that he was trying to correct his wife's sloppy riding habits.

"Never pull on your reins steadily. Give and take like this, see. Give and take," Gizy often said critically.

He was readying her for a hunting party he had long planned. He had imported a pack of hounds from England, and also a red master's coat that fitted his figure "like the paper on the wall."

"We don't mold situations to fit ourselves, but ourselves to fit situations . . . [we are] adaptable to an almost pathological degree," Cissy would later say. The hunt would be her first performance as wife-hostess. Somehow she had to transform their dilapidated quarters into a shining and welcoming home. She had as many servants as she needed, and her imagination. The next weeks were frantic, but she felt purposeful and important.

She found large silver serving dishes, stored and forgotten for years, and planned a hunt breakfast of roast chicken and *kasha*. She had uniforms made for the servants and had the shabby furniture repaired, recovered, and polished. She took as much care with herself as with her home, since she knew that she too was on exhibit. Her mirror told her how handsome she looked in a velvet-collared black habit she had bought in Paris.

They had invited fifty guests, some from the surrounding area and others from Vienna and Warsaw. As the guests arrived, Cissy watched it all go smoothly, her great concern gradually easing. An older woman guest surveyed her quickly and told her, "You are very attractive to men, but perhaps you don't know it yet."

Cissy mounted her horse for the hunt, determined to keep ahead of the field at all costs. Her last advice from the trainer was: "Give the mare all the head she wants at the jumps, and save her when you can. She might be a little hard to hold at the start."

The hounds were in the field that skirted the forest. There they were, all waiting for the cry of the huntsman: "Gone away!" And they were off.

Cissy felt her horse move "as if electric wires had galvanized suddenly her long and massive legs." Her horse reared and then sprinted across the field to the trees.

"How I hated the first run through the forest when the trees rushed by like live crazy things and my horse almost got away from me!"

Cissy described the hunt in *Fall Flight:*

They came to a ditch and bank, yawning as if with the jaws of death. She could see the hounds pour down over the brim, disappear, stream up again and over. She saw the horse in front of her, all four legs high in the air. . . . Right upon the long, yawning ditch they came. She clamped her knees to the pommel . . . they landed. Her head jerked so far back that she felt as if it were attached to the end of a long elastic band. But she managed to settle herself in the saddle again before they picked up speed, and started once more at full gallop. The lovely hounds slipped into place. So smoothly they ran, so fast, they seemed stuck like toys upon some painted sliding scene. Turning sharp to the left, they plunged into the dark of the forest like porpoises plunging down through the waves of the sea.

The forest tore by. Flung out hard, crooked limbs which miraculously did not sweep her from the saddle; she wondered why. Single file, they streamed along the winding trail. . . . She sat there, breathing short. Sometimes she raised an elbow to ward off the branches. But mostly she sat, a bewildered passenger clamped to her saddle. . . . It was lasting a long while, this wild ride through the dark and awesome forest, filled with living, thrusting, jabbing things. It was like ringing doorbells in the old days in Chicago; like climbing church steeples, and walking down Clark Street in the dark. It was like all the forbidden excitements of her childhood, intensified a thousand times, and it seemed to be going on and on forever.

Suddenly she sighted a stag, a magnificent stag, the stag they had been hunting all day. In the distance she saw the hounds pouring over the rim of a low, long hill, and she heard the repeated "Haloo." Ignoring the stag, her horse made stubbornly after the hounds, but Cissy decided to go after the stag alone. She frantically sawed on her left rein, fighting for control of her horse. They came to a wide, ragged ditch; Cissy was still pulling at the reins, and the mare, out of its stride, took off late. On the rise, Cissy saw a green boggy patch on the far side. Her mare saw it too, and high in the air seemed to make a supreme effort to propel itself across. They landed. The horse's forefeet plunged in, stuck fast, and the great body collapsed on the grass. Cissy lay dazed near her fallen mount.

The big belly with its queer-looking girths, seemed enormous, grotesque, within a few inches of her eyes. She pulled herself up and began stupidly to wipe the slime and mud from her eyes and mouth. A sickening gurgling sound, a choking grunt and groan. She watched the luminous eyes glaze over, saw the massive legs shudder and lie still. A ragged cut on the right foreleg, where the mare had overreached herself in falling, dripped red with blood. Distracted, she unwound the long white scarf from her throat and bound it clumsily around the horse's leg. She used a diamond hairpin—a wedding gift—to fasten the ends together. But the mare was dead; her back was broken.

On the long walk back to the house, she wondered how Gizy would greet her. Would he be delighted that she had escaped unhurt, or would he be angry, believing that she had caused the horse's death? His response shocked her. He seemed almost to ignore her. His hunt so far had been a great success, and his humor was high. She would have understood his anger, but she could not tolerate his unconcern.

She came into dinner late, something that would have normally infuriated him, but tonight he hardly seemed to notice her. The second-floor ballroom, which had looked like a barracks, was transformed—the crystal chandeliers with their hundreds of candles reflected in the highly polished floors, both fireplaces in full roar, oil lanterns hanging from all sides, and a half-dozen violinists playing in the corner. The air was perfumed by two footmen who poured aromatic vinegar over live coals in a copper brazier.

The room was filled with music and laughing conversation, but Cissy heard only the brutalizing silence of her husband. She had helped make his hunt party a smashing success, and not a word from him, not a look. No kindness, no appreciation, no anger, only silence, devastating silence. She tried to forget her hurt by draining glass after glass of champagne, dancing with one man after another. She danced until dawn with abandon, "resting in somebody's arms as if she already belonged there, dancing with her eyes closed." Her mauve satin slippers were frayed, her train torn, her mind numb with exhaustion as she finally escaped to bed.

Gizy grew restless during the first year of their marriage. He found reasons for frequent trips from his estate. He often left without any explanation, once going to St. Petersburg for three weeks. When the Czar had insisted he quit the Austrian cavalry if he wanted to retain his newly inherited Russian estates, Gizy found himself living a life of loose ends, with nothing fixed to do. He had more time for gambling, and there often seemed to be no limit to his losses. Gizy once wagered a racehorse and lost. When the winner came to claim it, Gizy told him, "I'm afraid you're out of luck because the horse is dead." Within months of the wedding, Cissy's ready cash, as well as his own, was gone. Gizy asked her to sign promissory notes. When she occasionally complained, he answered, "Don't be silly. You always knew I had mortgages. Your father talked of nothing else but mortgages for weeks before we were married. Mortgages, women, and illegitimate children. I was never so bored in my life."

She often thought of the difference it might have made if he had managed to get an embassy post in Washington. Knowing so many prominent people, she would then have been his major asset. They would have fulfilled each other so much more, enriched each other.

One night, as they sat reading after supper, he dropped his paper and stared at her with unwinking, inscrutable eyes.

"Why is it you have no babies, my little filly?" he asked her. "There must be something the matter with you. You see, my little filly, a man marries to get something he has not got. Otherwise, why should he marry? Now, besides the charm of your company, with which of course I am delighted, I want to have some children. And besides children, I want to improve my property, buy more land, pay off more mortgages. . . . We should have babies and a little more money to be quite happy. Anyway, we will need more money when we have babies. You should write Papa and get him to come to Vienna as soon as he can. He is so devoted to you. You might tell him that you don't feel very well. As a matter of fact, my little filly, you have grown quite thin and pale."

He stood and drew her into his arms. She welcomed his embrace, knowing that, as always, she would do what he wanted. Her parents did pay them a visit in Vienna, while on a European tour. But Robert Patterson greeted his son-in-law with nothing more than cold correctness. Gizy was disappointed in his great expectations of a flood of money from his American connections. After they left, Cissy found herself alone even more.

When Gizy left on his frequent trips, "he took with him even her sense of reality, leaving her empty, blank and drained of herself." Since Cissy still knew little Polish or Russian, she was a stranger in her own home, cut off from the easy household chatter. The winter was the hardest time for her. She could not ride her horse, visit the neighbors, enjoy the countryside. She would eat little. Gizy had taught her to enjoy burgundy, and she found that a glass of wine relaxed her while she waited for

99

the postboy's shaggy pony. A letter from Gizy was a kind of lifeline; a letter from home only deepened her depression. It made her remember too much and heightened her loneliness. She read every book she could find. She devoured *War and Peace,* identifying with Natasha, just as she saw herself as the tenderhearted prostitute in Dumas's *La Dame aux Camélias.* She read Anatole France's *Thaïs* twice, once for its story and again for its style. "Purity of style . . . exquisite. Cold. Like frost upon a windowpane." But when talking books to the occasional visitor, she would say, "I haven't any education. I don't know anything at all."

What she knew, she had learned herself, and there was nothing shallow about it. Cissy had developed the kind of mind that absorbed everything, retained sights, sounds, words, scenes.

When the silence of the house became too oppressive, she would wrap herself in furs, draw a knitted woolen veil over her mouth and nose, and go out on her sleigh behind her four new dapple-gray Moscow trotters. But the woolen veil would freeze stiff, and the cold would soon force her back home. "It kills the soul," she said of the Russian winter. The silence and loneliness of the snowy landscape overwhelmed her. Cissy needed conversation and laughter more than food. She knew that even the green heat of July would not drive the harsh isolation of winter from her mind. She kept remembering the summer songs of the peasants in the fields, "tender, compassionate, but heartbroken and resigned. . . . Listen how hopeless it is."

Cissy tried harder than ever to please Gizy whenever he was at home. He hated all cosmetics, and so she used only a touch of nail salve to freshen her lips. She was careful to plan the menus around the foods he liked, and she made sure that when he awoke after an evening of heavy drinking, his favorite remedy—tea with a bit of lemon—was at hand. She even joined him more often in his drinking. She talked to him about the books she read. Gizy was a great reader, but he never read novels. "Why should I?" he told her. "My own life is all the novels of the world rolled into one."

The first year passed slowly for Cissy. Her great diversion

was visiting the Potockis, a noble family who lived many hours away. Their large estate, Antoniny, was as luxurious as any princely house in Europe—and far more entertaining. It was the kind of place Cissy had imagined Nowosielica would be.

Antoniny's exterior resembled a sprawling French chateau. A great hall was two stories high. There were eleven dining rooms with guests eating in a different one every night. Fifty guests might come from all over Europe for a weekend party, some staying on for weeks at a time. They played everything from tennis to croquet, and an entire polo team might be invited from England to play a single match with a team of guests. A fifty-piece orchestra played every evening. Guests were served breakfast in their rooms. Luncheon was at two in one of the dining rooms with coffee on the terrace afterward, and the guests gathered in the great hall for tea at five. Then there was time to dress for dinner, which was served at nine. Afterward the ladies in their elaborate gowns and the gentlemen in their elegant evening clothes often gambled or danced the night away.

Cissy came alone to Antoniny more and more often when Gizy was away. Countess Helene Potocka became the motherly confidante Cissy badly needed. She was a kind woman and spoke excellent English. The Countess encouraged Cissy to amuse herself, to flirt. She had almost forgotten how to flirt. But she now lived in a world where a married woman was expected to flirt and even to have love affairs. There were always handsome men available, and if the lovers were discreet, romantic entanglements were regarded with benign amusement. Cissy spent many evenings in the library, with its soft lights, low voices, gentle piano playing. "Sometimes a pretty lady would rise . . . float by small stages out of the room. One of the velvet jackets might yawn, then stretch a little . . . peer into a book, yawn again and so gradually fade away. And when this interesting double maneuver had definitely been accomplished, everybody smiled at everyone else."

Cissy was not yet ready for an affair, but she had a yearning deep within her. She had physical love from her husband, but she wanted more; she wanted adoration and affection. "You are made for love," one of her escorts told her, "with your dark excitable eyes and your passionate mouth." She needed to hear things like that. She was a child-woman in love with her husband, but she enjoyed admirers' words just as she liked knowing that their eyes followed her when she walked.

The atmosphere at Antoniny fortified her. The time she liked best was tea after a hunt, most of the men still in their muddy boots and their splattered pink hunting coats, a few of them already changed into their velvet smoking jackets, the women wearing tea gowns, so languid and utterly relaxed. Sometimes tea was served in a large lounge in the stables by fierce-looking footmen in Cossack dress. The walls were covered with paintings and saddles, and the huge open hearth and leather chairs gave the room a warm, welcoming air. The soft whinnying of the Potockis' sixty horses could be heard under the animated chatter.

Cissy often watched the peasant women beating the brush to drive the golden pheasants into the air for the guests to shoot. The tired peasants would then drink vodka and dance a fierce, weird dance. The more they drank, the fiercer they became.

Cissy gradually learned more about her own peasants in Nowosielica. She observed their feet tied in rags for lack of shoes. In a land of salt mines, she knew they often borrowed salt from each other to boil their potatoes. Serfdom had been abolished long ago, but not feudalism. These people were a conquered, oppressed people, utterly dependent on their landlord. To survive they had to step lightly and think fast. Servants with disagreeable news for people in the main house usually reported it as indirectly as possible "like the caroming of a billiard ball."

Cissy found them strong, hard-working people of unswerving uprightness and absolute honesty. She never had any thought of hiding jewelry or fastening a latch or bolting a door. They were part of the family, and they depended on their squire for security, as their fathers had before them. Gizy had told her how much they prized physical strength and despised tolerance as a sign of weakness. He said that their strain of Tatar blood made them repay injuries with savage revenge, that beneath their torpor and peace was a raging tempest that could break out at any time.

Cissy felt a sense of power as she walked through the village, bowing right and left to the servile residents. Whenever she stopped, a peasant would come to kiss her sleeve, "not daring to touch my hand . . . like the clumsy fawning of a great strange dog." She later described the peasants as "conservative, suspicious, shrewd and selfish," adding, however, that they were the heart and strength of the country. Years later she horrified her aristocratic Polish friends by telling them, "Keep the peasant prosperous, give him a voice in the government . . . give your peasant more land, land of his own for which he'll fight and die and you will make for a stronger Poland."

Cissy liked to take her four trotters down the forest roads, some barely wider than the carriage. She had favorite clearings where the only sound was the crack of a twig, the rustle of a small animal, the twitter of a bird. She also rode along the black Tatar Trail, distinguishable even in the mists by its chain of mileposts; discovered the peace of the deep blue of Krasilovski Lake; found an abandoned riding school, supported on large columns, surmounted by a great horse sculptured in stone. Close by was a deserted ancient orangery with camellias and lemons and some stray peacocks.

Still concerned about her childlessness, Gizy took her to a woman doctor in Vienna. Cissy hardly resembled the bride of the year before. She had become very slim, and her features had taken on a chiseled quality. Her neck did not seem strong enough to support her extravagant masses of burnished hair. The doctor diagnosed an anemic and nervous condition and recommended rest. But rest was not what Cissy wanted. She wanted fun and people. She wanted parties and dances. Since it was Vienna's social season, she soon had all of these. They stayed at the Hotel Sacher, across from the Opera House, and Madame Sacher herself greeted them, jangling her bracelets and her long earrings, bowing her dyed head with its smart coiffure. She gave them a high-ceilinged suite at the end of a labyrinthine hallway.

Gizy often went out alone in the evening. Cissy watched him

moistening the palm of his hand with his favorite perfume, Peau d'Espagne, stroking the shining waves of his hair, wetting the tips of two fingers to twist up the ends of his mustache. She had noticed that her husband was a man who could not resist looking at a reflection of himself, whether it was in a triple-sided mirror or a rain puddle.

"Don't wait up for me, little filly," he would tell her. "Such a lot of old friends are here from all over Europe. I must just put on a proper coat, and I'm off."

If she saw or smelt some evidence of a woman on his clothes the next morning, she would angrily accuse him of having a mistress.

"I do not happen to have a mistress," he would answer. "I went to see a girl I know. I shall go to see any girl I like, anytime I choose to. You have no money, you have no children, you have no sense. You are no good as a wife. You bore me to death. And when your papa returns, I'll ask him to do me the favor of taking you back to America with him."

When he made her weep, he would imitate her, thrusting out his lower lip, wrinkling up his nose and eyes, and sniffing loudly.

She lived and relived in her mind one particular fantasy: she discovered Gizy's favorite bordello, bribed the madam, dressed up as his favorite whore, and surprised him when he arrived. So vivid was this fantasy that she later told it to friends as an incident that had actually happened.

In an entry in his diary, Gizy wrote: "Cissy made a big scene about my being with another woman. I do not understand. She knows I care for her. Why should she object to my occasional affair with other women?"

Cissy discussed this problem with a friend, "a most intelligent Polish lady," who said, "The last thing I want to hear after my husband has been absent from me is the whole truth of what he has done."

"But that is the first thing an American woman would want to find out if she possibly could," Cissy answered.

"Yes, I know, and I think it's a great mistake. I am his wife. I am the mother of his children, and with him, at the head of the house. We are very devoted friends. Our interests and our work are in common. That is enough."

It was never enough for Cissy.

To return all their party invitations in Vienna, Gizy and Cissy had a dinner-dance at their hotel. It started splendidly. The dining room was worthy of any palace, and the food was superb. But at the evening's peak, at the height of its gaiety, Gizy left, saying he had to get up early to watch the workout of a horse he intended to buy.

"But, my dear, you know his *esprit contradictoire*," a guest consoled Cissy. "If we'd wanted to go to bed, he'd have kept us all up, and now that we want to stay up, he's going to bed."

Her guests danced till six in the morning, and Cissy danced with them, losing herself in music and champagne.

"Gizy should not leave you alone at dances like this," an admirer whispered to her. "You are much too young and too giddy, my dear."

A handsome young officer who had danced with her a good part of the evening, kissed her hand; his face pale, his hands trembling, his lips quivering, his eyes wet, he said, "I cannot live without you."

This thrilled her. In her whole life no one had ever said to her, "I cannot live without you."

Before they left Vienna, Cissy suffered an acute attack of peritonitis. She was so ill that both her mother and brother hurried to her from the United States—as the newspapers dramatically put it—"in a race against death."

Despite her fluttering and complaining, her mother comforted Cissy and reminded her of the world she increasingly missed. Her brother brought with him a strength and a sureness, as he always did; she could always count on his love. She knew how much he disapproved of her marriage, but he never criticized Gizy. Instead, he refreshed her with all the warm, funny stories of their yesterdays. He told her, too, that he had discovered that their father had made a political deal with the local party boss to insure his (Joe's) election to the state legislature. When he learned about this, he had resigned in a fury. The new mayor had appointed him commissioner of public works, but he was irritated by the inertia of the municipal bureaucracy. Medill, he said, was establishing himself solidly on the paper, even though Ruth didn't like Chicago. Bertie had gone to law school at Northwestern and was learning how to play polo. To Cissy, it all sounded so faraway.

Her recovery was slow, and the Count prolonged their stay in Vienna. When her mother and brother had gone, it suddenly seemed to Cissy as if Gizy were courting her again with charm, flowers, love. Gizy was not a man to linger over guilt feelings, so it was more than that. His love was not hers, but it was a love, and it was there. Cissy was never more dependent, nor more grateful.

Soon after their return to Nowosielica, Cissy discovered she was pregnant. Gizy's tenderness increased. He was still not a doting husband; he never would be. But their home now had a happier air. There was more laughter in it.

There was not, however, much laughter in Russia then. Peasants who had gone without protest to fight for "the little father" in a faraway war with Japan, now grumbled about poverty and revolution. On a bloody Sunday, troops opened fire on a crowd assembled in front of the Winter Palace. They had come to beg their "little father" for bread. Revolutionists were soon assassinating government ministers and other prominent men. Moscow and St. Petersburg saw riots in their streets.

"I remembered myself as very young and very ignorant of the realities above or below the pleasant surface of things," Cissy said years later.

Cissy had a difficult pregnancy, and Nellie came to stay with her. There was no doctor in Nowosielica, and Nellie insisted that they move to a friend's home, the Blansko Castle in Moravia, where Cissy could receive proper medical care.

"I was very sick," Cissy said afterward, "and Gizycki suddenly announced that he was going away. He never gave any excuse or said what he was going to do. My mother . . . begged him not to go. But he went, and like every good wife, I suppose, I was very suspicious as to why he went; so I opened his desk and there I found a diary."

The crises in her marriage were not precipitated by her disappointment in Nowosielica or by her husband's constant need for money. Cissy took most difficulties in stride, but two incidents, which were turning points in her marriage, wounded her deeply. The first was finding that the bedroom chosen by Gizy for her at Nowosielica had been that of his former mistress. The second turning point was her discovery of his diary.

Gizy's diary was almost an inventory of women: names, dates, places, reactions, comments of sexual pleasure. She felt her pride pulverized, her shame absolute. Determined to keep the diary, she mailed it to a cousin in the United States, because she knew Gizy would otherwise force it from her. But he returned that day, found that his diary was missing, and confronted her with such anger that she told him what she had done with it. He went to the post office and retrieved it.

Gizy considered her action unforgivable. This was the most private part of his life, the deepest unshared part of himself, which belonged to him alone. He regarded her intrusion as a brutal exposure of his soul.

Seven days later Cissy's birth contractions started. "My mother was a very nervous woman. I did not want her. I knew she could not help me but only make me more nervous. So I never sent for her. But I sent for him. He was two rooms down the corridor and I sent my nurse to him directly. He simply said, 'Don't bother me. I can't do anything. Don't bother me.' And he would not come. . . . I was five hours in agony and he never came."

"There was no doctor, and he knew it. He knew that I was absolutely alone, that I was very frightened."

They had come to Blansko Castle to make sure that Cissy received proper medical attention, and yet, when her time came, the doctor was elsewhere and unavailable.

Gizy came only after their daughter had been born— September 3, 1905. Gizy felt no guilt about leaving her alone during childbirth. Although his anger about the diary was still intense, this was not the reason he stayed away. Men of his class never involved themselves with childbirth.

They named the child Leonora Felicia. She was a quiet and lovely child. Cissy felt no rush of mother love for her baby. Servants swooped in to care for it. Cissy saw in the child the pain of its birth, the fright and loneliness, the indifference of Gizy.

"I was absolutely distraught," Cissy remembered about the following winter at Nowosielica. "I suppose I cried a great deal. I may have made scenes. I was anything but pleasant. I reproached him naturally for his treatment of me. I was jealous. I was not the easy companion he cared for."

Gizy's trips now lasted longer. Her solitude became more profound. Warsaw seemed a salvation. They always went together for the start of the social season. Poland was the home of his father just as Austria had been his mother's home, and so Gizy felt at ease in both. The races were on, the restaurants and cabarets were crowded, the theaters were sold out; the noise of droshkies rattling over the cobblestoned streets never seemed to stop. Warsaw was crowded with returning travelers: mothers showing off their marriageable daughters; young married women, secluded for the winter, now hungry for frivolity; and young men from everywhere, most anxious to please.

Poland's aristocracy had a long history, and the great Polish families were related to almost every other royal dynasty in Europe. One Polish king, John III Sobieski, had saved Vienna from the besieging Turks in 1683 and had thereby probably saved the Holy Roman Empire. It was not, therefore, unusual to find Turkish saddles, taken during this great victory, displayed in the homes of Polish nobility. Poland had since been split up among Austria, Germany, and Russia. Russia controlled Warsaw, and the city was then full of Russian officers in their smart white drill jackets. Russia had sucked dry its part of Poland and had compelled Poles to sell their land only to Russians. The Russian nobility in St. Petersburg had open contempt for its Polish counterpart, and consequently the Polish nobles refused to learn Russian. The Polish aristocrats also stubbornly resisted Germanization. They were sympathetic only to the Austrians, who flattered their vanity and gave them places of honor in their court, their army and their church.

The Potockis were one of the greatest Polish noble families. Count Josef reigned at Antoniny and his brother, Count Alfred, maintained Lancut, outside Warsaw. Lancut was a sixteenth-century castle, with a moat and Byzantine domes. The estate's 100,000 acres produced everything from wool to orchids for the Paris market. Count Alfred entertained his guests by racing his six-horse carriage through the main gate into the courtyard with only inches to spare on each side of the wheels.

The Lancut Hunt was a most elaborate and festive occasion. A white-haired Frenchman began the *chasse à courre* by sounding a silver horn. After the hunt, the spoils were laid out in neat piles around a bonfire of huge logs, and a different hunting song was played for each type of game. Then came the traditional ceremony for the new Knights of St. Hubert. These were the men of the hunt who killed a wild boar with their first shot. Only two kinds of shot were mortal for a wild boar—the brain shot just behind the ear, and the heart shot just behind the foreleg. During the knighting ceremony a sword dipped in boar's blood was used to make a cross on the nose and forehead of the kneeling hunter. At last came the feast.

In Warsaw itself, there were social events every noon, afternoon, and evening, and few went to bed before the early morning hours.

"Do you remember the supper parties and the balls at the Bristol?" Count Michel Komorowski asked Cissy years later. "The maddening music and the champagne, and we never left till broad daylight."

Cissy called the blond Komorowski "the big cat," and he was her favorite escort when Gizy was away. Cissy later made him the hero of a short story and had him kill himself for love. Komorowski laughed at this. "But if I had killed myself for love, I should have been dead a long time ago."

It was only afterward that Cissy would realize that the jealousy and rivalry of Polish nobles had helped ruin the country and make it ripe for conquest. Only later, too, did she have the courage and the understanding to tell them, "The majority of your kind are too well educated and have too many ideas and talk too beautifully."

Cissy loved Warsaw. She delighted in the gay tea parties where cossack menservants passed salvers piled with fruits and biscuits. She was enchanted by the dinners and dances, the Paris gowns and the jewels heavy with heritage. She liked waking up to breakfast coffee served in a tall old-fashioned pot and accompanied by a little earthenware crock of clotted cream. She loved the spirit of this city "where everyone is a little mad." She felt that anything could happen in Warsaw, that anything could be said, and that she could do anything that came into her head. She drank more champagne than she ever had before, and she began to enjoy the brandy she had once hated. It seemed no matter that she drank as much for escape as for enjoyment.

She had been married only two years, but already the pattern that her life would take was plain. The future held noisy children, uncommunicative servants, and a restless husband. Cissy suddenly felt a great longing for home, her old home and her old friends. Instead of going to Warsaw for the "season," she and Gizy had been invited to the wedding in Washington of Alice Roosevelt and Nick Longworth in February 1906. Gizy liked Alice, and they decided to go, taking their daughter, Felicia, with them. Felicia was a lovely-looking child, hardly six months old, with her father's face. Gizy obviously hoped that their appearance as a happy family, complete with child, would soften the Pattersons and make them more generous. His debts were mounting, his creditors increasingly impatient.

The Pattersons loved seeing Cissy and enjoyed their grand-child. But Nellie Patterson could not forget Gizy's conduct at the time of the child's birth, and Robert Patterson's distaste for his son-in-law remained unchanged. The money mission was not successful.

One would never have guessed this at the wedding, where Gizy was his most ebullient self. Friends complimented Cissy on her marriage, and she kept her complaints quiet. She might well have envied Alice's new life with a man Cissy still found attractive.

Nick, like Gizy, was fifteen years older than his bride. Alice had wired: "I always told you that old Nick would get me and he has." Cissy would have reveled in the wedding that Alice had: the international pomp, the mountain of presents from all over the world including a pedigreed Boston terrier, a carload of coal, a Gobelin tapestry from the Government of France, a pair of trotting horses. "I'll accept anything but a red-hot stove," Alice had said.

Alice's cousin Eleanor Roosevelt was not there, because she was pregnant, but Cissy saw her husband, Franklin. Nick had tonsillitis and could hardly talk, but he introduced Cissy to one of his ushers, a handsome lieutenant named Douglas Mac-Arthur. And, of course, Alice had to compete for attention with her father, the President of the United States. Alice laughingly told Cissy, "Father always wants to be the corpse at every funeral, the bride at every wedding, and the baby at every christening."

Cissy's Chicago family was there in force. Joe told Cissy how unhappy he was in public office and talked about socialism and writing. Alice teased Bertie about his riding a horse up the steps of the house she stayed in when she was last in Chicago. Bertie had followed Joe into politics, had been elected alderman, and was then president of the Sanitary District. Medill seemed content at the paper, working for Cissy's father, but Ruth talked more and more about an eventual political career for him.

Their short time in the United States was not a happy one for Cissy. She was filled with too many memories, too many regrets. She was not, however, about to give her mother, or anyone else, the satisfaction of saying, "I told you so." The Countess Gizycki was the role she had chosen to play, and she played it well. But never before had she felt her future so uncertain.

Embittered by his parsimonious in-laws, Gizy vented his anger on Cissy when they returned home. Cissy later said that he did not like her to read. "He would take books out of my hand. He did not like me to think. I could not order a carriage from the house. I could not order the servants. He did not want me to learn Polish. I was nothing at all in the house. He drank always, every day, a great deal of drink . . . brandy before lunch and after lunch and in the afternoon, as well as the champagne and wine at dinner."

She admitted, however, that he always maintained his control, that she never had seen him really drunk, never once even saw him stagger.

"He was a sensualist," she added. "He lived simply for his senses, exercising and wine and women, that's all he cared for." She also told of his "perfect contempt for everything American, for my education, for my principles which differed from his."

Even if Cissy exaggerated, there was still no denying Gizy's sensuality or his contempt for her background. But Cissy herself had become a sensualist, drinking more, making more-frequent visits to the Potockis at Antoniny, flirting more freely with other men. Her marriage now seemed to have been based more on sex than soul, and with much of the sexual excitement gone, she thought about writing her own diary of conquests.

Cissy knew she was no longer "amusing" to Gizy. She was "boring." His financial difficulties had grown increasingly serious, and his temper now was more easily triggered, particularly when he had drunk more than usual. Cissy knew his strength. "I have seen him take his coachman off his box and hold him with one hand, hold him and punch him in the face. He was a big powerful man. And he could be cruel. I have seen him use the whip on stableboys."

Then one night, after a violent argument, she herself felt the force of his anger. He struck her a hard blow on her head. He grabbed her by the hands, crushing them, and then he jerked her forward, her head snapped back and her throat "arched rigid to the breaking point and she sank upon her knees like some trapped creature of the wild; moaned with futile rage and shame."

She crept upstairs to her room and locked the door behind her, feeling nauseated. Feebly, then, she began to collect her things, piling them in a heap on her bed: her nightgown, her toothbrush, the pictures of her parents in a red morocco frame, a comb, a small jewel case, a pair of walking shoes, a few underclothes, a thin woolen wrapper, a box of face powder, a jar of cold cream. She called in her maid and told her to dress Felicia and have a sleigh readied.

But now that she had her belongings together, what should she wrap them in? Her eyes fell on a brown-silk petticoat. But she had no string. It would take lots of string. A pillowcase? One of the great stout linen pillowcases with a scalloped embroidered edge. Why, yes, that was just the thing. And when she filled it, she tied up the ends as best she could with a shoelace. And she slipped into her sealskin coat and a small black travelling cap, stuffed a black-lace veil and a pair of gloves into her pocket.

By now she was beginning to think quite clearly and carefully, her mind burned white with excessive emotion. She remembered the passport the Czar had written for her on lambskin; she remembered some money she still had in a bank in Vienna. She slipped her hand in a water pitcher to remove the streak of blood. She could feel the cut on her forehead but did not take time to look at it in the mirror. She slung her pack over her shoulder, turned to the left along the corridor down the narrow stairs, groping her way to the basement floor with only the faint light of one oil lamp in the corner.

She heard the snoring of the houseboys and stablemen as she passed their common room. The stink of their unclean boots and bodies sickened her nostrils. She . . . walked on tiptoe up another short flight, opened the door at the top . . . just below Gizy's room.

Her maid arrived with Felicia, all bundled in furs. Another servant was at the reins of the sleigh. Cissy later wrote that champagne had given her the courage and strength to flee from Nowosielica on that cold December night in 1907. Never again did she expect to see the forest, the pond, the village, the cross on the church.

"It's all over," she said to herself. "All over. Finished."

5

*I had a longing to get away from this man, whom
I hated, and whom I wished dead—or myself
dead—anyway, to be free from this man who had
become my master from the first day I saw him.*
                                    —Cissy Patterson

Freeing herself from Gizy was not easy for Cissy: her hate was
mixed with so much love. He was her first love; her sexuality,
her youth. Cissy was only twenty-six. Her background, education, religion, told her to try to salvage this marriage. She had
to consider the child—and the social stigma of divorce. Divorce
would be even more difficult for Gizy, a Catholic, to accept.
And perhaps harder for him to bear would be the amused
comments of his friends when they discovered the great lover
had not been able to keep his wife.

Gizy followed Cissy to Paris. There he was at his most
charming and persuaded her to attempt a reconciliation. She
said later, "I guess I never had much character."

They went to Pau, a fashionable winter resort in southwest-
ern France near the Spanish border. Gizy took a villa facing the

spectacular Pyrenees, near a small stream flowing through a deep ravine. For a while, they had a second honeymoon. Cissy received word of her mother's arrival in Paris, and they went to see her. Gizy had fresh hopes for her financial help.

"My mother refused," said Cissy, "and he came back in a perfectly beastly temper, and was never decent to me after that at all." She recalled a remark Gizy made about the recent marriage of heiress Gladys Vanderbilt to the Hungarian Count Laszlo Szechenyi. "Look what that boy has got. Look what I have got. Nothing."

They returned to Pau, where, as Cissy recounted, "he started to do something he had never done before. There was a very pretty woman in Pau, who was more or less respectable. He would simply walk out with her and leave me alone, dine with her in public, take her out in public." One evening, as he was about to go out, he glanced at a mirror and asked Cissy, "Aren't you pleased to have such a handsome husband?"

Gizy finally "insisted on my asking this woman to a dinner party . . . and I refused. He pulled me out of the dining room, threw me down on the sofa. I began to cry."

She also began to fight back. When Gizy's *petite amie* did come to dinner and Gizy was openly attentive to her, Cissy began "sarcastically criticizing the techniques he was using to seduce his dinner partner."

Gizy countered later that evening by telling Cissy he was going hunting with his new friend the next morning. Cissy pleaded with him not to go. He slapped her face hard, then slapped it again. Then he started beating her with his fists. "I fell down and he pulled me up and beat me just the way he beat his stable boys. Then he flung me away."

In the midst of her hysteria, she managed to tell him that she was leaving him. "I am only too glad to get rid of you," he answered as he turned and left her.

Cissy lay on the floor, broken and crying. It was all so hopeless now. She could stand his insults, even his neglect, but not his beatings. She would not take that from anyone. She called her maid and ordered her to pack.

Cissy's father was still in London, and she sent him a

telegram, asking him to meet her in Paris. He was not a man who would remind his daughter of how much he had opposed her marriage. Bitter and vindictive toward Gizy, Patterson tried to envelop Cissy with care and affection. He was now the one who made the decisions, and they all returned to London.

Patterson decided that Felicia needed a quiet stay in the country while Cissy settled herself. Mary Gernat, Felicia's nurse, took the child, who was not yet three, to her home in nearby Hampton, Middlesex. Cissy stayed with her father at the Savoy. Cissy's feelings for her daughter then were more possessive than maternal. She was more concerned with her own pain than with Felicia's. When she went to Middlesex, she talked with the nurse and made sure everything was all right, but she spent little time with Felicia. There were few hugs and kisses or bedtime stories. When she looked at Felicia, she saw the face of the man she now hated.

Cissy was emotionally drained. Her mind was in a turmoil. She did not know what was going to happen, and she did not even know what she wanted to happen. Her father became her warm, loving protector. He made her feel that there was nothing to worry about, that somehow everything would work out.

Cissy had always loved her father, but now she felt closer to him than ever before. Both were delighted to be free from the hovering presence of Nellie Patterson. Her father comforted her, made her laugh, took her to the theater, escorted her to parties. They had long dinners together, and she learned more about him then than she had ever known. She took care, though, not to tell him too much of her own bitterness. But suddenly, they were more than father and daughter; they were good friends. They found they had a remarkable number of things in common; they were constantly surprised by the likes and dislikes they shared. Robert Patterson had been a silent man at home with his wife, but with his daughter he was bright and sophisticated, and so tender, so concerned. It had been a long time since anyone had really needed him.

Her father's advice to Cissy was to cut her losses, put Gizycki behind her, and come home with her child. But she was reluctant to take these sensible steps. The men she had met in London seemed pale compared with Gizy. Despite everything, he was always in her thoughts.

In Pau, Gizy had his own regrets. He wrote to Cissy, apologizing, asking for understanding, explaining the tension caused by financial difficulties, and insisting that his brief flirtation was meaningless. Cissy answered his letter in a cool but receptive tone. He wrote again, inviting her to meet him in Paris, at the Elysée Palace Hotel. He suggested she leave Felicia in England with her nurse. Her father protested. Cissy, however, had made up her mind, and in March 1908 she met Gizy in Paris. Their reunion did not prove to be a happy one for Cissy.

I was there a few days with him, only a few days. . . . He came to my room one night and I was in bed. I don't know where he had been. He came in late and—oh, I don't know how those quarrels started. It was just nothing. And suddenly he jumped on me in bed and put his knee on my chest, and took me around my throat and said, "Now I am going to kill you." Then he started to choke me, and then he said in German, "Why should I go to jail for a thing like you?"

He suddenly announced to me that he was leaving me again. I was in a distracted frame of mind. I felt broken up. . . . My health was gone, everything was gone. . . . I saw I was going to be left alone again, my life just up in the air. I didn't know what he was going to do or how long he was going to be gone, and I went to the railroad depot with him like a fool crying there before everybody and begging him not to go away . . . [saying] that we should try once more, that he should come back to America.

Gizy gave a less emotional account of this argument. He said that Cissy had agreed to return to Russia with him, and that the two of them had planned to go to England for Felicia. Cissy then changed her mind about Russia. "Let us drop all this," she had said, "and let us begin again. We will go to America and start over again." Gizy told her he hated America and would never go. After a heated exchange, he left her.

Gizy went to London alone. He knew where Felicia was staying. He had had detectives follow Cissy after she had left him in Pau. His detectives took him to the house of Mary Gernat. Newspapers all over the world soon carried the headline COUNT KIDNAPS BABY and reported that the Count and his accomplices, disguised in furs and goggles, had arrived in Hampton in a large car and had snatched the child from her nurse.

Mary Gernat told a simpler story: "The Count came to the house and told me that his differences with the Countess were over, and that they were going back to the villa in Pau, and that I was to go to Paris with him, with Felicia; then I asked where the Countess was, and he told me that she was already at Pau, already in the villa."

Gernat did not doubt the Count's explanation. She dressed Felicia and packed her clothes, and they set out with Gizy. After they had checked into the Hotel Vendôme in Paris, the Count told Gernat that he was taking Felicia for a drive that morning. She volunteered to accompany them, but Gizy told her, "Don't trouble yourself. She is a big girl." He then asked the nurse to pack for the trip to Pau.

Late that afternoon, Mary Gernat went to the Count's room to ask if Felicia was ready for dinner. The Count said that the child was with her mother. He then told Gernat that her services were no longer required since they planned to put Felicia in a convent. He gave the nurse her salary, some extra money, and a letter of reference. Before leaving Paris, however, the suspicious Gernat called a number of Paris hotels, unsuccessfully trying to find Cissy.

Cissy already had returned to London, discovered that her child was gone, and went in a frenzy to her father. It was then that the story broke in all the papers. Her newspaperman father saw to that.

A letter from Gizy, from the Jockey Club in Vienna, dated March 30, 1908, presented his case:

My dear Cissy:

Before leaving Vienna, I want to inform you I hope you will understand that after your behavior during my last stay in Paris, and especially the charming plans you explained to me at the Gare du Nord, it is quite impossible for me to live with you any longer. I took the baby away from London, as the most important point in that whole business is to secure for that child a decent future, and I don't want Felicia to have the kind of education of which, my poor Cissy, you are yourself a victim. For the final settlement of our affairs, please apply to my lawyer, Dr. Emil Frischauer, Wien, Whiplenstrasse 6. Good-bye. And best love, last time.

When her father left for Vienna to attempt to recover Felicia, Cissy insisted on going with him. They stayed at the Sacher, and she learned that Gizy was at the nearby Grand. She began to think that if they met, he might be touched by her appeals. They had so many mutual friends, but the circle was small, so it seemed an encounter was almost inevitable. Patterson, however, was set against a meeting between Cissy and Gizy. He didn't want to subject her to any more emotional stress than necessary. He conducted all his discussions with Gizy's lawyer.

By the time Cissy and her father arrived in Vienna, Gizy's lawyer had already filed in the Austrian courts for a legal separation. In his petition he charged that Cissy had spent most of their $20,000 annual allowance from her parents "upon her dress." Among her other extravagances, he mentioned her partiality for lavish suppers and fine wines.

The child was the prize in this contest of wills. For neither Cissy nor Gizy was parental love the moving force. Both were self-centered and wanted only to hurt the other. A child would have interfered with Gizy's freedom-loving life-style. And for Cissy she would have been a constant reminder of pain and failure, her lovely face a mirror of her father.

The New York *World* reported that Patterson had offered a large sum of money for the child's release.

"Is it a question of ransom?" a reporter asked.

"Yes. The Count had said that he would not sell his flesh and blood for millions of dollars, but of course I can't read his inner consciousness."

Vienna became alive with American reporters. The story had become an international scandal. "The gossip of society is that the trouble between the couple is not due to any money difficulties, nor has the Count brought any charge of infidelity against the Countess," reported the New York *American*.

To get a formal divorce, Gizy would have had to go before an ecclesiastical tribunal in Russia. The process was long and expensive, and Cissy's lawyers generally agreed that "he has not a shadow of a case."

Reporters asked Robert Patterson why Cissy was not divorcing the Count. "Because of the fact that a divorced woman has little standing in Europe," he replied, "and being the mother of a European nobleman's child, she does not wish to do anything that might cause the child unhappiness and annoyance in later years."

The real reason, which Cissy wouldn't acknowledge, was that she still hoped, deep within her, that there might be a reconciliation. She played the part of the distraught mother for reporters, and she played it well. The real drama, however, was the one she acted every night alone in her room, the reliving of her years with Gizy. In this drama he was both the villain and the hero, so much of a mixture that she was torn by conflicting feelings.

There is no record of who approached whom, but Gizy and Cissy were seen one afternoon, "driving together . . . apparently on friendly terms." An enterprising reporter discovered that the two had arranged to have supper together. Cissy's mother in Washington received a telegram from Cissy, dated that day, from the Grand Hotel: "Excellent friends. Going to see baby tomorrow."

It is likely that Gizy found Patterson too difficult to deal with and decided to contact Cissy directly. Gizy's cousins and friends in Vienna all favored a reconciliation. Gizy himself might have decided that the publicity had been too embarrassing, the scandal too distasteful. And there were his own feelings for

Cissy, stirred up again at seeing her. He knew that she wanted this madness even less than he did.

At this critical juncture, Cissy's brother, Joe, arrived. There was now no need for Joe to hide his feelings about his brother-in-law, who had wronged his sister. His Socialist philosophy intensified his antipathy to the European aristocracy. Joe's mood was such that he would have happily gone after Gizy with his fists. He felt as his father did: There would be no more meetings of Cissy and Gizy until the child was returned. Cissy was to see Felicia at a house in the city's suburbs the next day. Joe had a plan of action, and his father agreed. Six detectives and two cars were to be stationed behind the nearby shrubbery. The detectives were to move in and take the child away with them.

Cissy was hesitant, but the combined force of her father and brother persuaded her. Joe was in his element directing the drama. He set the scene, the detectives in position ready to rush in. A tense Cissy arrived with her father. They went into the house and waited. Felicia never arrived. Gizy had somehow learned of the plot. Infuriated at Cissy, he broke off negotiations. His lawyers told reporters that "her family upsets any arrangement that she is willing to make with her husband."

A livid Patterson angrily called in the press, told them that Gizy was an inveterate liar. "You can judge for yourself the needless heartaches and the suffering to which my daughter has been subjected by this man. . . . Cissy, I fear, has tied herself into a double-bow knot. . . . The Count is not molded after our ideals."

Cissy's brother was less polite. He called the Count "a blackmailer, baby-snatcher, a drunk and an adulterer."

Gizy's answer was immediate: a million-dollar damage suit against Joseph Patterson. The case was never brought to court.

There now seemed no reason to stay in Vienna. Joe Patterson returned home, and Cissy and their father went back to London. The scandal had made Cissy a celebrity. Conversation stopped when she entered a room. At parties, people crowded about her, staring, wondering, admiring. London society saw her as a symbol of embattled motherhood. Everyone wanted to hear her own story in her own words. Cissy basked in her new glory, yet maintained considerable poise for a young woman, keeping private the details that would have aroused pity or scorn instead of admiration.

"I will never live with him again," she dramatically told a reporter, "[but] what a terrible whip he holds over me—the child!"

Cissy soon had a string of noble English escorts, several courting her so ardently that the press reported she would marry as soon as she divorced the Count. But Cissy had made no legal overture for a divorce, and neither had Gizy. Gizy's financial plight had been eased considerably for a while when an uncle died, leaving him two large estates. But soon, as a newspaper account reported, Gizy was losing $9,000 at the Jockey Club in one night and he was seen betting heavily at the races every afternoon.

Gizy had put Felicia in a convent in Austria, but he refused to tell Cissy its location. As Cissy's attorneys pointed out, Gizy had solid legal ground for custody since under Russian law Felicia was a Russian citizen. With an agreement with Gizy now less likely than ever, the desperate Cissy hurried to St. Petersburg to visit her American friend and benefactor, Princess Catacuzene. The Princess's husband was aide-de-camp to the Czar's brother. The Princess was warmly sympathetic to her tearful young friend but explained that women in the Russian court had no influence in such affairs. As Cissy continued pleading, the Princess thought of a possible course of action. Even in Russia, women could maneuver through other women. She arranged for a meeting between Cissy and the Czar's mother, the Dowager Empress, Maria Fedorovna.

The Empress was a formidable survivor who believed in absolute authority. After listening to Cissy's story, she proposed an immediate solution: she would have Gizy put in jail for six months to think things over. Cissy demurred. She wanted Felicia, but she shuddered at the thought of Gizy in some dank, dark jail. She was not yet that vindictive. The Empress was impatient. Cissy quoted her as saying, "Child, I have had people beheaded for absolutely nothing!"

Cissy protested that she did not want to punish her husband, that she only wanted her child. The Empress promised to discuss the matter with her son, the Czar. If she did, nothing immediately happened.

Months passed without action, and Aunt Kate volunteered to help. As the former ambassador to Russia, her husband still had considerable influence there. Kate felt great affection for Cissy. During the McCormicks' stays in Vienna and St. Petersburg, Cissy had been part of their home and their family. Aunt Kate also set a price on her assistance. She told Robert Patterson that she and her husband would help all they could if the Chicago *Tribune* promised to promote her husband's diplomatic career.

Patterson was not in the best of health. The long negotiations on his daughter's behalf had driven him almost to the breaking point. Now he exploded at Kate, whom he called "The Witch."

The newly elected President, William Howard Taft, had been Patterson's classmate at Yale, and the indignant Patterson wrote him a five-page letter, stating in part:

Mrs. Robert McCormick has formally proposed to my wife to help my daughter with the Russian government in some of her domestic troubles if I will agree to assist McCormick to get another ambassadorship. . . .

I shall do nothing of the kind. On the contrary, I protest against the appointment of McCormick to office, if his appointment is supposed to be by way of recognition of the Chicago *Tribune*.

Mr. McCormick failed disastrously in business 25 years ago, and has since been dependent on his wife. He has no independent status and no merit . . . certainly he has no qualification for an important diplomatic office.

He has never written a line for the *Tribune*, never made a campaign speech, nor even given a dollar to the campaign fund; nor has his wife, unless she has done so this year "in the lively expectation of favors to come. . . ."

Patterson went on to say that while McCormick was ambassador to Russia, he had been disloyal to President Roosevelt, calling him that "madman in the White House." Patterson stated that Roosevelt had removed McCormick because he was incompetent.

"As for the wishes of the other stockholders," Patterson continued, "I think I may say they are unanimous in *not* wishing to have the influence and character of the paper pawned in order that the McCormicks may enjoy a social distinction which they have done nothing to deserve."

Cissy again returned to Vienna, this time with her mother and her cousin Medill McCormick. Medill again was her white knight, her handsome defender. For him, it was fun, a fresh adventure taking him away from Chicago. Cissy was his favorite cousin, and he felt righteously indignant about her situation. Beyond that, he enjoyed the chance to use his fluent languages, and he liked the jousting with lawyers and diplomats. At the *Tribune,* he had moved from editorial writing to the business side. Things had seemed quiet and dull until he got Cissy's call for help. Medill soon discovered that Gizy's heavy gambling losses that year made him more receptive to a financial settlement. The figure rumored was 400,000 rubles, about 200,000 American dollars at the time.

One of Cissy's lesser demands that had been relayed to Gizy's lawyers was the return of her silver tea service, a family heirloom. Medill related that as he and Nellie talked in their hotel sitting room, "the door burst open and the Count ran in with an armful of tea silver and pieces of that sort and hurled them on the table and floor, exploded adjectively in French, cussed a little and dashed out."

Gizy paid a much more mysterious visit to Cissy in her hotel room. He made a quiet entrance, chatting smoothly, as if nothing had ever happened. "I got up and pretended I was taking my hat off because I was very frightened," said Cissy. "I sort of walked around, got hold of the bell and rang it, and when the waiter came in, I said, 'Send my maid.' And then he left. He didn't say what he came for. I did not know. He was there. less than ten minutes." Just seeing him again had made her heart pound, and not simply from fright. She knew his hold on her, and so did he. His visit might have been a matter of impulse and curiosity, but perhaps it was an expression of affection and regret.

Again, there was no agreement. Medill decided to approach officials in both Poland and Russia. He received his most sympathetic reception from Baron Budberg, chief of the petitions department of the Russian court. Cissy had told Medill that the Baron had been one of her most open admirers. Indeed, the Baron profusely promised to give the matter his personal attention.

Nellie Patterson grew impatient with the slowness of the Russian bureaucracy and made her own move in December 1908. She wrote a letter to President-elect Taft, whom she had met. She wrote as a mother pleading for help, and Taft's answer was immediate. The President-elect sent a handwritten letter to Czar Nicholas:

Your Imperial Majesty,

Miss Eleanor Patterson, the daughter of Mr. and Mrs. Robert W. Patterson, was married in Washington by a Roman Catholic priest to Count Josef Gizycki, and thus became Countess Gizycka of Russian Poland.

One child, a daughter, has been born of that marriage. Since that time, in a quarrel, the Count struck the Countess. She left him, taking her baby daughter with her. He followed her, and succeeded in securing possession of the baby against the mother's will. The Countess has now been deprived of even the sight of the child for many months. The child has been placed by its father in a convent in Russia.* Both the Countess and her mother are in danger of a nervous breakdown because of the strain and worry attending these circumstances, unless some arrangement can be made in which the baby will be restored to its mother, at least for a period of time each year. There is no question of divorce proceedings whatever.

*The President-elect mistakenly wrote Russia; the child was actually in a convent in Austria.

I am advised that the only recourse of the Countess is an appeal to the sovereign will of Your Imperial Majesty, and I write on behalf of the mother and grandmother to appeal to Your Majesty to direct an investigation into the circumstances, and to make such order to Count Gizycki as shall seem to Your Majesty equitable and merciful.

I retain the pleasantest recollection of the audience which Your Majesty was good enough to accord me, and the feast of the Second Regiment of the Guard, and of the luncheon to the officers of the regiment given by Your Majesty, at which, by your gracious courtesy, I was a guest.

Hoping that I do not trespass upon the proprieties in thus addressing Your Majesty personally, I beg to subscribe myself, Your Majesty's obedient servant.

Wm. H. Taft

P.S. Mr. and Mrs. Patterson are prominent citizens of Chicago and Washington, and Mr. Patterson is the proprietor of the Chicago *Tribune*, one of the greatest papers in the United States.

"I am not at all certain it will be effective," Taft wrote to Nellie, enclosing a copy of his letter. But it could not have been more effective. A letter from the President of the United States to the Czar of Russia received its proper attention. Baron Budberg submitted a dossier on the dispute, recommending a ruling in favor of Cissy; the Dowager Empress added her own strong approval; and perhaps the Czar remembered the ambassador's piquant red-haired niece pinning her skirt behind a marble column at his Winter Palace ball. Although Russian law supported the Count, the Czar could bend the law or break it. He signed an order directing Count Josef Gizycki to release the child to the custody of her mother.

Gizy delayed his return to Russia, but in the summer of 1909, he had to visit his estates to collect rents. The Czar's police were waiting. Gizy was given the choice of complying with the Czar's order or facing criminal prosecution. Gizy, who had his own temper and his own righteousness, loudly refused to obey, and the police promptly put him in jail. Gizy had been in odd situations in many places but never in jail. His humiliation was profound. He spent forty-eight hours in prison, where he realized that since the Czar's power was absolute, he had no options. He finally agreed to surrender Felicia to Cissy.

Cissy found it hard to believe that she had truly beaten her overpowering husband. Yet, deep within her, she knew that this was a Pyrrhic victory: she had won her child, but she had irrevocably lost her husband. The possibility, however remote, of a reconciliation was now gone. She knew that his pride had been dealt a crushing blow, one that he could never forgive. But even though her custody of Felicia had been established by the Czar's order, she was afraid that Gizy could and would kidnap their child again.

Cissy told her mother of her fears. Nellie's lawyers were of the opinion that the imperial order protected Felicia while she was with her mother, whether in Russia or on foreign soil. To ease Cissy's mind, however, Nellie agreed to deposit 400,000 rubles to Gizy's bank account in Odessa.

Medill insisted that Nellie ask the Count to sign a receipt for the money. Gizy agreed. But when he came to sign and saw Medill there, he left in a storm without signing, saying, "Your nephew is here!" He kept face to the finish.

He finally signed and then paid an unexpected visit to Cissy's hotel room. Cissy described him as "amiable as pie . . . rather flirtatious." Was he pleasant because his financial problems were now finally resolved? Or had he realized that his daughter did belong with her mother, that a child would only complicate his independence, that he did not want such responsibility? Or was he impulsively saying good-bye in a gentle and affectionate way? Gizy had always been a man of the grand gesture. Part of the receipt must have been a pledge by Gizy that he would never attempt to see Felicia, that he would never write to her or communicate with her in any way. Gizy kept his word.

Gizy's surprising visit cast a bittersweet tinge on Cissy's triumph. Ruth Hanna McCormick had arrived to be with her, and Cissy could tell her things she could not tell her mother, or anyone else. But she was grateful to her mother, more grateful than she had ever been before. Despite the distance between them, her mother had been a pillar of support and had come quickly when she was needed. Cissy's father's loving help was instinctive; Cissy's mother's presence had perhaps been prompted by guilt, as well as by a taste for excitement that would break the boredom of her life. If Nellie could not be a man in a man's world, she could prove herself an effective force fighting for her daughter.

The climax of the long, dramatic struggle was the arrival of the blue-eyed, golden-haired Felicia. She was a little stranger, almost four years old. Felicia didn't remember that meeting, but Cissy never forgot it. She had promised herself to maintain emotional control—she did not want to frighten Felicia—but it was a promise she could not keep.

Mother and daughter arrived in New York on the *Kaiser Wilhelm der Grosse* on August 17, 1909, and the reporters were waiting.

"I am weary," Cissy told them. "I do not wish to talk of the past. I wish to forget it. Now that I have my baby, I am satisfied. . . . I am almost afraid to let my baby girl out of my sight. . . . I shall remain in this country six months and shall spend all of the time with my parents in Chicago. Then I shall return to my home in Vienna."

Why did Cissy want to return to Vienna, the scene of so much unhappiness where she didn't really have a home? Was it possible that she still refused to believe that her marriage was cold and dead? Did she feel that Gizy still loved and wanted her? Had she been touched by his enigmatic last visit?

She walked off the ship wearing a gray traveling gown and a large elegant hat with a birdlike feathered ornament atop her upswept red hair. Her appearance was still girlish, "though her eyes bear a look of sadness that is relieved only when she smiles." Felicia, a white sailor hat on her yellow curls, clung to her mother "and would not consent to release her hand for a moment."

Her father

Her mother

Eleanor Medill Patterson

She loved her brother Joe
more than anyone

And her grandfather, Joseph
Medill, was her hero.

Chicago's lake shore at the turn of the century

Cissy and Joe and their home in Chicago

Family heritage: (standing) Cissy and Medill McCormick and (seated left to right) Robert McCormick, grandfather Medill and brother Joe

In Washington, D.C., she was the belle
of the ball—

and her best friend was the President's
daughter, Alice Roosevelt Longworth.

In Vienna, Cissy fell in love with Count Joseph Gizycki.

Application for License.

No.

DISTRICT OF COLUMBIA, ss:

Count Joseph Gizycki, applicant for the issuance of a Marriage License, the persons named herein, do solemnly swear (affirm) that the answers to the following interrogatories are true, to the best of my knowledge and belief: So help me God.

	MALE	FEMALE
Names	Count Joseph Gizycki	Eleanor Medill Patt...
Ages	37 years	23
Color	White	White
Relationship	none	none
Former Marriages		

Witness :

Joseph Gizycki

Subscribed and sworn to before me, this 13 day of April, 1904

John R. Young Clerk.

By _____, Assistant Clerk.

No. _____ ### Marriage License.

To *Rev. Thomas S. Lee*, authorized to celebrate marriages in the District of Columbia, GREETING:

You are hereby authorized to celebrate the rites of marriage, between *Joseph Gizycki* of *Russia* AND *Eleanor Medill Patterson*, of *Washington D.C.* and having done so, you are commanded to make return of the same to the Clerk's Office of the Supreme Court of the said District within TEN days, under a penalty of fifty dollars for default therein.

Witness my hand and seal of said Court, this 13 day of April, anno Domini 1904

John R. Young Clerk.

By _____, Assistant Clerk.

No. _____ ### Return.

I, *Rev. Thomas S. Lee*, who have been duly authorized to celebrate the rites of marriage in the District of Columbia, do hereby certify that, by authority of license of corresponding number herewith, I solemnized the marriage of *Count Joseph Gizycki* and *Eleanor Medill Patt...* named therein, on the 14th day of April, 1904 at No. 15 Dupont in said District.

Thomas S. Lee

RECORD OFFICE, WASHINGTON, D.C.

And then they were married

PRIVATE COLLECTION

They lived in Russia, Poland and Vienna
and had a daughter (below) named Felicia.

В. Шехтмейстеръ   Староконстантиновъ

Her cousin Medill helped
Cissy arrange her separation and
regain her daughter and she
moved to Lake Forest,
Illinóis—

CHICAGO TRIBUNE

Residence of Countess Gizycka,
Lake Forest, Ill.   2405

where her daughter grew up.

Cissy became an actress.

And there were soon other men in her life: her psychiatrist and friend (above, left), Dr. Alvan Barach; Senator Borah (above, right), about whom she wrote a novel; Freddie McLaughlin (below), the polo player;

and Count von Bernstorff, the German Ambassador.

But the man she loved longest was a cowboy named Cal Carrington.

Jackson Hole, Wyoming, was then a small and dusty town

and her best friend, who helped run it, was Rose Crabtree (bottom, second from left).

She loved the beauty
and, for a while, the hunting—

but most of all, there was Cal . . .
and her ranch in Flat Creek.

She later married a New York lawyer, Elmer Schlesinger, while her daughter (below) married a newspaperman, Drew Pearson.

She now spent more time in her Washington home on Dupont Circle and saw more of her brother.

Her father confessors were newspaper columnist Arthur Brisbane (above) and William Randolph Hearst (below), who made her a newspaper editor.

The Washington Herald

CHARACTER · QUALITY · AMERICA FIRST! · ENTERPRISE

AN AMERICAN PAPER FOR THE AMERICAN PEOPLE

Vol. VIII. No. 241. WEDNESDAY, JULY 23, 1930. 20 pages PRICE THREE CENTS

The Weather

Fair today and tomorrow; cooler today; gentle winds. See Page 19.

Today

Weather, Money, Fun
Standard and Shell
Cover Head and Spine
Mr. Coolidge Smiles

By ARTHUR BRISBANE

THREE THINGS INTEREST human beings most, interested them 10,000 years ago, will interest them 1,000,000 years hence—WEATHER, MONEY AND AMUSEMENT.

Of the three there are many kinds. In winter we complain of cold, in spring we complain of summer's delay. Real summer comes and we complain.

Beautifully a few pages in Jean's book on astronomical physics would comfort us.

Inside the sun the temperature is 50,000,000 degrees centigrade, above. A few miles above our heads, outside of the atmosphere and the thermometer is just about zero, 217 degrees centigrade, below.

And miraculously, our cannot is kept at 98 degrees at the North Pole. Be grateful for our comfortable home.

There are many kinds of money, honest and dishonest, made and lost in gambling, accumulated in hard work.

If the money is $10,000,000,000 amount or about $40,000,000,000 represent fairly honest money. Not bad for our kind of civilization.

The history of mankind can be written in a history of his innumerable amusements. Some watch prizefights, some play miniature golf, a few contemplate the starry heavens.

Mr. Reese, of New York Standard Oil, asking permission to continue with the Vacuum Oil Company, asks his company wants a nation-wide distribution of all petroleum products. No American concern equals the famous "Shell" company, but a nation-wide distribution. Move beam to Mr. Deterding and his energetic associates.

But, why not allow an American concern, even if it is called "Standard Oil" to do what a foreign company is allowed to do?

In hot weather be careful, beware of tainted food, meat especially.

That warning was sent from Washington by Surgeon General Cumming of the Public Health Service on Monday. Yesterday thirteen more were poisoned in New York's Parker Hospital, presumably ptomaine in tainted veal.

Keep your hat on in sunshine. Acting rays are bad for the brain. Protect your spinal cord. Don't expose it to hot sunlight too long at a time.

Drink much good, cool water.

It will please Calvin Coolidge's millions of admirers to learn that, regardless of weather, he always makes up smiling. He inherited and served through the period of majestic prosperity caused by the pouring out of war billions. Then he handed the job to Mr. Hoover.

And now for twelve 110 words a day telling of things that happen to the people to support him Mr. Coolidge is paid $150,000 a year, at least please upon the people just to Mr. Hoover to worry. Tough work indeed. "I do not complain."

Eager, callous civilization in the world" cannot perhaps Metropolitans tolerate brushing through the misery of the world an all nation.

Ingenious citizens seek to make, in our insides, set fire in the brain and blow up insides, destroy one's health.

The British coast with sunset sewers call it European count on its own kingdoms when can you do?

But when the lightning spreads to the boy in Canal, that is something our Britain will not ignore a reason to ignore.

His bailey cost is in the British prime ministry what the Bure Canal was a short cut for ships. If the British Empire.

A committee of Congressmen will be properly recognized Reds' in the list countries at their summer room.

The Congressmen looked wisely, discovered in "shorts" accounted "experiment yelled 'Moscow's' Communist' at the communists which on more captaining of any experience.

If "Reds" could get any of the "capitalism" that worried Karl Marx, him would they feel? Have sought by on some barbaric automobiles, more made roads, dustily or good gas cell.

But these things will be the products of capitalism.

10 ARE KILLED, 100 HURT AS ITALY SUFFERS EARTH SHOCK

Naples Bears Brunt of Temblor; Damage Elsewhere Is Great; Towns in Darkness

Storms Precede Quake; Melfi, With Population of 12,000, Reported Almost Destroyed

NAPLES, July 23 (Wednesday).—A disastrous earthquake rocked Naples and southern Italy early today.

Naples bore the brunt of it, but damage elsewhere was great.

The first crack up here showed at noon and 100 injured. In smaller towns and theatre reports were beginning to come in of deaths throughout the area. Few reports of fatalities were obtainable at Naples time at Naples hours, though at half a dozen points, several of miles about were literally shaken from the funeral.

TOWNS IN DARKNESS

The temblor threw towns into darkness, disrupted telephone and telegraph communications and hampered railroad. All authorities could do in the long night hours of confusion and inadequate switch of thousand for tinted buildings.

Reports at 9 a. m. when communication was broken, was Rome and some other points, several persons of rooms and all of Southern Italy from Rome to Catania were rocked by the quake.

One of the first reports to come in at this hour was the Melfi, in the province of Potenza, with a population of 12,000 almost had been destroyed. Casualties were unknown. The houses and, like the others, in larger the quake by fire and fell or the people trapped in the buildings.

Then at 1:55 a. m. came register of large-sized fire great shock. Two more followed. Bold man rocked Electric light cables and telephone wires broke, and the entire territory was shut into darkness.

The Casamota Ridge here cost from another and many buildings in the vicinity of Castelnuovo and Pot area crumbled in ruins. Two towns were killed when an distance bodies, and eight hours was fatally injured.

The hospital thereafter sag out monsoon. A room collapsed at the Bernardin Hospital. No one was hurt but the wish of saving for the victims was obvious.

Police, firemen and soldiers rushed to rescue work, and in guarding against fire.

2 Killed and 2 Hurt In Locomotive Blast

SCRANTON, Pa. July 22 (UP).—The engineer and fireman were killed when a locomotive on passenger train No. 6 of the Lackawanna Railroad exploded today.

John L. Lynch, engineer, and Ray Whitman, fireman, were buried in their deaths. Both lived in Scranton.

DETROIT VOTES MAYOR RECALL

DETROIT, July 22 (U.P.).—By the decisive figures of 2:15 to 1 the Detroit electorate today approved the recall of Mayor Charles Bowles.

Tabulation of the city's 877 precincts tonight showed 126,843 in favor of the mayor's recall and 88,073 favoring his retention in office.

Under the law" Bowles gains materially becomes a candidate at the special election which will be held the latter part of August.

The movement to recall Bowles started a few weeks after he took office last January. His proposal to increase the trolley fare gave an increasingly postal boast drew immediate fire, and when he followed this with dismissal of a number of high police officials, the movement grew.

B and down, popular and was revived and carried on when he summarily dismissed Harold R. Emmons, police commissioner after Emmons surged widespread catch his operation in the gambling establishments in the mayor's absence from the city.

J. E. How Dies In Staunton Of 2-Day Illness

'Millionaire Hobo,' Chronic Sufferer, Easy Victim Of Pneumonia

JAMES EADS HOW

STAUNTON, Va., July 22.—James Eads How, the millionaire hobo, died at King's Daughters Hospital here today, following a two days' illness of pneumonia. His body was sent to Washington late tonight for burial. He will meet three probable tomorrow a brother, Louis How en route to Washington from his home in Massachusetts to arrange for the funeral.

How came here from his lodge in St. Louis last Friday.

Friday at Dr. J. F. Wine ask, who attended him here, he was emaciated and evidently run down, having been, though at it appears to him eating due to a chronic organic trouble.

How was about 48 years of age. He had long been studious, and for years and fare and other enemy had participated in the prosperity of his father of the unemployed, as leader of the largely ban the their cause. It was his often on that was for him the workingmen. 'The millionaire hobo.'

38 DIE AS SPAN FALLS, ENDING FETE ON RHINE

Celebrants of Evacuation Are Victims of Crash; Tragedy Turns German Joy to Woe

COBLENZ, Germany, July 23 (Wednesday) (U.P.).—Many were drowned as they participated in the closing of the Coblenz Rhine land liberation ceremonies early this morning, when an old span condemned long before, as on which they were passing gave way under their weight and three more than 100 merry makers into the Rhine.

Twelve along the bank of the broad river, which Tuesday afternoon had taken on a jubilation illuminated a mask it swept at the shape in the suburb of Laubel shedding a flickering light along's town at crimson chartered from the mile for the festival.

38 BODIES RECOVERED

Thirty-eight bodies, had been recovered by dawn moments the dead, it was feared, would the recent their toll. Twenty-eight are badly hurt.

Two children were among the dead.

President von Hindenburg was planning to have consulted his visit of his Rhineland fold, in mourning for the disaster.

The news of the tragedy spread rapidly through Coblenz when the police ordered all saloons to close immediately, despite the private special effort establishing this day of observing the feelings of real jubilant hours that she will bring to the eager the highest qualities of a trained intellect, the skill of a keen observer, an intimate knowledge possessed by few of the National Capital, and in addition to transmitting thoughts into words, endowed by journalistic greatness and experience, that will redound to her benefit and our success. They've made a marvelous choice, and most heartily I congratulate her. And I congratulate more of all of us who must have the pleasure and benefit of her work.

FLAGS HALF-MASTED

Flags way struck at half mast. The scene had 16 by more of the place where the climax was tables unto the river.

Twelve along the pack were immediately used to did no moat Jubilee Later, dragons were used to forests.

President von Hindenburg and other notables had participated in the festivities being held through out the Rhineland all seen a celebration of the final evacuation of the border country in the Allied forces. The French, the last to leave, departed June 30.

MRS. PATTERSON IS NAMED CHIEF HERALD EDITOR

Descendant of Journalistic Leader Assumes Duties In Washington August 1

In an advancing column, The Washington Herald today announces the appointment of a new editor-in-chief, Mrs. Eleanor Medill Patterson, who thus most again prominently becomes an active member of the Fourth Estate. She is a grand-daughter of Joseph Medill the founder of the Chicago Tribune, a niece of Joseph Medill Patterson, the publisher of the New York Daily News and Liberty Magazine, and a cousin of Col. Robert R. McCormick, the publisher of the Chicago Tribune.

In official and social circles Mrs. Patterson and her family have been known in Washington and the National Capital always has deeply engaged her interest as a city and community. Mrs. Patterson will assume her duties as editor-in-chief of The Herald on August 1.

The following comments were made last night on the appointment of Mrs. Patterson as editor.

Hiram Johnson

Editor of The Herald

How fortunate are we that I can conceive of an selection as editor of The Herald better or with more journalistic and potential possibilities than that of Mrs. Patterson. We who have enjoyed her writings, who have just the privilege of observing...

Senator Moses

Editor of The Herald

Permit, me heartily to congratulate The Washington Herald upon its recent step in securing Mrs. Patterson as its editor.

A journalist by inheritance, by instinct and by training, with contacts and public experience both broad and useful, she should be able to give to The Herald qualities of attainment which must inevitably be reflected in an enlarged sphere for the paper.

Senator Shipstead

The Herald presents an editor who is brilliant with a never paper tradition a century old. Many women have achieved high places in the various professions and the halls of Congress. This, however, is the first instance within my knowledge where a woman has been selected to preside over the destinies of a great metropolitan daily. Men man can only view with alarm these usurpations of power by members of the stronger sex but can only bow to the inevitable. I congratulate The Herald of its new editor-in-chief.

New Editor-In-Chief

MRS. ELEANOR MEDILL PATTERSON, who will become Editor in Chief of The Washington Herald, August 1. Her appointment was announced yesterday.

ANNOUNCEMENT

The Washington Herald makes the following announcement:

Mrs. Eleanor Medill Patterson, beginning August 1, will assume the direction of The Washington Herald as editor-in-chief.

Mrs. Patterson and her family have long been known in Washington in official and other circles.

The new editor of The Washington Herald comes naturally by journalistic ability. Her grandfather was Joseph Medill, founder of the Chicago Tribune, and she has been very successful as a writer of novels and signed articles. Mrs. Patterson is a first cousin of the late Senator Medill McCormick, and of R. R. McCormick, publisher of the Chicago Tribune. She is the sister of Joseph Medill Patterson, publisher of the New York Daily News and Liberty Magazine.

Mrs. Patterson has long been anxious to engage in active newspaper work which has occupied members of her family for three generations.

For a long time she endeavored to purchase The Washington Herald, of which she now becomes the active editor. But Hearst newspapers are not for sale.

Mrs. Patterson will work as editor of The Herald under the regular Hearst newspaper contract.

Mrs. Patterson, who was formerly the Countess Gizycka, and who subsequently married the well-known lawyer, Elmer Schlesinger, at her mother's request has resumed her maiden name which is the same as her mother's, Eleanor Medill Patterson.

Mrs. Patterson's mother is one of the two daughters of Joseph Medill.

The Washington Herald feels sure that Mrs. Patterson, who, in accordance with Hearst's law, inherits the genius of her grandfather, will be very successful and INTERESTING as editor of a Washington daily newspaper.

GLOTH MOVES TO GRILL WIFE OF SUSPECT IN BAKER MURDER

Left Son at 7 Instead of 6, He Now Says; Still Insists He Is Innocent of Killing

Barrere Jubilant as Police Admit He Is Nearly Clear; Pistol Expert to Eye Gun

Herbert M. Campbell yesterday was maneuvered into making further admissions that his "fair tight" alibi of his movements on the night of April 11 when Mary Baker was murdered were false during a three-hour grilling by Commonwealth Attorney William C. Gloth and Lieut. Edward J. Kelly.

The once suave Oakwood, Va., real estate operator, who began to chance on with the murder of the Navy Department worker, appeared to be a victim of shattered nerves at the end of yesterday's quest mining. Week from two days of grilling. Campbell readily admitted that he who put all his home as he previously said he ran at the time Mary Baker's bullet-shattered body is believed to have been dumped into a culvert bordering Arlington Cemetery.

LIED ABOUT TIME

Campbell, who previously had admitted I was sitting in a car with a woman about 100 feet from the culvert on Connery Road, two hours before Miss Baker was attacked and that he had passed fourteenth and B Sts. N. W., about the time she was seen struggling in her machine, said he had earlier I had lied when he told investigators he had gone directly to his home the night of April 11 after taking his son, Edward, to a Boys' meeting in Washington about 6 o'clock.

He told Gloth he brought his son to town about 7 o'clock instead of 6 o'clock, and after killing him at Fourteenth and B Sts. N. W. and Mary Baker both under came hours at a nearby store and then drove out to 610 Hamilton St. N. W. where he visited with Mrs. Mary Barr Smith until about 9:30 o'clock. After leaving the Smiths, Campbell said he drove direct to his home about 9 o'clock and Mrs. Ray Smith and stayed in bed.

The Smiths since have left for Arkansas, and Gloth announced he would have some one see them at an early date to check on Campbell's story.

GUN TO BE EXAMINED

Gloth with confidence over the latest developments in the 13-week-old murder mystery, announced he would send the Baker death gun to which Campbell admits ownership to Major Calvin Goddard, internationally known ballistic expert in Chicago. Although Bureau of Standards experts have examined Campbell's 32-caliber revolver and declared it to be the gun from which the fatal bullets were fired, Gloth said:

"I'm not taking any chances.

(Continued on Page 4, Col. 1.)

Shamrock V Bravely Speeding to America

LONDON, July 22.—The steam yacht Erin, conveying Sir Thomas Lipton's America's Cup challenger Shamrock V to New London, Conn., today radioed that an average speed of eight knots is being maintained and that the Shamrock is now 208 miles on its transatlantic journey via the Azores.

The Shamrock is expected to take a month for the crossing.

Four Murderers Die In Electric Chair

TRENTON, N. J., July 22 (U.P.).—Four murderers were put to death tonight in the electric chair at the State prison. They were:

Victor Giampietro, Frank McBride, Joseph Makaus, and Joseph Rado.

The four participated in the murder of George B. Lee, cashier in a Newark car barn, during a hold-up in October, 1928.

5 HURT WHEN 4 AUTOS COLLIDE

Five persons were hurt when four automobiles collided on Scott branch, between Decatur and Emerson Sts. N. W. last late night. John Dallas (Adv.) 61, a real estate agent, of 2900 Newark St. N. W. was arrested and charged with driving while drunk.

Alkphath he suffered a fractured rib Grady passed hired with his left Emergency Hospital. The other injured: Meridan Hess, T. Catherine Hess and Mrs. Charles Hess, all of 3660 block Harvey Place S. E.; Mary McDonald, 13, 1100 block Blair Place N. W. All suffered cuts, bruises and shock. They were treated at Walter Reed Hospital.

Traffic on Sixteenth Street was tied up 30 minutes. Police said Grady was driving north and the cars southbound, piled up in a heap in the middle of the street.

1 Dies, Three Stricken As Heat Wave Wanes

The heat wave, which has pushed the temperature up to and beyond 100 every day for the past four days, finally broke down last night as short but hard, rainfall yesterday put the mercury down 24 degrees in less than three hours—from 100 to between 12:30 and 1 o'clock and from 90 to 76 between 3 and 4 o'clock.

The temperature will be about mean 74.9, tonight of had a little above it, according to the Weather Bureau, sometime this evening.

(Continued on Page 2, Col. 7.)

Hourly temperatures as recorded by the Weather Bureau yesterday were:

8:00 A. M.	81
9:00 A. M.	85
10:00 A. M.	88
11:00 A. M.	91
12:30 P. M.	98
12:30 P. M.	100
1:30 P. M.	98
2:30 P. M.	98
3:30 P. M.	93
4:30 P. M.	88
5:30 P. M.	87
6:30 P. M.	85
7:30 P. M.	78

Day's

100

Hottest

HAMER IN LEAD IN AIR DERBY

CINCINNATI, July 22.—Herman Hamer, of Chicago, flying Plane No. 5, won the 400-mile New York to Cincinnati third lap of the All-American Air Derby in 5 hours 2 minutes and 45 seconds.

Lee Gehlbach came in second, and Lowell Bayles, Springfield, Ill., was third.

GIRL DIES OF RABIES

QUINCY, Mass., July 22 (U.S.).—Barking and growling like the savage police dog that attacked her and snapping at all who came near her, Esther Campbell, 14, died in agony at Quincy Hospital tonight, a victim of rabies.

WIFE DIVORCES GATES AT RENO

RENO, Nev., July 22 (U.P.).—Mrs. Dellos M. Gates, of Washington, D. C., was divorced today by Catherine Davis Oates.

Mrs. Oates, July 1929, in New York, York, Oates included a former sweetheart to dinner in their hotel room.

Mrs. Oates said she later found him occupying a room with the former sweetheart.

TENNESSEAN VISITS POPE

VATICAN CITY, July 22 (U.S.).—Pope Pius again granted an audience to Robert M. Gates of Nashville, Tenn., which lasted 10 minutes.

She did some reporting on her own, posed as a penniless woman in search of a job.

She was a woman in a man's world. She even tried to buy the *Washington Post* at an auction.

he was a tough editor...and the men on her staff respected her (standing, left o right) H. A. Robinson, circulation director; J. Irving Belt, mechanical uperintendent; Frank Waldrop, editor-in-chief; Edmund F. Jewell, adverising director; Michael Flynn, supervising managing editor; (seated, left to ight) Mason S. Peters, night managing editor; William C. Shelton, general nanager.

Two later men in her life: William Bullitt, Ambassador to Russia and then France and (top right) Tom White, Hearst's general manager; and her older friends: Bernard Baruch (left) and Herbert Bayard Swope

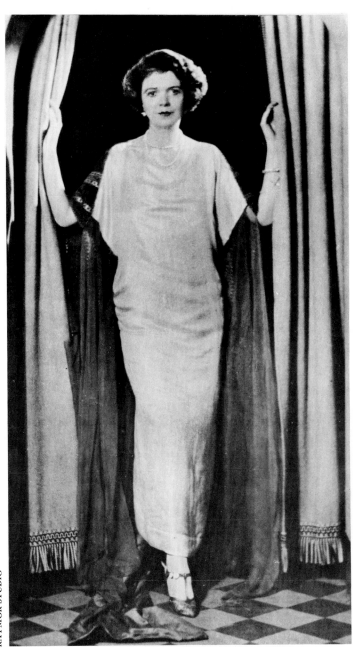

She admired Eleanor Roosevelt more than any
other woman but there was soon a growing
distance from President Franklin D. Roosevelt

Lissis

Mrs. Patterson

being removed from a

Cherry-Tree

F.D.R.

Her brother's death was her
greatest loss (Cissy front right,
Felicia extreme right in next
row, and Colonel Robert Mc-
Cormick at Cissy's right)

War Chief and Eleanor Patterson. The Round House 1941:

Her motto might have been: "Why not?" and "What the hell!"

6

My lines have fallen in pleasant places;
Yea, I have a goodly heritage.

—Psalm 16:6

It was hard coming home. If only she could have slipped in quietly and gone straight to Lake Forest and disappeared. If only she could be a little girl again and ride the horses on her grandfather's farm, or drive in the victoria to Monaghan's chocolate shop. If only she could forget the last ten years and slip back into girlish innocence. But the blaring newspaper headlines announced her arrival. She was an international celebrity. Notorious. Awesome to the younger set; anathema to old society. Cissy was too tired to care much.

The town of Lake Forest had changed little since her childhood. Lettuce sandwiches and iced tea were still served at lunch; the books in the library smelled of citronella; the social life revolved around the Presbyterian Church. Perhaps there were more polo matches and croquet tournaments, but most lawns still had no fences, and horses and cows still browsed where they pleased. The Meekers, a prominent Lake Forest family, had a pair of buffalo which escaped and had to be shot after they terrorized the neighborhood. They also had five hundred cows carefully tended by Dutch boys who wore wooden shoes. They even had their own milk-bottling plant. Felicia liked the Meeker farm because it had a menagerie for children—peacocks, pheasants, foxes, ponies, ducks, bull terriers. A Meeker pride was the red mule that had beaten Medill McCormick's white mule in a race.

"We lived in a little white cottage that I loved," said Felicia. It was a rented cottage in Lake Forest. Her first memories of her mother were "of a delicate woman who went to doctor after doctor, spent a lot of time in bed, took rest cures and went on different diets. I was not allowed to make a noise in the morning because she slept late."

Cissy's illnesses had their roots in her mind and heart. She didn't realize that she had the cure in her own home. She and her daughter desperately needed each other's love. Felicia was not yet five years old: she spoke German and Russian and the French that she had learned in the convent, and knew very little English. During her first months in the United States, she was shy, frightened, lonely. It took time for her to feel free with the children she met. Felicia's closest friends were her cousins—Uncle Joe's daughters—Elinor, who was two years older, and Alicia, a year younger than Felicia. Joe had a 400-acre farm nearby at Libertyville, and there the three girls raced about barefoot. A detective, however, was always with Felicia even when she played hide-and-go-seek in the cornfields.

"I remember that detective always did that magic trick of pulling a quarter out of our hair or out of our noses," recalled Felicia's childhood friend, Jane Dick. "I always thought how fabulous it was to have him around. It made everything fascinating and scary."

The detective treated Felicia with great affection: he often tossed her in the air and carried her on his back. But she received little of this playful love from her mother. "I only have memories of two times when my mother showed any warm, physical affection for me as a child," said Felicia. "I remember when I was a very little girl, cuddled in her lap, cuddled against her. That is a very distinct, warm and special memory. Another time, when I was afraid that she had wanted a boy instead of a girl, she consoled me and told me she really wanted a girl—and she hugged me and kissed me."

One other tender memory from those years was the soft, sweet way her mother sometimes sang "Tit-Willow" to her at bedtime. Cissy said her father used to sing it to her when she was a child.

Felicia needed mothering and never got it. Cissy regarded Felicia as the prize in the contest with her husband; now that she had won her, she was of less value. Cissy saw in her child the features of the husband who had beaten her and left her. She saw Felicia as the fruit of a failed marriage. She felt little spontaneous affection for her daughter, and she left her to her governess and detective.

Friends noticed that her years in Europe had changed Cissy. There was a new bitterness in her. "It wasn't until after she left your father and came home that she got nasty," Grandma Patterson later told Felicia.

Horses helped relieve Cissy's painful restlessness. She raced on horseback through the countryside, feeling a sense of profound freedom. These lonely rides eventually proved more effective in curing her than medicine and doctors. But what she really needed was to feel like a woman again, a wanted woman. She was twenty-eight years old. She wanted to be held by a man, to hear how beautiful she was, and to be told what a fool Gizy had been to let her go. She wanted reassurance. She wanted flattery. She wanted love.

She found all these in Freddie McLaughlin, the admirer of her younger years who had married shortly after she did. His marriage too had been unhappy, and he and his wife were discussing divorce. The handsome Freddie was then a nationally ranked polo player. Women thought he was dynamic and liked him more than men did. Cissy knew the laughter inside Freddie and knew how to get at it. They enjoyed each other and made no secret of how they felt.

Freddie was no Gizy. He was a much blunter man, with less sophistication. But he took her on long rides along the lake, offered her reassurance, warm memories, and adoration. She needed all these. They could not laugh about their failed marriages, but they could help each other forget.

Cissy's father died of an apoplectic stroke in April 1910, in a Philadelphia hotel room; he was as alone in death as he had been in life. For Cissy, the loss was real. When she was a child, he had been a cozy lap; when she was a young woman, he had been an indulgent father who denied her nothing. But she had known him best and loved him most during the last two years, when he had been the main source of her sanity and strength during her time of crisis. He was her buffer with the lawyers and her shield from the press, and his love and presence had nourished her. She had never known a man to be as gentle and charming as her father was when he escorted her to dinners and parties in London.

Robert Patterson's long obituary listed his accomplishments as a newspaper publisher, including his pioneering use of four-color presses for printing comics. It didn't mention the disappointment at not becoming a United States senator, the tragedy of his drinking, the sessions in sanatoriums, and the highly publicized legal suit years before by a New York woman who claimed that Robert Patterson had assaulted her, "tearing her clothing." The case was dismissed.

Patterson died within an hour of his mother, and the telegrams announcing their deaths crossed each other. There was a double funeral. He left an estate of $7,000.

Nellie Patterson did not pretend grief. She had lost an unwanted husband. Her sister remarked at the funeral, "Well, she got ahead of me again," thinking of her sister's new freedom as a widow. After leaving the diplomatic service, Kate's husband had had a series of mental breakdowns. Kate kept him out of sight in a nursing home in the quiet Virginia countryside where he had been born.

It was Bertie who accidentally discovered that before Patterson's death he had planned to sell the *Tribune* for $10 million. "If Mr. Patterson had lived a day or two longer, the sale would have taken place," Bertie later wrote. Bertie was then the unpaid treasurer of the *Tribune*. Bertie alerted Joe and Cissy, and the three of them campaigned among the directors, urging them not to sell. Their mothers had little inclination to keep the paper. "You ruined your husband," Cissy bluntly told Aunt Kate. "You ruined your oldest son. Do you wish to ruin this one, too?" (Medill had been on the edge of a breakdown and Cissy had blamed much of this on his mother.)

Some of the other directors agreed to delay the sale if Medill would leave in the near future and Bertie take a more active role in the paper's management. They regarded Medill as emotionally unfit to run the paper. The sisters then agreed with the others not to sell.

Nellie and Kate had decided that the time had come to settle more permanently in Washington, D.C. No matter how much they sniped at each other, the two were close. Kate called Dupont Circle, where Nellie had built her house, "a swamp at the wrong end of town" and predicted her sister would soon get malaria. Nellie said that Kate had moved "out in the sticks" on Massachusetts Avenue because she couldn't find a house among the proper people. She gleefully predicted that Kate would one night be murdered in her bed.

Cissy felt freer without a meddlesome mother. Freddie's divorce became final that year, and he pressured Cissy to sue for her own divorce. Her lingering reluctance disappeared in September 1910 when Count Gizycki formally applied in the Austrian courts for an official decree of "separation from bed and board," an added legal step to his initial application two years before. The only parallel in this country was a separation-maintenance suit. Gizy asked for no money, but Cissy had to pay court costs of 750 kronen, 10 hellers, or $141.

During the past year her wounds had begun to heal, but now Gizy had rubbed them raw again. Cissy regarded his suit as an indignity. He had thrown her out and now he was kicking her. She had managed to organize her broken pieces of life into a neat package, and once again the headlines had scattered them. Now she would finally finish it.

Cissy quickly sued for divorce in Chicago. *The New York*

Times surmised that Cissy's action was prompted by the fear that the Count would again attempt to kidnap his daughter "as he did before, and take her back to Europe."

Cissy charged in her divorce complaint that she had been "beaten, struck, kicked and choked at divers times in divers places," and that the Count had thrown her on the floor "and dragged her out of the room." She also listed three women with whom the Count had been "unduly intimate" during their marriage, and added that there were others whose names she did not know.

Gizy's lawyers quickly responded, legally indignant. "I beg to report to the knowledge of Countess Gizycka," warned Gizy's lawyers, "that I have taken the necessary precautions that this rascally attempt upon the honor of Count Gizycki, supported by bribes and perjured witnesses, will have no success." They deplored "the rascally character" of "two vagabond detectives" who had followed the Count in Vienna and "an equally unqualified scamp who has been trying to watch the Count in St. Petersburg." It would not work, they said, because even if there was proof that he was unfaithful, it all happened *after* he had got his initial Austrian separation two years before. Besides, they said, they were greatly distressed because they were not notified in advance about the proposed divorce action.

Then Gizy countered with his own charges: "It was impossible to get along with her. . . . This was due to the quarrelsome nature of my wife, to be ascribed possibly to her intense hysterical disposition, her domineering way, her absolute lack of tact and incapability to accommodate herself to the new conditions of life. She frequently tormented me with scenes of jealousy in an unheard-of manner, and often disappeared from our common domicile in Russia without deigning to give any reason therefor. Even after yielding to her wishes and going to Vienna to live, it was impossible to get along with her." This was a reference to the time they had lived in Vienna during her illness.

Gizy's lawyer added: "The Count did not receive a dowry [and] as admitted by the Countess, he has spent considerably more for the personal needs of his wife than the amount of the appendage allowed by her parents."

Count Gizycki only had a few friends to whom he would unburden himself. One of them was Countess May Wurmbrand, and in a letter to her he speculated on whether Russia or America "shelters the most scoundrels." He concluded that "America holds the record in this." Gizy went on to say that what angered him most was not that Cissy had taken away his daughter "by illegal and shocking means" but that Baron Budberg had helped turn the whole thing around "so that it had looked like I had 'sold' the child." "For this purpose he wanted me to sign a record . . . that I was the beneficiary of the dowry . . . and deposit my daughter to the custody of Mrs. Patterson. In spite of being pursued by Police and others, I refused to sign this protocol. By the way, Mrs. Patterson *never* deposited this dowry." What he had signed was a receipt for the money—technically to be used for his daughter's interest. He had never signed any receipt for a dowry.

Gizy then claimed that a St. Petersburg editor had confessed in court that Baron Budberg had dictated an article that called Gizy "a completely ruined swindler and adventurer." Gizy had sued the publisher, and the editor recanted. Gizy insisted that Baron Budberg had courted Cissy "and was very much in love with her, as I have already established through evidence."

Gizy then detailed the troubles he was having with his American lawyers. He had instructed them to "turn down any money offers from the Patterson family and [to] assure me the upbringing of the child." His Chicago lawyers, however, had answered "that they could not believe the guilt of my wife because she was utterly faultless."

"I have thought of other ways and means of destroying these people," Gizy wrote, explaining that he had fired these lawyers. "If Cissy's good reputation is lost this way, then she only brought it upon herself. Bluffing is of no use anymore."

Gizy then asked for the advice and approval of Countess Wurmbrand, adding as a postscript: "The hunting was superb today."

But, after the divorce, Gizy never bothered Cissy again,

never contacted Felicia. Despite all the hurt of memory, Cissy did nothing to discourage people from calling her "Countess." She startled onlookers at a horse show by wearing white silk hose with the Gizycki family crest worked in an inset of filet lace. "Society gasped," a reporter wrote, "then rushed to the books of heraldry to get the design to be worked into their stockings."

This public attitude made it less surprising that the next man in Cissy's life was another European, another count. He was Count Johann Heinrich von Bernstorff, and he was everything she had hoped Gizy would be.

He was the German ambassador to the United States. A handsome, well-built man in his late forties, he had a long, thick, curling mustache and enjoyed dressing rather flamboyantly. His wardrobe included yellow shoes, a black-and-white-check suit, a white silk shirt with red hand-embroidered panels down the front and along the cuffs, and socks that matched the shirt. He also fancied a wide-brimmed Panama hat with a band of the same embroidered silk. And his ties were extraordinary.

President Taft was horrified when he saw Bernstorff playing golf with a lady in his shirt-sleeves. He didn't object so much to the lack of a coat as to Bernstorff's pink shirt and red suspenders.

Unlike the private, cynical Gizy, Count von Bernstorff was an extroverted bon vivant, neither violent nor quarrelsome nor morose. He had a hint of deference in his tone, a general sweetness of manner.

"The secret of his success was his willingness to be bored," observed a fellow diplomat. Von Bernstorff could sit for hours through dinners, lingering with his cigars, letting others do the talking "while he listened with an understanding smile kept in constant play over what was otherwise an oddly baffling countenance."

For six generations, the Bernstorffs had been diplomats and government leaders. Before coming to Washington, Johann had served in Cairo, Constantinople, Belgrade, Dresden, St. Petersburg, Munich, and London. He told his American friends that he himself was part American since one of his ancestors had married Amerika Riedesdal, a resident of New York, in 1801. Bernstorff himself was married to an American, but his marriage did not prevent him from being a notorious ladies' man. "I think a man is a fool who denies himself any good thing in this life," he said. "I'm very lenient, especially towards sins of the flesh when the temptation is great and the results unimportant. . . . I try to play fair and get what I want, while causing as little pain to others as possible." He won the ladies with his waltzing, his laughter, and his warm blue eyes. Washington gossips listed Cissy's mother among his conquests. As a trustee of the Chicago *Tribune,* she was a key contact for Bernstorff. As relations with Germany gradually worsened, the State Department tapped Bernstorff's telephone and recorded many amorous conversations. One lady caller compared him with the hero of a current play, *The Great Lover.* Bernstorff protested that the comparison was not fair, because he had stopped pursuing women.

"Perhaps you have taken a rest," replied his caller, "but not *stopped.*" She then added sharply: "Besides, you *needed* a rest."

It was almost inevitable that Cissy and Bernstorff would gravitate toward each other. Cissy had met him at her mother's parties. Cissy had become nostalgic for Europe and was full of warm memories that Freddie neither understood nor appreciated. But Bernstorff could talk, in several languages, about all the subjects that interested her. When Cissy became more openly involved with Bernstorff, Freddie became increasingly jealous.

Freddie McLaughlin created a minor scandal when he raced his roadster into a lover's lane after the Count and Cissy. In front of witnesses, Freddie beat the Count with his riding crop until Bernstorff managed to drive away.

Bernstorff was stationed in Washington, but he found many reasons to come to Chicago, just as Cissy suddenly had a renewed interest in visiting Washington.

Chicago's major attraction for Cissy was her brother Joe. She had never stopped being his adoring sister. Joe was settled on his farm, writing stories, plays, and novels. He was an enthusiastic Socialist. His father had called socialism "one of the wildest fanaticisms of the age" but had insisted that Joe was "perfectly competent to form his own ideas of life." Joe felt guilty because he had had a valet when he was fourteen years old. The valet helped him dress, shined his shoes, and brought him coffee in bed in the morning.

In a novel he wrote, *A Little Brother of the Rich,* the hero expressed Joe's feelings at the time. "My whole life is a horrible lie, a poisonous blunder, a soul-destroyer. . . . I know it's all rotten and false but it's too late." "It's getting pretty tiresome," he wrote in another novel, *Confessions of a Drone.* "Same old people; same old food; same old booze; same old bridge; same old racket; same old staying up all night; same old horrible changeless deadly boredom. I've lost interest. It's all over with me, inside of me. Nothing matters much anymore; at least nothing around here."

Joe told Cissy about the hundreds of children he had seen in South Carolina working in the mills "burning out their little lives in order that his palms might be softly white." He talked about her years in Poland and Russia, stressing that she had lived a life of wealth in the midst of poverty. Joe, more than anyone else, developed Cissy's social conscience; made her see the needs of others. He tried to awaken her to what he regarded as the corruption of the upper classes.

"They can't sing, they can't dance, they can't sew, they can't cook, they can't educate," Joe had written of Cissy's friends. "They are inept, unthorough, inconsequential, rudderless, compassionless, drifting. They don't know life because they never lived life. . . . Helpless, hapless, hopeless, nervous, disappointed, cloyed and cowardly, they exist a few years here, seeking to have all their living done for them by paid dependents. They delegate all their living functions in life, save one—and even that, they don't do well or often."

Joe often talked to Cissy about what they should do with all the money they had and discussed giving it all away. "You may think of it sometimes," she had told him, "but you'll never do it." He said that he knew that money could get almost anything—but "Happiness, happiness, what is it? Who has it?"

Neither Cissy nor Joe was happy. His marriage was not going

well. His wife, Alice, barely five feet tall, was a "Dresden doll . . . but she had the guts of the damned." Their Liberty- ville farm was a battleground. She wanted it to be an English park with deer tripping over the green; he wanted it to be a working farm. She kept planting lanes of trees in the cornfields and he kept cutting them down. When a load of manure arrived, they could not agree whether it was to go for the farm or the garden. But more than that, she resented his socialistic ideas, his affected shabbiness, and his absorption in his writing.

Through all their years, Joe had been Cissy's protective brother, substitute father, and shining knight—the perfect model of the man she would have wanted to be. Now it was Cissy's turn to help Joe. She understood the pain of a broken marriage, and she gave him boundless sympathy and affection. She encouraged him to continue working on his novels and plays, and he in turn suggested that she might also have a talent for writing.

Cissy was twenty-nine, and she very much felt herself one of the rudderless, inconsequential, drifting women her brother had written about. Her romance with Freddie had quieted, mostly because of her affair with Bernstorff. But he was a high-ranking diplomat and would never jeopardize his career with a divorce. Cissy was bored and restless when Joe brought her the manuscript of a one-act play he had written. He insisted that she read some of it aloud. The characters captured Cissy. She saw herself in the unhappy young heroine, and she felt that her brother had based this character's vindictive mother on their own mother. His cynicism about sex and men rang true for her. The tenement in which the play was set was a hovel she had heard him describe many times. Joe was enthralled by her reading and excitedly told her she had to act in it. The Aldis Theatre was producing it in Lake Forest. Cissy caught his excitement, and agreed.

Mrs. Dorothy Aldis was a neighbor of Cissy's, a slight, earnest woman who wrote poetry and plays. Friends described her as "spirituelle" and "delightfully impractical." Her theater was a small green ramshackle building on her estate; fifty friends, and some critics, were invited to attend amateur productions there. Since there was no director, the performers criticized each other. Cissy refused to regard the performance simply as an interesting experience. Determined that her brother's play should have the best performance possible, she gave it all her intensity.

"The actress did it," wrote an enthusiastic Chicago reviewer. "The audience began to listen, and from listening, it proceeded to surrender. . . . She took her own time in creating her effects. She was as easy and as confident as a veteran, and yet underlying all she did was a manner that hinted her indifference . . . whether anybody liked her or not. The audience meanwhile was following her with pious attention. She held it in her slim hands and she did with it about as she pleased. When she finished, there was a smash of applause that wasn't merely polite, but that had the real thrill in it."

Critics were taken with Cissy's insouciance and the quickness with which she moved from arrogance to pity to twinkling laughter. The play was so well received that the Aldis Players agreed to give several benefit performances in Chicago. Again the newspaper critics praised Cissy.

"If he did not write the part of Mary Kearney for his sister, it is the opinion of the critics that he could not have found a professional actress better qualified to play it."

"The Countess Gizycka, if she wills, may become a star in the theatrical firmament."

"That girl ought to have gone on the stage," a critic told Joe Patterson.

"I wish she would," Joe answered. "She's wasting a great gift. You tell her so. I want her to act on the professional stage."

Cissy laughed at all this. She could not see herself as a professional actress. She could not see herself acting in the same play night after night. That year, however, for Aldis, she did play a variety of parts, including Queen Elizabeth. She found a unique feeling of release in being someone else, and she found it easy to achieve this sublimation.

The Aldis Theatre became so successful that Mrs. Aldis replaced her rundown playhouse with a more splendid one seating ninety people. This new building had dressing rooms and reversible flats—brown on one side, gray on the other. One of the actors, Charles Dewey, remembered there were only two rules in this company: "Keep your temper" and "Do not move while you speak and do not speak with your back to the audience."

In *The Stronger* by August Strindberg, a two-character play about love and infidelity, Cissy sat silently on the stage; without having a single line, she conveyed a mood of confrontation.

"The way the Countess handled the cigarette and the facial expressions she displayed could not have been equalled by Bernhardt herself," commented the Chicago *Inter-Ocean*. And the Chicago *Examiner* added: "She seemed to be able, with a single glance of her eyes or a fleeting expression of her face, to express fully all that she might have said to the taunts, pleadings and denunciations of Madame X."

Drama critic Percy Hammond thumped the arm of his chair and said, "Either acting is easier than I believed it was, or that girl is a genius!" He went to see Cissy and told her he could get her a job on the professional stage the next day. And the manager of Chicago's Majestic Theatre offered to produce any play in which she wanted to star.

Cissy was elated—she had finally proved herself. She had found something she could do well, very well; something at which she could make a living. Cissy always walked "as if the air parted in front of her," but now her natural grace was accentuated by a greater self-confidence. Acting had done that for her. Mrs. Prentice Coonley remembered arriving for dinner at Cissy's Lake Shore cottage. A servant let the Coonleys in, but after an hour passed, there was still no Cissy. Mrs. Coonley finally went upstairs to find her annoyed hostess vainly trying to fit herself into a new dress.

"Finally she threw the dress aside," said Mrs. Coonley, "picked up a piece of green silk, wrapped it around her and tucked it under her shoulder, walking down the staircase looking like a character in a Greek play."

Immersed in the theater as she was, Cissy had a growing curiosity about the family newspaper. Medill had delayed his departure from the *Tribune,* but, finally, the time had come. He had had his run at it as editor. He was unsuited for the hard daily newspaper work and was restless and detached from his job. Harold Ickes remarked that although Medill had a great deal of ability, he was "supercilious and snooty" and meeting him was "like biting deeply into a green persimmon." More and more, Medill left the paper in the hands of editor James Keeley, a ruthless, brutal man who looked like a bulldog and often acted like one. Keeley called the *Tribune* "the world's greatest newspaper" and added: "The *Tribune* has no friends and wants none."

Cissy spent a good deal of time with Medill and Ruth McCormick. Next to her brother, Cissy felt the warmest feelings for this tall, sandy-haired cousin. She heard about Medill's intention to publish the names of Chicago's "respectable" people who owned whorehouses and gambling places. But his health was poor, and he went on a trip, a long one. Shortly after he left the paper, he was hospitalized for a nervous breakdown. His list was never printed.

Bertie was still the treasurer of the *Tribune*. Cissy had never really liked Bertie McCormick, but she respected him, and it was mutual. Bertie was not a "likable" man. His height accentuated his aloofness, and he was generally dour and unsmiling. "He is too shy of contact with human beings, and too arrogant in his dislike of the people ever to think of becoming a public figure," wrote the noted journalist George Seldes, who once worked for him. "Nor does he enjoy secret manipulation of secret events." But Seldes, who became a caustic and constant critic of newspaper power and corruption, gave McCormick high marks for listening to his correspondents and for being easy to get along with. "Power, money, fame, egotism do not seem to be [his] motives in making the paper what it is," he added.

Bertie gradually gained control of the *Tribune*. He had concentrated on the business and mechanical departments, bought vast timberlands in Canada to guarantee a future supply of paper, as well as a fleet of lake freighters to haul it, and encouraged improvements in printing. He then became absorbed with editing the paper and asked Joe to join the *Tribune* as Sunday editor.

Joe had by now lost his passion for socialism. He had joined the national executive committee of the Socialist party and soon discovered that the party was torn by factions and splinter groups. He saw that the members were interested in talk, not action. Finally, and reluctantly, he bowed out, disillusioned and convinced that the only thing that would make people work was the profit motive. At this point in his life, he found Bertie's offer attractive.

Cissy encouraged Joe to accept, because she felt that this job would take him away from his unhappy home. Perhaps he would find the same consolation in the *Tribune* which his father had. And, in fact, Joe was soon captured by the excitement of the newspaper. The staff had considered Robert McCormick "patriarchal," but they thought Joe Patterson was "a great guy." Joe knew the names of all the pressroom apprentices and the night cleaning women. He stopped to talk with everyone, and his invariable greeting was, "What new ideas have you got today?"

Joe and Bertie soon implemented an unorthodox system of management. Joe ran the paper for one month, and Bertie assumed control for the next. This alternating leadership caused some editorial chaos, but somehow it worked. Under their joint guidance, the *Tribune* became a lively paper of columns and contests.

Every time Cissy saw Joe, he was bursting with new ideas: Should he hire former President Theodore Roosevelt as an editor, or should he spend the money for a comic strip called "The Katzenjammer Kids"? (He bought the comic strip.) What did she think about his hiring Lillian Russell to write about beauty; would women be interested? (Of course, said Cissy; and he did, for a while.)

Cissy heard about his circulation-building contest to pick Chicago's prettiest girl, and she got all the gory details about the *Tribune's* circulation war with Hearst's *Examiner*. In an earlier war, each side had hired gangs of thugs to terrify news dealers into boosting sales. Before the episode was over, twenty-seven news dealers and newsboys had been killed and many others wounded. One man had been beaten, thrown down an elevator shaft, and shot at. But no member of either the *Tribune* or the Hearst "wrecking crews" was ever arrested.

Cissy listened to everything, filed it all away in her retentive mind, forgot none of it, and later used most of it. She also remembered Joe's description of Grandfather Medill's newspaper crusades: "He never started one unless he had won it first. He made a deal with the feller he was having a crusade against, for whatever the feller wanted, if it was reasonable. So it was all cut and dried before it got started. That way, everybody was happy, and the paper wasn't made to look bad in the end. . . . That was his hard and fast rule."

Under Joe the *Tribune* launched crusades against political grafters, loan sharks, and clairvoyants. Cissy was now an avid *Tribune* reader. She liked seeing an idea her brother had mentioned at the dinner table develop into a series of headlines. But although he would talk to her about the newspaper, he did not want her involved. When she tentatively suggested that she try writing for the *Tribune,* Joe answered her with a firm no.

His health recovered, Medill McCormick also wanted to start working again for the *Tribune.* Joe discouraged him, too. "Make good elsewhere for a period. . . . Demonstrate that you are strong enough to do continuous, steady and difficult work." Joe used himself as an example of someone who had got "sort of a bump a time back . . . and it was a fine business for me inside."

Medill agreed and switched gears. That year, 1912, saw a bitter and dramatic fight for the Presidency between two former friends: Theodore Roosevelt and William Howard Taft. Roosevelt had picked Taft to succeed him to the Presidency in 1908. Now, still young and politically restless, Roosevelt decided he wanted the job back again. The normally good-humored Taft, unwilling to give up the White House, bristled. "Even a rat in a corner will fight," he said. As the incumbent President, controlling patronage and the party, Taft won the Republican nomination. Roosevelt, however, was still a man of "pure act." He accepted the Presidential nomination of the newly formed Progressive party. Medill not only joined his bandwagon but also became the Progressive party candidate for the Illinois State Assembly.

Cissy was torn. She had known Roosevelt from her young years and had seen him often in the White House, and Alice was one of her closest friends. On the other hand, Taft had been a Yale classmate and good friend of her father's, and Taft's letter to the Czar had helped her regain Felicia. Medill's fervor probably tipped the balance for her, and she went with him to the Progressive party convention in Chicago on the night of the nomination.

The hall was packed to near suffocation with cheering supporters; flags hung everywhere; a glee club sang patriotic hymns; bands played; the gathering had the high-pitched hysteria of a revival meeting.

"What happens to me is not of the slightest consequence," Roosevelt said in his speech. "I am to be used, as in a doubtful battle any man is used, to his hurt or not, so long as he is useful and is then cast aside and left to die. I wish you to feel this. I mean it; and I shall need no sympathy when you are through with me. . . . We fight in an honorable fashion for the good of mankind, unheeding of our individual fates; with unflinching hearts and undimmed eyes; we stand at Armageddon, and we battle for the Lord."

"We stand at Armageddon, and we battle for the Lord"— Cissy and millions of others never forgot this ringing phrase, and the roar in the hall.

"What makes him great," Medill explained to Cissy, "is that he understands the psychology of the mutt."

Cissy worked hard on the campaigns of Medill and Roosevelt. One of the men she worked with was an old Chicago friend of Medill's, a young lawyer Cissy had met at the McCormicks' home, Elmer Schlesinger. His father owned one of Chicago's largest department stores; his uncle was one of the city's most prominent lawyers.

Elmer was a tall, lanky man, not really handsome but very attractive. He had gone to Harvard and played marvelous tennis. But what Cissy liked best about him was his way of talking to her without condescension. Freddie had been fun, and Bernstorff was absolutely charming, but neither of them talked to her seriously about significant things. To Elmer, she was not just a woman but an intelligent person whose opinions he listened to with respect.

Cissy would have found little new in going to parties and dances and even to bed with a man. But working alongside a man for long hours, with high spirits and much laughter, was a strange and exhilarating experience for her. She worked with a fervor she had seldom felt before, even in acting. She wrote press releases, handled publicity, acted as an audience for Medill's speeches. She learned that political volunteers are tied together by a most powerful bond—a dedication so deep that they forget family, friends, love, sleep, time, memory. The political campaign, short and intense, becomes their whole world, a world open only to those whose blood is true, whose eyes are wide, and whose hearts are full. In this world there is more heart than head, more hope than knowledge, more fervor, more faith, more love than anybody deserves.

Alice Roosevelt Longworth had a troubled time. Her husband, Nick, was running for Congress as a Taft supporter, while she campaigned for her father. Four years before, Alice had had a much happier, gayer time during the convention. She had ridden round and round the city on a hot night singing "Only a Bird in a Gilded Cage."

Her father was shot during the campaign, and with the bullet still inside him, he told the crowd, "They're going to operate when I get back to the hospital. . . . I want you to know that whatever happens to me, I've had a helluva good time on this earth, for which I'm grateful alike to my God, my friends and my enemies."

Roosevelt lost, and Medill won. The Progressive party vote split the Republican party, and Woodrow Wilson, the Democratic candidate, was elected President of the United States.

After the whirl of politics, Lake Forest was too quiet for Cissy. She was thirty-one, and she now wanted a change. With family income, she had no money worries. Alice urged her to move to Washington, and so did Bernstorff. Cissy had no illusions that her mother had changed, but she hoped the 30-room Dupont Circle house was big enough for two women and a small girl.

Felicia was then seven, old enough to remember her mother and grandmother clearly. "They quarreled fiercely when they were together. Grams was striving vainly, and too late, to mold her character. Grams did not approve of her beaux . . . and tried to control her by spying on her. Mama finally moved and bought her own house."

A four-story red-brick house on the corner of 16th and R Street, it was an unpretentious place with a narrow, winding stairway. Cissy thought her third-floor bedroom would discourage early morning visits from her mother and Aunt Kate, but it didn't. Felicia often saw the two of them, puffing up the stairs early in the morning with their newspapers—while her mother was still in bed—and asking straightaway, "Now, what do you think of this piece of gossip?" At that point, Felicia was sent from the room.

"Little children are a terrible bore," Cissy told Felicia in anger once, almost the same words that her mother had said to her when she was Felicia's age.

"She left me with Grams as much as she possibly could," said Felicia. "I was such a constant visitor at Dupont Circle that I had the best bedroom in the house, an enormous, sunny, charming room on the third floor. It had been intended for Grams but the fact that it was next to the backstairs made it too noisy for her. Sometimes I would awaken at dawn to see Grams there on the balcony in front of the house, looking plump, lonely and forlorn. She herself used the word 'forlorn' when she wanted to speak tenderly to me. 'You poor forlorn little orphan,' she'd say."

Felicia would sometimes see her grandmother wandering restlessly through her marble palace, a lone stroller in a homely old wrapper, making her own coffee at five o'clock in the morning on an ill-smelling spirit lamp because it was too early to ring for a servant. Felicia would hear her talking to herself and replying to herself with indignation, sometimes exclaiming with surprise, or startling herself, or voicing anger at her children for neglecting her.

"I used to think she chose to be disagreeable," said Felicia. "I could not make allowances for her." To her granddaughter, Nellie was a scold and a tyrant, "full of shan't's and must's," whose favorite phrase was "I demand instant obedience!"

Cissy had not exaggerated the way her mother had grated on her; Grams grated on Felicia too. But Felicia never forgot that when she was sick, it was Grams—not Cissy—who sat up all night with her.

Back at her brick home on R Street, Felicia met the small parade of men in her mother's life and often sat with them while her mother finished dressing. She liked Count von Bernstorff because he was always charming and funny with her and always brought her presents she liked. "He laughed very heartily. The house was alive and noisy when he was there." And she liked Shane Leslie, a tall, broad-shouldered, smiling man, who sometimes wore kilts. He and Bertie and Medill had gone to school together in England. He was the nephew of Lady Randolph Churchill.

Cissy's taste in men had changed somewhat. Like Gizy, she did not want to be "bored." She wanted a man not only to be entertaining and intelligent but also to respect the intelligence in her. Although she was highly sexual, she disliked men who prized this quality above all others. She wanted the give-and-take of conversation, and she proved her ability to hold her own. Friends found it difficult to categorize her intellectually. She was conservative on some issues, liberal on others, and highly progressive on many questions. Her opinions showed the mixed influence of Gizy, her father, her grandfather, Medill, and Joe.

Cissy was strongly for women's suffrage, but she did not support the feminists who went on hunger strikes or chained themselves to lamp posts. She was most interested in Margaret Sanger's new magazine, *The Woman Rebel.*

As war loomed in Europe, Cissy's emotions made her sympathetic to Austria. The assassination of the heir to the Austrian throne, Archduke Francis Ferdinand, at Sarajevo on

June 28, 1914, put Austria at war with Serbia. A network of military alliances soon entangled all Europe in the war.

Behind the headlines, Cissy saw familiar places and people, her friends in Austria fighting her friends in Russia. She learned that Gizy had enlisted in the Austrian army the night before the declaration of war. She knew that because of his decision his Russian estates would be lost to him. A mutual friend who had been with him that night said that it was the first time she had ever seen Gizy dead drunk.

Bernstorff was having his own problems, and Cissy shared them with him. He had been born in London, where his father was then ambassador, spent half of his most impressionable young years in England, and considered British life almost perfect. "I can hardly realize even yet that we are fighting that nation. It is dreadful," he told her. After England and Germany were at war, they were at a dinner party where someone started singing, "It's a Long, Long Way to Tipperary." Bernstorff not only joined in the singing, but also applauded loudly afterward. "I have no hate in me," he said. "The worst of me is I cannot hate."

Cissy's family believed as she did about the war, favoring United States isolationism. Her mother said she had met the German Kaiser when he was "a bumptious youth and I did not like him." However, she added that "the hysteria against Germany leaves me calm. I do not believe the English stories that Germany wants to conquer the earth." Cissy's brother went to Germany and wrote a book, *The Notebook of a Neutral*, indicating how impressed he was with the German might. "Any American in a position of power or influence who allows any consideration but the selfish interests of America to guide him is a traitor," he wrote.

An editorial in the *Tribune* complimented Count von Bernstorff on his efforts at preventing a rupture between Germany and the United States. This led to snide rumors that the *Tribune* had been influenced by Bernstorff's relationship with Cissy. This was not true. Joe had made up his own mind.

Patterson denied accusations that the *Tribune* was pro-German. "We want to keep out of the war, but also start preparations for it." He then added, slowly: "It might be said that we were not pro-British."

"The *Tribune* proprietors may have earned abuse for being wrong-headed, perverse, selfish, cowardly, stupid or hypocritical," wrote Bertie McCormick's biographer, Frank Waldrop. "They may have deserved to be called poltroons and scoundrels on general principles one time or another . . . but pro-German, in the sense of adhering to a foreign power against the United States between 1914 and 1918, they were not."

Pro-war hysteria mounted with the increasing stories of German atrocities. Then in May 1915, German submarines sank the British liner *Lusitania*. Of the 1,198 people drowned, 28 were Americans. Bernstorff cabled his government: "For God's sake don't submarine any more Americans: it means war!"

As anti-German reaction grew more intense, Nellie Patterson dropped Bernstorff from her guest list. Cissy did not. If anything, she was even more open about their relationship, not only inviting him to her dinners and parties but also seating him in the place of honor.

Cissy never had been a crowd follower. She did not like to be told what to do or whom to do it with. Two of her strongest traits were stubbornness and loyalty. With Bernstorff, of course, it was much more. He was not just a man she admired; he was her lover—a lover who reminded her strongly of Gizy but who had shown her the tenderness and understanding she had vainly sought in her husband.

Woodrow Wilson campaigned in 1916 on the slogan "He kept us out of war" and was reelected. But then the Zimmerman telegram was intercepted and decoded. This message from the German Ministry of Foreign Affairs to the German minister in Mexico suggested a German-Mexican alliance. The uproar caused by this revelation was heightened when the German Government advertised in American papers that it intended to sink all enemy ships without regard for the nationality of the passengers on board.

Bernstorff said good-bye to Cissy and his other American friends and headed for Germany to try to convince his superiors how wrong they were. He spent the rest of his career in Germany and never returned.

America's entry into the war was now only a matter of time. Bertie McCormick had been to Russia and Poland and reported to Cissy that her friends there were working in the hospitals during the day and still socializing at night by candlelight. Of Gizy he had heard nothing. Bertie had hurried to get his commission as major in the National Guard, and Joe had enlisted in the Army as a private. Medill was at the Mexican border, reporting for *Harper's Weekly*. Freddie joined a machine-gun battalion.

Cissy felt frustrated, unhappy, lonelier than ever. All her men were in the war, and on different sides. She wanted a change of scene. A Chicago friend, George Porter, suggested a dude ranch in Wyoming. Cissy was undecided. "I begged her and begged her for us to go," said Felicia, who was then eleven years old, a pretty girl, tall for her age, with thick blond curls. About this time, on one of the rare occasions when they were alone together, Cissy sighed and said to her daughter, "Life's a bore."

Porter promised Cissy she would find fun, and maybe even adventure in the West. She was ready for it.

7

*Make your own peace, no matter what. . . . [It's]
like having your own electricity from your own
power plant when you're off and alone somewhere.*

—Felicia Gizycka

The sign inside the hotel read "LOBY." The cowboys in the
room were quietly chewing tobacco, contemplating the low row
of brass spittoons. The town was Victor, Idaho, in the late
spring of 1916, "as stark and ugly as an old bone." Cissy, Felicia,
and an uneasy, unhappy maid had just gotten off the train
from Salt Lake City, the last leg of their long trip from
Washington. Their supper in the hotel dining room was as
appetizing "as boiled bedroom slippers."

Victor was not the town of Cissy's romantic imaginings. She
had come West expecting to see handsome cowboys riding out
of the sunset into picturesque hamlets full of adventure. She
found herself in a shabby hotel that looked over a dusty street.
The cowboys of Victor were not dashing, modern-day knights,
but plain-featured, taciturn working men.

The three slept fitfully, and the next morning at six they were up and waiting for the Bar B C ranch wagon. The driver was hours late and gave no apology. This silent young cowboy wore his sombrero at a rakish angle and stared at the three women "with an absent eye as at an everyday dish which had lost its savor."

Facing them was a ten-hour ride over a dusty, winding, narrow road that cut through the Teton Pass, creeping up one side of the mountain ridge and plunging down the other. The three women and their six trunks were a heavy load for the rough-hewn wagon. The three soon felt smothered by the heat and dust, exhausted by the endless lurching, dazzled by the brilliant light, dizzied by the altitude. Thirsty and hungry, they seemed to be slipping into a kind of trance. Finally they reached the top of the pass. Cissy looked out and saw the whole of the valley. In the distance was the swelling of the Continental Divide, rugged, blue, but less austere than the Tetons through which they were passing. Below her were many masses of mountain flowers, the delicate lavender rose of Sharon, the white-flowered hawthorn, the black and red haws. The most luxuriant hay meadows she had ever seen were bordered by trees—light green willows and aspens stood out against the deep-green pines and firs. The valley was no more than twelve miles wide and sixty miles long, and wriggling through its floor was the Snake River.

The spectacular view cleared her head, wiped out her fatigue. She was pleased when the driver said they would all have to get out and walk because the grade was too steep, the load too heavy for the horses. In her long-skirted tweeds from Paris and her custom-made walking boots from London, she hardly resembled a pioneer, and yet she felt like one. "She looked like a big wildcat and her red hair flamed in the mountain sunlight," Felicia remembered. Felicia skipped along in her own ecstasy, while the bewildered maid hobbled along in misery.

Long before they reached the floor of the valley, the rains came, turning the dust on their clothes and faces into mud. It was dark when they got to the zigzag switchback road to the Bar

B C. They were drenched and exhausted when they reached the ranch. Cissy knocked on the door of the main house. The door opened, and an oddly dressed creature laughingly said, "I'm a cave woman!"

They had arrived on the night of the dudes' annual costume party. The bleakness of Victor, the interminable hot dust of the road, the sudden superb view of the pass, the drenching rain, and now a party of absurdly dressed revelers—it had been a long day for the three travelers.

Given a single wish, Cissy would have been in a hot bath in her Washington home. Instead, she now had a small cabin with no plumbing, no electricity, and a tin basin hanging outside to serve as a tub.

Cissy awoke the next morning, looked out of the window to see her maid Abigail unlocking one of the six trunks, which sat on the bare ground, strange objects from another world. As Abigail was lifting out a large drawer, a gust of wind caught a lace petticoat. Abigail grabbed for it, dropped the drawer, spilling everything, then burst into tears. "I want to go home," she cried. So did Cissy. In the cold morning light, the Bar B C did not look like much: seven sleeping cabins, four bunkhouses, a large central cabin with kitchen, dining room, and some smaller rooms, a few storehouses and corrals, some cows and saddle ponies, and that was it. It seemed suddenly depressing.

"But there was this very odd thing about Cissy," Felicia later observed with admiration. "When she was really licked, she invariably calmed down and behaved herself."

She told Abigail that she could leave alone the next morning, and take five of the six trunks. But the driver couldn't leave the next morning, because the horses needed shoeing. The next day, a wagon wheel needed repairing. The day after that, the driver disappeared. When the wagon was finally ready a week later, Cissy saw Abigail leaning on a rail fence, sniffing a small bunch of wild roses, looking with open admiration at a few young cowboys working some spirited horses in the corral—cowboys whom she now knew well.

"The air is very healthful here," she told Cissy. "I've been thinking . . . I'd like to stay."

Cissy, too, had been captured by the place. She had wandered all over the ranch site, the nearby half-moon of aspen and pine, the beginnings of a meadow to the south of the ranch. She had watched antelope running in packs of fifty, deer and elk grazing. The small lakes she saw really did look like fluid sapphires. She was dazzled and soothed by the towering Tetons. She had found her peace.

Felicia was also happy. She had met a girl her age on the ranch with whom she was soon riding, exploring, and fishing. They had only one rule: Be home in time for dinner. Her friend called it "a pearl of a summer."

The Burts—Struthers and Kate—who ran the place, had a simple theory about dude ranches: People are like horses in a corral. Give them space and they are calm and relaxed; crowd them and their worst instincts surface. Their rules for dudes were few: Don't ride horses near the cabins: don't tie them to trees, because ropes kill trees; treat your horse as you would like to be treated yourself.

The first dude ranches had been opened at the turn of the century. Struthers Burt had been a Princeton professor and writer who came to Jackson Hole on a holiday in 1908 and didn't want to leave. His was one of only two dude ranches in the area, seventeen miles north of Jackson, when Cissy arrived.

During her stay her fellow guests included a Philadelphia family of five—on their morning ride, the father sat backward on his horse and read Shakespeare to the others; a woman who could get on a horse but was terrified of dismounting and had to be lifted off; and a mild-looking man, an excellent horseman-hunter who became a good friend of Cissy's—Francis Biddle, later attorney general of the United States.

The foreman of the ranch and chief guide was Cal Carrington. George Porter had told Cissy that Cal was the best guide she could get. He said that there wasn't a horse Cal couldn't gentle, there wasn't a wild animal he couldn't outwit, there wasn't a river he couldn't cross on a horse. (Cal often remarked that he had never learned to swim because his horse could do it better.)

"He nursed me with infinite gentleness and patience," Burt

added, "instructing me in the ways of ranching, livestock, and the hills, although I had already worked on various ranches . . . and was by no means a tenderfoot."

When Cissy met him, Cal was in his early forties, his face seamed and lined like a walnut. A tall, powerful man, he was rangy and ruggedly handsome. Cal had first drifted into Jackson Hole in 1897, only seven years after Wyoming had been admitted to the Union. There were only a few log houses in Jackson then, built in a rough square. Later they formed a stockade, the buildings touching each other, not for protection against the Indians but to save fuel in the winter. Only later were there wooden planks serving as sidewalks in front of the stores.

Jackson had been named for a fur trader who arrived with Kit Carson and Broken Hand Fitzpatrick in the 1820s. Settlers came sixty years later; cattle owners were soon fighting sheep owners because cattle would not graze on land closely cropped by sheep. The Indians had gone—the Blackfeet and the Flatheads and the Shoshone—but the rustlers arrived. Cattle barons hired killers, such as Tom Horn, who got a bounty for every rustler they shot. Horn identified his work by placing two stones under the head of each man he killed. When rustling became more widespread, cattle owners sent out bands of fifty hired gunmen—accompanied by a doctor—to wage open war. One such group was attacking a noted rustler, when other rustlers arrived to attack the attackers. It took a cavalry regiment to stop that war in the eastern part of the state.

Cal belonged to a gang of six rustlers, identified by the red squaw bandannas they wore. They specialized in stealing horses, rebranding them, then selling them over the state border. Of the group, only Cal was never caught and jailed.

Cal had been born Enoch Julin in Sweden. When he was six, his family sent him to the United States with Mormon missionaries. (Cissy once told Felicia that Cal's mother had sold him to a ship's captain.) Two years later he was adopted by a couple with a small ranch in Idaho. He described his foster father as "a hard, mean man . . . and so when I was sixteen, and big enough, I beat the hell out of the sonovabitch and ran away."

Cal became a cowboy; he wore big spurs, fancy-stitched

high-heeled boots, a ten-gallon hat to protect him from heat and rain, leather chaps, a flannel shirt, copper-riveted blue denims, and a neckerchief to cover his face in the dust and cold. For guns, he favored two Colt single actions. Since he wasn't a ranch hand who did ditching and haying, he wore leather gloves to keep his hands soft.

He worked the long cattle drives in Montana and roamed from Canada to Mexico as a top cowhand. He learned the challenge of bucking horses, the thrill and fear of stampeding cattle, the many uses of a rope, the cold and heat and wide horizons and loneliness.

"California" was the nickname of a cowboy he admired, so he adopted it, shortening it to "Cal." "Carrington" was the name of an Englishman who had treated him well. With the help of many friendly women, he had learned to read and write by the time he was twenty-one.

Rustling horses had gradually become his business until a California sheriff started to close in on him. Cal then took a packhorse named Quincy and made the long trek across the West to Jackson. Quincy would come to Cal every morning for a piece of breakfast hotcake. "When I came to Jackson Hole," said Cal, "I didn't have nothin' but a long rope and an old buckskin horse."

The valley was a country of capricious climate. A sudden blizzard could sweep through with sixty-mile-an-hour gusts. A warm, dry chinook wind from the Rockies could melt a three-foot snowbank in hours and change biting cold into mild spring. Although spells of intense cold were short, the mountaintops were covered with snow for eight months of the year, and summer nights were wondrously cool.

Cal saw the area around Jackson as "hole-in-the-wall" country; its hidden valleys tucked away among mountains made ideal hideaways for rustlers. He found his perfect place in Flat Creek, a rough ride of fifteen miles from Jackson, up hills and down gullies, across a rocky riverbed, then up a high hill. His valley was a quarter of a mile wide and a mile long, and it lay at an altitude of eight thousand feet, under the head of Sheep Mountain. From a distance the mountain looked like a sleeping Indian. The meadows, lush with sage grass and wild geraniums, were nestled among stands of lodgepole pine, aspen, balsam, and willow. Cutting through the valley was Flat Creek itself—sometimes flowing with the force of a river—its deep pools filled with cutthroat trout. The cabin he built looked out over this serene land.

Flat Creek was an ideal base of operations for his gang of rustlers. "All I had to do was to put up two pair of boards and that shut the whole canyon off," said Cal. "The horses stayed in there." There was pastureland for the horses, and if the sheriff and his men decided to drop in, "you could see them a'comin' and a-goin'." The road Cal had cut into the valley was so narrow that a wagon had barely a half-inch clearance on each side. As an intruder's wheels clipped the standing trees, the noise telegraphed a warning to the outlaws.

After all his partners had been put in jail, Cal joined the Bar B C "because it was time to get respectable and go into dudin'."

Cissy entranced Cal. The ranch always had dudines, willing and ready and rich, silken women with soft centers, quickly gone and forgotten. Cissy was a much different, more complicated woman who challenged his understanding. Her self-assurance matched his, and he liked the way she laughed. She didn't make a show of her money to impress him, as a lot of wealthy women did. She knew her horses. She asked good questions. She didn't talk all the time. She listened to him, and he enjoyed being with her.

Cissy had come West to find someone like Cal. He was his own man, someone she could not dominate. He was completely indifferent to her money and title and position. She was charmed by his quizzical, inquiring smile and his quick, graceful movements. Here was a man who believed in action instead of conversation. He made her feel so relaxed and comfortable. She had never met anyone like him.

Social life in Jackson centered on the saloons and the Saturday-night dances. To "shake a foot," families would come from forty miles away. After leaving the children in an upper room of a saloon, the adults would head for the second floor of an old building on the east side of the square, dance until dawn, stopping only for the midnight lunch they had brought along. A courtly man from Texas called the square dances, and if there was a shortage of women, men would tie handkerchiefs on their arms and substitute. Nobody worried about social standing. The best dancer on the floor might be the chambermaid from the hotel. And the richest man might be a woodchopper who had been lucky in a card game. Dudes usually arrived wearing Levi's and sneakers.

Wearing britches and laced boots, Cissy went to her first Saturday-night dance accompanied by Cal. Jackson was too small for secrets: the whole town then had fewer than two hundred residents. The courtship of Cal and Cissy was closely watched. Whenever the two appeared together, someone would say, "There goes Cal and his countess."

Cal monopolized Cissy as usual at this dance, "dancing around her even when he wasn't dancing with her." A new arrival saw Cissy, requested an introduction, and asked her to dance. Afterward, he said, "Oh, she's a great lady, but my God, *the Count!*"

"My God, the Count!" was a phrase Cal was never allowed to forget; it became part of Jackson folklore.

"Back East, my mother was considered a fascinating, lawless creature, a charmer and a menace," said Felicia. "Nobody could oppose her without getting hurt. Out here, people weren't afraid of her at all. Jackson Hole was full of characters who could be themselves without benefit of psychiatry or interference from the law."

One of these characters was Ma Reed. Born Maude Lillian Asbrough, Ma was a small, tough, part-Indian woman from Osage, Oklahoma. A fine cook, she ran the local hotel. Ma had a tender heart for needy people and brass knuckles for stubborn types. Cissy decided to spend a weekend at Ma Reed's so that she and Felicia could enjoy hot baths, soft beds, and some of Ma's famous food.

The hotel was a two-story frame structure on a corner of the main square. Its neighbors included a hardware store, a grocery, a drugstore, two livery stables, and several saloons.

Cissy and Felicia did not sleep well. Cowboys tromped into the hotel from the bars all night long, often accompanied by noisy female companions. And the walls were thin. Unsettled by this rough-and-tumble environment, the young Felicia had an accident. When Ma Reed charged Cissy an extra dollar for the wet sheet, Cissy became indignant. After a hot argument, Ma Reed yelled, "Git out!"

"We *got*!" recalled Felicia. "Ma bundled all our possessions into a sheet, putting them out on the front stoop."

One of Cissy's first friends in town was Rose Crabtree, who worked for Ma Reed. Rose Crabtree divided human beings into two categories: she either liked them or didn't.

"We just loved each other, oh my, yes," said Rose. "I think Cissy loved me more than anybody, and I loved her. I couldn't have had a better friend than she was. We talked together about everything and we did enjoy each other. We had a lovely life together. . . . Cissy and I laughed our heads off. We laughed all the time. I can still remember hearing the echo of it, going along the trail, laughing and telling stories."

Rose and Cissy were two of a kind; about the same age, they had the same wit, the same frankness. Rose spoke her mind directly, seldom softening her words with tact. She said what she wanted to say, what she felt she had to say. She didn't tell people what they wanted to hear but what she felt they ought to know. She didn't have Cissy's fine figure. She was plump, of middle height, and gray-eyed, and her hair was cut boyishly short. She had a high voice and a throaty laugh. Like Cissy, she loved to ride; but unlike Cissy, she also loved to gamble and didn't like to drink or shoot.

Rose had come to Jackson from Weeping Water, Nebraska, and had married Henry Crabtree, a quiet man and a good carpenter. He would have been happy living in his own home on his own land. Not Rose. She loved the tumult and complications of interesting people.

Soon after Cissy's run-in with Ma Reed, her hotel became the Crabtree Inn. Ma Reed had asked Rose to take care of the place while she and her husband went on a two-week vacation. Seven years later Ma Reed returned, a widow, in a big car. In the interim Rose had discovered that Ma had been stealing supplies from the grocery next door. Rose and Henry had gradually paid off all the debts and bought the place.

Cissy always headed for Rose's kitchen when she was in town. "She'd like to sit among the help and pretend she was one," said Rose. "I guess she just liked to pretend."

Rose's kitchen was the heart of her house. The large, black wood-burning stove divided the room into two parts with the dining table in front. For nine dollars a week, Rose gave each guest a room and three meals a day, "three of the biggest darn meals you ever saw." New arrivals would come to the kitchen first, get their food ladled out, and take a seat at the twenty-four-foot maple dining table. Rose had red-and-white curtains in her kitchen and red geraniums. She covered her floors with red, white, and black Navajo rugs, hung pictures of family and friends on the walls, and filled her shelves with everything from old copperware to Indian jars. She always had a red-and-white checked cloth on the table for breakfast and lunch, a snowy-white cloth for dinner. At night the big lamp in the center of the room converted it into a reading and writing room where the guests shared their mail. It was homey.

Rose kept the hotel register hung on the wall. If nobody was around, the guests simply signed themselves in. The only heated room upstairs, with a potbellied stove, was Number 7, where Cissy always stayed.

Rose had a beautiful black horse, and she and Cissy often went riding through the hills. Cissy had single-mindedly, stubbornly decided to become a crack shot, and she kept practicing until she was one. When it came time for lunch, while they were riding, they would both look for a bird. Cissy would then shoot it, and they would dress it, cook it, eat it. And they would talk.

Cissy talked to Rose as she did to no one else. After one long session, Cissy wrote her a note:

It has been on my mind a little all that *filth* I spilled. . . . I think I just wanted to laugh and be gay.

That isn't the real me. You must know that. . . . You must make allowances for me this year.

All this because I respect and value your opinion.

Sometimes, if they hadn't finished talking in the woods or back at the hotel, Rose would come back to the Bar B C and share Cissy's cabin. Felicia, who had her own cabin, was awakened one night by a noise that frightened her. "I was rigid with terror and then I raced to their cabin and knocked on the door and woke them up. I told Ma I heard noises and I was scared. Ma was annoyed at my waking her up in the middle of the night, but Rose said, 'Just climb in with me,' and I did."

Rose believed that "Felicia was terribly abused when she was a little girl. Her mother didn't understand her. . . . Felicia was a lovely child. Everybody loved her and felt sorry for her and was good to her, *everybody* was. Everybody but Cissy. They were always at each other. Maybe most mothers and daughters are. But this was bad. The thing was that Cissy wasn't mean to anybody else."

Conflict between a daughter growing into adolescence and her mother is not unusual, but the clash between Cissy and Felicia verged on war and was tinged with hate.

"She loved me but she couldn't show it," said Felicia afterward. "She hated me because she hated herself, and took it out on me. I know I was a spoiled brat, and difficult, but I still think one of the main things she subconsciously resented was her pain at my birth."

Cal, who had the wisdom of his own loneliness, told her, "Little feller, it's all because your ma has taken a de-spite to your father." In pronouncing the word "despite" he gave it a special force by emphasizing the first syllable.

Cal took Cissy and Felicia on their first long hunting trip. They traveled with ten packhorses and a cook-helper named Al. Felicia "lagged behind, eating the dust and dying of boredom and fatigue," and the words she heard most from her mother were "For God's sake, hurry up!" The party set up a camp, where Felicia continued to be unhappy.

"Cal and Cissy would be gone all day and Al had no idea what

162

to say to a minor female dude," Felicia said. "So he said absolutely nothing all day long. There was lots of chocolate in the food supply. I made fudge every day. I'd put the pan on stones in the creek to cool. The pan fell into the water and so did I. Then I tried fishing. I finally caught a few. Twelve little ones on my twelfth birthday, and one big old fellow that we all ate with great relish. Cissy shot a young elk for meat. We enjoyed that, too. But then we had a snowstorm that lasted for a couple of days. Cissy enchanted Cal and me by reading Tolstoy aloud to all of us in her tent, where there was a stove."

Cal *was* enchanted by Cissy. Until he had met the Countess, he was just a professional cowboy, certainly the best of a breed, but with a simple set of standards, a fixed frame of reference. The Countess gave him new dreams, new fantasies. And he gave her a rough, intense love she had never had before. Cal was not a man for flowers and courting and quiet questions. When Cal wanted, he took, and few women ever objected. Certainly not Cissy. She could not be coy with Cal—especially not when the two went into the woods alone on a hard ride, or when he was guiding her quietly in the tenseness of a hunt, or when the campfire was low and she was too excited to sleep.

The summer was long gone before Cissy could force herself to leave Jackson and return home. That winter, in January 1917, she went through the ordeal of her divorce trial. She wrote Rose that it was "one of the worst experiences of my life. . . . [I] have been rather in pieces since then. . . ."

The trial dredged up all the details Cissy had tried to forget—Gizy's desertion at the train station, his violence, his women. The newspapers had a heyday, headlines and pictures retelling the story of her unhappy marriage. The peace she had gained during the summer in Jackson Hole now disappeared. As the divorce became final, she wondered if Gizy was still alive. The Germans were withdrawing on the western front, but the casualties on both sides were still enormous. There had been a revolution in Russia, and the Czar had abdicated. What would happen now to all her Russian friends? Had the peasants taken over Nowosielica? Who was now sleeping in her bed?

General John J. Pershing had arrived in Paris to head the American forces. Cissy knew that Bertie was on his staff. He was a major, and surely safe. She was glad that her cousin Medill, now almost forty, was out of the war. But Joe was just a private in the Rainbow Division, and she worried about him. His letters were short and infrequent, always making things lighter than she knew they were. She tried to imagine the horror of shells and bombs and gas. It terrified her to think that her brother might be killed.

It was not a happy winter. She kept replaying the divorce trial over and over again in her mind. She sent Felicia to boarding school but still had no feeling of freedom. There was no full-time interesting man in her life. Her mother in Washington was as impossible and as domineering as ever. One of the most interesting men she met in Washington was Senator William Borah of Idaho, a large, impressive man. When he spoke on the Senate floor, his voice was like the roar of a lion, and when he threw his head back, his long hair shook like a mane. She had met him at a party in Alice's house and was quick to see how much Alice was smitten by him. Borah was a political maverick, and Cissy liked him instantly because he looked directly at her, and admiringly. He also answered questions directly and simply. She noticed, too, that he had the same stillness that Cal had, the same sense of strength. Alice mentioned casually that Borah might be President one day.

Cissy spent much time with Medill and Ruth. Medill had just been elected to Congress, after two terms in the Illinois General Assembly. He and Ruth were full of the excitement of Washington, and Ruth talked confidently of someday soon seeing her husband in the U.S. Senate. At their house, Cissy again met Elmer Schlesinger, the dynamic Chicago lawyer she had known during Teddy Roosevelt's campaign for the Presidency in 1912. Their paths had intermittently crossed since then, and their mutual attraction was obvious. He had become highly successful and represented some of the country's largest corporations, including the Chicago *Tribune*. But he was a married man with two children.

In her restlessness, Cissy went to New York. The city's gaiety could not relieve her anxiety about the war, and she soon left. She was glad when the summer came again, and she returned to the peaceful honesty of Jackson Hole. She felt, however, that she had outgrown the dude ranch; she wanted a place of her own with more privacy. She persuaded Cal to work for her. Cal explained to Burt why he was leaving to go with Cissy: "She don't know nothin'. She's a mighty nice woman, and someone might get the better of her."

Cissy leased the White Grass ranch for the season. White Grass had three log cabins, a tent, and a big barn. Nestled close to the Tetons, White Grass occupied a remote and beautiful site, where only the sound of running streams broke the silence.

Cissy's cook was Pearl Deyo, a local woman. "The Countess said we could eat anything in the kitchen except the goose livers. They came in little jars from France. But she was real nice to work for. Most of the time I was on my own. She let me cook what I wanted to cook. She wasn't fussy. Of course, every once in a while, she might want something special. As for Cal, he sure kept close to the Countess!"

Cal took Cissy to his own ranch at Flat Creek. Once she saw it, she was determined to have it. Cal was reluctant, highly reluctant. But Cissy was persistent, incredibly persistent. Cal seldom surrendered, but he finally agreed to let Cissy have a lease on Flat Creek for several years.

Back in Washington that winter of 1917 as a fully freed divorceé, Cissy was very much at loose ends. So many of the men she dallied with were married, from Senator Borah to Elmer Schlesinger. So many of the others she knew were on their way to war. American troops had landed in Europe in force. Her greatest fears were still for her brother, and then for Freddie, and, much less, for Bertie. And, surely, there was her secret concern for Gizy, of whose fate she had heard nothing.

Ruth and Medill had bought a house in Washington, and they discussed their plans with her for Medill's race for a Senate seat. Cissy knew that Ruth's ambitions for him did not stop there.

The Senate had defeated a proposed constitutional amendment to give women the right to vote—but they had passed an amendment for national prohibition against liquor. Cissy and Ruth were also indignant that forty-one more suffragettes were put in jail for picketing outside the White House.

The next summer could not come quickly enough for Cissy. She took over Cal's cabin, with its porch facing the meadow and the mountains, and a creek running nearby. Cal had a smaller cabin directly behind hers. The cook and the new Swedish maid, Aasta, lived in another nearby cabin, and the chore boy slept in a cabin a quarter-mile away near the red barn.

Cissy was contented in this hidden valley; she felt protected by the great cliff north of the cabin and the tall timbered mountain to the south. It was so still that as Cissy sat silently on her porch, the animals came down from the woods to drink and feed—the elk and the bear and the antelope and the moose, and a multiplicity of birds.

Life on the ranch was simple. Water was drawn from the creek, and kerosene lamps provided light in the evenings. There was an outhouse a short distance from the cabin. Getting supplies from town meant a day's trip by horse, packhorse, and foot. There were no horse trails then, but Cissy often rode in the woods, making her own way up the surrounding hills. She spent long stretches of time by herself. Billy Wells, who once worked for her, recalled that she would go off and sit on a stump, gazing out over the valley. Everyone knew that she wanted to be alone, and nobody bothered her. If Cal could make himself feel like one of the animals he was tracking, Cissy began to feel like part of the trees and the mountains. Most of all she loved the wildness of the land. Rose had told her, "Every man to his country, but I always pray—God bless mine, and keep it wild."

Felicia, at first, loved Flat Creek. She took long walks in the woods, hard rides up the mountain with Cal. "Loosen up your reins, little feller. He ain't a-goin' to fall if he can help it. A horse hates to fall down. He's got four legs and twice as much sense as we have."

But Felicia was no longer "a little feller." She was a tall, attractive girl who soon became bored, missing the company of people her own age. She had friends in Jackson and was soon spending more and more time there. As a teenager, she was most mature for her age, and her friend, Ellen Dornan, recalled how all the boys at the Saturday-night dance asked her to introduce them to Felicia. The dance floor was too rough for the participants to slide their feet, "so they all hopped around like grasshoppers to a squeaking fiddle."

When Felicia returned to Flat Creek, she and her mother quickly resumed their round of cutting quarrels. She once told Cal, "I don't know how you can work for my mother. For fifteen minutes I wouldn't work for my mother." Years later, more reflectively, Felicia admitted, "As a child, I was an awful drag around adults. Really, I can't blame Cissy for some of our roundups. Even a normal mother would have had a hard time of it."

And Cissy had never been a normal mother. In a hotel lobby in Idaho, she once saw a baby alone on a sofa, screaming. She picked it up "rather awkwardly" and unsuccessfully tried to soothe it. The cowboy-father soon arrived, his mouth full of safety pins, to diaper his baby. Cissy watched his swift, delicate gestures. In comparison, she felt "as if my whole ten fingers were made of cotton flannel."

Cissy never felt at ease hugging and kissing babies, much less her own daughter. Yet she liked children, and she was particularly fond of Rose's son, Hank. Hank recalled going with his mother and Cissy to the Bar B C for lunch. "But I wouldn't go inside because all the other kids were wearing Levi's and I had on these big overalls. My mother was so mad she was trying to drag me and I was crying and crying, and Cissy said to me, quietly, 'Keep on crying a little harder and you might get that toy gun you wanted.'"

Like Felicia, Hank never received much physical affection from his mother. It seems that Rose and Cissy were alike in this, too.

Cissy was no longer a dude; she was a westerner. She wore a man's shirt, boots, britches, and a five-gallon hat, often tying her hair back with a bandanna. She long ago had earned the town's respect. "Anybody who can ride from town to Flat Creek on a horse is *really* a rider," remembered Ed Lloyd, a Jackson resident who knew Cissy well. On impulse, Cissy would often ride from her ranch the fifteen miles to Jackson to have lunch with Rose, and then ride back the same day. Cissy loved a hard ride, but she soon loved the thrill of the kill even more.

Elk and moose were in excess in the area; the herd of 15,000 had to be regularly thinned or the animals would starve. In the winter, hunger brought them into town, hunting for hay. Townspeople joked that one old buck held a lantern while another elk broke down the hay rick.

Cissy had an unsentimental view of the natural world:

Life was intended to destroy life. All nature is cruel. Big fish eat little fish; hawks kill sparrows; even in this country, bears, wolves, wolverines, coyotes kill when they can. Wild animals die a tragic death anyway. They die of starvation and cold when they are old and weak, the prey of others. Wolves eat wolves. . . .

The passion of the chase lies deep beneath the consciousness to kill. To the natural-born hunter, the mere sight of game stirs to the roots an ancient fundamental instinct, inherited through the ages, probably from the days when a fight between man and beast was a fight on both sides of deadly consequence. It is the same animal instinct which throws a setter dog, for instance, into a trembling ecstasy at the sight or scent of a grouse.

She added that she believed man is more inhuman and degenerate in the slaughterhouse than in the forest.

Cissy used a 6.5 mm Mannlicher carbine with a short barrel, the same kind of rifle Gizy had given her at Nowosielica. She found it a wonderful gun for long-distance shooting, "but it shoots high like all high-power guns at short range." Al Johnson, a guide who hunted with her, said, "Cissy could hit an elk at four hundred yards. She could shoot the head off a grouse at seventy-five feet." Another guide, George Ross, called Cissy the best shot of all the women he had met.

"Women make the best hunters," said George Ross's son Rex,

who once worked for Cissy. "They listen to you and do what they're told. The trouble with men hunters is that they know a little bit about hunting and they think they know it all, and they're not apt to take advice from anybody."

When Cissy went hunting with Cal, she listened, almost always.

"My mother could not be independent of him in the woods," said Felicia. "She tried to leave camp alone once and got lost. Cal could leave you in the woods at a certain point and come back at the day's end to that very same point."

Cal was an intuitive hunter. "He hardly bothered to track an animal or follow it directly," said Struthers Burt. "He would smell the wind, reflect, and then take off, frequently at right angles. Presently he would stop. After a while, the game would appear. What he had done was to submerge himself in the weather, the wind, the lay of the land—putting himself into the mind of an elk, a bear, a moose."

The hunting season opened in September, often with the screaming bugle of a rutting elk.

"Bull elk in love have some of the same characteristics of a man in love," Cissy noted. "They mope along a little to the side of the herd, half-hidden in the brush, engrossed in their own emotions." But they sound different: the elk gives a guttural roar, then a series of trumpetlike calls followed by a shrill, screaming whistle, the guttural again, and a final grunt. Cissy compared the high notes of this mating call to "an eerie silvery whistle."

A bull elk weighs up to 800 pounds, with antlers up to five feet in length from tip to burr. Cissy was determined to shoot one of these majestic creatures.

With Felicia, a cook, and a chore boy, Cissy and Cal headed into the mountains. They spent twenty-one fruitless days before they heard the bugling of a bull elk about a quarter of a mile away.

She and Cal "jumped off without a word," Cissy wrote, "tied up the ponies, pulled out our rifles, and started down the canyon, Indian fashion, avoiding brittle twigs and dried leaves as best we could." They caught the elk's scent:

. . . a kind of stale animal smell, like cattle, and yet different, wilder, more elusive.

We crept unseen to within a few hundred yards of this particular herd. And then, round the corner of some brush, we came face to face with an indignant elderly matron. We looked at each other for a second or so, as if all three had turned to stone. Then, with a warning snort, she dashed up the opposite side of the canyon, a bunch of cows and calves at her heels. The bull had not yet come in sight.

Then the bull arrived, more curious and courageous than the cows, and paused "like Lot's wife"—for a fatal look behind.

He paused, I shot, and he shied to one side like a horse shying at a scrap of paper. He plunged on. I knew he was hit; but I knew, too, that if he were not struck in a vital spot, he might run off and die in the forest, where we would not find him. . . . Within a minute, the air shook with a great roar of agony and rage. Down he came, rolling over and over to the bottom of the steep incline. We could not see him distinctly, for he was hidden in the brush, but he thrashed and raged and fought for his splendid life till the last breath left his body.

He was a magnificent creature, bigger than a western horse, stronger, heavier. He had fourteen points, and his horns were heavy, wide and long. He was fat and sleek, in the very prime of life—the most beautiful specimen shot in Jackson Hole that year.

Cissy's satisfaction was supreme. She felt as if she had grabbed the brass ring. She wanted to hang the elk head on the wall at home and astonish her sophisticated friends, who would find it hard to believe. They would find it hard to believe that their pampered Cissy could go anywhere an elk went, ride all day and never want to quit or pitch camp early, and camp anywhere without fuss or bother. They would find it hard to believe that this same Cissy who was used to elaborate, sophisticated menus absolutely delighted in a meal of bacon and eggs, hotcakes, sourdough biscuits, and coffee cooked over an open fire. She now had passed the final test in her own new world.

Cal's friends at Ben Sheffield's Hotel in nearby Moran had been kidding him about his "fancy dude." Now Cal brought them the elk's head, "and I told them fellers, 'All right. She done it. Look!'"

Cissy soon knew almost everyone in Jackson. She told her Washington friend, Evie Roberts, "I have seen taller mountains and larger lakes, but I love the people there." She loved them because they were there when she needed them, they were friendly when she talked to them, and they respected her privacy and let her alone when she wanted to be let alone. They didn't treat her like a freak or an outsider or a dude; they accepted her for what she was. And what was she? She was like Cal, a very private person, a loner. Anyone who wanted to make friends with Cal had to make the initial overture, and then he might, or might not, reciprocate. Although he knew everyone, was welcome everywhere, was respected by everybody, he had almost no intimate friends. His solitary nature made his relationship with Cissy all the more remarkable. Before Cissy, women had been transients in his life. He even had refused to marry the woman who had borne his child. Nothing was more important to him than his freedom. And now, suddenly, voluntarily, he had surrendered his freedom to Cissy. There was nothing abject in this surrender. He was still his own man with his own strength, and he knew he could walk away whenever he pleased. In his quiet way, he was as regal as she was. He had no false modesty about his assets, his value. He knew what she wanted and he knew what he gave her, and he knew he was as important to her as she was to him. His surrender simply meant that he would be with her when she came to Jackson.

Cissy surrendered nothing; she absorbed. She absorbed Cal's love as she absorbed everything else in her new world. She delighted in the high, sweet, cool, and clear way Cal whistled for his horse in the early morning; the delicate way a mule picked along an incline, snatching at grass, while a horse would pant and tremble; the drumming song of a hundred male sage hens, inflating their air sacs as they grunted and croaked and strutted, announcing the mating season.

171

Now that she had her elk, Cissy wanted the even greater challenge of a mountain goat. Out on the hunt, the morning was particularly cold and bitter, and Cissy borrowed a pair of Cal's boots so that she could wear two pairs of socks. That morning they found a game trail winding up the side of a canyon through the brush and rocks.

"My feet swam in those great high-heeled boots," she said. "My ankles turned in and they turned out. I fell continually, and the hurry and the worry and the high altitude knocked out my wind entirely."

She told Cal she was too excited to shoot, and he pulled out a dingy handkerchief, told her to blow her nose, which she obediently did, and returned his handkerchief. Suddenly ahead of her, 175 yards away across a small chasm, was a mountain goat, his head half raised, looking straight at her. At that instant, the big animal rose on its feet, and she shot. The bullet hit, but the goat lurched away and vanished. Because of her boots, she couldn't clamber down the rocks to find it and finish it.

It was her first ram and she wanted the head. "How you goin' to get it?" Cal asked. "I ain't noticed no airplanes around here yet."

"The sharp wind had stung tears into my eyes," said Cissy, "and I added a sniff or two." Cal went.

I heard no more . . . for the next four hours. The gigantic sky, the gloomy rocks, and the brooding plain swamped me. . . . I longed to sneak back home, under a roof, to familiar things. . . . Presently I found a little hole in the rocks. . . . By drawing my knees up, I could lie on my back out of the wind—in comparative shelter. Every once in a while, I'd poke my head up to look down . . . and at last I spied him far below, coming around a point in the slide rock. And yes—he carried something, for he walked lopsided. Finally, after an hour's struggle, he came suddenly from under a ledge into plain sight. And he held up the head—an unbroken horn in each hand—radiant and triumphant as the original Salome.

Cissy and Cal liked to be alone together. Cissy was the boss at the ranch, but Cal was in command in the camp, and Cissy did what she was told. Out in the wild, just the two of them, Cissy could be more feminine than she ever had been wearing a silk dress in a drawing room.

Cal bought her a pair of black angora chaps. The townspeople perked up—Cal had a reputation with women of taking, not giving. Leather chaps protected pants from sharp brush and branches, when mounted; angora chaps were for warmth and elegance. Her Jackson friends regarded the chaps amusingly as a kind of slave bracelet, but Cissy wore them proudly.

Cal also helped her pick out her favorite cow pony. She named it Ranger and said the horse had been "born with nineteen legs," as surefooted as a mountain goat. Ranger also had the gift of a hunting dog, the ability to point and flush. She remembered a wintry day when she had gone out alone from camp. Suddenly, "Ranger's ears pricked up and he pointed dead for a thick clump of mountainside brush." Not a leaf stirred, but Cissy's trust in Ranger was implicit, and she fired at the brush. Looking behind it, she found she had killed a bull elk. The next day, when Cissy rode out with a packhorse to carry the elk back, she got lost. She let Ranger have his head, and he went directly to the elk.

As much as Cissy loved to hunt, it would never occur to her to go for her gun when she sat on her porch in Flat Creek and watched the unafraid animals come down to feed in her meadow. "Cissy really loved animals," said Felicia. "I remember she and Rose were riding along when they saw this stray cow and calf, alone together. She went to the mayor of this little town and told him he had to find the owner, and he did. She could get very excited about things like that."

Rose would come up often to Flat Creek and spend a few days. Only Cissy called her "Rose"; the rest of the town called her "Crabtree." The two would occasionally squabble and indulge in real tongue-lashings. Rose's language was not profane, but it could be powerful. And when Cissy was angry, her words came right out of the gutter.

"I loved her to death and all that," said Rose, "but oh, she was all temper when she was mad. But who ain't? I've got a temper like a house afire myself."

Cissy still took more from Rose than from anyone else. Only Rose could look her in the eye and say, "You need a bath, you look awful." And Cissy would take a bath.

Cissy was amazed that Rose had never slept with any man except her husband. She wasn't happy until she found someone who had been mooning about Rose for years, without encouragement. She often teased Rose laughingly about her admirer.

Cissy had always been afraid that no one would ever love her for herself alone, that everyone always wanted something from her. But here was Rose, who wanted nothing but her friendship and her love. Cissy frequently tried to give Rose gifts, but Rose always refused. Rose's pride and independence were as great as Cissy's. Once when Rose admired Cissy's ruby and emerald earrings, Cissy offered them to her. Rose laughed and said, "When you die, you can leave them for me."

"Why wait till I die?" said Cissy. "All you have to do is have your ears pierced."

She finally persuaded Rose to accept the earrings, but Rose soon gave them to a niece. Instead of getting angry, Cissy laughed and loved Rose all the more.

Everyone in town knew that if you told Rose something, Cissy soon knew it, and vice versa. "They were right together as the leather on a baseball."

It was Rose who started Cissy writing. Like Cissy, Rose was outraged by injustice and inaction. She was especially angered by the sad mess of the town government in Jackson. Rose corralled a number of women friends, and they decided to run against the men in the next town election. Women around the country were struggling for the right to vote, but in Wyoming they had had it since 1896.

When the women won, Cissy was so pleased that she wrote a story about it. The Omaha *World Herald* printed it, under the headline "'Just Like Housekeeping,' Women Ruling Town Say."

"The spotlight turned full on Mrs. Crabtree of Jackson Hole," Cissy wrote, "when she ran against her husband for Town Councilman and beat him two-to-one."

After noting that Jackson was the only town in the country run by women, Cissy described Rose as "a handsome young woman with a broad, candid brow like a madonna. Her manner is trenchant, yet easy and welcoming." She quoted Rose:

The men had made just a mess of running this town. Seven hundred and fifty dollars in debt and nothing to show for it. Keeping a little town like Jackson is like keeping house. We women who were elected are all good housekeepers. Whoever heard of a good man housekeeper? Why, look at the old bachelors around here. Most of them live like wild animals. As for cooking, all they know is how to open a tin can into a frying pan.

Now, in Jackson, the men did the foolishest things. They built a two-foot ditch all through town, and put up one-foot culverts. Consequently our streets are flooded half the time. We women are goin' to have a town well before next year, too. It's all right in summer; we get our water from the irrigating ditches, but in the winter every drop used in this place has to be hauled in barrels from the river through the ice and snow. Did you ever hear of anything so ridiculous?

And we're going to level the grade to the cemetery. That's for sure. The way they've got it, the corpse has to be carried half a mile up the hill to be buried—wagons and cars can't make it in bad weather. Like as not, the men thought the corpse would oblige by getting out and walking just a little way.

Cissy waited almost until the snows came before returning to Chicago. Whenever she left Jackson Hole now, she left with a pang, as if she were abandoning the most important part of herself. Just before she left this time, there was a telegram: her brother Joe had been wounded and gassed. She was frantic until she learned that the wound was slight. Joe had fought in five major battles and earned a number of decorations, and

General Douglas MacArthur later called him "the most brilliant natural-born soldier who ever served under me." Her brother's wound was the kind of news that made Cissy realize that his was the real world that she was trying to escape in Jackson Hole.

8

Writers have to have two countries, the one where
they belong and the one where they live, really.
The second one is romantic, it is separated from
themselves. It is not real but it is really there.
                                    —Gertrude Stein

The Ogden Armours were giving an engagement party for
their daughter Lolita in the Crystal Room of the Blackstone
Hotel in Chicago. It was the high point of the social season, the
night the ladies put on their most elegant dresses, their most
expensive jewelry, their long white gloves. In the midst of the
party, there was a commotion at the door, the guards trying to
hold back a noisy and determined crasher. Ogden Armour
hurried over to the excited group. He soon returned, escorting
Cissy Patterson Gizycka, still in her western riding clothes. She
had just arrived from her Wyoming ranch, Cissy explained.
Her train had been late, and had she gone home to change, she
would have missed the party. A society editor observed that the
guests were startled by her defiance of convention, "but many a

dowager secretly wished she had Cissy's independence of spirit."

Chicago was always home for Cissy. Here she would always be the little girl with the lemonade stand who dared to climb to the top of the church steeple. Here she remembered what she wanted to—the good times, the good places, the good friends. The empty vastness of the 91-room Gold Coast home of her parents on Burton Place could not compare to her own preferred quiet cottage in Lake Forest. She was no longer afraid of her mother's bite or roar. She now had her own bite, her own roar.

That winter in Chicago, Cissy met Walter Crawford Howey. It seemed improbable that Cissy, who liked her men handsome or rugged, or preferably both, could have any interest in a man who was so conspicuously neither. Howey was a slight man with a round face and neatly combed hair. He looked like "a guileless, small-town merchant who never missed a mid-week prayer meeting." His left eye was somewhat bluer than his right; it was also glass. Ben Hecht, who worked for him, claimed that the glass eye was the warmer one.

Howey struck a chord in Cissy because he had a flamboyant sense of power, an extravagant imagination, and an ever present urge for instant action. He was as cynical and sentimental as she was. He could be as wild and uninhibited as she was.

The dapper Howey was then city editor of the Chicago *Tribune*. He had the same red hair as Cissy did, and she soon discovered that they shared the same quick temper. They also shared a consuming taste for drink and books.

Howey often took her to Schlogl's, a saloon frequented by most of the top reporters in town. Then, as reporter Adela Rogers St. Johns remembered, he would recite large parts of *King Lear* "without a break." He might spend a whole evening telling Cissy about a movie script he was writing concerning upper-class criminals. Or about the invention he later patented for transmitting photographs over the wire. What Cissy loved best, and remembered most, were Howey's stories behind the stories.

Howey had worked for Cissy's brother Joe and cousin Bertie

when the two alternated as editor. Howey preferred Bertie, the humorless autocrat, because Bertie left him alone. Joe, the hearty backslapper, was determined to exercise his authority. "You may be right, old boy," Joe would tell him, "but I was smarter than you in my choice of grandparents. Since it's my property, let's do it my way."

When Joe Patterson apologized editorially for a short puff piece Howey had printed, Howey felt his face publicly slapped. He quit the *Tribune* and became managing editor of Hearst's Chicago *Herald-Examiner*. Before going, he blasted Patterson and vowed revenge. And he got it, again and again.

Frank Carson, Howey's star assistant at the *Tribune*, had remained loyal to Patterson and stayed on with the paper. Howey, however, got Carson drunk enough to sign a letter of resignation that read:

Dear Mr. Patterson:

I address you as "Mr." because your phony pretensions of democracy, urging the help to "Just call me Joe," turn my stomach, as they do all who must lick your boots for pay.

I could stand your cousin, because the man is honest according to his lights. He is a Twentieth Century Quixote, tilting at windmills, visible to no one's eyes but his own. You are a common panderer, catering to the meretricious tastes of the masses.

I call myself a coward because I have hitherto lacked the courage to tell you what I think of you, and to ask you to stuff your pipsqueak newspaper up your overstuffed bottom.

Thank God, now that I have been given a contract as City Editor of the Herald & Examiner, I shall be able to use your paper daily for the purpose I have long felt it was meant—in the Men's Room of the Hearst Building.

Sincerely,
Frank Wesley Carson

The next morning, Carson groaned at the letter he had signed and went to work for Howey. The story became part of the folklore of the Madhouse on Madison Street—as Howey's Hearst paper was soon called.

Howey's thirst for revenge was so strong that he was reported to have said that his final humiliation of Joe Patterson would be his seduction of Joe's sister. Howey's attraction to Cissy, however, was stronger than his animus toward Joe. Cissy normally would have hated anyone who hated her brother. But Howey had caught her imagination and her affection. Had Joe been in Chicago, Cissy would have had to avoid Howey. But with Joe away at war, Cissy persuaded herself that neither man was serious in his expression of hostility toward the other.

Because she saw it through Howey's eyes, the newspaper business seemed like a wonderful game to Cissy. Howey was fast becoming a living legend in Chicago. "The top editor who ever was," said Westbrook Pegler, who worked for him. "If you weren't sure of Howey's reality, you would insist that some crazy liar just wrote him."

"He saw more news, more color, more features, got out a better paper with one eye than anybody else ever did with two," observed reporter St. Johns. "The cleverest editor in the newspaper business," commented William Randolph Hearst.

Howey was as ruthless as he was imaginative, as violent and coarse as he was irresistible. When his top reporter, Charles MacArthur, said he was going to New York, Howey gave him his watch as a farewell present. He then called the police in Gary, Indiana, telling them to meet the train, arrest MacArthur, and bring him back to Chicago. When he was asked what the criminal charge was, Howey shouted, "Why, that sonofabitch stole my watch!" (MacArthur and Ben Hecht used the incident, the line, and Howey in their hit play, *The Front Page*.)

To get a public official on the hook, Howey would have the official investigated. If any incriminating evidence was turned up, he would confront the official and say, "I do not mean to use the material now. I want your resignation, written and signed but undated. I will not publish it until the day when you do not cooperate with me."

The *Herald-Examiner* concentrated on murder, adultery,

scandal in Chicago, while carrying standard Hearst syndicated features on home, family, jobs, and church. Howey told Cissy that his formula was 90 percent entertainment and 10 percent information. It was a formula she never forgot. He saw his paper as a compilation of organized gossip—what he thought his readers were talking about, or would like to be talking about. Howey was fundamentally provincial. A foreign earthquake was never as important as a strong local story. When a little girl was reported trapped in a safe, Howey called the warden of a state prison and asked him to rush over his finest safecracker. The safe turned out to be empty, but Howey still ran a front-page story about the safecracker pleading with the warden to be allowed to try to free the little girl.

Every evening with Howey was an advanced class in journalism for Cissy. She learned that Chicago reporters fought and tricked each other to get a story; that Howey felt the end justified the means; that he was capable of creating a story when it didn't exist. He told one reporter, Burton Rascoe, "Don't ever fake a story. That is, never let me catch you at it."

Cissy also learned how Howey increased his newspaper's circulation. He once printed an article about a millionaire who wanted to distribute his fortune by putting dollar bills in random copies of the *Herald-Examiner*. People were waiting in line at their newsstands the next day. There were enough dollar bills in enough newspapers so that the lines doubled the following morning. In a short time, circulation jumped from 300,000 to a million. The whole scheme cost Howey $5,000.

Her constant exposure to Howey's enthusiasm about newspaper publishing whetted Cissy's desire to work as a journalist. Her brother had refused to let her write for the *Tribune*. Perhaps Joe thought she wasn't good enough and didn't want her feelings hurt; perhaps he felt that nepotism was wrong. He might not have realized that her ambition to write for newspapers was based in part on her wish to imitate him. This urge to be like him was a constant theme in the pattern of her life.

Howey was happy to give her an opportunity to write professionally. He had read her story about Jackson Hole politics and insisted that she could write, and write well. He persuaded her to describe her hunting experiences for him. He ran her picture above each article and made sure her byline read: "Countess Eleanor Gizycka, sister of the editor of the Chicago *Tribune*." Once more Howey had triumphed over his former employer.

Cissy was so pleased with her newspaper stories that she decided to write a magazine article. She once had visited Sing Sing prison, and Howey suggested she go to the Illinois prison at Joliet and compare the two institutions.

"The ventilation is equally bad," she wrote, "and the bucket system also prevails. But there was life and stir in the courtyard at Sing Sing. At Joliet, I saw men listlessly standing around, idle and vacant." She described a prisoner in solitary confinement, forced by his chains to stand upright—"his unnatural eyes and humble quick movements suggested the well-trained wild animal." *New Republic* magazine printed Cissy's article, and it shocked her friends. This was a Cissy they did not know.

Felicia was away at boarding school, at fashionable Foxcroft, where Cissy's mother had gone. Felicia showed an early talent for writing, which Cissy encouraged. "But whenever I got a thick letter from Ma, I'd shake because I knew it was usually vituperative. I don't know why. I guess sometimes she just hated herself and took it out on me."

Felicia joined Cissy in Chicago in 1919 to see her senile grandmother, who had just returned from a trip to Europe. Felicia was then almost fifteen. "Grams was really out of her head," Felicia said. "Ma couldn't take it and ducked out, and left me alone with her. Me and a maid. I was there a week with her, alone, until we got a nurse. I remember it terrified me to be alone with her because you never knew what she was going to do or say next. I remember I once went with Grams to a restaurant and she poured her soup in a water glass, saying, 'I don't want to embarrass my grandchildren.'

"Ma sometimes ducked out like that when things were too overwhelming for her."

Cissy's life was full of things she couldn't face. She could now run away from her mother more easily than she could run away from herself. Howey and his newspaper world were romantic and fun, great fun, but she was in her late thirties. She was always moving fast, but where was she going? And when would she get there? Howey had swept her off her feet, and their affair was intense. But Howey was not a marriage-minded man. He often lectured his staff on the follies of marriage, even reprimanding those who were foolhardy enough to enter this perilous state. Still, few men made her feel as alive as he did, few men kept her imagination as constantly crackling, and no one had ever made her laugh as loud and often as Howey.

The war was over and Joe was home, safe. He had come back a captain, a rank he had earned with pride, and was proud to keep using for a while. But he told Cissy about the degradation of war, the dehumanizing horror of it, the agony of the wounded, the rats in the trenches, the fear and purposelessness of sudden death, and the stench of the decomposing bodies in no-man's-land. He filled her with his own insistence that the United States must never again involve herself in any foreign war. Bertie McCormick also returned, with the rank of colonel, a title he used until his death. He had gone to war carrying a walking stick (for an injured football knee) and wearing a monocle. He had had morphine pills sewn into his coat; he had planned to use them if he found himself abandoned to die on a field of battle. Some critics claimed he had missed the first American offensive at Cantigny because he had gone to Paris to look for his lost dog. It was true that he did have his dog with him for part of the war, as well as his newly married wife, but it was also true that he had served with his artillery regiment under fire and had received the Distinguished Service Medal. In his book about the war, the Colonel favored the French over the English but attacked the bureaucracy of all nations. He joined his older brother, Medill, then a U.S. senator, in his attack on President Wilson's proposed League of Nations.

But Joe and Bertie were caught up in a new project: they decided to start a picture newspaper in New York City. In later years, the cousins liked to say they had made their decision while sitting on a manure pile on a farm in Mareuil-en-Dole. In fact, they had discussed the idea of a paper in New York years

183

earlier. The picture paper was Joe's idea, an idea he got from Lord Northcliffe's highly successful illustrated London *Daily Mirror.* Joe had earlier produced the first rotogravure section in the Chicago *Tribune,* and he would use this same tabloid form for the New York *Daily News.*

The two cousins agreed that the new paper would primarily be Joe's responsibility. He would continue to be coeditor of the *Tribune* until the *News* was launched; then he would move to New York. Joe told Cissy that he believed readers were most interested in sex, money, and murder and that he intended to fill his new paper with stories about all three. The renegade socialist was trying to keep close to the working people.

Cissy knew her brother's need for change. His marriage had broken down. The new woman in his life was Mary King, who had been his secretary and was now Sunday editor of the *Tribune.* Cissy resented Mary King, a resentment that was close to jealousy. As much as possible, Cissy wanted to keep her brother to herself.

The first issue of the New York *Daily News* was published in June 1919, with a picture of the popular Prince of Wales on the front page. The paper captured the spirit of the Jazz Age; it catered to its readers' desire to escape from the humdrum reality of everyday life. Joe Patterson commuted to New York from Chicago for the next five years, and Cissy often went with him. She shared the uncertainty and experiments of the paper's first six months. She and Mary King discussed his problems and his innovative ideas with him. A major crisis occurred when Howey's boss, Arthur Brisbane, Hearst's second-in-command, offered to buy the *News,* intimating that if his offer were refused, he would start a rival tabloid in New York. Joe and Bertie decided not to sell, and Brisbane and Hearst did start another tabloid—but not until five years later.

Despite their closeness, Joe still refused to let Cissy write for the *Tribune* or the *News.* He was not opposed to employing women reporters; in fact, he hired more of them than did most editors, and his respect for Mary King's editorial judgment, for example, was absolute. But even though Cissy had more than proved her ability in her articles for Howey, Joe was still reluctant to allow her to write for his newspapers. Was it simply because the management of the *Tribune* empire was neatly divided between him and Bertie, and a more knowledgeable Cissy might become a more powerful member of the board? Or did he simply want to keep her in the "little sister" category, always seeking his advice and help? In the same way, Joe later discouraged his daughter Alicia from going into the newspaper business.

While Joe discouraged, Howey encouraged. He assigned Cissy to report on the national political conventions in the summer of 1920.

Cissy was not an impartial reporter at the Republican convention, nor did Howey want her to be. Cissy supported the former governor of California, Senator Hiram Johnson. Howey approved of her choice—Hearst was also for Johnson. Cissy had known Johnson since 1912, when he bolted the Republican party to become Theodore Roosevelt's running mate on the Progressive ticket. But eight years later, the Republicans still could not forgive that defection.

In a speech before the Chicago Women's Club, Cissy stated that Johnson opposed secret agreements with foreign governments "who seem to be a great deal smarter than we are. . . . We are still like children with a childish desire to please rather than to be pleased." She told how Johnson had campaigned for governor in a ramshackle car saying he would "kick the Southern Pacific Railroad out of California politics . . . and he did!"

She followed up this speech with a pro-Johnson article in the *Herald-Examiner.*

Radical! Radical!—what is a radical?

I am sick and tired of having people denounce Hiram Johnson as a radical. When pinned down, they failed to prove that one single law advocated or passed by him as Governor of California, or as a member of the United States Senate, is unreasonable, impractical or not humane.

A blazer of trails, Johnson had supported the law mandating an eight-hour workday for women and the workmen's compensation acts. "Yet some delegates from the East told me today they weren't for Hiram Johnson because he is too close to the people," Cissy wrote. "Isn't that a funny thing for Americans to say?"

Cissy was proud of Johnson, whose supporters held a balance of power in the deadlocked convention. Approached with an offer of the Vice-Presidential nomination, he said curtly, "Go sing your siren songs to somebody else."

Cissy was not only a partisan reporter; she was a rich one. She was probably the only reporter there who could afford to have a dinner in a private dining room at the Drake Hotel for Senator Johnson and his wife and a dozen guests. Among them were Ruth Hanna McCormick, the William Wrigleys, the Joseph Pattersons, and Elmer Schlesinger. Elmer had separated from his wife and family and he and Cissy were now more often together.

Senator William Borah seconded Johnson's nomination at the convention, and Cissy was there.

> Everybody loves courage. A crowd loves courage most of all. Senator Borah faced his difficult audience like a lion—a good-natured and experienced lion. . . .
>
> I could hear the people in the galleries above milling around. There were catcalls and interruptions. The air was charged with disturbance . . . and pretty soon he picked up and held that audience in his hands as expertly and delicately as a woman might pick up and hold a peevish child.

Cissy interviewed him afterward about his speech, asking if he had found it fun.

"Ask any American boy of twelve whether he likes baseball," Borah answered.

Cissy's interview with Borah was almost adoring, and Howey headlined it "Borah: Countess Gizycka's Hero."

Despite Borah's support, the delegates rejected Johnson. After a lengthy deadlock, convention leaders met in a smoke-filled room, and agreed, "We've got a lot of second-raters and Warren Harding of Ohio is the best of the second-raters." For their Vice-Presidential nominee, they chose Calvin Coolidge, the slim, dour governor of Massachusetts.

When the distinguished-looking Harding questioned whether he was "big enough for the race," his campaign manager answered, "Don't make me laugh. The day of giants in the Presidential chair is past."

The Democrats also nominated an Ohio politician, James Cox, for President, and Cissy was there to cover that, too. Their Vice-Presidential nominee was the young, vigorous Franklin D. Roosevelt, who had impressed Cissy's mother because his dress was always faultless and he had "the correct manner of carrying gloves." Cissy had known him from Groton and Washington.

The election over, Cissy was drawn back to Washington. Chicago had become quiet for her—Hearst had sent Howey to Boston to rescue his papers there, and Elmer Schlesinger's work kept him close to New York—and Borah had become a new magnet.

Cissy began going to the Senate gallery with increasing regularity, particularly when she knew that Borah would speak. She described the scene:

> The Senate Chamber was packed that particular afternoon. On the floor itself, Senator Lodge, shadowy but erect, moved across with small drifting steps to drop a word to Senator Curtis. Senator Curtis nodded a stolid, swarthy head. Reed of Pennsylvania, square-shouldered, thin and flexible, leaned over his colleague, Senator Pepper of Pennsylvania, and while he spoke, his brilliant glance struck in twenty different directions. Senator Pepper was fatigued. He listened absently. Perhaps he was contrasting the stale air and staler futility of the moment with a vision of promise and early springtime on the countryside at home. Across the aisle, Senator Heflin, in his grand white waistcoat, was again on his feet. He was cribbing from one of his own speeches made five years previously, at the time of the Armistice. But nobody noticed it. Behind him, in the back row, sat Senator Wheeler of Montana, in the attitude of Michelange-

lo's Il Penseroso, his fine head sunk slightly forward, the forefinger of one pale, slim gambler's hand resting against his cheek.

A page boy presented Senator Walsh of Montana with a visitor's card, and he moved away towards one of the swinging doors leading to the reception room. A handsome gray-haired man, with a curved nose and relentlessly honest blue eyes. As Senator Walsh went out at one side of the chamber, the door of the Republican cloak room flew open and Borah of Idaho cautiously entered the arena. However, perceiving Heflin still on his feet, he changed his mind and turned to go, but paused first for a second, with one foot across the threshold, and from over his shoulder raked the ladies' gallery fore and aft with a bold, magnetic eye.

Cissy could describe these men in such detail because she knew them well. They all had been to her home many times. She had talked to them at a dozen dinners and countless parties. Everyone, that is, but Borah. Borah was married to a mouselike wife everyone called "Little Borah." He was simply not social; he never went to parties.

"Washington has no morals," Benoit Cobb, an Idaho newspaperman, had told Borah after the latter's election to the Senate. "It is the wickedest city in the world. You'll see women you've only dreamed about; and they'll try to make a monkey out of you. My advice to you . . . do not accept invitations . . . keep your nose to the work."

Cobb told Cissy's Chicago fellow-actor Charles Dewey years later, "I'd give my arm up to my shoulder to be able to withdraw that advice, for that's exactly what the sonofabitch did."

Cissy noticed that Alice Roosevelt Longworth, another frequent visitor to the Senate gallery, was also taken with Borah. There were few men in Washington who could withstand the determination and charm of both Alice Roosevelt Longworth and Cissy Patterson. Borah still went to very few dinners and parties, but he went to theirs.

Borah and Cissy were soon riding together in Rock Creek

Park. When they returned to her house for a drink, her riding breeches were mud-stained, and "the heavy knot of her hair had sagged to her collar's edge, an unbecoming accident, although it lent rather an appealing wet-kitten expression to her face." In a clumsy forward movement, Borah rose from his chair, "his great bulk towering like a moose in the hall, all out of proportion in the low-ceilinged room. With no other leave-taking than a rumbling goodbye, he walked towards the door, catching the panel of a red-lacquered Chinese screen with his elbow so that it wobbled as he turned the corner. . . .

"When the sound of the closing door reverberated through the house . . . [she] tilted her head back against the back of her chair, straightened her long legs out before her, toes down, and burst into delicious laughter and told her maid, who had entered, 'He really seemed to go out of his way to bump into that screen. . . . Did you notice?' "

Cissy was familiar with Borah's "stubborn silences . . . sometimes [lasting] an entire evening." But she also knew how emotional he could be. When they watched *Orphans of the Storm*, D.W. Griffith's noted movie about the French Revolution, Borah reacted "as though the scenes had been taken on the spot." He blazed with indignation at the cruelties, as if the film had recorded reality.

Borah was a man without humor and playfulness, a man of inflexible prejudices, a man who got all tangled up in a finger bowl. Asked if he wanted a cup of tea, he answered, "Do I look like a man who drinks tea?" "His evening clothes were certainly not of the smartest cut," noted Cissy, "but they sat well on his broad shoulders." She also reported that he went to bed in his underwear.

In the competition of Cissy and Alice for Borah, it was difficult for Washington to pick a winner. At a party at Alice's house, Borah arrived without his wife. After a while, he and Cissy disappeared together. The next day Alice sent Cissy some hairpins she had found in the library. Her note simply said, "I believe they are yours." Cissy answered quickly that, indeed, they were hers. "And if you look up in the chandelier," she added, "you might find my panties."

But it was not Borah who caused a break between Cissy and Alice; it was Nick. "If any man ever caused trouble between Cissy and me, it was my husband Nick," Alice said. "He adored her."

Alice's marriage to Nick had not gone well. Discussing it later, Alice admitted, "I hardly revelled in it." The small, gossipy town of Washington knew that while she and Nick lived in the same house, they led separate lives. Nick was known for his wandering eye. A Roosevelt cousin remembered a Longworth picnic where Nick was stretched out on the grass, holding hands with a pretty girl, when Alice walked by. "Oh, hello, Mrs. Longworth," said the girl. Alice passed without a word.

Nick was as successful in his political career as he was with the ladies. In 1925 he was elected Speaker of the House of Representatives, and many regarded him as a potential candidate for the Presidency. Divorce would have halted his rise, and this is perhaps why the Longworths stayed together.

Nick was in his early fifties, but there was "nothing gone of his youth except hair from his head. . . . He comes into a room in the evening time, jesting, gibing. . . . He has both irreverence toward others and humility about himself." While Alice was thought to have "a brilliant mind," Nick was widely admired because "after all, *he's a Prince!*"

Nick was often seen with Cissy when Alice was away from Washington. Friends saw them together at dinners, at the theater, at Dupont Circle parties. Nick was usually among the last to leave, he and Cissy having been drinking and talking together for hours. At one party, with Alice in attendance, there was "horseplay between Cissy and Nick." Not to be outdone, Alice "turned a somersault to amuse herself and us," remarked Agnes Meyer. "It was neatly done."

Something not neatly done was an incident in the bathroom of Alice's house during one of her parties. Somebody turned on the lights and found Cissy and Nick, both drunk, on the floor, making love.

Cissy was growing weary of the intrigues of Washington. She wrote to Rose Crabtree in Jackson Hole: "I'm discouraged . . .

by life. I can't find my way through. Anytime you want to change places—Henry and all—just let me know. I could give him nice pictures to look at, if nothing else." She added, in another note: "My dear—I'm so damn lonesome, I think I shall be sick. You hang on to Henry for you don't know (judging by your foolishness) a *real* good thing when you've got it. . . . Love to darling old Cal. Tell him I miss him almost as much as when I went away."

In Cissy's novel *Glass Houses*, the character based on Cal kills a Borah-like character. And in reality, Cal did supplant Borah. With Alice winning the battle of Borah, Cissy turned once more to her taciturn westerner. Cal was an unlettered, unmarried Borah. He was as forthright as Borah, as honest, and even more rugged. She knew that she would never find all the qualities she wanted in a single man.

Cissy was back again in Jackson Hole in the summer of 1921. But for all her closeness to Cal, this time he had competition.

When Cissy stayed at the Crabtree Inn, she had Number 7, a corner room overlooking the square. The room really belonged to Felix Buchenroth, who rented it by the month but was away most of the time. "Bucky" was a broad-shouldered, forceful man who was the area's chief forest ranger whom Cissy had known through the years. After one of his long trips in the woods, Rose greeted him with laughter. "It's lucky you didn't come back last night, Bucky," she said, "because Cissy was sleeping in your bed."

"Well," he answered, "I just would have told her to roll over."

Felicia remembered that Bucky felt so much at home at Flat Creek that he would simply walk in and sit down and eat. Cal was jealous of Bucky because he had reason to be.

Cissy had never completely forgotten Count Gizycki, and although Bucky was not as handsome as the Count, he did remind her of her former husband. Born in Germany, he was well educated, well traveled. Cissy teased him about his slight German accent, but it brought back a warm rush of memories when she talked with him in German or French. The painful memories had faded; she remembered only the happy times.

A graduate of Heidelburg University, Bucky had spent a

year at the Munich Art School and had seen most of the world, including Africa, by the time he was twenty-four. His travels brought him to the United States. Finding himself broke in San Francisco, and refusing to write home for money, he enlisted after seeing an Army poster. He was shipped to the Philippines, where he became an officer, and was then transferred to the Army base in Yellowstone Park, sixty miles north of Jackson. He explored the countryside and would occasionally ski into town. He liked the western life, and after he left the Army, he stayed on as a forest ranger.

Bucky was an artist, botanist, and expert mapmaker. He hated offices "where the people are so thick that you can stir them with a pencil." He was happiest when he was out in the woods, or gambling. He was not a woman chaser, but it was well known how hard some women chased him. It was said that his women friends, Cissy among them, helped finance his later transformation from forest ranger into town banker, but there is no proof of this.

Bucky was not a mean-mouthed man, but he was a hardheaded one, and half the town liked him while the other half didn't. Cissy found in him a man with whom she could ride and reminisce. He never flaunted his background and knowledge, but it was there to be tapped, and Cissy found it refreshing to do the tapping. Bucky found in her someone who helped make the present more pleasurable.

Cal still had the advantage of usually being the love "in residence." Cal, too, was the man who accompanied her when Cissy decided to be the first woman to ride the rapids of the roaring Salmon River. The Salmon was a wild river. Starting at the lower end of the Continental Divide at Hell's Canyon, between Idaho and Montana, it traveled through 420 miles of deep picturesque canyons and fell 8,000 feet to empty into the Snake. Lewis and Clark had considered it unnavigable. The Indians called it the Forbidden River, the river of no return. Cissy's trip was the 163 miles from Salmon City to Riggins, Idaho.

The scow for the two-week trip was thirty feet long, eight feet wide, and square at both ends.

Cissy asked the captain-guide, "How scary will it be?"

"How scary are you?" he asked.

"Oh, I'm scary. . . ."

"Well, you'll get a kick out of it, all right."

During the days the sun was so intense her hands blistered. "We fuss and fidget," she wrote in her diary. "My hair comes down. The sun scorched through my heavy woolen stockings."

The scow skimmed like a cork between the rocks and through the swirling rapids, sometimes flying out of the water as it went down the steeper falls.

Then, suddenly, "the rapids are wilder, more brilliant, more bewildering. The boat slaps down the white-crested waves, amazingly steady, and the spray splashes mockingly over us, soaking us all to the skin. We stand at the bow and laugh and shout, excited but not really afraid."

They found the empty boat of a man who had set out alone a few days ahead of them. The captain told of knowing two other men who had recently drowned, and of burying a man who had traveled down the river alone the year before.

"The whole scare comes in avoiding the rocks," wrote Cissy. "Sometimes in the narrows there's not six inches leeway on either side." She described the smaller boats—"treacherous undercurrent and swirling eddies pounce on them cat-like, spin them around, turn them over in one stroke, and suck them under and out of sight."

The boat stopped at a mining camp, and Cissy saw a careworn woman with a baby at her breast and a half-dozen children at her side. "They stare in a kind of ferocious silence. They hate us. . . . They hate us for having kept our teeth and hair; for having no visible babies; and for careering around the globe at middle age in riding breeches."

One girl said to her, "I wisht I was goin' in that boat way off down the river."

"Don't you like it here?" asked Cissy.

"I hate it," she answered.

Cissy then knew why she loved the western wilderness so much: unlike this young girl, she was free to leave. She could have her fill and then go on.

She slept on sandbars, and slept wonderfully. The river water was like a bath of iced champagne. The mountain trout tasted like young grouse. She devoured a breakfast of eggs, honey, two tin cups of inky coffee, two flapjacks the size of a frying pan, and laughed at the memory of sending her coffee back to the kitchen three times in Washington because "if it wasn't just exactly right, my whole day would be completely ruined."

Back at Flat Creek in September, Cissy sat on her porch and looked out at the quaking aspen, turning yellow against the dark green pines. She could close her eyes and see the violets and the bluebells and the grandpa-whiskers and the trillium and the timber mushrooms. She watched the animals come down each dusk to feed in her meadow and drink in her creek. Then she wondered why she always went back to the tumult and trauma of Washington, Chicago, and New York.

It seemed almost as if there were two Cissys. One belonged to Flat Creek, the other to Washington. Perhaps in this way Cissy was able to lead two lives. She loved both, and both enriched her. Her brother, in a dark mood, had once written: "Where I am not, there lies happiness." Cissy had a more optimistic philosophy: "Don't let's ask too much. But we can be happy most of the time, I suppose, when we have learned to compromise."

When Felicia was seventeen, and about to graduate from
Foxcroft in 1922, her mother wired her: "I'll come if you like
darling. What do you think?" This was warmer than the wire
she had once sent when Felicia was sick, perhaps with pneumonia, in Washington. Nellie Patterson had wired this news to
Cissy in Jackson. In her reply Cissy told her mother to get
another doctor's opinion, "because I don't want to come home
on a wild goose chase."

Cissy and Felicia needed each other, but neither had the
reach to bridge the gap. Cissy had few obvious maternal
feelings, and Felicia was a reminder of a painful past. "Cissy
hated me because I was Gizy's," Felicia said, "and loved me
because I was hers." Felicia herself hardly helped. She described herself as "a scared-to-death kid on the inside and a
spoiled brat on the outside." Felicia, years later, assessed her

mother's attitude toward her: "She was just dying to be loving and good and generous, and whenever she could, she was. But she was terrified of being vulnerable. Maybe that's the reason she was so fearful of giving love."

Felicia had fallen from a horse when she was fourteen. "I had a concussion and two busted eardrums, and I remember how very nice she was to me then, staying with me, hovering, taking me out afterwards for ice-cream sodas. But even then, there were no hugs, no kisses, no tears. We kissed whenever we met, but there was no real love in it. I remember her telling me years afterwards that one of her regrets was that she didn't always come in and kiss me goodnight. Even verbal expression of affection was hard for her."

When Cissy proposed a formal debut for her daughter, Felicia wasn't interested. A date was set, then postponed. The New York *World* commented: "It is doubtful if the former Eleanor Patterson will ever have the pleasure of directing the social destinies of a beautiful and accomplished debutante daughter." She did hold a semiformal party for Felicia in Washington, but Felicia recalled that "the men were mostly fags from the State Department." Cissy also wrote to Rose that Elmer Schlesinger—whom she was now seeing more and more—had given a large party for Felicia—there were fifty guests for dinner and a hundred more came later for dancing. As an adult, Felicia couldn't remember this party—perhaps because she never felt it was for her.

Although Cissy couldn't verbalize her affection for Felicia, or show it physically, it was certainly there, deep within her. Her affection was perhaps a strange kind of love mixed with guilt and resentment.

Cissy knew Felicia's innate shyness and once wrote Rose: "Rather think we will go to California as Felicia should see more young people—particularly make friends with some boys of her own age. It's time for her to learn to hold her own with them, and not be so shy. She looked lovely in Chicago by the time she went back to school. But she had the awfullest clothes when I came home, poor child!"

They went to Santa Barbara in May 1922. Cissy's grandfather

Medill had often stayed there. Joe's daughter Elinor went with them, and the two girls had "the most heavenly time." Cissy wrote Rose:

> They both have passionate beaux which of course makes me feel rather pleased and satisfied and also scared to death. Never on earth can I persuade them to go to the Sierra Nevadas with me—and it wouldn't ever do to leave them here alone. They howl and yell at the bare mention of leaving even for a day. A dance to them is as important as the Battle of Waterloo was to Napoleon. Well—that's youth.

Cissy stayed in California because of the girls, but she herself was not happy there. As she told Rose:

> Felicia's friends look on me as a kind of consumptive old party easily disposed of. I am not counting the days but the minutes to get away from this damn place. There are some nice people, I suppose, because there are some nice people everywhere—but I never see them. . . . I love vulgar people if they have just a little charm. But the Santa Barbarians are vulgar alright, and pinheaded besides. That's a poor combination.

Cal joined Cissy in California, and Cissy wrote Rose: "I am perfectly delighted to have someone to talk to." She also ordered a carload of furniture for the ranch because, as she wrote Rose: "It must be comfortable or poor Felicia won't be able to stand it—bring her friends there etc.—and can you blame her?"

Cissy's concern for Felicia was becoming more evident, but Felicia had moved too far away and was in her own orbit. Their relationship had become so poor that Felicia resented everything Cissy tried to do for her. When Cissy's mother was ill, Cissy hurried to her in Chicago, taking Felicia along. She wrote Rose that she had

> a perfectly vile time . . . between my poor sick mother and Felicia, who is about as easy to drive as a team of young bull

moose. However, on the whole, I must say she has improved. I let her have her own way because I couldn't very well help it and she has found out for herself that she is only human after all and capable of making quite a few mistakes.

Months earlier, at a Dupont Circle dinner, Cissy had pre-emptorily told Felicia, "Put on a dress and come down to dinner. . . . A woman dropped out." Her dinner partner was a twenty-four-year-old newspaperman named Drew Pearson. Felicia, sitting under a cloud of resentment, immediately decided that Pearson was "older than God." He came from a Quaker family in Pennsylvania and was then teaching at Columbia University and writing. The seventeen-year-old Felicia confided to him that she wanted to be a writer. After dinner they went to a nightclub, the first she had ever been to, and she drank her first planter's punch. Drew Pearson was smitten by this tall blond girl, but Felicia regarded him as "a stick-in-the mud."

Cissy's mother was declining rapidly, and Cissy decided to take her to Europe during the winter of 1922. She was not prompted by love or loyalty, but by the code of behavior she had been brought up with and by her own sense of duty. Surely there was also some gratitude for her mother's support during her difficulties with Gizy.

Felicia balked at joining them. She preferred spending the winter with her cousin Elinor. Impulsively, Cissy then invited Cal.

Cissy greatly enjoyed showing Cal Paris. He wanted to see everything, and they did, from the Eiffel Tower to the cancan girls. Cissy wrote Rose that when they visited Napoleon's tomb, "we both cried—just from the majesty and beauty of the thing." They also went to see a black singer from St. Louis, Josephine Baker, whom Janet Flanner described:

She made her entry entirely nude except for a pink flamingo feather between her limbs; she was being carried upside down and doing the split on the shoulder of a black giant. Midstage he paused, and with his long fingers holding her basket-wise around the waist, swung her in a slow cartwheel to the stage floor, where she stood, like his magnificent discarded burden, in an instant of complete silence. She was an unforgettable female ebony statue. A scream of salutation spread through the theater.

Paris was a playground for them. They sat at outdoor cafes, Cal in his cowboy hat and Cissy glowing. The French strolled by, smiling. Even the blasé Parisians must have watched as the cowboy and his red-haired lady rode in the Bois de Boulogne.

Cissy's mother, however, refused to be left alone or pushed aside. She seemed more senile. "Without exaggeration, she asks the same question ten times."

Cal wanted to see Italy, and Nellie Patterson didn't, so Cal went alone. "I really have begun to worry for fear something terrible has happened," Cissy wrote Rose, "although I'm sure the old simp is having the time of his life and too busy to write. Or else he's in jail."

Cal never stopped being his own man. He never regarded himself as simply the handsome escort of a wealthy woman. When he wanted to be with Cissy, he was; when he wanted to go elsewhere, he did. He had his own independence, his own dignity, his own restlessness. The grace of their arrangement was that Cissy never used her money to tie him to her, and Cal never would allow it to tie him. He knew the strength of his attractiveness to women, and he moved at his own pace to his own pleasure.

Marriage was not a subject of discussion between Cissy and Cal. Cal knew he belonged to only part of Cissy's life. Nor did he want more. He would be no woman's poodle. Cissy knew an eastern woman who had fallen in love with a cowboy in Jackson Hole and had married him and stayed there. This woman was Cissy's contemporary, wealthy but not as attractive. Cissy knew her well. She and her cowboy husband ran a ranch and seemed happy enough. It was a good life, but it was not the life Cissy wanted. Cissy wanted Jackson Hole, but she wanted more. Cissy wanted Cal, but she wanted others too. The truth was that, at forty, Cissy still wanted everything and still didn't know what she wanted.

Cissy spent her time alone in Paris looking up old friends. She shared her feelings with Rose:

> The people—old friends—I run into here make the effects of a character in a play—twenty years after—second act. Physically so much changed—much fatter—much thinner—wrinkled, puffy-eyed. They seem to think and talk and act the same—their personalities seem to be unchanged. But this queer, ghastly change of the body. Of course, it's just the same with me. [I had] a silly, fat, perfectly round face. And now I'm all wrinkled and skinny.

Despite Cissy's description of herself, a photograph taken at Longchamps shows a highly attractive woman, her striking figure set off by a black silk and lace dress.

Cissy dined one night with "a Polish lady I used to admire above all others. . . . How I used to try to copy her in the old days; used to try to dress like her, walk like her, talk like her . . . never did manage to *be* like her. . . . It's a great relief to be myself—a plain American." The dinner stirred Cissy's memory. She remembered what she wanted to remember—the beauty of youth and the dancing and the handsome men. She wanted to feel again as she had then. Cal was still in Italy, and she had sent her mother home with a visiting cousin. So here she was in Paris—a footloose, rich, desirable woman with no ties and no connections. She wanted to revisit the cities of her youth. But because of the political climate in Russia, she couldn't go to St. Petersburg, now called Petrograd. And she couldn't return to Vienna, because Gizy was still there. She had heard that he had again lost most of his money, that he was spending much of his time on the estates of his friend Count Kinsky, the two probably sharing their bitter thoughts about American women. Kinsky was bitter because Jennie had not left Lord Randolph to marry him.

That left Warsaw. Cissy suddenly decided that Felicia should come with her, that she should experience her paternal heritage. Cissy wired her brother to send Felicia. But Joe warned her that Felicia still held dual citizenship and that her

Russian passport might involve her in legal difficulties. So Cissy went alone, filled with anticipation and trepidation. She felt as if she were traveling backward in time, but she found that the world of her past had vanished. The aristocratic gaiety she had known was gone. Poland was now an independent republic. The Potocki palace still stood, but the Count had been swallowed up by debt and had committed suicide. Most of her friends had scattered, and those who had stayed gambled more, drank more, and laughed less. She missed the laughter most, that unfettered laughter, loud and free. Much of the conversation in Warsaw was now serious and cynical, all about land reform and revolution.

Whatever she had hoped to find in Warsaw wasn't there. No one swept her up and made violent love to her. Her old beaux were all grayed or gone.

She wrote an article about this trip, "A Sentimental Journey From Fifth Avenue to Warsaw," which appeared in *Harper's Bazaar*. In it she berated Polish aristocrats for living in the past. The American magazine *Labor* commented that "she has eyes and understanding." And the Hearst editor and columnist Arthur Brisbane said that she was "earnest and philosophical." In a puckish aside he noted that she had included the flattering assessment by an aristocratic friend: "But no, Countess Cissy, you have not changed at all."

Within a matter of weeks, Cissy had returned to Chicago, and Cal went back to Jackson Hole. Cissy wrote Rose that her mother was "really out of her head," and had moved into Chicago's Drake Hotel as a permanent resident. Cissy then sold her Washington house on R Street and moved into Nellie's Dupont Circle mansion. This four-story building of thirty rooms had ten bathrooms. There were fireplaces throughout, most of them unused; there were two libraries, filled with books, most of them unread. Cissy soon made this house her own. She had most of her mother's furniture removed and decorated the rooms to her own taste. She hung a Gobelin tapestry of a hunting scene in the foyer and put thirteen heads of animals she had shot on the wall along the marble stairway. She kept in the ballroom the two full-length portraits that were there. One showed her mother, self-assured and looking as if she didn't much care whether anyone liked her or not; the other of herself, dressed in chiffon, svelte, tall, "with no bones showing," in her hand a long cigarette holder.

Whenever she went into the ballroom, she remembered her wedding day. If there was someone with her who didn't know the wedding day story she would tell it. Her tone then was sometimes hard, but most often there was a soft sadness to it. "He was the only man I ever loved," she once said. "I should have stayed married and tried harder to make it work. I was a spoiled darling." It was a romantic mood that matched the crystal chandeliers, each lit with fifty flickering candles, the mirrors at the end of the room reflecting an infinity of them. When the room was ready for a party, with the candles lit, it was, as Felicia said, "enough to stop your heart."

Even as Cissy had her secret hideaways as a child, her quick mind now needed private places of peace to regroup its forces. Here at Dupont Circle, her hideaway was a small suite at the top of the house next to the servants' quarters, "perched up like a little nest under the eaves." She wrote to Rose:

> The walls of the [bedroom] are a sort of robin's-egg blue. The curtains are of yellow glazed chintz with a tiny little red border on them. . . . The sitting room has the same kind of walls and the same curtains with a very slight variation. These two little rooms and the bathroom between them are shut off from the rest of the house like a little apartment, by a hallway and an outside door. So, you see, whenever I get cross or tired, I can lock myself away from the world. . . . [From the windows] only the tops of the trees are in sight and they are covered with snow for the first time this winter. . . . Toto is lying on the carpet chewing a rotten old bone. He's got an old lemon with him which he runs around and bites and then gets mad when the taste comes out. He is just as cute as ever, which means that he is cuter than any pup I ever saw.

Washington in the twenties was a "company town," and it was Harding's company. Seldom had the country had a more handsome, more distinguished-looking President. When Cissy first met him at a poker game at Alice Longworth's, Evelyn Walsh McLean described Harding as "a stunning man." But as he was the first to admit, he was also a limited one. He had once been publisher of a small-town Ohio newspaper, and his mind had not grown much since then. A more noted newspaper publisher from Kansas, William Allen White, said that Harding was "a mere bass drum, beating the time of the hour, carrying no tune, making no music, promoting no deep harmony; just a strident rhythmic noise." And the more caustic critic, H. L. Mencken, wrote: "Harding, intellectually, seems to be merely a benign blank—a decent, harmless, laborious, hollow-headed mediocrity."

Harding called his wife the Duchess, and her haughty demeanor justified the title. She was five years older than he, and Washington was soon alive with rumors that Harding had a mistress, Nan Britton. It was said that he had met her when she was fourteen and he was the fifty-year-old governor of Ohio. She later published his voluminous love letters and claimed that Harding had fathered her illegitimate child "on a couch in his Senate office." She also described a White House closet "no more than five feet square where the President and his adoring sweetheart made love." She dedicated her book to "all unwed mothers and their innocent children whose fathers are not usually known to the world."

Harding left much of the running of government to a small set of corrupt cronies while he enjoyed the prestige of his office. The President sets the tone of Washington social life. The busiest social people were newcomers with "new-rich money," including a number of dawdling dowagers with lots of money and nothing to do.

Cissy had plenty to do. She used her money to keep the house humming with dinners, parties, dances, and teas. To spice the evenings, she usually invited people who were openly in conflict with each other. She even sat them next to each other to set off more sparks.

Invitations to formal dinners were then sent out a month in advance; the guests arrived at eight, men in white tie, women in *grand décolletage.* Dinner was finished at nine-thirty, and guests were expected to leave exactly one hour later. Cissy found these parties stuffy and held few of them. For her more informal gatherings, she usually wired invitations to her guests shortly before the planned party. Responding to such an invitation, a well-known newly arrived ambassador said he would come only if she had some other important guests. Cissy invited some of her newspaper friends, told them and their wives to come in formal dress, and then introduced them all to the snobbish ambassador as "leading foreign diplomats." He soon got the message and left.

Cissy needed a kindred spirit, and she found one in Agnes Meyer, an extremely intelligent, perceptive, and independent woman. Married to a wealthy economist, she was the mother of five children. She was interested in politics and had lobbied vigorously in Congress for the rehabilitation of the Washington slums. Cissy intrigued her: "Pug nose, red hair, a ready wit and charm, what more can a woman have? As she is extremely feline, I shall see to it that I do not get scratched, but with that in mind I intend to see what there is in it."

The two were soon seen everywhere together: sitting in the Senate gallery, enjoying the circus or the theater, riding their horses. Agnes recalled that after a horse rolled over on Cissy one morning, she still arrived for tea, although she was "a little bit wan . . . [with a] pathetic little face and hungry eyes." That same evening at dinner, Cissy had recovered, "looking divine in red chiffon." Agnes later said, "She appeals to my senses."

Agnes and Eugene Meyer took Cissy with them to the Jackson Day dinner held by the Democratic party leaders. The two women agreed that most of the great men were "funny little people . . . swelled instead of growing." Commenting on the evening's events, Cissy and Agnes criticized the banal ideas, the poor English, and the smoky atmosphere.

The two women agreed on much. They both liked Chinese painting, a subject on which Agnes had written a book: *Chinese Painting as Reflected in the Thought and Art of Li Lung Men.* They both thought Herbert Hoover was "shy and nice," and Agnes hoped he would become President and make her husband

Secretary of the Treasury. They both thought that American women were more beautiful than European women but perhaps "more cold and hard." They both felt that too many young British men were serving as escorts for older, eternally eager, but worn-out women.

Cissy—who was eager but not worn out—had her own British escort, John Joyce Broderick, the first secretary of the British Embassy, whom she had known in Europe. Agnes thought Broderick "extremely clever and likable and very good fun to talk to . . . his mind most alert." Agnes's husband told her that he thought Cissy and Broderick were having "a quiet affair." Both Cissy and Agnes agreed that Broderick's wife was "impossible" and that she had "nothing to recommend her but her hair."

Aside from Borah, the two senators who were constantly in Cissy's camp were Burton K. Wheeler of Montana and Henrik Shipstead of Minnesota. Both were tough, independent, and progressive. Wheeler had charged that Attorney General Harry Daugherty had refused to move against Harding's corrupt "Ohio Gang." The Attorney General resigned, but the Justice Department, in retaliation, charged Wheeler with conflict of interest. Cissy let everyone know where she stood by inviting Wheeler to dinner and seating him on her right.

"Men liked Cissy and enjoyed her company," said Wheeler. "She had charm and she also had guts and courage."

Wheeler and Shipstead, the rangy dentist-turned-politician, had both been guests of Cissy's at Flat Creek. She once told the two of them, "You westerners are all alike. You want a girl to be 'a pushover.' I like to be wooed and fussed over first."

Cissy and Agnes often lunched together "and gossiped outrageously." What one didn't know, the other did. They discussed the double suicide of a governor's wife and her lover who had talked with each other on the telephone while they died; the Dutch minister who had arrived with 3,000 bottles of wine, stating that he would stay in Washington only as long as these bottles lasted; the Supreme Court justice who left a dinner in a huff because the seating plan violated protocol; the Dictograph that had been planted in Bernard Baruch's hotel room because his lady companion was suspected of being an enemy agent; the persistent rumor that Harding's wife had poisoned him because of his scandalous behavior with Nan Britton.

On the death of Harding on August 2, 1923, the colorless, incorruptible Calvin Coolidge became President. He wanted to be "the least President the country ever had," and he succeeded in this ambition "by avoiding the big problems." His epigram "The business of America is business" is still quoted, but more typical of his style were near-ludicrous statements of the obvious: "When more and more people are thrown out of work, unemployment results." Alice Roosevelt Longworth was said to have remarked that the sour-faced Coolidge had been weaned on a pickle.

In the summer of 1923, Cissy, as always, was happy to head back to Jackson Hole. This time she had Felicia in tow. Felicia was now full-grown, looking older than her eighteen years. She had been increasingly reluctant to return to Jackson Hole and had skipped several of the previous summers because she wanted to be in Washington where she had more friends.

Cissy was now more determined than ever to buy Flat Creek from Cal. She used every persuasion on him, until he reluctantly agreed to sell the ranch to her. She quickly wrote the check. Again hesitating, Cal said that he had left the deed at his cabin in Driggs, Idaho, and that he would have to go for it. Cissy knew her man. If she let him go, he was sure to change his mind. So she sent one of her part-time employees, a local cowboy, George Ross, to Driggs to get the deed from the bottom of Cal's trunk.

Cissy finally had her way. The county records for 1923 note that "Enoch Carrington, an unmarried man . . . sold 140 acres to Eleanor Gizycka for $5,000."

Cissy was elated. She immediately hired Charlie Fox, Henry Crabtree, and a crew of carpenters to add a dressing room, twelve-feet square, to her own cabin. More importantly, she had them build four small guest cabins and a large lodge. This lodge had a kitchen, a cook's room, a dining room with a wall-size window, a living room with a massive stone fireplace and a floor large enough to dance on, and a porch overlooking the meadow and the mountains.

Furniture soon arrived from everywhere. Only a rough wagon trail connected the ranch with the outer world. The forest rangers did not complete a fire road to Flat Creek until six years later, and it was later still before a car could make the trip. Cissy's furniture was carried in wagons. It had to be taken off and hauled up gullies by the wagon crews; it was then reloaded onto the wagons. "And some of that furniture was so heavy," said Eddie Schultz, who worked for Cissy, "that when we finally got it there, it seemed like it was nailed to the floor."

Cissy kept the wagon crews busy; among the objects they hauled to Flat Creek were a grand piano, an antique Chinese cabinet, several Navajo rugs, a large Persian rug, and some driftwood.

Water still came from the ice-cold creek, and there was still no electricity and no plumbing. When her cook left, Cissy hired a temperamental Russian, who didn't last long. He carelessly poured some lye on the holes in the privy, and Felicia burned herself badly. Cissy's comment was, "Well, why don't you look where you sit?"

Despite her offhand manner, Cissy kept a watchful eye on Felicia. She arrived one night at Crabtree Inn to find Felicia having her dinner sitting with a park employee. She quickly ordered Felicia to join her for dinner. Cissy could talk to all sorts of people on their own level and in their own language; she was comfortable with cowboys and with queens. But she seemed incapable of talking with her daughter; she could only order her about.

Concerned about Felicia's lack of suitable beaux, Cissy invited Drew Pearson to Flat Creek that summer. He was then writing syndicated features, but he had to borrow money to make the trip. Because her mother had invited him, Felicia ignored him almost completely. And Drew himself seemed awkward and out of his element; he had very little to say. Rose, however, thought that he looked like the movie star John Gilbert.

The fights between mother and daughter intensified that

summer, and Felicia became tense and anxious. "I was always afraid of the next moment, the next sentence!" Felicia recalled "She wasn't reasonable; she had no emotional self-control. She couldn't control her animosities. And I always fought back. She couldn't bear opposition from me and perhaps my opposition frightened her because of her own opposition to her own mother. And, after it was all over, Ma always laughed at her anger and her fights, but I hated it."

Those fights reached a climax one day when Cissy fired her Swedish maid, Aasta. She had fired her before and would fire her again. This time Cissy not only fired Aasta but also refused to give her a horse on which to leave. She believed that Aasta, though fired, should stay on until she got another maid. Felicia took Aasta's part: "I told my mother that this was hardly the Dark Ages, or even Russia before the Revolution." Cissy had her own hot answer, and the two were soon screaming at each other.

"She and I had a knock-down, drag-out fight, which included hair-pulling and having my shirt half-ripped off," said Felicia. "I offered to ride Aasta out of there on my pony, which had *not* been given to me by Cissy." (Cal had given it to her.)

Aasta then burst into tears and said she was not going anywhere. Still incensed, Felicia packed all her own possessions into two duffle bags and left on her horse. She rode bareback because she wouldn't use the saddle her mother had given her. Felicia had reached a breaking point: "I told Ma that I was through with her for good."

Halfway down the twisting road, the pony bucked and the rear duffle bag slid off. "I left it there, too scared to get off because I thought Ma would send someone to bring me back. Besides I was in a rage."

Cissy did send Cal after her, but Cal could not persuade her to return. In Jackson, Felicia withdrew several hundred dollars from her savings account and told Rose that her grandmother was sick and she had to go to see her. "How did you get the message?" asked Rose. "By Ouija board?"

Felicia rode to Victor to get the train for Salt Lake City. Waiting at the train for her was Drew Pearson, who had been dispatched by Cissy. Although Felicia refused to speak to him, he stayed with her until they reached Salt Lake City. He left her there when she told him, "You bore me, and the more I see of you, the more bored I get."

While in Salt Lake, Felicia met Irvin Corse, who had just bought into the Bar B C. He asked what she was doing there.

"I'm running away to California," she answered.

When he discovered she knew no one there, he gave her the address of his cousin. He told Cissy of this encounter when he returned to Jackson. Writing to her brother about Felicia's departure, Cissy rationalized, "I think it will be good for her."

In truth, Cissy was caught up in guilty thoughts about Felicia. She wrote to Rose that Felicia had liked none of her friends. "You'd think I was running a bad house, and that all my friends are trollops, which they are, God bless them."

Since she had no telephone at Flat Creek, Cissy often wrote notes to Rose, which Cal delivered. "Her handwriting was so bad," said Rose's son, Hank, "that it took three of us to interpret it." Rose herself was so self-conscious about her poor spelling and grammar that she had a young friend type her letters.

That fall, Cissy decided that she needed a change of scene. Cal took her to Banff in Canada to hunt in the mountains. When she asked Cal where they would camp, he gave her a characteristic answer: "How do I know where we're a'goin' to camp? I ain't been there for a year. Maybe there's no grass left. Maybe it ain't there anymore! How do I know?"

Cissy had gradually started drinking more. Guilt about her daughter, frustration over her future, served as good excuses for getting drunk. In those prohibition days, she always arrived in Jackson with enough cases of liquor to last the season. Cissy and Cal put away an inordinate amount of gin on that hunting trip. "Cal was a quiet drunk," Cissy's chore boy said. "You wouldn't know he was drunk until he talked. But Cissy could be a mean drunk. The way she talked you thought she came right out of the alley."

It was a rough hunting trip; they spent eighteen days on the trail with little sleep. She missed her first shots. "Cal and the new guide (divine) were with me and kept jawing directions until it was a mercy I didn't shoot them," she wrote Rose. She killed the next ram she spotted and then shot another. "His white body lay prone, directly below us, but his head was still up. That was the sickening thing: the broken body and the head still up. The jet-black horns pointed our way, and the intense eyes gazed straight into ours. . . . Distaste for the whole proceedings swelled in me, a feeling almost of nausea. I'd never really wanted that goat."

The ram staggered to his feet, lowered his horns, made one mighty lunge forward up the trail, and then sank back again on the ground. "Why doesn't he die?" Cissy cried. His head was hidden, and she could not fire the killing shot. She heard it moan—sobbing, choked sounds. "I felt very sick indeed. . . . I had destroyed a perfect living creature. And to what purpose?"

At the camp, after finally killing the ram, Cissy discovered that her rifle barrel had cracked. She decided not to have it fixed.

Back in Jackson, Cissy spent more time with Rose. They had long rides and longer talks, with Felicia the most important subject of conversation. Cissy's guilt was immense, and her concern was real. There had been no letters from her daughter, but Cissy had hired detectives and knew that Felicia was working as a waitress in San Diego and seemed to be settling and surviving.

Cissy suggested that she and Rose open a new hotel, to be called the Eleanor Rose. Rose laughed off this proposal, but Cissy was serious. She even bought a lot in town, where she planned to build her own house, a few blocks away from the Crabtree Inn.

Rose once told Felicia that without Cissy "my life wouldn't be worth a damn." She considered Cissy "one of the truly great people of my generation." Felicia replied that her mother's life wouldn't have been worth much without Rose, that their times together were certainly among her happiest days.

Even when Cissy was happiest, there was restlessness within her. Whether she slept on a sandbar in the Salmon River or on a mountain in Canada or in Room 7 of the Crabtree Hotel, or even in the utter peace of Flat Creek, part of her mind now was always elsewhere, and most often in Washington.

Both Alice and Cissy supported Borah for President in 1924, even though Nick Longworth was also prominently mentioned as a candidate. Coolidge had approached Borah to tell him he was needed on the Republican ticket, but Borah had refused the offer of the nomination for the Vice Presidency.

Alice's preference for Borah instead of Nick took on added significance when she announced her unexpected pregnancy at the age of forty-one, after eighteen years of childless marriage. It was snidely remarked that there wasn't a Nick in her and that the child should be called DeBorah. Alice's behavior wasn't calculated to quiet the gossips. One night when she was in "a carnal mood," she ate three chops, told shady stories, and sang in a deep bass voice, "Nobody cultivates me . . . I'm wild, I'm wild!"

If Alice was growing more frivolous, Cissy and Agnes were becoming increasingly interested in national and international affairs. That year, 1924, was a relatively quiet one, and Calvin Coolidge was elected President with a campaign slogan of "Keep Cool with Coolidge."

The family's tragedy that year was Medill McCormick's failure to be renominated for the U.S. Senate because of a political power play. Medill and Ruth were crushed. There had been much joking in Cissy's presence that one day Medill would be President of the United States. He had cut a national figure in opposing American entry into the League of Nations. He was equally proud of his child labor bill, his proposed waterway from the Great Lakes to the Gulf, his plan for a national budget system. He could talk to a joint meeting of French senators and deputies in fluent French, and he could talk about crops and livestock with the farmers who were his constituents.

Medill had always been a light in Cissy's life. In her early years, he had been her romantic hero; later, when she needed his help to regain her child from Count Gizycki, Medill was at her side. But now he saw himself as a beaten man of forty-six, and all of Cissy's love and encouragement could not penetrate his dark world.

Joe and Bertie, meanwhile, had thrived. The Chicago *Tribune* was both popular and prosperous, and Joe's New York tabloid venture, the *Daily News,* was a rousing success. Joe still commuted from Chicago but planned to move to New York within the year, leaving the *Tribune* in the complete care of Bertie. For all its popularity, the *Tribune* had little political clout at that time, and its endorsement "couldn't even elect a dogcatcher." But Joe saw the *News* as a potential political force. He told Cissy that Lord Northcliffe's tabloid paper had made him a great power in England, a man who could make prime ministers and break cabinets. One day, he said, the *News* might give him a similar power.

Cissy had started writing short fiction, and *Harper's Bazaar* had published a short story based on her early days in Poland. Joe insisted that it was good enough to be expanded into a novel and encouraged her to begin this project. When they talked about Felicia, Cissy would say, "Oh, I don't care where she is." But Joe later told Felicia, "I knew her heart was breaking." Felicia was working as a waitress near the San Diego naval base. "I tell you I was good. I could swing a mean tray," she said. One of her bosses was a woman bootlegger, and Felicia shared an apartment with another waitress and her Navy husband. She used the pseudonym "Marion Martin."

Cissy's own life had some new stability and purpose. Besides her writing, she and Agnes Meyer organized a weekly luncheon group of "the most intelligent women in Washington." The group included Ruth Hanna McCormick and Mrs. Borden Harriman, among others, but not Alice. The members researched a particular issue for each meeting. Among the questions debated were: Should the Russian blockade be lifted? Should public officials lead or follow their constituents? Who was the most outstanding figure developed by the war—Hoover or Lenin? What was the real threat of Bolshevism? (Agnes and Cissy agreed that if revolution came to the United States, "she and I are going to kill instead of be killed.")

Most of the groups' members grew increasingly frosty as the discussion became heated, but Cissy, never a polite debater, was known for her quick flashes of temper. A hard listener and an omnivorous reader, Cissy was self-educated, and proud of it. She had learned much from the men in her life, but she had done her real growing on her own. She absorbed, selected, and remembered, and this discussion group prompted her to think and analyze. Had some of her social friends sat in on the group's meetings, Cissy would have flabbergasted them. They would have seen an intellectual depth Cissy seldom displayed in society. One trait they would have recognized was her stubbornness. Once Cissy's sharp mind had formed an opinion, it was almost impossible to shake her from it.

Cissy was forty-three, and the years had been kind to her. Her figure was still youthful, her curiosity wide awake, and her spirit restless and stirring. She decided to return to Paris; but this time she would go alone, and this time she would write her novel.

Cissy liked the pleasure of writing but not the pain. The writing, but not the rewriting. She loved the sudden imagery that jumped into her mind but hated the long search for the right word, the right rhythm. She was determined to write the novel, but she hated sitting and looking at a blank sheet of paper. Her stubbornness conflicted with her lack of discipline. She knew the price of writing but hated to pay it.

She did not live in the Left Bank colony of struggling artists. She didn't often eat a twenty-cent meal—an omelet, wine, and *fraises des bois*—at the Dôme or the Sélect. When Cissy went to the Left Bank, as she liked to do, she was slumming. She did not pretend to be what she wasn't. She was rich and she lived rich. She was a "lobster palace American" who lived at the Ritz and loved champagne and the superb chocolate cake from Columbin's.

Frustrated because of her lack of discipline, Cissy did what she would always do when she wanted to expedite things: she got someone to help. A French publisher had been intrigued by an outline of her novel and had found her a French collaborator. This collaborator, however, wanted to collaborate in everything.

"I had to . . . listen to his raving till I got to hate the very sight of his face," Cissy wrote Rose. Finally, he "got savage and tore up my very best tea-gown . . . said he was going to commit suicide and could not live without me."

The publisher was not entirely happy with the book Cissy and her passionate collaborator had produced. Cissy told Rose:

> He said he liked the cowboy part which is what I wrote but did not care so much for the political part [which her collaborator wrote]. . . . I said I would take out my part and he could go to hell with his. But I'd write my own book in my own way—and I *did*. . . . It is coming out in one of the first literary magazines in the world and later as a book. I will translate it back into English as soon as I have the courage to look at it again. . . . So I put Jackson Hole on the map of France. . . . You should be proud of your old friend, although I'm so conceited already over the whole thing there will be no living with me.

Cissy's novel *Glass Houses*, was given the French title *André en Amérique*, and was serialized in the *Revue de Paris*. Cissy, however, deplored the lack of French equivalents for some of her western ranch slang. "I write for myself and strangers," Gertrude Stein had said, and Cissy did too. She wrote about the Washington she knew and the Jackson she loved, put a literary dress on actual incidents, and gave fictionalized names to real people. Her cast included Alice and Borah and Cal and herself and a male character based on Gizycki and Bernstorff.

Cissy sent presents from Paris to Rose and Henry—a bare-bottomed marble statue of Salome for Rose's hotel guests to pat, and a painting of a female nude for Henry. "Hang this on your side of the bed when Rose is mad at you," she told him. She teased Rose, "Who does your type-writing? Is it that nice, good-looking young man in the Land Office? I hear he is quite rambunctious. *Stop. Stop. Stop.*" She threatened to write a novel about Rose—"all about how you had a baby by my brother, and Nick McCoy (your husband) never found it out." Then she added, "Will write as soon as I get someone to dictate to. Would that charming Mr. Ellis like to be my secretary this summer?"

But the man mostly in her thoughts then was Cal.

What do you hear from old Cal? Let me know if you see him and how he is. It always worried me to think of him living alone and his own horrible cooking and half dead of indigestion most of the time. I suppose he hibernates like an old bear in his cabin and sits there thinking the horriblest thoughts about women, which he punctuates by running to the window every ten minutes in the hope of seeing some go by. Give him my love anyhow.

As an American writer published in a French literary magazine, Cissy now had standing in the American expatriate set. At the center of this group was the squat, mannish Gertrude Stein "with her strange cold eyes," her hair close-cropped like an ancient Roman's. With her always was her companion, Alice B. Toklas, a slight, dark, whimsical woman who looked like a gypsy. Isadora Duncan's brother, Raymond, seemed to be everywhere in his flowing Greek robes and open sandals. The elfin photographer Man Ray had started painting without brushes, using a spray gun on such subjects as brassieres and shaving brushes to create "nudes of objects."

Cissy admired Picasso's work but found him "a small, dark, closed man," unapproachable even when he was drunk. A Polish friend of hers observed that James Joyce "smelled bad," but Cissy was intrigued by this frail-looking man who twirled his cane as he walked and wore his black hat on the back of his head, a patch over one eye, and rather grimy white sneakers.

Her favorite young friends were the Hemingways. The two had just returned from skiing in Austria and told Cissy about a lovely old inn with wonderful featherbeds and vast quantities of trout and kirsch. "Hem," then in his twenties, was distraught about the loss of his wife's suitcase, which had contained the original manuscripts of almost everything he had written that year. He was busy writing *The Sun Also Rises*, but he and Cissy talked more about guns and hunting. Hemingway's wife, Hadley, adopted Cissy as a mother confessor, and this relationship became critically important for Hadley when Hemingway abruptly abandoned her.

Cissy also enjoyed Scott and Zelda Fitzgerald, who were busy spending his munificent publisher's checks for champagne. On one drunken spree at a party, they threw ripe tomatoes at titled French ladies. What Cissy envied most about Scott, though, was his tight-minded discipline when he would suddenly stop drinking, stay cold sober, and "write, write, write."

Another Paris friend was the cosmetician Helena Rubinstein, who had left Poland shortly after Cissy did. She thought Hemingway "a loud mouth and a showoff," but she impressed Cissy by financing the publishing firm her husband founded.

Had she come to Paris earlier and stayed longer, Cissy herself might also have become a publisher. She had a special instinct for talent; she became very enthusiastic about the young James Thurber, who worked for the Paris edition of the Chicago *Tribune*.

In her talks with her new literary friends, Cissy often found herself on the defensive. She denounced those who claimed that the French embodied a glorious civilization while the Americans were barbarians. She did not believe, as Ezra Pound did, that America was "half-savage." Nor did she agree with those writers who insisted, "My country is where I feel at home." Cissy appreciated the grace of life without pressure, and her French was good, but she knew she would always be an outsider in Paris. She shared no expatriate dreams. "I feel at home in my country."

She was about to go home when she impulsively decided on a final trip to the Riviera. Once there, she became part of the social and literary set of Somerset Maugham at Cap Ferrat. Maugham told Cissy that he had bought his villa cheap because it was so hideous. A Catholic bishop had built it at the turn of the century; its Moorish cupolas and Renaissance loggias testified to his unconventional taste. Maugham soon adorned it with liveried servants, a yacht, a swimming pool, a Rolls-Royce, and avocado trees imported from California. And he surrounded himself with celebrities. Cissy intrigued Maugham because she was not the cliché American tourist. Nor was she the typical rich snob or the typical American writer or even the typical American. He liked the sensitive, earthy ring of her conversation, and some of her traits are evident in several of his short-story characters.

Roaming the Riviera, and always ready for romance, Cissy found it again.

"I fell in love . . . old fool that I am," she wrote Rose.

Ten years younger than she, William Bullitt was also divorced, also writing his first novel. Bullitt's background included Philadelphia's Rittenhouse Square, Virginia's Patrick Henry, and Russian Jewish immigrants. A dark-haired man with a lordly air that made him seem older than his years, Bullitt had been a member of Phi Beta Kappa at Yale; he had graduated from Harvard Law School and had worked as a war correspondent in Germany and Austria.

"I didn't suppose this world held anyone as fascinating—just for *me*—as that man," Cissy told Rose.

Bullitt fascinated Cissy with his unbounded enthusiasm. He described American success as "futility on the upgrade," but Cissy sensed how much he wanted it. He said that he was a coward who shrank from unpleasantness, that he had to force himself to do the hardest things, that he feared flying "so I had to do it." Cissy listened to his story of being sent by President Wilson on a secret mission to sound out Lenin after the war. He said he had met a brilliant man in Vienna named Sigmund Freud, and they planned to write a book together about Wilson.

Bullitt kept Cissy on the Riviera longer than she had planned. It was a memorable romantic interlude, but Cissy wrote Rose that she "left just in the nick of time." She was terribly vulnerable, and she did not want to be hurt. An older woman simply could not marry a younger man. It had been an intense affair, and she was determined not to drag it out to the bitter end. She was glad to be going home.

10

To marry a second time represents the triumph of hope over experience.

—Samuel Johnson

Psychoanalysis was still young in 1925. Interest in it had begun to grow in the United States with the lectures given in 1909 by Freud and Jung in Worcester, Massachusetts. When Cissy returned home from Paris, psychoanalysis had become chic. The phrase "My analyst said . . ." was often heard at fashionable gatherings. Lively dinner conversations explored the Oedipus complex, the id, and the superego. Yet this discipline was so new that only Vienna, Berlin, and London had psychiatric clinics.

Cissy had her problems, but she had a strong keel of common sense. During her months in Paris, she had given much thought to the pain and pleasure of her past. Now she needed an objective listener to prompt her exploration of her frustrations and repressions; she needed a sympathetic guide to help her understand her submerged past.

Alvan Barach had been a noted medical doctor before he became an analyst. The brilliant inventor of oxygen chambers for the treatment of pneumonia and cardiorespiratory diseases, he also later introduced helium for the treatment of asthma. Fifteen years younger than Cissy, he seemed much older because of his intensity. Cissy impressed him because of "her straightforwardness . . . the way she looked you right in the eye." Barach went on:

"Almost as soon as we met, she automatically seemed to transfer herself to me. I don't know why. But just by talking to her, I seemed to hypnotize her. In fact, when she came in for her regular consultation, it got to a point when I'd try not to look at her, at least for a few minutes. Sometimes if I would just look at her across the room, she'd go off into a hypnotic state. I often had to rap on a table to bring her back to herself. It *was* surprising how *completely* she did transfer to me. I guess she had never been able to do that with anyone else before, and she *needed* to do it. If a person has an unspent impulse to yield, and if someone comes along who's strong-willed, they yield to that person.

"I think Cissy's greatest problem was that she couldn't yield herself to anyone else, she couldn't surrender, she couldn't give all her love. And I think that was the great tragedy because she had so much love to give."

Cissy consulted Barach for the next five years, regularly for almost a year, and then intermittently. Barach had a favorite phrase from Goethe that he tried to pass on to all his patients: "Remember to live!" "And I think it had great impact on Cissy," he said. Perhaps Cissy and her friends flocked to Barach because he epitomized a life philosophy of optimism and security and certainty which they so much wanted for themselves.

Barach and Cissy talked much about marriage. He suggested that the Count, while he had caused her much pain, had served a vital purpose in her life. Gizy had revived her ability to love, an ability that had atrophied during the difficult years of her childhood. Barach tried to help her overcome her hatred of Gizy. "I told her that there was no hope in hatred, that the hope in living was to be able to love again after having once been hurt. Otherwise the bruised impulse comes out as a hatred, a sadism, or a masochism."

Some of Cissy's friends were skeptical of her ability to surrender much of her soul to anyone. But Cissy kept Barach close to her for a long period. Cissy was frivolous about things, but not about people. When people had meaning to her, she tightened her hold. If not, they were soon out of her life.

Cissy's return to America was a settling time for her. She had come back determined to translate her novel from French into English and to write short stories and articles. She had decided to stay awhile in New York because that's where the publishers were. She also returned to find tragedy. After another breakdown following his political defeat, Medill McCormick was dead. It was announced that he had suffered a gastric hemorrhage, but in fact he had committed suicide. For Cissy, Medill had been one of the few intimates who knew her whole story and who was always willing to listen, to sympathize, to help. She had loved him as a girl, and she later told friends that she felt he had returned this love. Bertie McCormick, however, observed coolly, "She always thought everyone was in love with her."

Medill had been one of the linchpins in her life, and now he was gone. It was not therefore so unexpected that she would turn, at this time, more and more to Elmer Schlesinger. Medill and Elmer looked very much alike and had been the closest of friends. Since Cissy and Elmer had met in 1912, he had played an increasingly larger role in her life. "He fixes up my life for me—arranges everything," Cissy wrote Rose. "Describes my troubles in two seconds—after I've been changing my mind for weeks and arrived at no conclusion."

In many ways they were two of a kind. They both loved races, prizefights, theater, intelligent people, and provocative conversation. They were both in their middle forties, Cissy in her prime and Elmer at his peak. A partner in one of New York's most prestigious law firms, Elmer represented some of the most powerful companies in the country and served on their boards of directors. He belonged to the most exclusive clubs—from Boston's Longwood Cricket Club to the New York Yacht Club—owned a sixty-five-foot yacht, maintained a private wine cellar at the Ritz hotel, and had a luxurious apartment at 1010 Fifth Avenue. In the day of raccoon coats, patent-leather hair, wrinkled socks, and bell-bottom trousers, Elmer owned twelve classically cut suits, all of gray herringbone tweed, and wore black knit ties. Unlike Cissy, Elmer wore a quiet, conservative face. He was a distinguished-looking man, with considerable gray in his wavy hair. Although he often drank a great deal, he always remained in control of himself. Few men were more pleasant in a long, tense poker game. Or more gracious when they lost. He had made his millions and picked up some of the snobbery that went with wealth. Yet he had Cissy's gift of "being real with real people."

Cissy knew well how kind and considerate he was. Long ago, their feelings had grown much deeper. She knew how much he loved her: he had divorced his wife in 1922. She knew he did not need her money. In their dozen years of friendship, they had shared moments of tenderness, of high-spirited gaiety; they had also survived the explosions of their quick tempers. She understood him as an ambitious, intelligent, giving person. She had shared his bed, his mind, and his heart.

Cissy had invited Elmer to Jackson Hole in 1924. She felt that since they shared so many things, so many people, so many places, he would be delighted by her western home. But Elmer found Jackson Hole an alien world. He was a fastidious man, uncomfortable with the primitive accommodations at Flat Creek. Elmer was a highly organized lawyer and lived a highly organized life. For relaxation, he liked a hard game of tennis and was a champion at it. Drinking also relaxed him, and when he traveled to Flat Creek, he brought along a large supply of whiskey. During the rough wagon ride to the ranch, he worried more about the whiskey than about himself. The thrill of the hunt was not his. Nor was he moved by watching the sun set, night after night after night. He loved peace and quiet, but in small doses. He thrived on the conversational challenge of bright minds, the liveliness of good parties, the stimulation of music and theater. He was a dynamic man restless for action, with a need for the excitement of people.

Elmer had come courting Cissy on unequal ground in Wyoming, which was Cal's country. Elmer knew all about Cal, and it had taken a certain courage to come West. But he felt that if he wanted to win this woman, he must win all of her. Cal led them on rougher rides than usual, through wild woods without trails, and Elmer often returned to camp bruised and scratched by underbrush. Cissy, disappointed by Elmer's awkwardness and lack of enthusiasm, remarked to a friend, "And to think I almost married that sissy . . ." Rose, however, liked Elmer, and Cissy had great respect for her friend's intuitive, uncannily accurate judgments of people. Since Cissy had no telephone, Rose had long been Elmer's telegraphic contact. At one time Elmer was so persistent in his telegrams that Rose answered, *"Oh shut up!"*

When they finally met, however, Rose quickly decided he was a genuine gentleman and a good human being. At first they seemed an odd combination, their mutual approval highly unexpected. Elmer could be stiffly formal, but with friends he was a relaxed man with a remarkable fund of stories, a sharp sense of humor, and a contagious laugh. He and Rose were soon laughing and talking like intimates. Cissy was amused at their quick familiarity, and she teased Rose in her later letters about Elmer being "your beau."

Cissy had little romantic resistance now. She was much more vulnerable because she was more lonely. Cal fulfilled one part of her, and Elmer another. Perhaps she needed both then. She and Elmer, however, were deeply entangled, and her feelings surfaced often. When Elmer got sick, Cissy sent a frantic message to Rose: "Come up with Dr. Huff and spend the night. *Please* do! *Please* come! *Quick*! . . ."

Elmer's world was in New York, and Cissy soon found herself part of it. One of his close friends was Herbert Bayard Swope, the celebrated editor of the New York *World*, a newspaper that combined literary flair with crusading zeal. The *World* exposed everything from the Ku Klux Klan to southern peonage to New

York political corruption. Swope instituted the Op Ed page, where provocative columns of varied opinion were published. Wearing a pince-nez and swinging a walking stick, Swope stalked through his city room. His journalistic philosophy was simple: "Pick out the best story of the day and hammer the hell out of it." To young reporters, he said, "There ain't no instructions: go there, get the story, get back . . . and don't make a fool out of the paper . . . don't forget that the only two things people read in a story are the first and last sentences. Give them blood in the first one."

Swope was a red-haired six-footer, ebullient, egocentric, and wildly charming. One of his columnists, Westbrook Pegler, wrote, "All gall divided into three parts—Herbert, Bayard and Swope." President Wilson called him "the fastest mind with which I have ever come in contact."

Swope knew all the wheelers and dealers of his time. They came to him to enjoy the play of his mind. More than advice, encouragement, stimulation, and amusement, they wanted access to his thoughts. Cissy called him "Swopey," and their mutual attraction was almost instant. "My father had a world of friends, but he didn't have many of their pictures framed," said Herbert Bayard Swope, Jr. "But he not only had Cissy's picture framed—he had it prominently displayed. She adored him and he adored her."

Dorothy Schiff, later the publisher of the New York *Post,* remembered Swope as "very male, a large man, interesting, very opinionated. He pounced on other girls, walked out with them at a party, but I don't think he got very involved. I don't think he had affairs. His wife Maggie was very strong and he was scared of her."

Maggie Swope was expert at pulverizing people who said the wrong thing. A weekend guest once complained about the flies in the sunroom, saying, "I don't know how they got into a nice house like this!"

"They came in with the guests," Maggie retorted.

The Swopes entertained on a large scale. It was not unusual for Maggie to casually tell her housekeeper, "May, there will be thirty-four for dinner tonight."

Maggie liked Cissy as much as her husband did. She adopted her as a friend, sister, companion. The two lunched together, shopped together, and talked about everything.

Elmer was Swope's attorney, and Swope and Maggie both encouraged Elmer's courtship. The Swopes maintained a lavish Manhattan apartment and a splendid weekend home in Sands Point, Long Island, and Cissy and Elmer were often their guests. Swope loved to talk, and Cissy loved to listen to him, entranced by his probing mind, astonishing memory, and biting wit. His was a giant ego that insisted on being stage center. If someone in his living room was talking quietly thirty feet away, Swope's voice would boom out, "I do *not* like to be interrupted in my own house."

Cissy and Swopey did a lot of riding together on his estate. One of his most expensive hobbies was horse racing. He owned horses, bred them, raced them, and bet on them. Cissy often went to the track with him in the early morning to watch his horses work out. Swope always remembered the way she looked wearing a sable coat over a turtle neck sweater and slacks.

Cissy spent many evenings learning to play croquet on the Swopes's floodlit court, with the dictatorial Swope telling her how to hit the ball. She played tennis and golf and even Murder. Murder was a favorite game at Sands Point: everyone getting a blank card except the murderer and the district attorney. The lights go out, the murderer picks a victim, the victim screams; the lights go on. The district attorney questions everyone and everyone has to tell the district attorney the truth—except the murderer, and nobody else knows who he is. Swope kept complicating the rules so that a murder often stayed unsolved for most of the weekend. Cissy loved being the district attorney, or the murderer.

The one game Cissy did not play was poker. She stayed with the players, though, giving Elmer or Swope moral support, having a supper of grilled frankfurters and champagne with them at four o'clock in the morning. A newly-arrived film producer announced he didn't like low-stakes games and wanted to "shoot the works." He asked for 10,000 worth of chips. Swope looked at Elmer and said, "Throw him a blue chip."

Swopey kept a record of his bets with Cissy, particularly at prizefights. First-night Broadway theater was a must of the Swopes, Cissy invariably with them. The Swopes and their two children loved Cissy. "She had a happy funny monkey face," said Swope's son, "and she had this wonderful laugh and used to laugh at her own jokes as well as everyone else's. She really liked to laugh." Her loyalty to the Swopes was absolute. The sure way to see Cissy's anger was to make a disparaging remark about any of the Swopes.

The Swopes gave Cissy a sense of family she had never had before. She had become part of people who wanted her, and wherever they went, she went. She felt completely at ease in their homes, genuinely secure in their affection.

"You give more happiness than you get so the world is your debtor and I for one would like to help repay the obligation," Swope once wired her. In his papers, he kept a card from Cissy that simply says: "To my darling Herbert." Such acceptance was particularly important at this time. She was familiar with the loneliness of a luxurious hotel suite, but now she also had a spartan flat where she went to write, a fourth-floor walk-up at 6 East Sixty-first Street, unknown even to her closest friends. She still found writing difficult; she felt painfully isolated when she worked, and she badly needed the warmth of the Swopes.

Elmer Schlesinger's work took him all over the country, and Cissy often found herself alone. Whenever her writing was most difficult or her hours most lonely, Maggie Swope was a cheerful voice at the other end of the phone with an invitation to lunch or a party. Swopey introduced her to a group of his friends who met regularly for lunch and became celebrated as the Algonquin Round Table. (Dorothy Parker, one of the members, described this group as "just a lot of people telling jokes and telling each other how good they are.") Swopey and many of this circle also went to Dr. Barach. Dorothy Parker caused much laughter when she announced that she finally understood why the doctor kept telling her to work at least five hours a day: "I just got his bill!"

Cissy now had her brother in New York. The *Daily News* was an unqualified success, and Joe had made his move permanent.

Just as she had shared his early editorial days on the Chicago *Tribune,* so was Cissy now joined in Joe's excitement about the *News.*

He aimed his paper at "Sweeney," a lower-middle-class reader with upper-class dreams. The working girl who skipped lunch but bought a fur coat. The man whose salary was small but who spent eighteen dollars for a bottle of bootleg whiskey. Joe gave them "Real Love Stories," offered them prize money in all kinds of contests: "The Ideal Mate," "The Most Beautiful Child," "The Queerest Boss I Ever Worked For," "Your Favorite Movie Actors." His Letters to the Editor column was called "Voice of the People." He published advice on health, horoscopes, and comic strips (nobody laughed harder at these than Joe himself).

Cissy often went with Joe when he visited newsstands, taking notes on which papers the customers bought, what kind of clothes they wore, what brands of cigarettes they smoked. He would peer over readers' shoulders on the subway to see which section of the *News* had caught their attention. Cissy was no longer startled when he would say, "Let's go to Coney Island and study people." Given his attention to detail, it was not surprising that the circulation of the *News* had passed that of the *Journal,* the Hearst paper, and was edging close to a million copies a day.

Joe's personal life was not as successful. His wife, Alice, would not give him a divorce, and he and Mary King lived in their unsatisfactory limbo. While he was a lenient boss and a generous friend, Joe (who was often called "JMP" or "Jomp") could also be iron-willed and vengeful when defied. Cissy, too, was like that. They both had an impishness, with enchanting smiles; but if they were crossed, they became ruthless, mule-headed, and unforgiving.

Joe kept his hair close-cropped, regularly played handball with anyone available on his staff, from the office boy to the cartoonist, and went to the movies almost every afternoon. Of his four children, his son James wanted to be a soldier, his oldest daughter Elinor, an actress, and the other two girls,

Josephine and Alicia, newspaperwomen. Felicia had often stayed with them. She and Elinor were particularly close.

Felicia had been in San Diego almost eighteen months. She had kept working as a waitress, spent little, and survived. She had proved her independence, her ability to come to a strange city, find a job, and pay her own way. But she was still not yet nineteen. She ached for the familiar.

Felicia wouldn't write to her mother, but as she said, "I had to write to *somebody*." She wrote to Drew Pearson, "making him promise not to tell anyone where she was."

Drew was working as a writer for the United Publishers Corporation, mostly doing interviews, for the then-respectable salary of $125 a week. In her letter, Felicia wrote: "I always wanted to make my own way." She included some literary sketches she had written in longhand and said she was saving her money to buy a typewriter. Pearson promptly sent her a portable typewriter, and their correspondence flourished.

One of the few ways of escaping from her mother was marriage.

Encouraged by her letters, Drew Pearson was determined to pursue his courtship in person; he approached Cissy and got her blessing. In San Diego he was persistent and persuasive, and he and Felicia were married there by a justice of the peace in March 1925, without any members of their families in attendance.

"We wired ma," said Felicia, "but we refused the money she offered us."

The Chicago *Tribune* account of the marriage noted: ". . . in her veins, the blood of Russian Polish nobility with its burning fire and brooding moods." The report observed that the couple would stay in California for the rest of March and would spend Easter with the bride's mother in New York.

"Felicia is really happy," Cissy wrote Rose. "If she isn't, it's *her* fault, for she has a *lovely* boy."

Felicia's marriage relieved some of Cissy's guilt about the gap between them, but it gave her a sudden feeling of age. She was forty-four years old. With her immersion in the frenetic life of

227

the Swopes, with the progress of her own writing, with the ardent attention of a man who loved her—the specter of future loneliness had temporarily faded. Now Felicia's marriage brought it into a shivering sharp focus.

Drew urged Felicia to be "good to your mother," and she wrote her a warm and loving letter:

Dearest Mama,

Now that your notorious child is wedded to the right son-in-law I hope everything will be happy ever after, as the fairy tales say.

I didn't write you at once because I feel so funny, and didn't know what to say. I am so glad you like Drew so you will be contented and happy about your newly-acquired son.

We spent a lovely honeymoon in Long Beach, Los Angeles and Catalina Island . . . there are glass-bottom boats and seals lying on rocks. . . . I am enclosing a letter from my newly-acquired Mama. Isn't it too cute? She's all jealous about Drew because he's her favorite. I'm scared to death.

Just think, Dearie, isn't life funny? I have squirmed under the regime of one Mama and now I have acquired 2 and that ain't the half of it!

Well, you know when I'm not busy hating you, I love you a lot. Even though I ran away.

All this softness is because my Pa-in-law sent two clippings this morning. One was a picture of you—a lovely one—beneath which was enscribed—Mrs. Drew Pearson. The other, from another paper, was one of me looking like a bull. Well, my Pa-in-law wanted to know *which* was me. Yours is so lovely. I'd deceive him if I thought I'd never see him.

Well, we're going to have a tiny flat in New York for a while. I'm going to cook. Don't laugh, it's terrible. . . . Well, I make good coffee, bacon, hotcakes, tomatoes and steaks and prunes. Poor Drew! . . .

Who is your new beau?

She signed it "Much love," and under that, "Mrs. Pearson—Tee! Hee!"

Cissy kept the letter, adding her own affectionate comment, "Just a *kid!*"

Immediately after their arrival in New York, Felicia and Drew had dinner with Cissy and Elmer. Felicia was radiant, and Cissy said she had never seen her looking so well. The mood was high, and Drew smilingly suggested that Elmer and Cissy should follow the example set by Felicia and him.

Felicia and Drew found a small furnished flat near the Cathedral of St. John the Divine. Felicia had not yet learned how to cook well, and Drew's salary was slim enough to keep them on a tight budget, so they were delighted whenever Cissy called and said, "You come and have dinner with us tomorrow."

"My mother-in-law did everything possible to bring happiness to a match which had few ingredients of success," Drew wrote afterward. "Among other things, she offered us a fabulous income, which we refused."

They did not refuse the $250 wedding-present check sent by Agnes Meyer. "We hugged and I laughed," Drew wrote of their reaction to the gift. "She served chicken in sour cream; I poured wine. We sat on sofa cushions eating on a table top supported by ten textbooks; no rug, no shelves, no furniture. . . . My wife is a red wild strawberry; I love her dearly."

"I have a feeling this thing is going to work out," Drew told a friend, "because I know the Poles pretty well."

"Yes," said his friend, "but do you know the Pattersons?"

Cissy's most patient beau, Freddie McLaughlin, had married the celebrated dancer Irene Castle in Chicago. Cissy sent her comments to Rose:

> He is her third husband, and everybody predicts a near calamity, but as a matter of fact, it may work out all right, as they have both reached the normal age of discretion; but whether they really have acquired a little sense or not remains to be seen. She gave her age as 29, but she is really 34 or 35, and he (so coquettish of him) clipped off a year or so too. They were married in his apartment—the apartment you saw. . . . But whether it turns out all right in the future or not, I am sure they will have a most *interesting* and pleasant honeymoon."

229

These marriages, of her daughter and of her longtime suitor, were surely a spur to Cissy. She had once told her friend Senator Wheeler that if Elmer asked her while she was in a gay mood, she was "afraid" she might agree to marry him. And she later said, "Drew talked me into it." But Princess Raspiglioci, who knew her well, said that Cissy "was in love with him . . . seemed crazy about him." And Cissy later agreed with another friend, Frances Marion, who said: "All my life I've been trying to find the man I didn't have to lie on my back to look up to." Cissy now felt surely that Elmer was that man. And when he proposed again, for the umpteenth time, she accepted.

Elmer would help fill her life, give her someone to think about, worry about, plan for. They would tour the world. They would entertain the most fascinating people in Washington and New York. They had all the money they could possibly spend, and they would spend it. She might even publish a magazine—and he would help her edit it. He would not work so hard. She would write more books. Both of them would drink less. They would have a solid life, full of purpose. And she would no longer sleep alone.

Elmer saw in Cissy a kindred spirit. But Cissy also brought spice with her; she brought an exhilarating excitement. Her imagination soared far above his, her impulses were more unpredictable, her sensitivity was deeper. How she would enrich his life!

Cissy called Felicia and Drew. "We're getting married this morning. Come on over." Felicia refused to believe that Cissy was serious, and stayed in bed, but Drew went. Elmer and Cissy drafted him as the only witness.

The newspaper account on April 12, 1925, was brief:

There was no crowd of titled and fashionable folk, no train of bridesmaids, no pages, no flowers, no distant droning of organ, nor beat of wedding march. Only the Countess and her bridegroom, Elmer Schlesinger, and the City Clerk reading the marriage ceremony. And, after the reading, no rice and old slippers, only a hurrying away to an unnoticed boarding of the

Italian steamship *Conte Verde*, which sailed at three o'clock, the day of their wedding.

Before sailing, Cissy told reporters, "I'm happier than I ever was before."

She wrote Rose from Versailles: "Elmer sends you and Henry his love. He is the kindest, most intelligent and patient man in all the world. And he has made me happier than I ever was before."

However happy she was, part of her was still in Jackson and always would be. She urged Rose to tell her everything of interest.

For the love of Mike, write me a long letter and tell me all the news. First of all, the gossip and scandal, and second, *business*. Let me know if the old German is still taking care of Flat Creek. If he drank up most of the whiskey and gave the rest away when he was drunk. What work has been done on the road? I really will turn their forest office inside out and upside down if they don't make good when I get back to Washington. *I will!* . . . Also about my beloved horses—Ranger first of all? I am very anxious about them. . . . Still expect to be west for a few weeks in August.

Elmer had his own concerns. He sent his former father-in-law a telegram: "Will you please keep an eye on the children?" His daughter Halle was twelve; his son Peter, six.

"Married men make very poor husbands," quipped a friend of the new couple, Frank Crowninshield of *Vanity Fair*. But Cissy was most content. She was more than willing to let Elmer take charge—make the choices from the menu and the wine list, decide where to go in the evening, organize the frenzy of her life.

Swope had written to some European friends: "For their own sakes, as well as mine, I know you will be glad to do what you can in the way of having them meet interesting people." But there was little need for Swope's friends, since the Schlesingers had so many of their own. The wining and dining seemed continuous. Cissy thrived on her new life, and during their three-month honeymoon, she found time to begin her second novel. (Her first was being readied for American publication in 1926.)

On their return they planned to visit Cissy's mother in Chicago. She would not have approved of Elmer, but she was now too senile for judgment. Cissy also wanted to see her niece Elinor make her stage debut in Milwaukee. They would then stop off in Flat Creek for a reunion with Rose before traveling to the Orient. But they got only as far as Chicago before Elmer's work pulled them back to New York.

Meeting Elmer's family, in Chicago, was a memorable experience for Cissy. She had known so few Jews. Except for the Leiters, there had been no Jews in her social set when she grew up in Chicago. She had met no Jewish girls at Miss Hersey's School in Boston nor at Miss Porter's School in Connecticut. And her beloved grandfather Medill, the great friend of Lincoln, had been outspokenly anti-Semitic. A man of high principle in so many areas, he despised most minority groups because they opposed him politically. Although her father shared this bias, he did not verbalize it. Her mother, however, loudly voiced the prejudices she shared with most of her class. Even her brother, who had tried socialism, was not free of such elitist feelings. He had been bitter about her marriage. "If she marries a Jew, she's also a Jew." It was many months before Joe made his first social overture to the newly married couple. They were then living on Fifth Avenue, in an apartment opposite the Metropolitan Museum of Art, and "Joe dropped by early one morning, wearing track shoes, a turtle-neck sweater, and a check-cloth visor cap. He was on his way to trot a couple times around the reservoir."

Whatever Joe felt about having a Jewish brother-in-law, he was not about to sacrifice the society of his sister. His was not a blanket bias. Despite his general antipathy toward Jews, he had a deep affection for his circulation manager, Max Annenberg, whom he considered one of his closest friends, a man he greatly admired. When Annenberg died, Joe wrote a moving personal tribute in a *News* editorial, saying: "I shall miss you and I shall see you soon."

Cissy had known some Jews in Washington. Agnes Meyer was not Jewish, but her husband was. Cissy had found him a warm, intelligent, kindly man. She remembered him at a dinner, hurrying over to a young boy faced with his first lobster. The boy was crying, and Meyer consoled him, saying, "I don't like them either, Peter," and told the waiter to bring roast beef instead. He then wiped away the boy's tears and told him about the ice cream they were having for dessert.

Then, of course, Bill Bullitt, to whom she had given her love, was half-Jewish. And Herbert Bayard Swope had introduced her to a whole range of Jews, from the Marx Brothers and Dorothy Parker to George Gershwin and Bernard Baruch. She had never really known any Jewish women, and she accepted without thought the stereotypical view of them as totally absorbed in home and children. But now she met a group of women in Elmer's family as sophisticated and fashionable and knowledgeable as herself, graduates of Smith and Vassar and the best schools, some of whom traced their roots to the American Revolution. She afterward said that they were the first Jewish women with whom she had had any intelligent conversation and that she had thoroughly enjoyed herself.

Of course, as Elmer's nephew said, "Elmer himself wasn't much of a Jew." He was not a member of a synagogue, nor did he observe any Jewish traditions. But he was always conscious of his heritage and once confided bitterly to Rose, "I'm only a Jew."

Nor was Elmer close to his own family. He once traveled from California to Chicago without discovering that his mother and sister were on the same train. Nor was he a good father. He shared Cissy's disinterest in young children. So seldom did he see his son that Peter recalled getting physically sick from excitement when his father was about to visit. But he recalled, too, how Elmer had let him take the wheel of his yacht on Long Island Sound.

Peter also remembered visiting his father and Cissy in their apartment. His father was lying on a couch drinking brandy, and Cissy was wearing a flowing green chiffon dress.

"She patted me on the ass and gave me two bucks," he said.

It was said that Cissy didn't want Peter in her house because he looked like Elmer's first wife. "This doesn't make much sense," said Julian Bach, Jr., who married Elmer's daughter, Halle, "because Halle looked even more like her mother, and she and Cissy got along just fine." What made the new relationship even easier was that Halle and Felicia became friends, too.

One of the first things Cissy and Elmer did together was to buy a forty-seven-acre estate from Vincent Astor in Sands Point. Cissy soon discovered the estate's romantic history. The land had once been owned by King Charles II of England. Some 250 years later the estate had belonged to Bourke Cockran, a flamboyant congressman and onetime lover of Jennie Churchill. Her son Winston visited there, and her nephew Shane Leslie, an admirer of Cissy's, had been married there.

Cissy was happy in the great white clapboard house with green shutters and a porch all around it. It sat on the top of a hill overlooking a lawn that swept down to Long Island Sound. She could look out and see the dock where Elmer's yacht, on which he commuted to Wall Street, was often moored. On the wooded grounds there was a saltwater swimming pool, a greenhouse, and a cottage where Cissy retired to write. They could walk to the Swopes, a circumstance that heightened their delight in their new home. Although Sands Point was meant to be a country retreat, Cissy and Elmer lived in high style. One night as Dr. Barach, their visitor, was getting ready for bed, "her butler arrived with a silver flask on a tray and said, 'Your nightcap, sir.'"

Cissy soon learned to expect the unexpected from Elmer. As she wrote Rose:

We got back from Paris last Tuesday. Maybe you didn't know we had sailed? I was at the dressmakers having some clothes tried on when Elmer telephoned and said that some frightfully important business had come up and we had to sail the *next day*! We were half moved in from the country, everything just at the worst disorder, and I had no maid, having just got rid of that elegant lady who was too dainty to empty slops out in Jackson. Well—my God it was awful. We *had* to go to dinner and dance that night at Elmer's partner's house, and then up early and out to the country and tried to give five million orders about shutting up the house for the winter. (All nice, good, reasonable orders—and all carried out just about as sweet and well as the orders I left behind me in dear Wyoming.) That was in November—the first week—about two months ago. The post-card I sent you was from Florence—beautiful Florence—Italy. We had a good time in Paris the first three or four weeks and tore around to restaurants and theaters, seeing our friends—up all night, and shopping all day. But got sick afterward.

One night we went off on a bat with some old friends—about four in the morning Elmer wanted to go home but I had a lot of champagne by then and felt pretty gay and wouldn't go with him. We went to one place where the men all painted up were dancing together, some in women's costumes. I gave one 20 francs to go over and kiss Elmer, which he did right on the mouth. Elmer turned green and came over absolutely foaming—said he probably got a disease and I must be drunk and better go home where I wouldn't disgrace myself. That's when *he* left. Then we went to a place where the women were all making love to each other, some in men's clothes. Half very masculine and half very fluffy ruffles. The head girl had a lovely face, like a young boy, and a deep, deep voice and a tiny mustache. She was *very* well dressed in a tuxedo (excepting for a little black straight skirt) high stiff collar and a white gardenia in her buttonhole.

I thought she was grand and would have loved to talk to her, but they dragged me on to a Russian place where there were some of the oldtime Russian gypsies (the kind the Grand Dukes and nobles used to ruin themselves for, before the war). I will never forget the voice of one oldish fat woman. It was the wildest, most passionate heart-broken thing you ever heard. Then we went to a nigger joint, all American coons—singing their heads off too. We ate waffles there and drank coffee. It was about 6:30 a.m. Then we thought we'd go to the great central market, which supplies (just think of it) the whole of Paris, and buy some flowers. All those big noble horses, three in line, were standing about with their carts, having walked in—miles and miles from the country—and hundreds of peasants muffled up in warm woolen stuffs, wearing wooden shoes—huddled over braziers of charcoal, lots of them for it was bitter cold, and acres of food stalls. And there we were, among these simple, poor, hardworking people—me in a white ermine coat and rose satin slippers walking through the slush and mud.

We came back to the Ritz—it was 7:30 by then, or later—arms full of the loveliest flowers and straight up to Elmer's room (not any *too* straight!) He was asleep in bed. We showered him with roses and voilets and mimosa and tulips—all *over* the bed and floor. But do you think he was grateful for this lovely sentiment of ours. Not a bit of it! He didn't hardly speak to me for a week.

Cissy was sensitive enough to feel uncomfortable about wearing an ermine coat among freezing peasants in wooden shoes in the open market. She thought nothing, however, of using epithets such as "niggers" and "coons." Her language was that of her social peers, the "smart slang" of the day.

Although Elmer was impulsive and fun-loving, he was no match for his high-spirited, energetic wife. She was always able to startle him, just as he often surprised her. It has been remarked that when Americans die, they go to Paris; Cissy certainly found the city delightful beyond measure. Like other wealthy American visitors, she and Elmer were caught up in a dizzying round of tipsy evenings. Their suite at the Ritz was a scatter of roses, silk stockings, and fragments of toast.

At Cissy's Dupont Circle mansion, where she and Elmer spent several months a year, the parties continued. She wrote to Rose:

Sunday night we had a big party here and brought down from New York three quadroon girls and two men and a big band to do "The Black Bottom" dance after dinner. One girl wore an enormous wig and nothing but a few bananas around her waist. When she came in, I thought I'd die of shame. But everyone got used to it mighty quick. The girls dressed upstairs in one of the bedrooms before the show.

I knocked on the door before the show—they said "come in"—I opened the door—they hadn't a stitch on any of them—excepting one girl had a napkin. About every two minutes, without any knock, the door would open quick and one of our *gentleman* guests would stick his head in, and seeing me, pull it out again. Don't know how all those men knew where the girls were. Guess they just smelled them.

Although it seems odd for the sophisticated Cissy to write of dying of shame, her remark indicates the puritanical strain in her character. She was very aware of the boundaries of taste and propriety. She believed her sex life could be as wild as she wanted as long as she kept it under covers, as long as she "didn't do it in the middle of the street and frighten the horses." Drinking could be excessive as long as one didn't strip naked and chase little boys. Language could be coarse, and jokes dirty—up to a point, and depending on the company. She knew exactly where her fine line was—but few of her friends did.

Cissy was still seeing her analyst, Dr. Barach. He told her Nathaniel Hawthorne's definition of happiness: "to live through the whole range of faculties and sensitivities. . . . Be true! Be true! Be true! Show freely to the world, if not your worst, then some trait whereby the worst may be inferred." "And I think she really believed that," said Barach.

President Calvin Coolidge knew little of Hawthorne's formula and nothing about the wild parties at Dupont Circle. He did know that the White House needed a new roof, and so he needed a temporary residence for six months. Cissy volunteered her house, and in 1927 the President and his wife moved to Dupont Circle while Cissy and Elmer stayed at their New York apartment.

Cissy showed Grace Coolidge through the house, and the President's wife noted that it was bigger than the White House and had more bathrooms. She was impressed with the size of the pink and white ballroom, with its Louis XVI chairs in gold taffeta, and an eighteenth-century Aubusson rug. She was even more impressed with the dining room, with its white marble fireplace and red-tapestried walls, a room that seated sixty easily. But she wrote a friend, Mrs. Hills, that she still preferred the big square rooms of the White House to Cissy's odd-shaped rooms. "Like most of the Washington houses," she wrote, "this one was built with more thought given to the entertainment side than to the living side." The Coolidges were not overly concerned with entertaining. When Cissy and Elmer dined at the White House, the portions were so small that Elmer told his daughter he felt "like a peanut rattling around in its shell."

The Presidential couple changed little at Dupont Circle, the President bringing only his desk and his bed, and Mrs. Coolidge the White House linen and silver and servants. The President also brought 30 pairs of shoes and a hundred pairs of woolen socks, a pair of which Felicia took as a souvenir for Drew.

President Coolidge was generally regarded as a deadweight at the dinner table. It was said that a woman guest had once pleaded, "You must talk to me, Mr. President. I made a bet today that I could get more than two words out of you."

"You lose," said Coolidge.

Even Grace Collidge later wrote: "I wonder if Mr. Coolidge would have talked to me more freely if I had been of a more serious turn of mind."

Cissy preferred the pleasant-faced, kindly Grace, who loved people and prizefights and had been a teacher of the deaf. Cissy's good friend Ethel Barrymore reported that the President had told her, "I know some funny stories, but I think the American public likes to think of their President as being a sort of solemn ass, and I think I'll just go on being a solemn ass."

Even Coolidge found it difficult to stay solemn at his first large dinner party in Cissy's house. It was in honor of a twenty-five-year-old blond, curly-haired, lanky man called "Slim" who was a houseguest for two days. The shy Slim had designed his own single-engine plane and had then made the first nonstop solo flight from New York to Paris. By the time his plane landed, Charles Lindbergh had already become a legend.

Cissy was a guest at this dinner, and she heard the crowds outside yelling, "We want Lindy!" and singing "America" and "Onward, Christian Soldiers." Lindbergh made a dozen trips to the balcony to wave at the crowd, the President going with him once. "They call me 'Lucky,'" Lindbergh later said, "but luck isn't enough," and then he gave the great credit to his plane. Writing of Lindbergh's feat, F. Scott Fitzgerald noted that "for a moment people set down their glasses in country clubs and speakeasies, and thought of their old best dreams."

Cissy had a plaque commemorating his visit placed in the room where he had slept (there was no plaque noting the Coolidges' stay), and she named her favorite horse "Lindy."

Cissy and Elmer were not entirely happy with their Presidential tenant. Coolidge fed his dogs on her expensive dining-room rug.

Felicia and Drew had gone on a prolonged trip to Europe and Asia shortly after their marriage. Drew had worked as a foreign correspondent, writing syndicated articles on every place, from the Gobi Desert to Outer Mongolia. On their return Cissy again offered them a generous allowance, and Elmer proposed setting Drew up in the printing business in Philadelphia. Drew instead took a job as foreign editor of a new Washington magazine called *United States Daily*, which later evolved into *U.S. News & World Report*. (Years later, publisher David Lawrence revealed that Cissy had prevailed on him to hire her son-in-law and to keep this request confidential so as not to hurt her daughter's pride.)

One of Cissy's reasons for living in New York with Elmer at this time was to leave the Washington scene clear for the young couple. For a while, Felicia and Drew lived at Dupont Circle, but they later bought their own house in Georgetown, then a rundown and unfashionable area. Felicia began reviewing movies for the Washington *Post*, then owned by friends of Cissy's, the McLeans. Felicia felt that Drew was not social enough, and so he gave a sumptuous Washington party, complete with celebrities. Cissy came from New York, and

Drew beamed at her. "It's a wonderful party, mother," he said. Felicia made it more wonderful by announcing her pregnancy.

"The cutest, darlingest little girl you ever saw—only weighed six pounds two ounces," Cissy wrote Rose later. "But that is what Felicia weighed exactly, and she grew to be a big girl." The baby was named Ellen after Drew's great grandmother, but she had Cissy's red hair. Cissy's natural joy, however, was coupled with a painful sense of the passage of time. She became more determined than ever to do more writing.

Barach helped her generate enough discipline to keep at her writing in her cottage at Sands Point and her walk-up studio in New York. The celebrated Snyder murder so intrigued Cissy that she was finally able to persuade her brother to let her write for the *News* in 1927. The murder would be her first assignment for that paper.

Ruth Brown Snyder was accused, with her lover, of killing her husband with a sash weight while he was sleeping. Her husband had been a magazine art editor who preferred fishing to parties. The chief witness against Ruth Snyder was her lover, Judd Gray, a former corset salesman, who detailed their previous attempts to kill her husband with sleeping powders, knockout drops, gas, and mercury tablets.

Cissy started her story by telling of young Indians qualifying as braves. They slit their flesh on either side of the big chest muscles and then ". . . pulled through one end of a rawhide thong and tied it fast. They fastened the other end to a young pine tree. Then they competed to see which boy could tug until he uprooted the tree and which boy would burst his chest muscles.

"Sometimes they tested themselves by hanging by the armpits on long poles from sunrise to sunset. They stuck it out without a whimper."

Cissy compared Ruth Snyder to the young Indians.

Strong nose. Strong-jawed implacable woman, sitting there, hour after hour, almost motionless, her hands nicely clasped like a lady's one upon the other . . . a white seductive skin. One of those indestructible Scandinavian white rose skins. Neither heat nor cold affects it, nor five pounds of chocolate, nor a quart of whiskey . . . answering questions in that same inflexible, defiant voice, sometimes louder. Never softer. . . . What do we know of the soul of an Indian?

Cissy's brother bylined her story "Eleanor Gizycka," and Cissy quickly explained to her husband that it was a professional name, the one under which she had written her novel. Joe Patterson ran her photograph alongside the story.

Joe wanted his photographer to get a picture of Ruth Snyder being electrocuted. This was accomplished with a miniature camera fastened to the photographer's right ankle, tripped by a shutter release in his trouser pocket. Never before had there been such a picture printed of a woman strapped onto an electric chair. Joe ran the picture on the front page of the *News* and delightedly told Cissy how his circulation jumped 250,000 on that day. Reprinted in the Sunday rotogravure section, sales were again up, 400,000 copies this time.

Cissy was soon in the thick of New York newspaper activity. Swope told her about his problems with the publisher of the *World*, Ralph Pulitzer. The paper seemed more and more "like an old car going up a hill." He had tried to buy the *World*, but Pulitzer wouldn't sell. He and Cissy talked about starting a paper of their own.

Arthur Brisbane and Walter Howey were then both in New York. Cissy had first met the tall, athletic Brisbane in Chicago, where he was Howey's boss on the Hearst paper. Hearst had hired him away from the New York *World*, where he was the sensationally successful Sunday editor. When he went to work for Hearst, Brisbane asked for a small salary plus a bonus for every thousand increase in circulation. When the circulation zoomed, this contract soon made him the highest paid newspaperman in the country, then earning more than fifty thousand dollars a year.

In 1928, Brisbane was slightly paunchy and in his middle sixties, but he still had a good right hand that could rock anybody in a fight. Most people felt he was a forbidding man with cold eyes and a hard voice whose admitted favorite sport was "putting one dollar on top of another." Cissy was one of the few for whom his eyes warmed and his voice softened.

Brisbane had not impressed Cissy at first. His speech was rapid and his movements staccato. He had a short nose, a querulous mouth, and a bomb-shaped brow—he was called "Old Doubledome." Then Cissy learned more about him. The son of a prominent Socialist intellectual, he had been educated in France; he worked like a drudge, neither smoked nor drank, and spent two hours a night reading the classics. Some considered him "brilliant . . . but without conviction . . . a mass of insincere sincerities . . . an adjustable conscience." But few knew better than Brisbane how to mirror the mind of the average man, how to put complex politics and philosophy into the language of the truck driver. His daily column, "Today," was the most widely read column in the country. And now Hearst had sent Brisbane and Howey to New York to help revitalize his sick papers, the morning *American* and the *Evening Journal,* and provide some tabloid competition for Joe Patterson's *News.* Cissy greeted Howey with friendly affection but no more, and she welcomed Brisbane like a respectful daughter. Brisbane, Howey, and Joe had urged her to write a novel, and she had dedicated it to all three.

Cissy's first novel, *Glass Houses,* had appeared earlier under the name Eleanor Gizycka. Her descriptions of her Washington friends, thinly disguised, were witty and satirical, occasionally showing a certain cruelty; her account of her rivalry with Alice Roosevelt Longworth over Senator Borah was graphic and detailed; her presentation of Jackson Hole and Cal was warm and loving.

The reviews were warm. "A remarkably good first novel. . . . The part which is set in Washington and deals with political and social life there, is as good as any novel of its kind . . . ," wrote Fanny Butcher in the Chicago *Tribune.* "The characters are supposed to belong to smart society, and you know that they do. They are supposed to have distinction, and they have. There is nothing in the least false about them."

"All Washington is laughing," said the Baltimore *Sun.*

"Real distinction, real style . . . more closely allied to Mrs.

Wharton than to any other writer I can think of," said a third review.

Cissy reveled in this warm reception. She was no longer a dilettante. She had climbed the church steeple again, but this time everyone was applauding. Her money had not bought this success; she had purchased it with the quickness of her imagination and with the haphazard discipline she had some-how forced on herself during the painful hours of writing. This book was a child of her talent and determination, and she had lavished more of herself on it than she had ever lavished on Felicia.

She and Elmer were vacationing on a houseboat in Sarasota when she saw a snide review of *Glass Houses* in the New York *World*. Cissy fired off a letter to Swope.

> The *Times* gave me a swell review Sunday, and I don't even know anyone at all on the *Times*, and look what my own *World* has done to me. This comes from acting like a lady—special privilege—it's the only hope for amateurs like me when we step off into the professional class.
>
> Was the young feller who wrote this review ever fired by Joe? I bet he was—maybe twice.
>
> Well, I'll have to defend my rotten little book as we defend liberty—it sold 25,000 within the first week of publication.
>
> Love to Margaret.

She added a postscript: "Yes, I am sore." Swope wired an immediate reply:

> It serves you right. Why in the hell didn't you tell me something about your more-or-less illegitimate and to me secret offspring. You didn't even send me a copy. I had heard only vaguely that you were supposed to have written a book before you went away. Apparently book was received and criticism printed during my absence. To show how ignorant I was of the matter, when Albert Lasker told me in Miami you were the guilty authoress, I immediately wired to have news story printed and review prepared, only to be told criticism had already been printed.

This should teach you hereafter to take me and God into your confidence and if there is any real trouble you can leave out God. Why don't you write answer to review. I will print anything you want to say. I haven't read book, but it must be pretty fair because Alice Longworth at my house other night said she thought it was pretty good. How can I help? Perhaps review won't hurt, because it will tend to balance over plus on other side in way of beautiful hair beautiful eyes pert nose kissable mouth delightful skin wonderful figure and reasonably attractive husband. Bayard

Swope also forwarded a letter from a reader who disagreed with the *World* review: "Its characters linger long after you put it down. . . . [It] ranks among the novels of the day . . . a really fine work."

Cissy finally wired Swope: *Well, I guess, I must forgive you. . . .*

The success of her first novel gave her the final push to finish her second novel. "I want to do a better one," she told an interviewer, "I'm not at all satisfied." She had a Murphy bed in the walk-up studio where she worked, and sometimes, when Elmer was away, she slept there. "There isn't a clock in the place," she said. She had furnished it with some old brocade draperies and simple furniture. "I get real satisfaction out of this place. Very few people know where it is."

She called her new novel *Fall Flight*. ("My poor mother tried so hard to make me say 'autumn' in the old days. But I never would.") It was almost entirely autobiographical, concentrating on her childhood, her youth, her marriage to Count Gizycki.

One night, in the midst of her work on this book, she had a dramatic dream. "This was no drab, gray dream," she told her friend Ruth Montgomery afterward. "It was bright technicolor. And I was awake."

Standing at the foot of her bed was Count Josef Gizycki, wearing his red hunting coat. The next day she received a cable informing her that Gizy had died suddenly in Vienna. His death had occurred at about the time she had seen him at the foot of her bed, and the Count had requested that he be buried in his red hunting coat.

244

Cissy's reaction to his death was shock without tears; for Felicia it was even more muted—a father she only dimly remembered, who had never written to her.

Cissy had never buried the Count within her, and never would. But no matter how much she later emphasized the glowing romance of her years with Gizy, she never blotted out the painful times.

Rose once told her, "When I was running barefoot in Nebraska, you were a princess in Europe."

"The hell I was," Cissy answered. "I was being spanked, and pulled by the hair, kicking and screaming, all over Europe."

Writing her new novel, much of it about her life with the Count, had been a kind of therapy, and she persuaded Dr. Barach to read it and write a preface. When she read what he had written, she told him that he had made clear to her, for the first time, the real meaning of her novel. So personal, so revealing was his preface that she told her daughter, "What a fool I made of myself letting him write that!" But she had committed herself and would honor her commitment.

The printed preface, analyzing her heroine, was a public analysis of Cissy:

Made continually conscious of her physical unattractiveness by a mother whom she originally loved, she developed first of all a feeling of inferiority, which tended to remove her from the world of reality, leaving her with an exaggerated respect for power, no matter how acquired. Riches, pomp, and rank were influential with her, far more than she could understand or prevail against.

Perhaps more important in this early influence was the mother's cruel indifference to the love of her daughter, with its inevitable arrest of emotional development. Instead of the child growing up to put faith in loving others, she curbed her feelings, being sure only of the rewards of loving herself. . . . When our love instinct is deeply hurt early in life, it fails to undergo the normal differentiation. . . . As adults, we love someone most unlike ourselves, someone of the opposite sex, and in that love we experience the greatest loss of self. In this girl . . . no example of a love characterized by loss of self was afforded to her. When, therefore, as a young adult, she began to use her love instinct, we find it defined by all the characteristics of an infantile feeling. . . .

The child is mainly concerned with sensation, the adult is concerned with sensation, feeling and thinking . . . the girl's love for the prince in our story is concerned with sensation, feeling and thinking. . . . She is stirred to the roots of her being by the contact with his shoulder. Her feelings are concerned with the effect he has upon her. There is no loss of self, no concern for his happiness. . . . The man whom she loves is a man far more than herself a sensationalist, representative of a primitive, archaic, infantile capacity for love. It is easy to see that such a marriage could only end in extreme failure, each one thinking of himself, each relying on sensation, with no possibility afforded for that unfolding of self of which a mature marriage offers us the greatest opportunity. The girl happened to have more innate capacity than the man, and so she is hurt more. But because we are so truly aware that her love is essentially a manifestation of narcissism, we are not more profoundly torn. We see the pathos of her situation, her helplessness, her terrific defeat, and are humanly moved by her flight, but the note of greatness in that human soul is not sounded. . . .

The fountain of youth lies, not in romantic sensationalism, but in a love that loses itself.

Barach was telling Cissy in print what he had told her often in private: that her mother's lack of love had crippled her emotionally, that she had never afterward been able to give any man the fullness of her love.

This inability had become apparent in her marriage to Elmer Schlesinger. She had once written Rose: "He is so smooth and so sure of himself that it is quite impossible to ever get mad at him, and with my kind of disposition, these are very unusual characteristics. . . . Elmer is reading the financial section of the paper in bed next to me. He's got an old striped wrapper on and specs, and he looks too homely and cute and contented for anything." Now she wrote Rose: "Elmer sends his love. He is still sweet and reasonable—but one *couldn't* say that the seasons are as damp as they once were."

Elmer, of course, brought his own problems into the marriage. As the youngest child in his family, and as one of the youngest men ever to graduate from Harvard, he had been spoiled, self-centered, willful. Both were passionate people, but like Cissy, he could not surrender himself to a loving marriage. Both were domineering people, but neither could truly dominate the other. Both were empathetic enough to understand the other, had enough charm and consideration to captivate the other, and both genuinely respected, liked, and even loved the other. But their love was not the "love that loses itself" that Barach had written about.

The reviews of *Fall Flight* in 1928 were emphatically good.

"When a second novel shows such a marked improvement over a first . . . and when the first was in itself a first book of unusual skill and brilliance, the author may be said to be established as an American novelist of note."

The book was serialized in newspapers throughout the country, and there were even discussions about a movie.

In an interview, Cissy said that a woman in Europe mattered less than a man's horse, a little more than his dog. She disagreed with the author Rebecca West's statement that women in England were incapable of rising to men's intellectual level. She felt that men achieved more than women simply as a result of their wider experiences and interests. "In this country, we feel no inferiority to man. Once women become educated, they lose the idea of inferiority."

She was thinking of writing another novel, this one exploring the difficulties of being wealthy and the burden of possessions. "Some women may enjoy servants and clothes and hostessing and beauty shops. I don't know. I only know I find it hard work, which keeps me from the things I'm really interested in."

What Barach had said about Cissy and power was true. Unable to fulfill herself fully through love, she now wanted power. Elmer's nephew, Bill Friedman, who became a good friend of Cissy's, felt that she had "a man's mind."

Barach had told her again and again that discontent with one's character breeds hate. Cissy's discontent came from her restlessness: she wanted more in her life, more passion, more purpose. Felicia wanted the same things. She and Drew had married without really knowing each other. They soon discovered that they preferred different friends, different life-styles. Felicia felt that Drew was too self-centered and refused to consider her important as a person. "The two of us never really could communicate."

While Drew was away on an overseas trip, Felicia left Ellen with a housekeeper and went to Reno for a divorce. Cissy called her repeatedly, but Felicia refused to talk to her about her decision. Nor would she discuss it with Drew when he returned. In an elevator back in Washington, Drew glanced at a headline on another passenger's newspaper: it announced his divorce. It was August 1928, and they had been married only three years.

Cissy was bitter about the breakup. She was genuinely fond of Drew and put the primary blame on Felicia. "I've got to remember every minute that Felicia is half-Polish." Cissy's relationship with Felicia had not improved much. Felicia did visit Cissy and Elmer at Sands Point and Washington, but there was always a boiling antagonism under the polite pleasantries. They still could not break down the wall between them. Cissy even urged Felicia to consult Dr. Barach, and she did. After the doctor-patient relationship with Felicia had ended, Barach was intrigued enough to continue seeing her. Cissy warned him, "You can have an affair with her if you like, Al, but don't marry her. She's not very responsible."

This was a hard, cutting thing for a mother to say about her daughter, and yet that was often the state of the bitterness between them. Still, Cissy was concerned about her daughter and tried to serve as a matchmaker. She introduced Felicia to Bill Friedman, Elmer's personable nephew, and they dated occasionally. But Felicia decided, finally, to go to Europe to "contemplate her novel." With a generous allowance from her mother, she took her baby and a nurse with her. She sailed a day before Ellen was to be turned over to Drew according to the custody agreement, which divided the child's time between them, six months for each. Drew was on the next ship, in hot pursuit. After months of chase and negotiation both again accepted the original agreement. A despairing Cissy saw it as a replay of her own flight with Felicia so many years before. Only this time, the story stayed out of the papers. And, this time, Cissy sided with the husband.

Felicia's failed marriage might have affected Cissy's own. But a stronger factor was Elmer's absorption in his legal practice. He was working too hard on too many important deals; he was traveling too often to too many places. The pace was exhausting, and Elmer was nervous and irritable. Cissy's friend Burton Rascoe said that Elmer was then "an argumentative maniac," who treated some of his guests as if they were defendants "under cross examination."

Cissy no longer wanted to accompany Elmer on his business trips. Even in New York they seemed to be going their separate ways. "If he wanted to go one place," remembered Elmer's nephew, "and she wanted to go another that same night, why that's what they did."

Elmer, however, kept trying to please Cissy. When she was impressed by the food served at a Vanderbilt dinner, he went into the kitchen to persuade the Vanderbilts' French cook Clementine to come and work for them. And when Cissy seemed tired, Elmer took her to Treasure Island, an island owned by friends in the Bahamas. When she spoke of missing her horse Ranger, he had him shipped to Washington. Cissy wrote to Rose, describing her meeting with Ranger.

> Went to see him yesterday for the first time. He didn't know me *at all!* And when I led him out of the barn, he started rarin' and tearin' and bucking and jumping and he pulled the rope clean out of my hand—and he about sawed my hand off doing it. They say down at the stable he bucks so they're afraid to take him out. Well, *can* you beat it? . . . But I was so lonesome for him.

To please Cissy, Elmer even arranged for Cal to sail on a freighter to join a safari in Africa. Again Rose was told the whole story.

He is the only passenger. They sailed for Mozambique, British East Africa, by way of the Suez Canal and Arabia. I went down to see the ship—and it is certainly a Romance ship if I ever read of one. The whole crew are black East Indian. Cal wrote us . . . said he had an Indian boy just to wait on him every morning—the boy turned his socks and fixed them for him. But he had to wait until the boy left to turn them back again to get them on. Also, so he could throw the hot water out of the porthole. [Cissy was the only person who could make Cal take a bath; he claimed that baths weakened the constitution and robbed a man of his manhood.]

Cal took his old gun with him, bought a secondhand Model T, and slept in the car.

"I shot two elephants for myself," he said. "If you shoot 'em where you stick a pig, straight on, you hit the heart. You're allowed two on the first license. After we kill 'em the natives eat 'em. I got four dollars a pound for the ivory. They weighed fifty pounds apiece. Those pieces of ivory was six feet long. . . ." About the gun he used, he said, "The Countess give to me."

Cal had never asked Cissy for anything. He accepted gifts because he knew how much the givers wanted to give. If Cissy had given him a gun, or paid for an overseas trip, he knew how little the money meant to her and how much pleasure the gift gave her.

Elmer brought Rose and Henry to Washington. Elmer and Cissy met them at the station, and Cissy asked Rose if she had any immediate wish. Yes, she did, answered Rose. She wanted to meet the President of the United States. Cissy laughed. Knowing Rose, she had anticipated this and had already arranged for it.

Rose and Henry were impressed by Washington but not by Cissy's friends. Cissy could not persuade them to extend their stay, but soon afterward she did induce Rose to go to Europe with young Hank.

"She coaxed me and coaxed me," remembered Rose, "and then said that anybody with any brains at all wouldn't cheat a boy out of the trip."

When Rose finally agreed to go, Cissy was unexpectedly in Nassau, but Elmer met them at the station in New York, took them in his yacht from Wall Street to Sands Point, and gave them a great time before their tour started. The five-week tour had been carefully planned; Cissy had even arranged fittings for custom-made riding boots for Rose in London.

President Coolidge, meanwhile, startled the world by saying, "I do not choose to run." Cissy later heard the story behind Coolidge's decision from Agnes Meyer, who had heard it from North Carolina's Governor, A. W. McClean. The Coolidges had gone on an inspection trip to the Black Hills of Dakota. Mrs. Coolidge returned to camp late for lunch after being away all morning with a handsome Secret Service man.

"Coolidge lost his temper completely," claimed McClean, who was there, "accused her of infidelity before everybody, dismissed the poor Secret Service man, and generally carried on like a lunatic . . . threatening an open scandal of the matter. In the midst of this, a message came that he must declare himself on the presidency, and before he or anyone else knew what he was doing, he sent out the statement: 'I do not choose to run.'"

The Republicans took him at his word in 1928 and nominated and elected Herbert Hoover, who promised the American people a car in every garage and a chicken in every pot. "The poorhouse is vanishing from among us," he insisted. The people elected the "Great Engineer," who, they hoped, would establish prosperity on a permanent basis.

Colonel Robert Rutherford McCormick, now sole publisher of the Chicago *Tribune,* had supported Hoover, but when he read his inaugural address, he said simply, "This man will not do."

Cissy had seen Bertie only on her infrequent visits to Chicago. Their relationship was correct but never warm. Cissy did not like Bertie, and Bertie knew it and was always wary of her. Cissy suffered him because of her lasting affection for his mother, her Aunt Kate, and his brother, Medill.

The aloof, arrogant Bertie had a vast knowledge of his paper's mechanical side, a generous policy toward his employees, and a long list of "hates" headed by the "burocracy," pacifists, Bolsheviks, "liberal crackpots," and the idle rich. "He knows what he believes and is willing to go to hell for it." Only a few family members knew that "an almost impish smile" sometimes broke through his grave courtesy. He was also a shrewd businessman, shrewder than either Joe or Cissy. He wrote his mother in 1928 that the stock market had gone "beyond the bounds of reason."

In that year the market made a gain of $11,385,993,733 and *The New York Times* predicted that 1929 would be even better for investors. It was a time of excesses. Movie star Lilyan Tashman confessed that she had an ermine-covered toilet seat. Mayor Jimmy Walker's wife made a stir when she bought $2,472 worth of shoes and handbags. A reporter revealed that a Pekinese occupied a Park Avenue suite while its mistress went to Europe—a chauffeur giving the dog a ride each morning, and another employee walking it at night. A man named John Markle moved alone into a Fifth Avenue apartment with forty-one rooms, fifteen baths, and twenty-six extension phones. Asked what he planned to do with all that space, he answered, "It's nobody's damn business." And Elmer and Cissy bought a luxuriously fitted private railroad car with gold-plated bathroom fixtures. Alice Longworth said, "The golden calf was giving triple cream and nobody seemed to care much about anything else."

A popular song was "My God, How the Money Rolls in," and the *Ladies' Home Journal* ran an article entitled "Everybody Ought to Be Rich," which pointed out that a $10,000 investment in General Motors stock in 1919 would be worth $1,500,000 in 1928. Even brainless, chinless comic-strip character Andy Gump made his fortune in the market.

The moneymaking madness only intensified Elmer's work. Some friends now commented on the shakiness of Cissy's marriage and speculated about the possibility of separation or divorce. Others insisted the two still had too much in common to break up and neither one truly wanted a split.

Elmer was tired. He took time out to go to Aiken, South Carolina, to play golf with a friend. On a February morning in

1929, Cissy got a call that Elmer had felt ill on the golf course, had collapsed in the clubhouse, and had died minutes later.

"What can I say to you?" Cissy wrote Rose. "I have lost above everything else *my child*. A woman can get over the loss of a man she loves but not over the loss of her baby. Outside business—at home—Elmer was my baby. You know that. All day and every waking moment of the night I want to put my arms around him and tell him not to be frightened—that I'll take care of him."

This is a revealing and startling comment. Did the dynamic Schlesinger have an unsuspected private face? Or had the shock of his death forced Cissy to recognize the unselfish love that she had for him, the true tenderness that she expressed in this maternal way? Cal had one face, always the same, always relaxed because he had been a solitary child, thrown out on his own at an early age. Elmer was different. He had been the youngest, spoiled child, and his work had involved complex decisions involving vast fortunes. When he relaxed completely with the woman he loved, perhaps he felt the simplicity of a childhood without responsibility. Perhaps this was why Cissy was able to assume a maternal role in her mind and feelings. He relaxed in her tenderness to renew himself with her. The paradox again was that Cissy could feel this maternal feeling toward her husband while never showing it to her child.

Her ex-son-in-law, Drew Pearson, volunteered to accompany her to South Carolina to bring back Elmer's body. On this trip Cissy must have contemplated the contrast between the two men she had married. One had been chosen by a romantic girl and the other by a mature woman. Gizy had given her passion, and Elmer had given her love. Gizy had treated her like a chattel, and Elmer had welcomed her as an equal partner. Only at Elmer's death did she recognize his great importance to her. Their marriage had lasted less than four years. She wept openly at the funeral.

Drew arranged the details of the simple but impressive funeral. Honorary pallbearers included senators and cabinet members as well as Joe Patterson and Colonel McCormick. Those present included Speaker of the House Nicholas Longworth and a justice of the Supreme Court. Cissy's grief was dramatic. She even bought black sheets for her bed. In her despair, she decided that she and Elmer should share an impressive mausoleum. She hired the architect of the Chicago *Tribune* building, Raymond Hood, to design a miniature Taj Mahal, and the two spent hours going over his plans at her home in Dupont Circle.

Like many busy lawyers, Elmer had not prepared his own will. He had left an estate of $2,225,000, including the Sands Point home, which would be divided equally among Cissy and Elmer's two children—seventeen-year-old Halle and ten-year-old Peter. Cissy had no need for the money, but she felt that the house should be hers. She had loved that house; it represented the early happiness of their marriage. She felt that it should be absolutely hers as a point of principle. She was angry that Elmer, who had arranged so much of her life, had not taken care of this. Grief over a loved one's death often contains elements of anger and guilt. Cissy felt angry at Elmer for leaving her when she still needed him so much. And she felt guilty because she believed that the difficulties in their marriage might have hastened his heart attack. But her anger over the Sands Point house eased her guilt. She sued to get it back, and did. As impulsively as she had ordered the mausoleum, she now canceled it. "No more Taj Mahal," she told Hood.

But she still told a friend, Arthur Reilly, about Elmer, "He was the only man I ever really loved." She had told others the same thing about Gizy.

The rooms were so lonely again, the bed empty.

She was forty-eight years old. How could she know that still another beginning of her life—perhaps the best and most important—was yet to come?

11

Emancipation has to do with power, not love.
—Dr. Alvan Barach

Arthur Brisbane wrote to Cissy:

I am sorry that you are going to Nassau. Why? To put on a fancy bathing suit, and not like yourself in it after you get it on. To supply cocktails to thirsty nobodys, supply them with dinners, bore yourself talking to them. . . .

If you must go to Nassau, why don't you refuse to see more than one person, sit down and write really seriously, and try to write a novel with ideas. *You* can do what you please. Why not write something that will represent your thinking in connection with a scattered life. . . . Write a book called "Spilling The Wine." Let it be the story of a woman's life, thrown away here and there, with laughs and a good deal of sadness scattered through it. Imitation laughs, and real sadness.

Then, if you *can*, make a climax that would make the life and all its disappointments well worthwhile. And, afterwards, make it real in your own existence. . . .

It's better to stay in New York, even if you have to suffer, *trying, trying* to do something.

Cissy answered, still discouraged, and Brisbane replied:

I have read your letter with sadness, because it seems a great pity that you should not be as happy as you might be. You have not taken time to search in life for what you ought to have. You take .what comes. You cannot do that, those who amount to much cannot do it safely. . . .

You are very much mistaken when you say that we don't know anything about anything. We know that we were put here to work and improve the race, just as a microbe was put in a cheese to give it better flavor.

And it is our business to be good microbes. . . .

Come back, start something that will be useful to the world in a big way, if you can; to a few people near you, if you can't. And be happy.

Brisbane had touched a tender nerve. She had been needed and she had been used and she had been loved, but she had never felt herself fulfilled. She needed something that would make her feel excited about waking up in the morning.

Despite Brisbane's advice, Cissy went to Nassau, where she rented a cottage with three miles of private beach at Lyford Cay. She stayed away from the Porcupine Club and the cocktail parties and spent much of her time swimming, thinking, and walking on the beach. In the largest sense, she was a loner like her brother. They both found it difficult to surrender themselves to people. She knew how intuitive he was, "suspicious as an old grizzly. You just can't fool him and it's dangerous to try." But then so was she. She knew how brave he was, and she too had that kind of courage. But she knew what a shambles of indirection his life had been, just like hers. He had suffered from the fiasco of his commitment to socialism, the frustration of his marriage, the faint praise for his novels. But when he started the New York *Daily News,* his new power had changed his world. He was now satisfied and self-confident.

She knew that her brother was "a man born with genius"; yet Arthur Brisbane had told her, "You have your brother's brain, only more and better and infinitely more active." And Brisbane was a man her brother considered "the greatest newspaperman of our time." If Brisbane's assessment of her ability was accurate, why couldn't she be a publisher too? She had the same printer's ink in her blood, the same taste, the same money. If anything, she possessed a greater aggressiveness than her brother, more iron in her will. She would never keep a hatchet in her bathroom as he did. If she got locked in, she would have banged on the door with her fists and yelled.

"Think there is actual chance of buying little more than a third of common stock of magazine we discussed. I shall be happy to see you have it. In fact I hate to see it get away. Wire me your wishes. Affectionate regards."

This wire from Herbert Bayard Swope in early 1929 seemed providential. She hurried back to New York to talk to Joe about this project. He tried to discourage her. He and cousin Bertie had bought *Liberty* magazine, and they were losing millions. He pointed out all the hazards of magazine publication and stressed her complete inexperience. They shared a common stubbornness and a common temper, and she exploded.

"You know, I love you very much, always will, *anyhow*," she wrote him afterward, "and I'm just bursting with pride of you. When you get into one of those ugly and oh so mean streaks, it is hell, bewildering and turns a feller roller sick. Now *stop it!* "

Once convinced then that Cissy had made up her mind, Joe gave her all the help he could. Max Annenberg had been his circulation manager in Chicago and had been pivotal in the quick success of the *News*. A man of great energy, Annenberg not only gave Cissy a compressed course in circulation but also found her an editor. He was Burton Rascoe, the former literary editor of the Chicago *Tribune*. Cissy planned to convert the magazine into a Washington weekly of political satire, sticking pins into such people as Alice Roosevelt Longworth. Unhappy, unwilling Rascoe tried to persuade Cissy to drop the project, telling her she could lose $300,000 a year for many years before the magazine made money. Cissy was not concerned.

Bertie McCormick wrote his mother about Cissy's magazine intentions. The New York *American* described Cissy's "dickering" for a "liberal" magazine, and added: "Long ago, in fact, she threw in her lot with the Liberals." At a critical point, however, the magazine was withdrawn from sale.

Again, rootless and alone, Cissy headed West for Flat Creek. Rose was waiting, and Cal. Rose was the same Rose, the same salt in her speech, but Cal had changed perceptibly, edging into age. Close to sixty, he was still strong and erect, but Cissy looked at him now with more warmth than passion, more memory than anticipation.

Still, Flat Creek was better than an empty Nassau beach. She needed friends now. Her failure to acquire the magazine had deflated her badly, and she needed Rose's laugh and encouragement. Rose had hired a caretaker for Flat Creek who was a local legend. He was Forney Cole, the toughest man in town; he had been a hired gunman in the old war of the settlers against the cattleman, "who could beat up any four or five men in the country." When a bear once knocked Forney down with a blow of her paw and bit a chunk from his thigh, he grabbed a club, stunned the bear, "and just beat her until I was all tired out." The club earned a place of pride over Jack Dornan's bar in Moose.

Cissy was aghast when she saw him. He was not only the ugliest man she had ever seen, but also the dirtiest. "His underwear wasn't just gray, it was black." He and Cal bristled at each other. In a showdown, Forney told Cal, "By God, one of us better go, and it ain't gonna be me." Cal laughed, but he went. Forney afterward confided that he had tried to "make it" with Cissy. He felt "she couldn't have been too particular after being with Cal." But he admitted that "she wouldn't let me have any." Forney did complain to her about the loneliness of the long winters at Flat Creek, and Cissy suggested he invite a woman to stay with him. Forney brightened. "Maybe I ought to have two?"

A telegram arrived from Swope: "I miss you. Where are you?"

After her magazine debacle, Brisbane had suggested that

Cissy persuade Swope to buy a newspaper with her. Swope was now ready. Pulitzer had decided to sell the *World* without giving him a chance to buy it, and he had resigned. Hearst was then conferring with Swope about editing the *Evening Journal* in New York, and Swope was also talking to Bernard Baruch about joining him to buy the Washington *Post*, which Ned McLean was supposedly ready to sell. Cissy returned to New York, and she and Swope had long talks. They went to his Sands Point estate, which was still "an absolutely seething bordello of interesting people" who followed Swope's rule that "no one in my house goes to bed before 3 A.M." Cissy, as always, felt completely at home with the Swopes. But she had decided which paper she wanted, and Swope disagreed with her choice. She wanted to buy the Washington *Herald* from Hearst.

Brisbane also tried to dissuade Cissy. "Washington is a childish place. . . . You ought to be working and living in some other city and INFLUENCING Washington." He opposed her proposed purchase of the *Herald*.

Take the advice of an old man with some wisdom, and don't load yourself down with a newspaper in Washington. If you must do anything of the kind, *buy the Washington Post*, or even the Washington *Star*. Money will buy anything from some people— and your brother and your cousin, with the Chicago *Tribune* backing, organization and advertising power could easily make either of these papers pay, even at an extravagant purchasing price. If you bought the *Herald*, which I would never encourage, you would literally lose millions. What's the use?

Cissy persisted, and Brisbane asked William Randolph Hearst if he was interested in selling the *Herald*. Hearst answered that he liked to buy newspapers, not sell them. Cissy decided to appeal to Hearst himself. Through Brisbane, she got an invitation to visit San Simeon in the summer of 1929. She arrived in high style in her private railroad car. She had named it the "Ranger," after her favorite horse. This car had three bedrooms and three baths and an observation platform. As with yachts, anyone worrying about the cost of a private railroad car was not ready to own one. The car had cost $100,000 and she spent $50,000 a year on its maintenance. She kept a cook and porter on duty year round.

Hearst had a band playing when Cissy arrived; his other guests stood on the terrace holding bouquets for her as if she were an arriving queen. From then on, whenever she went to San Simeon—and she went often—she always received the same elaborate greeting.

Cissy was seldom in awe of anyone, but she was nervous about meeting the Lord of San Simeon. Swope had told Cissy that Hearst was the most remarkable genius the profession of journalism had ever known. He owned an empire of newspapers, magazines, radio stations. While he never achieved his ambition of becoming President of the United States, he had the power to make or break Presidents. He also had the power to tell a reporter in Cuba, "You furnish the stories; I'll furnish the war!" With a wife and five sons in New York, this man was mighty enough to live with his young mistress, Marion Davies, in this California castle, presenting her to presidents and prime ministers.

Cissy had heard that Hearst was blunt, tactless, ruthless. She found a shy man who didn't like many people. A carefully prepared wall of courtesy and aloofness protected his kingly ego. To guests, he was unfailingly gentle, the old world gentleman. This tall, heavy man with a thin, squeaky voice, then sixty-six years old, was a law unto himself. Nobody raised an eyebrow when he played tennis wearing ordinary shoes and a shirt with a high, stiff collar. When his pants drooped, he looked like an elephant from the rear; when he flailed in his pool, he looked like an octopus. But his eyes never lost their great dignity and presence and power.

Cissy found it surprisingly easy to talk with him. Once she understood his innate shyness, which she herself shared, the awe was gone. She pentrated his reserve and made him laugh. The Lord of San Simeon seldom laughed. In turn, Hearst saw Cissy as one of his peers. Her family, wealth, and position were almost as exalted as his, and her newspaper heritage even more prestigious. He and Cissy were soon riding together every morning, and Cissy marveled at how splendid this sprawling man looked on a horse, how gracefully and well he rode.

Hearst called San Simeon "The Enchanted Hill," and he took Cissy on a private tour. Backed by the mountains, the estate covered several hundred thousand acres—it was almost half as large as Rhode Island—and boasted a sweeping view of the Pacific Ocean. He showed her his zoo, the largest private zoo in the country. The dangerous animals were caged, but all the others wandered free. New guests were often flabbergasted to find an ostrich or a yak in their path.

Hearst was particularly proud of his castle and his collections. A critic called him "the grotesque gargantua of our collecting era" and said he couldn't discriminate between "the awful and the awesome." "I think he went out and bought things whenever he was worried," his wife once explained. Most of his acquisitions were stored in two five-story warehouses in New York; a staff of thirty was kept busy cataloging and restoring his purchases. One such cataloged item was the ancient Cistercian monastery of Santa Maria de Ovila from Siquenza, Spain. It had been taken apart stone by stone, each one carefully marked and crated. It took ten ships to transport the monastery to New York.

Two guests at San Simeon once discussed the rumor that an uncrated castle had been lost somewhere on the grounds. "That wasn't a castle," the chauffer interrupted politely, "that was just a chateau."

Cissy saw all of San Simeon: the breeding farm and dairy with 10,000 cattle, the private airfield, the stable full of horses, the thirty-five cars, the movie theater, the tennis courts, and the roomful of fur coats for women who wanted to go walking in the chilly California evening. In the dining room there were life-size figures of saints from a Milan cathedral, decorative banners from Siena, Gobelin tapestries, and an ancient refectory table that seated 150. Cissy was delighted that Hearst kept bottles of chili sauce and ketchup on the table and used paper napkins. She was amused to see that a spirited guest had put a brassiere and panties on a statue of a water nymph. And she was impressed that the gardeners worked all night long under

261

floodlights so that his guests could look out on thousands of blooming lilies when they woke up on Easter Sunday.

Cissy got nowhere in her personal appeal for the Washington *Herald*, but she had won this man's friendship and she had touched his heart, as few ever did. "Nobody could have been kinder and more gentle than W. R.," Cissy wrote Brisbane. "I don't think I will ever be nervous with him again." There were those in the Hearst family who felt that the warmth between them might have grown into much more if there had been no Marion Davies.

Marion Cecilia Davies was a younger Cissy—eighteen years younger. Barely thirty, she was a hoyden full of fun. She and Cissy took to each other immediately. Marion felt Cissy was a sympathetic spirit in a castle full of power-hungry sycophants. She told Cissy that she once rushed into her room after dinner, looked in the mirror, and said, "Marion, you p-p-poor kid, it's a shame, they're a bunch of d-d-dull old bastards." When she was anguished, she stuttered.

Hearst first saw Marion in the 1917 Ziegfield Follies when she was just a nineteen-year-old chorus girl. He reportedly returned every night for eight weeks simply to stare at her. He promised to make her the biggest star in Hollywood, and he did. Marion told Cissy she knew she couldn't act, but she did it to please Hearst. He installed her at MGM, hired top creative talent to write for her, and direct her films, and the biggest acting names to co-star with her, built her a 14-room bungalow for a dressing room, even hired a six-piece orchestra to play her favorite tunes during film takes. In 1928 she ranked ahead of Greta Garbo and Joan Crawford as the moneymaking movie favorite.

Hearst built her a "beach house" at Santa Monica—a 90-room mansion with two swimming pools, three drawing rooms, two dining rooms, and a private theater. With all this, she felt like "a butterfly with glue on her wings." This was one of the reasons she drank so much. Because of her, Hearst gave his guests anything they wanted—except a second drink, and there were no drinks at all before five o'clock. But Marion made her arrangements with obliging servants who poured champagne instead of water into her rose-colored goblet at dinner. She also had bottles of champagne hidden in the toilet tanks of the castle's countless powder rooms. As she told Cissy, "Pops can't follow us here." She and Cissy once tried to leave the castle for some less inhibited drinking in Los Angeles, 200 miles away, but Hearst had them intercepted at the door. Marion cried on Cissy's shoulder, "Don't get married, don't get married, don't get married. . . ."

For all purposes, Marion felt she *was* married. She told Cissy that she didn't want Hearst to divorce his wife and marry her, that she didn't want to be confined by legal marriage, that no husband could be more faithful and considerate than Hearst was. Yet when she drank too much, she often became angry and ugly and once chased Hearst with a pair of scissors, yelling, "I'm going to cut your balls off."

Cissy talked to Marion as she talked to Rose Crabtree. They matched their quick wits and quick minds, and their stories were often ribald. They traded unvarnished judgments on all the Hearst guests from Charles Chaplin to Calvin Coolidge. Marion told Cissy that after she had spiked teetotaler Coolidge's fruit punch with wine, Grace Coolidge had remarked that she had never seen her dour husband so cheerful. They laughed about George Bernard Shaw's nearsighted wife, who had eaten a white orchid from a floral arrangement, having mistaken it for the salad.

They talked about Felicia. She was still in Paris with Ellen, but there was little word from her. They had a flat on the Quai d' Orléans near Notre Dame, and Felicia did write that Ellen liked to feed the pigeons in front of the cathedral. She refused money from Cissy for herself, but she did accept some for Ellen's expenses. Felicia told Cissy that she had a job on a magazine and that she was writing a novel. Ellen was three years old, and Cissy missed her granddaughter more than she missed her daughter.

Drew Pearson was still foreign editor of the *United States Daily;* he had also become the diplomatic correspondent for the Baltimore *Sun* and even picked up a fat fee for promoting the Irish sweepstakes in America. He was so successful that more sweeps tickets were soon sold in New York than in Ireland. With his new prosperity and position and a chauffeur-driven limousine (provided by the Irish Hospital lottery), Drew became a Don Juan, a heavy drinker, and a social lion in Washington. Cissy saw him whenever she came to Washington, and he no longer called her "Ma."

Felicia returned from Europe with her daughter in 1929. She had been living the life of a gay divorcée in Paris, and Ellen's presence had been burdensome. Felicia was happy to leave her with Drew for a while. Meanwhile she went to Cape Cod, Massachusetts, and finished her novel. Cissy reported to Rose in August:

> There isn't any news—except that Felicia is going abroad this month—I guess I will have to join her later and pick her out of any new love affair she has fallen in. She is as beautiful as the day—and so sweet and good nearly all the time. Her baby is with us now. But she's kind of skinny and long like her grandma and will never have her mother's beauty.

Cissy had never written so warmly about her daughter. Perhaps her grandchild had mellowed her.

Cissy found the world turned upside down in New York that fall. Her friends all had been multiplying their money in the skyrocketing stock market until the day came when everybody wanted to sell stocks and nobody wanted to buy. That was Black Thursday, October 24, 1929.

Cissy's money was so conservatively invested that she was hardly hurt. She had offered $160,000 worth of stock to finance a psychotherapy clinic at the Presbyterian Hospital, where Dr. Barach practiced. Before the board of directors could agree to accept the gift, the stock had fallen from 199½ to 3. An angry Cissy refused to make up the difference.

Barach was one of those frantic friends caught short of margin money in the panic. He telephoned Cissy in desperation and told her he would be wiped out unless he could get ten thousand dollars immediately. Cissy gave a check to her chauffeur, telling him not to stop for any lights. "He arrived too late," said Barach, "but the important thing was that she wanted to help. She was a real friend."

Swope, however, had managed to salvage most of his fortune, and his parties were more popular than ever. The 32,000 speakeasies in New York were crowded every night. Cissy went to the parties and frequented the speakeasies, but she felt more and more as if she were sitting on the sidelines, watching a performance.

Cissy was still possessed by the ambition to publish her own paper. She and Howey met occasionally, and he kept her fired up, assuring her that she could do it, that it would be fun, and that he would help her. He also told her that the Washington *Post* was again for sale. Ned McLean had become an unmanageable alcoholic. He had shocked Washington society by urinating on the leg of the Belgian ambassador and in a fireplace at the White House. Moreover, he had left his wife to live with Marion Davies's sister Rose in Beverly Hills. Now the *Post* was foundering.

Joe again was discouraging, even more so than he had been about the magazine. But Bertie McCormick was surprisingly enthusiastic, even recommending a business manager to help her "make up the books." He also promised to put her on the inside track with major advertising accounts if she did buy the paper. Cissy soon learned, however, that cousin Bertie was seriously interested in buying the *Post* for himself. Joe later told her that he and Bertie once had agreed that if *Liberty* ever made money, Joe would start a tabloid newspaper in Los Angeles and Bertie would go to Washington.

"Gee, Bertie, what does it all mean?" she wrote.

It meant that money was thicker than blood. It also meant that Bertie never seriously expected her to buy the *Post*. This all became academic when McLean withdrew the *Post* from sale.

Brisbane wrote her consolingly: "Please remember me to your brother. Tell him that in his next cycle, when he turns radical again, he and you and I will buy a paper, run it anonymously and have some fun with it. Then you will be able to do anything you like with Alice and your little *bêtes noires.*"

Cissy had begun to have her own second thoughts. "Although realizing 'puffickly' that my judgment is based on next to nothing of knowledge or experience, I still think the small class paper is my best bet."

Howey had told Cissy that Hearst had been hit hard by the Crash, that he had to sell two million copies daily of his twenty-five papers just to pay the daily $100,000 interest on his enormous debts. Howey thought Hearst might now be more interested in selling the Washington *Herald* —one of his papers that had never made money.

In the summer of 1930, Hearst and Marion were going on a holiday in Europe. They asked Cissy to meet them in New York before they left. Cissy made her plea personal and passionate. This time she was talking to good friends. Hearst was still adamant about not wanting to sell. Selling represented a psychological blow to him. He had never sold any of his papers. But Cissy stirred an idea in him. That night, after Cissy had gone, Marion Davies surely continued to press her friend's cause.

The next day, June 30, 1930, Brisbane wrote Cissy: "You must have taken a lot of trouble with him last night. . . . How would you like to be co-editor of the Washington *Herald,* with a modest salary and no expenses. That would be better than being owner with no salary and a gigantic loss."

Cissy made it plain that she must be editor, not coeditor, and Hearst immediately agreed. Brisbane's formal letter spelled out the details: She would be chief editor; she would receive two hundred dollars a week and would get one-third of all net profits that the paper might earn during the three-year period of her contract. Hearst cabled from Europe: "I would be delighted and honored to have you edit the *Herald.* Hope you will be as much pleased as I am."

Cissy was not simply pleased; she was exultant. Even her brother could not object to such an arrangement. She had no illusions about Hearst's decision. "He probably didn't care very much who ran the paper," Cissy reflected afterward. "He probably thought anyone would do." Perhaps. But, perhaps, also, Hearst sensed in her a spirit that might somehow raise the *Herald* from the dead.

Cissy now changed her name legally from Eleanor Schlesinger to Eleanor Medill Patterson. She would begin at the beginning.

12

You're younger than your daughter, and I can prove it!

　　　　　　—*Arthur Brisbane to Cissy in* 1930

Cissy arrived in Washington, D.C., in great high spirits. Almost fifty, she felt like one of the "hotsy-totsy girls"—the name the newspapers had given her circle when she had been in Washington as a young woman. So infectious was her joy that someone said, "She's not an atmosphere; she's a climate." Most of her snickering friends felt she was flying too high, and they waited expectantly for the fall. Did this sybaritic socialite truly expect to succeed as a newspaper editor? Had she ever done a disciplined day's work in her life? Brisbane publicly heralded Cissy's arrival, stating that she had inherited her grandfather's journalistic genius, but privately he worried: "I hope, and I am not sure, that you will work hard. Enjoyment is one thing, work is another."

August 1, 1930, was the sort of sultry Washington day Cissy

hated. She arrived at the *Herald* in her chauffeur-driven sixteen-cylinder Cadillac limousine wearing a big straw hat. The three-story building had been a warehouse, and the city room looked like a loft. There was no air conditioning, but some of the reporters had put on their jackets when they knew she was coming. The *Herald* had at that time a reputation as being the final refuge for the more alcoholic reporters in town. Most of them were tough, cynical, amused by the idea of working for a rich widow. Cissy did not know that Frank Knox, the general manager of the Hearst newspapers, had been there earlier to tell the *Herald* staff, "You know, she won't be around long. She won't last six months."

No one knew how apprehensive this tall, elegant redhead was; there was no hint of nervousness in her languid walk and regal bearing.

"All right," she said in her rich contralto, "they say this is a stunt—a joke! Well, if that's their idea, let's show them—let's go to work and put it over!" Then came her warm smile. "And you don't have to wear your coats when I'm around either."

They offered her a distant executive office, but she refused it, saying she wanted to be close to the staff. She took over the small sports office, which gave her a good view of the city room. She wanted the reporters to know she was with them, just as she wanted to catch some of their excitement. One of the first things she did was to write an editorial on the back of a telephone book, which happened to be on her lap.

"Put that in a box on the front page, signed with my name," she told the managing editor. "Be sure it's on the front page. Mr. Hearst says that's the only place people will read it."

The editorial read:

Arthur Brisbane told me in New York yesterday that I've got to say something.

"Did you ever hear the story," he said, "of the parrot that spoke five languages? A man bought a prize parrot for his wife. Next day, when he came home, he found the parrot on the supper table, boiled, ready to serve. 'My God,' said the man, 'what have you done? Didn't you know the parrot spoke five languages?' 'Well,' answered his wife, 'why didn't he say something?' "

Now, Mr. Brisbane, I've said something.

If this was whimsical, enigmatic, zany, it gave the staff a taste of things to come. The front page that day also included news about a British dirigible that landed in Montreal after a stormy flight from England and about a middle-aged real estate man in nearby Virginia who had murdered a girl, and the plans for the upcoming Washington bicentennial.

Washington, D.C., in 1930 was a southern town with a touch of New York sophistication, some western friendliness, and a liking for French cuisine. It was an extraordinarily easy town, very pleasant and quiet, and a great many people downtown actually knew each other.

But Washington was a graveyard for newspapers. The *Evening Star* was comfortably tied in with big business, the banks, and the local merchandisers. The tabloid *News* was in a sad state, and so was the once-saucy *Post*. Hearst's morning *Herald* and evening *Times* shared the same building on 13th and H Streets, their city rooms separated by a wooden frame of two by fours. Both had histories of financial disaster under such owners as Herbert Hoover and Arthur Brisbane. (Hearst had bought the *Times* from Brisbane in 1919.) Before Cissy's arrival, since the paper began, some thirty publishers and managers had come and gone. The two Hearst papers shared the same circulation and advertising staffs, but their reporters were more competitive with each other than they were with rival papers.

Cissy liked to say that the first words she learned at her grandfather's knee were "circulation" and "advertising," but the fact was she knew little about either. She had learned all kinds of odds and ends about the newspaper business from her grandfather, father, and brother, from Hearst, Howey, Brisbane, and Swope, but she knew nothing about the day-to-day management of a newspaper. "Out at sea in a tub," was the way she described herself then.

The great gifts she did have were an instinct for recognizing talent, a sure feel of what the public wanted to read, and an unquestioned courage. These talents would give the *Herald* its quality and its character.

"There is nothing to worry you," wrote Brisbane. "There is, especially, no possibility of 'humiliation.' . . . Don't let any inferiority complex creep in. . . . I think you will be running the paper for ten years, that is, if it continues to interest you."

"Hang your idea on a peg that all can reach," he told Cissy. "You can't drag people up to a subject and make them think about it. You've got to talk to them about things they really care about." People were interested first in themselves, he told her, then in their families, and, finally, in their race or country. He gave a final warning: "Work in fire."

Work in fire. She had never done that, except during the short spurts of intense effort that had produced her novels. She had had her pain and defeats, but her life had largely been a world of indulged impulses: another trip, another house, another lover. Could she abandon this soft life-style to work in fire, to work every day with discipline and enthusiasm? Deep within her, she knew she could. She would because the prize was power, and power was the royal jelly of the queen bee.

Her small office soon became home: a worktable, a leather couch, and, later, a marble-topped coffee table, refrigerator, hot plate, air conditioner, venetian blinds, black carpet, and violets—Gizy always had given her violets. On the wall, for inspiration, hung a portrait of her grim-faced grandfather, Joseph Medill. In the tiny anteroom sat her secretary, and the Washington joke was that Cissy paid her secretary more than she herself got from Hearst—which wasn't true.

Before Cissy's arrival the *Herald* was "pro-Americanism, pro-Hearst, pro-Marion Davies, and anti-everything else." Cissy knew that she did not have the authority to transform the paper. "There is only one boss, and he is not only supreme, but also strangely understanding and patient beyond expression." In another front-page editorial, a week after she came to the *Herald,* she wrote:

271

All kinds of people ask me if I intend to change the policies of The Washington *Herald*.

I would not if I could. I could not if I would.

Everyone should understand from the beginning that Mr. Hearst is first, last and all the time his own editor.

Aside from this rock-bottom fact, the other newspapers with which my family has for so long associated stand today with the Hearst papers on nearly all the major issues. AGAINST prohibition. AGAINST the League of Nations. AGAINST the World Court. AGAINST the recent naval treaty. FOR an adequate defense and FOR the general debunking of our foreign relations.

Dozens of other inquiries have come in as to how a woman proposes to boss an office full of men. But why should it be a worse job to boss men in the office than to boss them in the home? Men have always been bossed by women anyway, although most of them don't know it.

Still others want to know what ideals, if any, are peculiar to the female editor. The ideal of all true newspaper folk, regardless of sex, is to keep a paper interesting, inspiring, honest and successful. . . .

"Perhaps a woman editor is resented because an editor is supposed to possess wisdom, and something in the masculine mind objects to the suggestion that a woman can know anything except what she has already been told by a man," Cissy said later in a radio talk.

"A woman editing a newspaper is a novelty, as a woman in Congress once was, or a woman smoking a cigarette, or especially, a woman voting." She said she believed most men regarded women editors as Samuel Johnson had regarded women preachers: "Sir, a woman preaching is like a dog's walking on his hind legs. It is not done well; but you are surprised to find it done at all." But Cissy insisted that "there is nothing in the contents of a newspaper that a woman cannot understand. No part of the paper to which she cannot contribute, no part of a newspaper management that need necessarily be beyond her power to control."

272

Cissy had learned from her family that a successful paper had to be an autocracy, run by a single mastermind. At one of the first meetings she called, her executives crowded around her as she sat on her couch, one leg tucked under her, a copy of the *Herald* in her lap. She saw so poorly without her glasses that the paper was a blur, but she kept her glasses off to get an overall physical impact of the page. She turned the pages, shaking her head and pursing her lips, and finally said to them, "I *know* what I don't like, but you gentlemen won't agree with me."

Their silence was absolute.

"It's too black," she said.

How could they answer that? Every newspaper is white paper and black ink.

She pointed to the display advertisement of a downtown store. "This ad is too black," she said firmly. Her department heads stared at her blankly. They thought she had been referring to the news columns. None of them had looked critically at the *Herald*'s ads.

"Mrs. Patterson," said Irving Belt, in charge of the printing, "the advertisers are paying for black ink. This is what they want."

"I know," said Cissy stubbornly, "but it is *too* black. What can we do so that it will *still* be black—but not *so* black?"

After considerable pause, Belt, who was not only the printing genius but a scholar, said, "We can screen it."

The result was astonishing. Suddenly there was no more black in the paper, not even in the headlines. Everything now was a very very dark gray, and Belt had found a type called Ryerson that Cissy found easier to read. The *Herald* looked so distinctive that other publishers in coming years would send their printers to Washington to discover Cissy's secret.

Stirring her printer to think of something unorthodox was typical Cissy. She wasn't arrogant, but she was willful. It never occurred to her that anything she wanted could not be done. She didn't want excuses. She wanted her staff to say, "Yes ma'am, we will do it." She was so naive that she suggested to reporter Eddie Folliard that he get "a scoop a day." This was like asking a chef to produce a great new recipe every day. But future Pulitzer Prize–winner Folliard was so awed by her that he actually produced a news scoop the next day. If she sometimes acted the *grande dame*, she was always an earthy *grande dame*. She never fired a reporter for drinking unless it caused him to miss a story. She once stormed at a city hall reporter, "I don't give a goddamn how much booze you drink, you goddamn rummy, but, first of all, you *are* this paper. This is *your* paper. When you don't feel like that, get your ass out of here."

Long after midnight, after looking at an early edition of the paper, she called Bernie Harrison of her staff to find a lithographer at the plant. She had noticed a wrinkle in a model's dress and wanted it removed. There was never any question of cost. "She wanted perfection," said Harrison, "and you had to respect her for that."

When Cissy walked into the city room every day, "gorgeous, casual and possessive, the air became electric. Suddenly everybody seemed to be moving at a half-run, with shouting and bustle as if they were getting out an extra on a Presidential assassination." Cissy couldn't stand tranquility. She liked everything kept in ferment; she repeatedly said that she would rather raise hell than raise vegetables. Her day didn't end when she left the office. She had direct lines installed from her home to every department of the paper, and her reactions were swift and direct. The resulting spirit at the *Herald* "was ridiculous . . . and wonderful."

Cissy was soon hammering at Hearst, telling him her editorial page was "flat dead" because she had to run Hearst syndicated editorials about New York graft which were "not interesting to Washington readers in August." She told him that she wanted "to reorganize [the] editorial page combining first class local editorials with your national editorials."

Brisbane had told Hearst that Cissy "is an ambitious young woman and there are a great many people in Washington she wants to hit over the head." Alice Roosevelt Longworth expected to be an early target because their feud had never stopped simmering. "When Cissy got hold of that paper," she said, "I knew she'd do something to me." The "something" was another front-page editorial concerning their mutual friend, Ruth Hanna McCormick, who was running for the U.S. Senate seat of her dead husband, Medill. Elected as congresswoman-at-large in 1928, Ruth McCormick was described as "the only woman in America with a political technique." She had learned some of it as the first Republican national committeewoman from Illinois. The editorial read:

INTERESTING BUT NOT TRUE

Reports that Mrs. Alice Roosevelt Longworth will manage the Senate campaign of Mrs. Ruth Hanna McCormick are interesting, but not true.

Mrs. McCormick takes no advice, political or otherwise, from Mrs. Longworth.

Mrs. Longworth could not possibly manage anyone's campaign being too lofty to speak to newsmen and too aristocratic for public speaking.

Mrs. Longworth gives no interviews to the press.

Mrs. Longworth cannot utter in public.

Her assistance, therefore, will evolve itself as usual into posing for photographs.

Eleanor Medill Patterson

If a city can collectively gasp, Washington did. Cissy's attack was so personal, so provocative, so unorthodox. Alice was a Washington institution. Cissy could thinly disguise her and satirize her in one of her novels, but it was quite another thing to print caustic comments about her on the front page of the *Herald*. Wire services picked up Cissy's editorial and gave it national circulation. Alice refused comment but privately claimed it was "very amusing." Her friends insisted that although she might go to Illinois to advise Ruth McCormick, Alice had never intended to play a major role in her campaign.

Joe Patterson considered his sister's attack highly unprofessional, and so did Brisbane. "Scrapping with Alice is all very well," said Brisbane, "but you must keep it on the high Joseph Medill level." Hearst, however, was delighted. Cissy had wired him in Germany: "I wrote a little piece about Alice, which to my surprise ran like wildfire all over the country. Even Ruth approved it. I have her telegram. Only King Saul Brisbane took a slam at me."

When Cissy's editorial became a popular town topic, Brisbane changed his mind. He wrote her that Swope had spread the word that Brisbane had written the Alice editorial for Cissy. "I am much elated," Brisbane wrote. He included a drawing of himself with a broad smile on his face. Heywood Broun once told Cissy, "Never go to the typewriter to do an editorial unless you are angry at something," but it was from Brisbane that she learned how to hit like a battering ram by using plain words in a terse and energetic style.

When Brisbane heard that Cissy had another Alice editorial planned, he advised, "Sugar better than vinegar." But when he read it, he confessed, "You are best in that piece of gentle venom like God Almighty addressing a black beetle." He also sent her a photograph of a newspaper in a jungle with the inscription, "Eleanor Patterson . . . Jungle Editor." The second Alice editorial read:

WILL SHE? CAN SHE?

Some weeks ago, I wrote that Alice Longworth had no real gifts to bring to Ruth Hanna McCormick's campaign. Ruth McCormick is Alice Longworth's close friend.

I was in error. I spoke hastily.

Senator Borah, another *close* friend of Alice Longworth, has said that if Ruth McCormick is elected, he will vote to unseat her because of her excessive campaign expenditures. Mrs. Longworth may now present her real gifts. She may use her political influence, of which the country has for so long heard so much. She may soften this decision of the frugal gentleman from Idaho. . . .

But it is for Alice to come now bearing her offerings. Will she? Can she?

The editorial exploded like a fragmentation bomb all over Washington. The town talked of little else, and everyone bought the *Herald*. It seemed unbelievable that Cissy had exposed such a delicate situation, one in which she was so intimately involved. Washington insiders were well aware of Cissy's heated rivalry with Alice for Borah's affections; Cissy herself had detailed it in her novel.

Their mutual friend Arthur Krock discussed the editorial in his column in *The New York Times*. Observing that the three women—Cissy, Alice and Ruth—had been girlhood friends, he questioned whether Cissy's "cutting disparagement" of Alice "represents a woman colleague's idea of what is of first importance."

Krock missed the point. Cissy was not only having fun, not only making the *Herald* a personal paper, but she was also making circulation jump. Hearst responded immediately, cabling Brisbane from Germany: "Tell Cissy fine news about the Herald. I guess she's not only our star editor but our star business manager."

Cissy had little time for anything but her newspaper. Parties were pallid unless they produced some kind of story idea. She had no qualms about picking up ideas anywhere, if they were good ideas. "Newspaper people must have flash, intelligence, and a certain amount of ruthlessness," she said. "Their work must come first, always first before anything else. . . . One can't be a good reporter and a lady at the same time. I'd rather be a reporter. I think newspapermen are the most interesting people in the world."

Hearst's syndicated services supplied his twenty-five papers with national and international news stories, editorials, and a full quota of columns and features. Cissy could have put out a complete newspaper merely by using Hearst's "canned" material. But Cissy often decided to give a good local story a page-one preference over international stories, and grudgingly gave space to foreign news. She kept her staff pushing to get local stories, on the presumption that life was mainly something that was happening in Washington and hardly anywhere else.

One of Cissy's constant questions was: "What's going on and what are we going to do about it?" When her brother started a campaign in New York against syphilis and gonorrhea, Cissy followed his lead, using these words in print for the first time in Washington. Until then, venereal disease had been obliquely referred to as "social disease." Cissy sent reporters into clinics to interview prostitutes and doctors; their stories were illustrated with a great many pictures. And she used her paper to spotlight other local problems. Editorials demanded that civic leaders clean up the Potomac, get home rule for the residents, eliminate police department corruption, get a new airport, and rebuild the slums.

Cissy followed Brisbane's maxim: Print what you think 90 percent of your readers want to read and let the other 10 percent "look elsewhere for its fodder." She soon learned that 70 percent of her readers were women. They were the government girls, forming the working base of Washington. Cissy sensed how anxious they were to better their lives, how hungry they were for beauty and romance and excitement, and she was determined to meet their needs.

"Mrs. Patterson created—I truly believe it—*created* the modern Woman's Page," insisted Mason Peters, who worked for her for many years in a variety of jobs. "A great many people have taken credit for it, but I know better. *Nobody* in this business ever approached the concept of a Woman's Page that Mrs. Patterson brought to success. Her rule was: Is it beautiful? Is it worthy of a magazine? Is it tremendously effective?"

Cissy read all the fashionable magazines—*Vogue, Vanity Fair, Harper's Bazaar*. When she was struck by a story, an idea, a picture, a layout, she would tear the page out and send it to the appropriate editor, with a scrawled query: "Why can't we have things like this?" She called in a woman reporter and asked what she knew about beauty culture. "Well," said the young lady, "sometimes I have trouble getting my lipstick on straight."

"Tomorrow you will start a column of beauty hints." It became one of the most successful columns in the paper.

"When Cissy took over the paper," said Marie McNair, "there were only two women on the staff, me and an alcoholic who was sleeping with someone in the sports department. Then, suddenly, we had women all over the place."

Cissy went through women reporters "like she was eating

popcorn." Chic young socialites pleaded with her for a chance to work, and she sprinkled them through the paper like English lavender. But she expected too much. She was searching, she said, for reporters who had "the technique, the flash, the bloodhound news sense and nose, the quick pencil, the true judgment, the intuitive sense of mass psychology." And when the young women she hired failed, as most of them did, she could be petty, brutal, bitchy. Some of them left her office distraught and in tears. The survivors, though, became superb reporters.

Cissy believed that a good-looking woman could sometimes get a story that a man couldn't. Brisbane once told her that he someday hoped to see a paper published and run only by women. Her brother had a liberal policy on hiring women reporters, and so did Hearst. Swope had hired women with the warning: "I'll raise you or fire you at the end of the month."

Cissy raided the Washington *Post* for the best society editor in town, Ruth Jones. A handsome, sophisticated woman who had gone to the best schools, Jones knew not only the current crop of debutantes but also their mothers. President Woodrow Wilson's press secretary once told Jones that he read her social columns religiously since the guest lists of Washington parties often indicated developing political alliances. Cissy also hired Cecilia "Jackie" Martin as picture editor, heading a department of eight male photographers. Jackie was a very demanding, wild-tempered woman. Photographers were then called "rats," and the stocky editor often said that the only way to keep them in line was to keep her foot on the backs of their necks. But they respected her because she was a better photographer than any of them, and she fought to get them new equipment and higher salaries.

Cissy hired Francis Troy Northcross, an expert home economist, to start *Herald*-sponsored cooking classes and homemaker clubs. Mabelle Jennings came in to cover drama and movies. Cissy rarely questioned her reviews. Once, however, Mabelle dismissed a Mae West film as vulgar. Cissy, who had seen it and loved it, persuaded Mabelle to see it again and reconsider. Mabelle reconsidered and rewrote. Soon the *Herald* was carrying fashion columns, health columns, and several columns to "share the gossip." Cissy once wrote that Washington was a city of talk, a city that talked about itself and almost nothing else. She also editorially defended women on talking:

> Men have always accused women of talking too much. Talking their heads off. Driving men wild. The truth is that men accuse women of talking too much because men want to talk 100 percent of the time. I know two girls who went to a party and, on a bet, said nothing all night excepting, "Not really!" and "How wonderful!" They weren't pretty girls but they were belles of the ball.
>
> Men around the office talk like women around the home. You know what I mean. No woman can spill language around like a man once he gets started. . . .

When Cissy editorially supported her friend Ruth McCormick for the United States Senate, she made a sharp point, "I do not think that any appeal should be made to women, when a woman is the candidate." She added, however, "I believe that both men and women in Illinois, men especially, will be glad of the opportunity to send from Illinois the first woman ever elected to the United States Senate." Ruth lost the Senate race, and Cissy felt her editorial should have been stronger.

"Don't scold me about it," she wrote Brisbane, saying that she had wanted to send it to him for his approval, "but I thought you might be annoyed if I pestered you too much." Then she added, "I take my job terribly hard and worry myself half sick about everything I write."

"I don't need to tell you that you can write, and you don't need anybody to help or direct you," Brisbane answered. At the same time, he advised her to stay away from slang, double negatives, the first person pronoun, and any language that Coolidge wouldn't use, "except in quotes." A chastened Cissy promised, "From now on I'm going to be a *femme serieuse.* "

The relationship between Cissy and Brisbane was now at its high point. Brisbane was not only the richest newspaperman in the country, but he was also probably the most widely read. He had a reputation for ruthlessness. Hearst people would talk affectionately about Hearst but not about Brisbane. Subordinates would quake when he called them in, staring at them with his hard, blue eyes. Cissy was one of the few with whom he was loving, witty, wise, and charming. He punned with her, laughed with her, shared a large number of private jokes with her. His continual stream of letters was full of suggestions and advice.

He thought her idea for an article on what Americans do to influence votes was "excellent"; he sent her a book on Stalin to read "because whether he succeeds or fails, it is important to know about him"; he proposed a series on mothers of famous men, including Olympias, who "danced with snakes around her, no other costume"; he sent an article she had done on Edison to her brother to publish "because it is better than anything his paper published, or ours either." He liked the small sketches of people she drew in her letters and wrote, "I am thinking very seriously of having you illustrate your articles, and to get Mr. Hearst to use his commanding influence to MAKE you do it." He asked for a photograph of her—"an intellectual one with an eye to frighten and command." He urged her to do a series against Prohibition, and he approved of a proposed article about women's superiority to men as ambassadors. But when she discussed subjects he thought dangerous, he warned her, "Lay off, girlie."

Cissy was delighted to be Brisbane's disciple and sent him everything she wrote. Brisbane, however, worried not only about her professional problems but also her personal ones. He was concerned, perhaps even jealous, about the many men in her life—"at least two who would marry you if you would let them. Whatever you do, don't marry again without asking my opinion this time. I know husbands."

"You should have married me twenty-five years ago," Cissy replied puckishly. "We would have got along very well. You would have married again and been happy as you are, A.B., but you should have married me first."

As much as Cissy relied on Brisbane's advice, he was too far away. The *Herald* was a daily challenge, and many decisions had to be made immediately and instinctively. She had learned too much too quickly, and she was full of questions. She needed Howey. He came, as he promised he would, and he brought his excitement with him, prodded her imagination and let her share his. What Cissy loved most about Howey was the air of the unexpected that surrounded him. Yet, on the job, he was cool, professional, superb. He became her surrogate and gave the scene a sudden order she couldn't. Howey was Hearst's troubleshooter; he was uncannily skilled at getting ailing newspapers back on their feet. He told Cissy his first commandment: Get the story and keep the other fellow from getting it.

Howey believed that a newspaper must have "humanity." He told of a letter a little girl had written to him, asking, "Please find me a home—I have never slept in a bed." He soon ran a story about the girl and a photograph of her staring at a child's bed in a store window. Hearst himself sent Howey a check for $10,000, saying, "Please buy the little girl a home. You're breaking my heart."

Howey also capitalized on people's fascination with the repentance of a wayward sinner. He once ran a series of articles by a woman about to be executed for the murder of a policeman. She had signed a contract with Howey's paper, and her daughter was to receive a generous sum after the execution. During the six-day series, the newspaper's circulation increased 54,000 copies.

Cissy was a raptly attentive pupil. Her lessons continued at Dupont Circle, where Howey was now "in residence." Howey hated pomposity, pretense, stupidity, and society cocktail parties, so the two of them usually spent their evenings alone together. This did not necessarily mean that the evenings were always quiet. Howey was as exuberant in her home as he was unfettered in her office. They had a guest one night, a Chicago newspaper friend, and their mixture of reminiscence and champagne lasted until dawn. When Howey heard the clanking approach of two milk wagons, he challenged his friend to a "chariot" race around Dupont Circle. The three conspirators edged quietly into the street and waited until both milkmen were away from their wagons. Then the two men ran for their wagons and the race began. While the milkmen chased and cursed and milk bottles crashed, Cissy cheered and laughed uproariously.

"Walter Howey has been here, cute as can be," Cissy wrote Brisbane. "He had two or three grand ideas, none of them fit to send over the wires."

When they had first met in Chicago, Cissy was still troubled by her divorce, and Howey had diverted her by persuading her to write for his paper. As their friendship warmed, she might have thought of marrying him. But Howey believed in love, not marriage. Now he saw Cissy differently. His spirited rich girl had flowered into a woman of dimension and imagination. He was fifty years old, tired of being a jumping jack for Hearst, solving other people's newspaper headaches. Cissy offered him more love and laughter—and money—than he had ever had in his life.

"Cissy and Howey were really in love," said star Hearst reporter Adela Rogers St. Johns, who moved into the Dupont Circle ménage and watched the affair at close hand. "I asked Howey if he was in love with her, and he said, 'Yes, I am . . . I'm just plain nuts about her.'" Adela never saw Cissy happier either. "I have been lying on a bed of roses," she wrote Brisbane. "Flattery, incense, the grandest time of my life . . ."

Hearst was having a celebration for Marion's birthday at San Simeon, and Cissy and Howey traveled there in her railroad car—her "chintz boudoir," as Brisbane called it. They found that this enforced confinement did not diminish their enjoyment of each other. St. Johns insisted, "Cissy wanted to be dominated so badly . . . all of us dominating women are like that. I'm sure Howey won her because she was completely sure that he would kick her right in the teeth and throw her out of the window if she crossed him. Here was another man she did not have to lie on her back to look up to."

Marion, Cissy, and Howey kept their own close circle, surrounded by the usual crowd of celebrated guests. Hearst joined them when he could, and he and Cissy took their "lovely rides in the hills" every morning. He was touched when she gave him a painting she had bought in Florence. As close as they became, Cissy always felt as if she were a little girl being watched over by a gentle giant. When she told Hearst how much she liked California, he promptly got his real estate people busy finding a ranch in the area for her. But Brisbane warned her not to buy a house, "because when you came out here, Mr. Hearst would absolutely compel you to come to his ranch so that you would never see your own."

Hearst had planned a picnic supper for his guests in an isolated area of the estate. Loaded on the pack mules were champagne, Japanese lanterns, caviar, shrimp flown in by chartered plane from Louisiana, sleeping bags, and the instruments for the hillbilly band that would play that evening. For Cissy and Marion, Hearst himself made scrambled eggs and bacon, his specialty. But he would not permit any trees to be cut for campfires; with forests all around him, firewood was hauled in from thirty miles away. So morbidly sensitive was he to the death of any living thing that his gardeners painted the yellowing leaves of dying trees so that they would look freshly green. Nobody mentioned death in Hearst's presence.

Cissy felt protective toward Marion, even though Marion seldom needed protection. Cissy watched Marion play Ping-Pong with Robert Maynard Hutchins, the *wunderkind* who had been recently named president of the University of Chicago. Marion complained that Hutchins had violated one of the game rules. Hutchins called Marion "stupid," and Cissy stormed at him, "How dare you insult our hostess?"

"They had this brilliant argument," Marion later reported. "Cissy was as brilliant as he was. . . . She cut him down to size . . . and told him to leave. He was glad to get away."

Cissy managed to get Marion to Los Angeles on the excuse that she needed Marion's help in selecting a present for Felicia. When Marion chose a necklace and bracelet set with aquamarines and diamonds, Cissy had it wrapped and handed it to her, wishing her a happy birthday. "This is the only way I knew of finding out something you wanted."

Even at San Simeon, Cissy pored over her daily copy of the *Herald.* She called her office every day, running up phone bills that her secretary remembered as "enormous." Cissy wanted to know all about everything, and she always had specific criticisms about pictures, headlines, and stories. As much as she enjoyed San Simeon for the two weeks, she wanted to get back to her paper. Most of all, she missed the ferment of the city room.

When they returned, Howey told St. Johns that he had proposed to Cissy and they were talking seriously about the pros and cons of marriage. "I thought it was great," said St. Johns. "I thought it was absolutely wonderful. I was so happy about it that I fell on the floor in hysterics. And I said to him, 'I give you my word that of all the things that I've done in my life, one of my greatest thrills will be to be your maid of honor or best man or whatever you want me to be. I hope you do it! I want to see it happen.'"

Joe Patterson was not happy about his sister's affair with Howey, and told her so. Joe's good friend and circulation manager, Max Annenberg, had told Joe that, during a circulation war between the Chicago *Tribune* and the *Herald-Examiner*, Howey had once hired a gunman to kill Annenberg. Both sides had gangs with guns and some were killed. Annenberg, who since had traded his guns for golf clubs, told Joe that Howey's hired gun was Dion O'Bannion and Annenberg had managed to see O'Bannion first and disarm him.

Joe also knew that Howey had a New York sweetheart who was a former gangster's moll. When Howey once came home too late, she dumped a chamber pot of urine on him. Adela Rogers St. Johns recalled a Howey visit to her Long Island summer place. "Well, this girl shows up with a gun while he was there, and she starts walking across my yard and shooting at him. Howey looked like he was going to die. Luckily my son managed to grab her gun away."

Had she known all this, Cissy might have been more intrigued than repelled. But there was something more immediate that she resented about Howey. With increasing intensity, he was making the transition from being her surrogate to being the boss at the *Herald*. One day Howey called the city desk and said, "This is Walter Howey." A new reporter replied, "Yes, and this is the pope." A furious Howey strode into the office, yelling, "Everybody here is fired!" This was reminiscent of the morning when the Hearst hatchetman "Long John" Hastings had arrived with a hangover and had announced, "Everybody on this side of the room is fired!" Cissy rehired everybody Howey had fired, but she was angry. The *Herald* was her paper, not his. She wanted his help, needed his help, just as she wanted and needed his love. She was willing to surrender as much of herself as she could, but she was not willing to surrender her power. She was the first woman ever to edit a major newspaper, and she was not going to sacrifice the substance of her position for its shadow. Given the choice of love or power, she chose power.

There was no sharp break, no final heated argument. The love stayed and so did the affection, all easily stirred up whenever their paths crossed, which was often. When Hearst sent troubleshooter Howey to revive another ailing paper in another city, Cissy was lonely, and relieved.

She now woke up when she wanted to, seldom before ten. She slept in different bedrooms in her mansion, but her favorite was still the hideaway bedroom suite in the corner of the fourth floor, near the servants' quarters. It included a sitting room with a fireplace, a large bathroom with a glass shower stall. She loved its feeling of privacy and remoteness. Breakfast in bed arrived along with her poodles, the newspapers, and the morning mail. When someone complained to Joe Patterson that he had not yet heard from Cissy about attending a reception for the British ambassador, Joe laughed. "Don't you know she never opens her mail?" he said. She usually did open it, but she seldom answered it. She had little patience for such matters. She not only failed to answer letters but often misplaced undeposited checks for large amounts in piles of correspondence. She seemed incapable of paying bills, and also constantly lost her glasses: her staff cached dozens of pairs of glasses in strategic places all over her various houses.

Her limousine took her to the *Herald*, where she usually arrived before noon. She usually wore simple tailored clothes at work.

Cissy's staff was soon divided into those who swore at her and those who swore by her. But the *Herald* bloomed. The personal journalism it represented was dying out. Newspapers were becoming more and more alike as their use of feature syndicates and wire services increased. Cissy, however, had a distinctive voice, and more and more Washingtonians were buying the *Herald* because they wanted to read what she had to say.

Brisbane wrote Hearst saying how much he liked Cissy's impact on the *Herald,* adding that it was a pity she wasn't a man. Hearst's retort was short and sharp: "Glad you like the Washington *Herald* but do not think Mrs. Patterson could be better if she were a man, or that any man could be better than Mrs. Patterson."

This prompted Brisbane to inform Cissy, "You have only one real boss and that is Hearst. And, in view of the fact that I can see that you are HIS boss, I should say that you might act quite freely."

And so she did. Her brother had strongly urged her to emphasize sex in her paper, a policy that had proved so successful in the *News.* Cissy mentioned this to Hearst. "Big brother is right about sex appeal," he answered, "but it is not responsible for circulation in a mighty good newspaper. Tell him that." But Cissy knew that Brisbane too relied on a formula of crime and underwear: a picture of the rape of the Sabine women tied into a somewhat similar story in Alaska; an article on a torture chamber; a picture of a woman holding up her dress while walking through a sewer; an article entitled "How I Fascinated Over Twenty Different Women"; a short story entitled "Love, Intrigue, Tragedy, and Mystery." Brisbane rationalized that this "ACTS AS A SAFETY VALVE FOR PUBLIC INDIGNATION." He also believed that every romance was really a sex story.

Cissy had her own way of giving the *Herald* sex appeal. She created Page 3. Page 3 was the fun page. Page 3 was shocking. Page 3 was Cissy's page. Washingtonians turned first to Page 3 to find out who was doing what to whom. The city was too small for social secrets. Page 3 had all the scandalous and outrageous news stories, all the sex, all the leg art, and the spiciest, meanest gossip columns ever printed. Cissy told her editors she wanted earthiness, but with humor and grace. Stories could be suggestive but not crude, flagrant but not vulgar, bawdy but not dirty. Cissy's own judgment on this was impeccable and decisive. Her editors, without her instinct, walked a daily tightrope.

Page 3 was truly Cissy's in the sense that she herself collected and uncovered many of the stories, mostly from a network of friends. She once called one of her editors, Mason Peters, about an item she had sent him.

"Yes, Mrs. Patterson, I saw it," he told her. "I have it on the spike, thinking about it. It seemed to me that it would be a little hard to make it look right." He meant that he thought it was too raw.

"Then I heard her chuckle over the phone," said Peters, and she added, "Well, I have a feeling you ought to try."

It took a delicate hand to transform a raunchy story into a spicy bit of gossip. "Sometimes I thought I had pulled off something that was pretty darn good, but it would offend Mrs. Patterson. A tiny bell would jangle in her mind. I had crossed the line of good taste, and, boy, would I hear from her!"

Cissy was not infallible. In one of his rare reproaches, Hearst told her that one of her editorials was "silly." Cissy quickly agreed. "I knew it before I wrote it, while I was writing it, and ever since. What happened was this: we were preparing to spring the idea in another two or three days. Somebody told us that we were going to be beaten to the story if we didn't come out with it immediately. I guess I don't write well enough to write in a hurry. Disgusting I call it."

Cissy was in Palm Springs in February 1931 for a short holiday when she learned that Albert Einstein was a guest at a nearby estate. She walked over and asked the butler where she could find him. He pointed to a steep, winding trail between the rocks.

"I looked up—and bang! There was Einstein," Cissy wrote, "wearing nothing but a white handkerchief knotted at each of the four corners which rested upon the famous shock of curly gray hair." Seeing the professor "relatively in the nude," Cissy beat a hasty retreat, "wondering what a regular determined go-getter she-reporter would do under the circumstances."

Brisbane told her. Nelly Bly, he wrote in his "Today" column, "would have got a blanket, put it over Dr. Einstein, and got the interview, if necessary sitting on the blanket and on Einstein to keep him from getting away."

But Cissy was not finished with Einstein. Several nights later she went to see Charlie Chaplin's *City Lights* and saw Einstein sitting directly in front of her. She watched him staring:

> bewildered, utterly absorbed, like a child at a Christmas pantomime . . . this look of astonishment never wholly left his face. . . . Suddenly, just at the end of *City Lights,* your heart is caught up, squeezed, twisted. I began to cry then, and pretty hard, but I choked, blinked, and managed to take one last look at Einstein. . . . An enormous handkerchief, maybe the same one which covered his head while he was taking a sun bath on the Mojave Desert, almost concealed his face, but you could see two big sorrowful eyes, still wide with wonderment, brimming with tears. . . .

> There didn't seem to be much need after that in trying to get an interview with Professor Einstein. Why ask him if universe, space, and time are finite or infinite? Isn't it more interesting to know that Einstein, who understands better than anyone else the sublime arrangement of the universe, can also understand, and weeping, see the heartbreak of a little clown?

Hearst reacted quickly:

> Your Einstein article was really a gem. You have the faculty for humor and pathos. A very rare faculty. So few possess it and so many strain for it. You also have the gift of observation and of simple and vivid description. I don't think you appreciate yourself. People read your stuff and enjoy it, and *talk* about it. These Pattersons surely have a strain of genius. . . . I hope you will write more for publication.

"Mrs. Patterson is a first-class reporter," echoed Brisbane in his column, and urged that her article be read by all young reporters. "Unfortunately," he added, "Mrs. Patterson has more than a million dollars income . . . so she won't do the things she might do. She will succeed, in spite of wealth, the worst of all handicaps." That day, all Hearst papers received the message: "If you have not already printed Mrs. Eleanor Patterson's article on Einstein, sent you last night under Los Angeles date, Chief instructs that you print it."

An unfettered Cissy was plumbing her potential, and she was thrilled. While vacationing in Miami Beach, she interviewed Al Capone, the gangster "with the scar on his cheek like the welt from the lash of a whip," whose gang had reputedly killed 227 men.

"He has the neck and shoulders of a wrestler. One of those prodigious Italians, thick-chested, close to six feet tall. The muscles of his arms stretched the sleeves of his light brown suit so that it seemed to be cut too small for him. . . . Ice-gray, ice-cold eyes. You can't any more look into the eyes of Capone than you can look into the eyes of a tiger."

They were small eyes, his mouth was too full, more purple than red. All he did, he said, was to supply a popular demand:

> If the people didn't want beer, they wouldn't drink it. . . . I don't interfere with big business. None of the big business guys can ever say I took a dollar from 'em. Why, I done a favor for one of the big newspapers in the country when they was up against it. Broke a strike for 'em. . . . I only want to do business, you understand, with my own class. Why can't they leave me alone? I don't interfere with them any. Get me? I don't interfere with their racket. . . . But they're forever after me.

Capone did not tell Cissy about the fourteen-year-old girls who worked at his Four Deuces bordello on South Wabash Avenue, but he did tell her about some of his other employees: "At least 300 young men, thanks to me, are getting from $120 to $200 a week . . . in a harmless beer racket . . . work that has taken a man out of the holdup and bank robbery business and worse."

Cissy wrote that the thirty-one-year-old Capone looked forty-five. He sat "impassive like a Buddha, yet you began to sense the painful, nervous intensity under the solid exterior. His enormous hands rested half-clenched on the table. Without raising his voice or looking around, he called for a servant. A man in a white apron simply tore into the room.

"My goodness," I half-whispered, "I wish I could get service like that at home."

His speech speeded up, his tension increased. "The stirring of a tiger," Cissy wrote. "For just a second, I went a little sick. I had to fight the impulse to jump up and run blindly away." She then discussed the special sympathy women have for gangsters, ending with, "If you don't understand why, consult Dr. Freud."

Cissy's success prompted another Brisbane editorial:

ELEANOR PATTERSON SETS A GOOD EXAMPLE
Having Brains, She Worked Hard
This young woman is one of the VERY few able and successful women editing newspapers. There ought to be many more, for women are particularly adapted to newspaper work. They know what interests human beings. And they possess INNATE INTEGRITY, which is the most important thing in newspaper work. . . . Mrs. Patterson, if she chose, could, like many other rich men and women, devote her life to pleasure, but that doesn't suit her. She wants to work, and she does work, HARD. . . .

Cissy had a more critical view of herself.

I'm always explaining, forever explaining. It seems to me I have to. Often I think I'm silly, and I say so. But it has gradually dawned on me that I never WILL be a SUCCESSFUL WOMAN unless I adopt a different attitude. So I decided to blow my own trumpet, fill my lungs and blast away with the others. . . .

Successful women brag more than successful men, and successful men brag a good deal. I guess the reason is that women are fairly new at the game, and are still suffering from an inferiority complex. . . . Alice Longworth never brags. On the contrary, she seems to take an odd, malicious satisfaction in poking fun at herself. She delights in setting off a whole room of people, like a bunch of firecrackers, at some story in which she figures as anything but a triumphant heroine, while she lies back in her deep armchair and lets go peals of true Rooseveltian laughter. The reason for this is that although Mrs. Longworth is one of the most celebrated women of the world, she believes herself to be a failure because she was not born a man. She cannot hope to be a second Teddy Roosevelt. No substitute for this particular choice of success has ever satisfied her purely dynastic type of ambition.

Alice had ambitions Cissy didn't know about. Brisbane reported he had heard from a mutual friend in Newport that "Alice seemed very interested in the Washington *Post* about which she had long talks with Mrs. Ned McLean. . . . It would be very interesting if you should find yourself as Editor of the *Herald* competing with Alice."

Cissy was not pleased by this news, and her comments about her girlhood friend became more stinging. Alice referred to herself as "just one of the Roosevelt show-offs," but she distanced herself from Franklin Delano Roosevelt by stressing that he was only a fourth cousin once removed. Cissy remarked that perhaps Franklin "wasn't crazy about the relationship either."

Alice and Nick were still living together, but theirs was a marriage in only the most formal sense. Nick's reputation as a womanizer had increased as he grew older. Still, with her feud with Alice at its peak, Cissy and Nick kept a respectable distance from each other. When they did meet accidentally at parties, he was always warm and affectionate. He was her unchanged friend, jaunty, full of jokes and games. His was a flippancy "so light and airy that it might be said to have the specific gravity of feathers." But as the Speaker of the House of Representatives, "he had the weight of lead shot."

Cissy heard that Nick was stricken with a heart attack in Aiken, South Carolina, the same city where her husband Elmer had died. She hurriedly called Dr. Barach to ask that one of his oxygen tents be rushed there, but it was too late.

"I'm afraid all the care in the world would not have saved

him," Brisbane wrote consolingly. "He had not taken sufficiently good care of himself."

"Nick was my friend for thirty years," Cissy answered. "He will be terribly missed."

She ordered his life story to be run in installments and supplied many of the anecdotes herself. In the midst of her grief, she was still the editor, and she discussed with Brisbane the possibility of getting Alice to write her memoirs: "She may be willing. . . . That would certainly be grand for circulation." Brisbane pointed out that her memoirs would be interesting only if Alice wrote frankly. He added that he believed it unlikely that she would be candid.

Alice retired from the Washington social scene. Political talk at parties indicated she might be offered Nick's seat in the House of Representatives, perhaps even a chance at the U.S. Senate. But Alice insisted she had "no temptation for office." She said that she was "hideously shy" about talking in public; she was "contrary and conspicuous" to avoid being "a pathetic creature." "I'm not witty. I'm just funny. I'm the old firehorse. I just perform. I give a good show. I like to tease . . . a sense of mischief gets a hold of me from time to time." Her agile mind spun from topic to topic, and her conversation seldom followed a charitable course. She feared being sentimental as much as she loathed self-pity. "I have an appetite for being entertained. . . . And I don't mind what I do, unless I'm injuring someone in some way."

In the small town of Washington, Cissy and Alice encountered each other on the street soon after Nick's death. Cissy instinctively rushed forward and said, "Isn't it time we made up?" Alice looked her over slowly, without smiling, and said, "No, it's too early yet."

Some months afterward, Cissy was sick with an undiagnosed illness that lasted weeks. Adela Rogers St. Johns was staying with her. Adela and Alice Longworth were old friends, and the two lunched together in town one day. "You know, Cissy's been ill," said Adela. "I'm staying at her house, and she knows I'm having lunch with you. And when I come back she'll ask me a million questions."

Alice said nothing. Adela leaned forward, took Alice by the hand, and said earnestly, "Why don't you come back with me? I think she's often lonely for someone who remembers the same things she does."

Alice hesitated, then smiled slowly and agreed. Adela called Cissy to alert her. Adela sensed Alice's nervousness, and she could imagine Cissy's. Cissy was waiting near the door when they came in, and the two women looked at each other for a long moment. Alice spoke first. "I should have believed you about the champagne—that was your weakness, not men." Cissy's eyes twinkled when she answered, "I don't remember how old you are, lovie, but you don't look it." Then they both laughed, and embraced. And they lived happily ever after.

There was something in Cissy that pulled people back to her. No matter how hard she hit, no matter how bitter the feud, almost everyone she crossed was willing to forgive and forget. And with few exceptions, Cissy's anger was a flash storm, which soon subsided.

Drew Pearson was one of the exceptions, but that break came later. She loved Drew. When Felicia divorced him, Cissy pulled him even closer to herself. And whenever she needed him, he was there. When Howey left, Drew became her "absolute chief advisor." When she feuded with Alice, he carried her shield and spear, even writing his own disparaging article about Alice. He encouraged Cissy with her writing, helped her with some of her final editing, even made flattering mentions of her on his new radio show. His magazine article on Cissy, "Our Leading Lady Publisher," was a lavish paean.

Perhaps partly because of the brouhaha that had ensued when Elmer Schlesinger died intestate, Drew wrote his first will in September 1930:

> I ask my parents to save that part of my personal belongings, my papers and my furniture which they think might help make my daughter better acquainted with her father and give them to her when she is of sufficient age. . . .
>
> I ask that my brother take charge of my personal correspondence and . . . save for my daughter all letters exchanged

between her mother and me. I know that my former wife will not only continue to be the thoughtful mother she always has been but will try to make up for what little I have been able to contribute to the baby's life. I hope that she (Ellen) will go to college and I would caution against too much money and too much attention from nurses and governesses. . . .

Drew ended his will on a note of self-contempt: "As I grow older, I become more shallow. . . . I am not worth very much concern or very much regret and I hope there will be none."

Drew showed the will to Cissy, and she cried when she read it. She also sent a copy of it to Felicia in Paris.

Felicia had become part of the European social whirl, much as her mother had thirty years before. Her life was one of too many parties and too many drinks.

Drew, too, was caught up in a feverish round of social activity; he had become a man of many women. Yet whenever Cissy called, he came. In her loneliness, Cissy found it easy to reach out for Drew. His Georgetown house was only a short distance away, and he soon became her favorite escort. Cissy had grown up wanting to be the belle of the ball, surrounded by adoring beaux. And in some ways she was still a shy romantic dreaming of being irresistible, still sure that no man wanted her for herself alone. Drew buoyed her ego, made her feel younger, desirable, glamorous.

Cissy gave him the run of her house. He stayed whenever he wanted, entertained his friends at dinners and parties there. "No matter what was going at Cissy's house, or how many people were there, or what the conversation, when Drew's radio talk was on, Cissy made them all keep quiet so they could listen. She thought he was wonderful. She adored him."

In 1931, Drew was thirty-four and Cissy fifty, but she felt more and more like his contemporary. When he had first married Felicia, she had signed her letters to him "Ma." She no longer did that. In many ways, they were much alike. They were both able to denounce someone in print with venom and "then be very sweet to that same person at a party, and *mean* it!" Both had a charming surface and a tough center; both were very private people with an impenetrable reserve. Perhaps Cissy had fastened onto Drew to show that she could succeed with him where Felicia had failed. There was much speculation about their relationship.

Whatever the nature of their friendship, now in the early 1930s it had begun to show signs of wear. "I can see Drew now as vividly as though it were yesterday, sitting in front of the fireplace in his Georgetown house one cold winter night," said Dorothy Detzer Denny, "a balloon glass of brandy on the table beside him—lyrically proclaiming the virtues of Cissy—her kindness, generosity, wisdom. And then within the space of only a few days, driving me to Capitol Hill, he almost wrecked the car several times in a blind rage at Cissy, calling her 'that rich bloody bitch . . . that goddamn vulture.' "

Cissy had become increasingly demanding of his time and attention. The more impressive Pearson's successes were, the more possessive Cissy seemed. But Drew had a great many younger, prettier women waiting in line, and he no longer felt it necessary to dance attendance on the queen. And, so, a certain distance grew between them.

When Cissy did not have Drew, she had her grandchild. Ellen was a quiet, delicate little girl, and she and Cissy took long walks. Cissy introduced her to dogs and horses, spending much more time with Ellen than she had ever spent with Felicia. "I love the enemy of my enemy," someone once said of a grandchild.

Cissy was most helpful to Drew with his own parents. She had a nonalcoholic dinner for his Quaker parents, saw their reduced circumstances, and asked Drew if she could try to get his father a political appointment. Drew was overjoyed at this prospect, and Cissy used her political contacts to help get the post of governor of the Virgin Islands for his father.

Robert S. Allen, correspondent for the *Christian Science Monitor*, invited Pearson to coauthor an anonymous book, exposing "the hypocrisy, demagoguery, cowardice and reaction that pervades Washington." They called it *Washington Merry-Go-Round*. They portrayed President Hoover as a vain man who didn't permit photographic closeups because his face was too flabby, attacked the House of Representatives as "a cross between a troop of monkeys and a herd of sheep," and described the social and sexual exploits of some of the city's leading lights. They gave a list of "Nick's girls," the women often in the company of Speaker of the House Longworth.

In a chapter titled "Boiled Bosoms," they told how Cissy's novel had shocked Washington, causing a breach between her and Alice Longworth. Cissy was described as "always too active to be idle and too intelligent to be content with the routine of society." Cissy liked this assessment, but she became annoyed when she read that she "pretended to enjoy coarse newspaper revelries at which she tried hard to be one of the gang" and that she often "dissipated her gifts on trivialities." And she was not pleased that Drew had printed a story she had told him about one of her romantic escapades.

Somehow, however, Pearson soothed Cissy's feelings.

Thanks to Cissy, the Washington *Herald* was no longer "a backstairs paper." Within a year, she had made it the most provocative paper in the nation's capital, perhaps in the country. She had converted Hearst's sickest paper into one of his most successful. On October 11, 1931, she notified Hearst: "We are running refined but sensational front page streamer tomorrow and forever after: LARGEST MORNING CIRCU-LATION IN THE NATION'S CAPITAL . . . easily 10,000 ahead of our competitor and going up." When Hearst wired his congratulations, she answered: "You made me what I am today. I hope you're satisfied."

Yet she had truly done it mostly with her own verve, her own personality, her own brains. Hearst delighted her by wiring: "Please put at top of editorial page: Eleanor Patterson, Editor and Publisher."

It was almost enough to ease her insecurity, for a while.

13

Women like to sit down to trouble as if it were knitting.

—Ellen Glasgow

"There is nothing mysterious about it," commented Arthur Brisbane, writing about menopause. "Women between the ages of 45 and 50 have their best days before them . . . a considerable enlargement of intellectual interests, developing their highest intelligence. They should refuse to let themselves sink down; they should interest themselves in politics, helping in the forming of sound public opinion, encourage and direct the young."

Charles Dewey, an old admirer with whom Cissy had appeared at Chicago's Aldis Theater in 1911, dropped in at Dupont Circle one summer day. He had now come to Washington to take a senior post at the Treasury Department. A handsome man, he walked into the living room, tall and straight and expectant. He had not seen Cissy for some years.

There she was, sitting on the couch, busily writing on a pad on her knee, unaware of his entrance. She was wearing a short dress, and had her legs crossed. After they kissed, embraced, and sat down, he said, "Cissy, from where I'm sitting, I wish I were an artist so that I could draw that good-looking leg of yours all the way up."

Cissy looked at her leg, smiled, and said, "Well, that is a pretty good-looking leg, isn't it?"

She was highly appreciative of her assets. She knew the richness of her red hair, and hairdressers arrived regularly at Dupont Circle. She converted the Lindbergh bedroom to an exercise room and persuaded some of her friends to join her for regular sessions. She was always searching for the perfect masseuse and finally found one "far and away the best of the lot. *Wonderful* masseuse of shoulders and neck and head. Marvelous when you are tired and her brushing is *the* best." She still liked to ride, hike, swim. She'd rather stay vital, she said, than be a vital statistic. She was personally fastidious, sometimes showering and changing three times a day.

At Cissy's fiftieth birthday party in 1931, she looked stunning in a black-striped gown, cut very low in the back, a billowy scarf effect around the neckline and the skirt so starched that it stood stiffly around her slender feet. Her hair—which could reach way down on her back—was off her brow as always, combed back and up; her youthful figure was much admired. She had the pug nose, but her flashing eyes, so vividly alive, gave her face not only a special spirit but almost a loveliness. Everyone laughed when a huge cake with more than a hundred candles was wheeled in. A smiling Cissy explained the candles, saying that she really couldn't hide her age because everyone knew all about her scandalous affair with Methuselah. For music, she had brought in the orchestra from the Miami Beach Surf Club. She had once heard this group playing Viennese waltzes, and Vienna was never far from her romantic mind.

Her Irish heritage had given Cissy a love of fine singing. Caruso had once sung at Dupont Circle for her mother, and this evening John Charles Thomas gave a program of sentimental Irish songs. She then made a graceful speech about the next performers: "Some singers with sweet old English folk songs. . . . They are very sensitive artists so let's have absolute silence, so quiet you can hear a pin drop." She waited until the room stilled, then gave the signal. In trooped a group of young black singers, and the rug was rolled back for jazz dancing.

She had all kinds of parties, and she liked to mix people; the young achievers with the old diplomats, two senators who were fierce opponents on the floor of the Senate, and lots of newspaper people. She often scandalized society editors by having newspapermen to dinner and asking the diplomatic set to arrive *after* dinner, a complete reversal of the usual arrangement. Cissy didn't return the invitations of people she considered dull. Her philosophy was simple: "If you owe a bore a dinner, send it to him." The population of Washington changed with any shift in the political winds, and one guest asked Cissy, "You know most of the people you meet aren't going to be here a couple of years from now, so why bother?" But Cissy had an intense curiosity about everybody, and as she said, "Everybody's *somebody* here."

At Cissy's larger parties, a dozen flower-decked tables were scattered around the great dining room and adjoining rooms. Each man was given a card on which was written the name of the woman he was to escort into dinner (and a description of the flowers on their table). In Washington, protocol was almost as important as gossip. But Cissy ignored the elaborate rules about social precedence. When Cissy's "very dear friend" Cal Carrington was her guest, he sat on her right in his cowboy clothes and his boots, while the Secretary of State in carefully correct formal clothes sat elsewhere. (Philpott, Cissy's butler, carefully followed Cal everywhere "because he chewed tobacco and spit on everything in the house.") Bernard Baruch summed up the seating silliness to Cissy, saying, "The ones who mind, don't matter; and the ones who matter, don't mind."

Many believed that political policy was frequently plotted at Cissy's smaller dinners. Cissy knew that Presidents were not made and unmade at dinner parties, but she also knew that anything could happen at a party, and she liked to help it happen. Political talk was the lifeblood of Washington parties, and Cissy knew how to keep it flowing. She also knew how to use these lively conversations as the basis for future news stories.

Arthur Brisbane felt that the *Herald*'s political coverage was too gossipy: "You need more depth in your political news," he wrote her. "Your desk is too easily persuaded to glorify a group of young Congressmen calling themselves The Mavericks, who are of no importance so far. St. Johns does not belong on Page One so constantly. On occasion, I find this occurs twice in the same issue. She is a front page of the second section feature writer."

Cissy tacked Brisbane's letter on the city room bulletin board. Adela Rogers St. Johns arrived later. There was a hush in the city room as she entered. Somebody whispered something about the bulletin board. She went to it, read the letter, took it down, and tore it into pieces. Then, as everyone watched in silence, she put the pieces into a wastebasket and set fire to them. Adela was not simply a star reporter. She had worked for Hearst since she was a teenager in San Francisco; she was a Hearst favorite and Cissy's friend.

A copyboy soon notified St. Johns that Mrs. Patterson wanted to see her.

"She wore a Chanel suit, and the emerald clip in her lapel was real, her hair looking redder than usual," recalled St. Johns. "In that drawl so low, it was hard to hear, she said, 'I understand you destroyed a letter I posted on my bulletin board.'"

St. Johns said she would not work in a city room with that "slush on the board."

Cissy's voice rose, "It was by *Arthur Brisbane!*"

"He's a columnist who ought to be in the real estate business," answered St. Johns. "I don't care if you're Queen of Rumania and Empress of India, you don't insult the captain in the presence of his troops. More than that, you haven't any right to put such temptation under the noses of the men who work for you."

"Temptation?" asked Cissy.

St. Johns caustically pointed out that an underpaid *Herald* reporter could sell the letter for a handsome price to one of their rivals. Brisbane's letter would then appear on the front page of a Washington newspaper under the headline "WHAT ARTHUR BRISBANE REALLY THINKS OF THE HEARST HERALD." Cissy sat quietly alone after St. Johns left the room.

"She came into the City Room soon afterwards," said St. Johns. "Except Isadora Duncan, she was the most graceful woman I ever saw." Confronted by icy silence, she stood in front of the city desk. "I have come to apologize," she said in that voice whose falling-away melody reached the remotest corner. "Ignorance is no excuse, but sometimes it's an explanation. I thought Mr. Brisbane's advice would help us to get out a better paper." Then she looked at Adela, her eyes twinkling, put an arm around her, and started to laugh, "I wish you had given me a chance to take it down."

"You stick with us, Mrs. Patterson," said City Editor Ray Helgeson, his eyes very bright, "and we'll get you out a better paper without any help from Mr. Brisbane."

This moment was memorable for Cissy. The *Herald* was not just her newspaper: it was her family, her world. Brisbane never stopped his stream of advice, and Cissy listened to all of it, accepted some of it, but no longer took his words as gospel. She had cut the umbilical cord. The *Herald* was hers, not Brisbane's.

Ray Helgeson had been one of Howey's legacies, a younger, more handsome version of himself. Within minutes of getting to the office, Helgeson had two cigarettes and three telephones going at the same time. He had a flamboyant theatricality, and his mind was so quick and creative that some swore he had second sight. He always acted on his hunches and took wild chances and was often proved right. He could read a story, dig out the smallest kernel of human interest, and expand it into a splashy, fascinating feature. His was the Howey tradition: If you can't find a murder, go create one yourself.

The lanky, six-foot Helgeson was an attractive, strong-featured man with a shock of blond hair. He always had a date waiting outside the *Herald* when he finished work. Once there were two women, and his reaction was quick. "Which one has the car?" he asked, and all three rode off together.

Cissy liked nothing better than to watch Helgeson go into high gear on a big story. One foggy night a bus full of high school students was hit by a train at a grade crossing in nearby Rockville. Helgeson gave specific assignments to reporters who raced away in their own cars. After learning that the area was deep in mud, he called circulation for a truck to transport the photographers and their heavy equipment. As Helgeson was directing his troops, a small, angry man walked into the city room, loudly claiming that he had been libeled by the *Herald*. Just before she took off, St. Johns pointed to the complaining man and asked, "What about him?"

"Hell, take him with you," said Helgeson, and she did.

The bus had been bringing twenty-seven chemistry students and their teacher home from a college show. More than half of the youngsters were now dead. Some of the broken bodies lay on the muddy ground; others were trapped in the wreckage. Helgeson stayed on the phone much of the night, suggesting story angles, picture ideas. News photographers make their living from disasters, but Cissy heard that even these hardened professionals were silenced by the carnage at Rockville.

As his staff straggled in, Helgeson barked on the phone to a lingering photographer, "Get it in here. It's no good to me in Rockville."

While St. Johns pounded out her copy, the man with the libel suit acted as her personal copyboy. "The *Herald* came up hot and smoking," said St. Johns. "It was a masterpiece of death and tragedy, but it *was* a masterpiece, a classic. We knew it. Cissy knew it. Washington would know it and Mr. Hearst would know it. . . . We couldn't go home, we were afraid to go home. Nobody would dare to go to sleep for fear of nightmares. We had to drink and make a lot of noise so we'd be sure we wouldn't hear again the cries and pleas and weeping of mothers for their children."

A big policeman strode into the city room. He had had a neighborhood complaint that they were disturbing the peace.

Some of the reporters began to argue with the overbearing officer. Suddenly one of them threw a punch, and the cop was out cold. Some circulation men were called in, and after they had carefully put the unconscious policeman on a newspaper delivery truck going to Virginia, the party continued.

The phone rang insistently, but the *Herald* staff ignored it. Finally, the little man with the libel suit plopped into Helgeson's chair, picked up the receiver, and barked, "City desk." The room quieted as he shouted at the caller, "Get it in here. It's no good to me in Rockville." And then the room roared.

Howey's other legacy to Cissy was Harry Arthur "Happy" Robinson. Cissy's Happy had come to the United States from Russia as a boy, and he had sold newspapers in Chicago during the circulation wars. He was a fighter with a fighter's face. An awestruck young woman reporter once asked him, "Are you a gangster?"

Happy had been Howey's circulation manager on Hearst's Boston *American*. He was happy there, and it had taken both Howey and Hearst to persuade him to help Cissy in Washington for six months. Exactly six months later, without saying good-bye, Happy and his wife returned to Boston. His wife had hated Washington.

Several days later, at two in the morning, Howey went into the mail room of the Boston paper and told Happy that someone wanted to see him. It was Cissy.

"Happy, why did you leave me?"

"Hearst told me I only had to stay six months," he said.

"You're coming back," she stated firmly.

"I'm not coming back," he said. "My wife doesn't like Washington."

"You're coming back," she repeated.

They adjourned to the editorial office. Cissy called Hearst and told Happy to get on the extension.

"You know I was only loaning him to you," Hearst said softly. Cissy replied with urgency. She needed Happy; she needed her own circulation manager. She would no longer share one with the *Times*. Happy was indispensable. Hearst then talked to Happy, promising him that he would be well rewarded for returning to Cissy. A highly unhappy Happy asked for time to think it over, but Cissy had already switched to another phone. She woke up Happy's wife to tell her they were all going back to Washington. "I'm not going!" yelled Happy's wife.

Hard-boiled Happy, who had survived the gang wars, found himself beaten by Cissy. And six months later his wife rejoined him in Washington.

To Happy, Cissy was always "The Lady." His loyalty was absolute. "I'll never lie to you, lady," he told her. "And I never did," he said later. In turn she told him, "I give you my word, I'll never interfere with you in Circulation." And she never did.

Cissy regarded Happy as a kind of citified Cal Carrington, a man of belligerent independence who never kowtowed, who always said what he wanted to say. She trusted his honesty, respected his judgment. When she asked him for advice during a crisis, he often urged her to do what she deeply believed in, to follow through, or, as he pronounced it, "Folly tru. . . ." Cissy had this phrase engraved on a gold watch she gave him. She also gave him a bracelet of gold dice from Tiffany's because she had found him in a crap game with some circulation men. Cissy could have fired them, but she got down on her knees and joined the fun. Happy was also the only man on the staff allowed to curse in her presence. Happy could do no wrong.

Shortly after the paper was put to bed, Happy might get a call from Cissy. "How about coming over, Hap?" When he came, they might talk about anything. A large number of blacks were then moving into Washington, and Cissy was worried that Hap's tough circulation men might get into fights with them. Hap promised her there would be no trouble. She even asked his help in personal problems. Talking about Felicia, Cissy wondered aloud about some of her daughter's men friends that Cissy felt were unsuitable. "What am I going to do with her, Hap?" It was Hap who arranged for a detective to check out one of Felicia's troublemaking escorts. Felicia's life was frenetic rather than happy.

Cissy talked to Happy as a friend because she knew his loyalty and his love. Cissy's intuitions about people were extraordinarily accurate. Close friends felt she could see them a block away and know what they were thinking. "It was almost a built-in radar. It was uncanny, frightening." Cissy knew that Happy needed nothing from her. He was not just a sounding board for her; he was a hard, practical man with a great deal of common sense. Most of the men around Cissy told her what they thought she wanted to hear; Happy told her what he believed she should know.

Cissy insisted that Hap attend one of her more formal parties. "It was the first time I ever wore soup-and-fish: tails, tight collar, the whole thing," Happy recalled. Happy stood beside her on the receiving line, sat on her right at the dinner table. To Hap, The Lady was "tops." "What guts she had. She would take on anybody. You couldn't beat her."

Cissy took over the advertising director's job when he was on vacation. "And I did it all by myself," she wrote Brisbane. First she went to all the expensive shops she patronized, virtually forcing them to place ads in the *Herald*. Then she concentrated on leading businessmen. "I did what you told me, you remember, about the parties," she wrote Brisbane. She made these potential advertisers part of the mix at the Dupont Circle parties, introducing them to Washington high society. She even invited their wives for tea. And then she asked for their advertising. "Jelleff's comes in with a nice contract on Wednesday. They are a key department store," she wrote Brisbane. In answer, he apologized for mentioning the size of her fortune in his column, but added that "it inspires respect in Washington advertisers which is what you want."

Howey had once told Cissy that an editor may be a genius on his ass but is always an ass on his feet. Cissy was an exception. She had a quiet, dramatic way of speaking to the public, particularly on the radio and to small groups. As part of her campaign to increase advertising in the *Herald*, she spoke to clubs all over Washington. After addressing a Jewish women's group, she reported to Brisbane: "The Chairman made a speech in praise of the retiring President. Everybody cried. The retiring President made a speech in praise of the new President. Everybody cried. The Postmistress proposed a moment of silence in memory of a defunct member. Everybody cried. I made a most touching speech about intermarriage between the Jews and the Christians—and everybody cried. This time I cried too."

It had been more than two years since Elmer Schlesinger's death. His body had been stored in a California vault, in accordance with his family's request. Perhaps Cissy's speech on intermarriage, which had moved her to tears, revived her love and guilt. In any event, she now decided to have Elmer's body buried in Washington. Cissy's secretary suddenly that summer of 1931 received a memo directing that the body be shipped to Washington and that arrangements for its burial be made. This was not a passing whim, because Cissy's memos to her secretary became persistent on this, all asking variations of, "What has been done about my former husband?" Her secretary had arranged for the casket to be met by a representative from a local funeral parlor. Cissy asked that photographs be taken of the available plots at the cemetery; she then selected one large enough for four graves near a curve in the road.

She ordered sketches of gravesite plantings, deciding on a ring of poplars, with smaller trees in front. After the trees were put in, a photograph was taken and sent to Cissy for her approval. Her secretary got another memo: "Please conduct burial. Please make sure that it is the right casket. It has a brass plaque on the front. I want you to look at it and make sure." She then gave the date when she wanted the burial, asked a friend, an alcoholic architect, to represent her. He arrived for the burial in formal mourning clothes "drunk as a monkey." Her secretary and two funeral parlor representatives also attended the ceremony. As the coffin was lowered into the ground, the drunken friend started sobbing and had to be held up to keep him from falling into the grave. The funeral directors found it almost impossible to repress their laughter. After it was all done, Cissy ordered a final photograph, then returned it to the secretary with an arrow pointing to a bush she wanted removed. She had decided that she would be buried there, too.

Cissy was still insecure; she always would be. During an hour's conversation, she told an interviewer: "Sometimes I think I haven't any sense. . . . I was a fool to do that; maybe I'll know better next time. . . . Don't read those books I wrote; they're no good. . . . I was wrong about that man; I should have known he wouldn't do. . . . I don't know much. . . . What a sap I was! . . . I guess I was taken in that time. . . . I don't know what was the matter with me, but my judgment was certainly off. . . . It was all my fault, of course. . . . My first year, I was really too stupid for words. For instance, I refused to run the story of the Kentucky Derby on the front page—a horse race—how vulgar! Can you imagine?"

She did know enough about sports to notice when a publicity handout from a college was published as a news story. She put a quick stop to this practice: "I don't know a damn thing about sports, but I want my reporters to be completely honest. There are no favorite colleges; nobody gets a free ride."

She was highly conscious of her own "free ride." Talking to a radio audience, Cissy stressed the importance of accomplishing success on one's own, and told them, "And you won't have to fall back on the record of your family, as I do."

But that time was long past. Although her heritage had helped open the door, her accomplishments had been impressive by any standard. Under her, the *Herald* had gained both readers and advertisers. Cissy knew that a successful newspaper informs and is informed by its readers. She had told a local group, "If an editor receives from a man or woman a letter saying, 'I read your article, and what you say I have said a dozen times,' he may be sure he has written an article useful to the paper. . . . The judgment of the public, like divine justice, is always right. . . . A newspaper owes its least important reader service as faithful and sincere as a great lawyer gives to his most important and prosperous client. A newspaper is a public servant possessing public influence." A joint wire from Hearst and Brisbane to Cissy stated: "We made you what you are today and we are more than satisfied."

The harder she worked, the more impatient she grew. Her first secretary, Betty Hynes, became so overwrought that she went to the society editor of the Washington *Post*, Hope Ridings Miller, and asked for a job, saying she couldn't continue to work for Cissy. After getting the job, she called again to say, "I know you must think I'm a perfect fool, but I just can't leave Cissy. . . . She couldn't be more wonderful."

Carolyn Hagner Shaw became Cissy's personal secretary when "Hynie" left her and went abroad in 1933. Shaw's aunt had been social secretary to President Theodore Roosevelt, and Shaw's mother published *The Green Book,* the Washington society bible, and wrote a column on dress and manners for the *Herald.* Carolyn Shaw previously had worked for Cissy's neighbors, the Leiters. Summoned to Cissy's estate at Sands Point, Shaw spent four days waiting to speak with Cissy—whom she had never met. On the fourth day, while washing her hair, Carolyn was told by the butler that Mrs. Patterson wanted to see her NOW!

"My hair was still sudsy, wrapped in a towel, and I started to apologize," said Shaw, "but she waved me to a chair with a languid hand and started dictating, boom, just as fast as she could go. This was our introduction."

Shaw called Dupont Circle "The League of Nations," since the eighteen servants represented so many nationalities. One of her duties was to supervise them. She quickly discovered that two maids were both in love with the English butler. She also found out that some of the servants were getting kickbacks on everything from food to cars. Cissy once caught one of them in the act of taking a large hoard home. Cissy said she often tried to come home early to catch the footmen buggering each other.

Shaw found memos from Cissy almost everywhere: on her desk, under a table, in a chair. She also found her impatient about money, hating to look at bills or sign checks or even deposit them. And, never, ever was her mood predictable. One morning there would be a friendly hello, a warm smile, a concerned question; the next she might be so preoccupied that she would barely mumble. She could be overbearing, and impatient when someone could not keep up with her.

"You got awful mad at some of the things she did," said Shaw. "Sometimes I wanted to choke her. But if she blew off steam, you knew it wasn't you she was attacking, just getting rid of steam. And she never held a grudge. The more you knew her, the more you respected her."

Shaw learned early to expect the unexpected. Sometimes a call from Cissy came after midnight: "I want to leave at dawn." That meant arranging for her private railroad car to be hooked onto a train ready to go wherever Cissy wanted. "We might start off for New York and end up in California." She also had to alert the car porter, Alonzo, to collect his staff, stock up on the champagne, and make sure to get fresh flowers. For Cissy, fresh flowers were not just a pleasure; they were a need.

Cissy and Shaw once made an unexpected trip to Sands Point and found Cissy's servants throwing a party for the servants of adjoining mansions, with her food and her liquor. Her servants recovered enough to invite Cissy to join the fun. She did, and she also fired them all the next morning.

Cissy wanted a rural retreat closer to Washington, a place of absolute privacy where she could recharge herself. A friend took her to the tobacco country around Upper Marlboro in Prince Georges County, Maryland. Leaving the highway, they drove down a private road, past a spring-fed lake, and through orchards and fragrant clover fields. After a mile's ride they came upon a fire-gutted section of a house with its fireplace intact, large enough for six people to stand in. It once was Dower House built in 1660 as a hunting lodge for Charles Calvert, later the third Lord Baltimore. Its architect reportedly had modeled it after a palazzo on the Grand Canal in Venice. A member of George Washington's family had been married here, and much later it had become an attractive restaurant, a place of many parties, several scandals, and lingering ghosts.

Dower House was only an hour's drive from Dupont Circle, and Cissy soon had it restored to its original design. Fortunately her secretary examined the blueprints in time to discover that none of the fifteen rooms had a closet. While Cissy had superb taste, she was a woman of whim. "Change purple bath at Dower to green." Down would come all the tiles. One bathroom was changed four times. She furnished much of the house with fine English antiques from Dupont Circle. She used flowered chintz and yellow-and-white-striped satin to give the house a cozy feeling. The drawing room was a cool, slate blue; valuable floral paintings were hung low over a fine walnut commode. The walls of the elegant dining room were covered with midnight-blue silk on which had been painted enormous birds and white flowers, a thin lacquer glaze giving the fabric a rich sheen.

Cissy also had the stables renovated, built a greenhouse to supply flowers year round, and installed a mammoth heated swimming pool. A week before her first pool party to open the house, one of her poodles jumped in and was electrocuted because of some faulty connections. Cissy's poodles were with her everywhere. She had started with six big black ones and a white one named Bo—these were standard poodles, but she later went in for miniatures. Bo was the only one who stayed in her bedroom at night, but all of them had the run of the house. They chewed draperies, played with rolls of toilet paper in the living room, nipped at people. Several occasionally accompanied Cissy to the *Herald.* Reporters learned to control the nipping by a sharp slap of a metal ruler on the poodle's nose—when Cissy wasn't around.

At Dower, Cissy wore whatever she wanted. When she went walking, her favorite costume was an ancient pair of patent-leather laced boots, a shabby buckskin jacket, a woolen skirt that reached just below her knees, and a shapeless tweed hat.

One of her first guests at Dower House was Arthur Brisbane. Her secretary noticed that he was getting absentminded; he dictated to her for an hour, then was ready to leave the house without noticing he didn't have his pants on. For more romantic guests, overnight male guests interested in overnight female guests, Cissy posted a hand-lettered sign: "BEWARE— THE STAIRS CREAK."

A member of the board of directors of the Tribune Company, Cissy made a trip in May 1932 to Chicago for the annual board meeting. Joe and Bertie were both in high spirits. The *News* was so successful, more and more so every year, that Joe had wiped out the memory of his $5 million loss in the stock market crash. He was pleased by Cissy's accomplishments at the *Herald* and told her that his daughter Alicia had said that she wanted to be an editor like her aunt. Joe had built an impressive building in New York to house the *News* (its architect was the same Raymond Hood whom Cissy had hired to design a memorial for Schlesinger). On the front of the building, Patterson had had engraved HE MADE SO MANY OF THEM—part of Lincoln's quip, "God must have loved the common people because he made so many of them." The secret of his paper's success, he told Cissy, was that he never forgot who his readers were.

Neither did Bertie. The *Tribune*, too, was enormously profitable, the voice of almost a million midwesterners. Bertie kept it a paternalistic paper: he paid his reporters the best wages, almost never fired them, always backed them to the hilt. Cissy noted that Bertie had mellowed slightly since he had married. Told that his rival Chicago publisher, Colonel Frank Knox, had ordered his staff to oppose the *Tribune* on every editorial issue, Bertie laughed and said, "He'll be at a disadvantage next week when we come out against syphilis!"

Cissy was en route home from Chicago when her secretary in Washington got a call from Brisbane. He wanted her to race to Baltimore, await Cissy's train, and join her in her private car. She was to keep Cissy so distracted that she would not notice the big ads in the Washington railroad station for a new book called *More Washington Merry-Go-Round*. Brisbane promised he would rush to Cissy's house, "and I just hope to the Lord that I get there before she gets that book."

The secretary went pell-mell for the train, made it, joined Cissy, but it was too late. Cissy already had a copy of the book. Had someone other than Drew Pearson written it, Cissy might have smiled wryly and shrugged. In a book of snide snipes, she was treated more kindly than most. Referring to her as "one of the most gifted women in Washington," it observed that "with no journalistic experience . . . Cissy had cajoled, stormed and goaded the staff of the Washington *Herald* into putting out a first class sheet." But then Drew told a Cissy story that she felt was purely private. It concerned an editor of the Washington *Daily News* who had been impressed by her stevedore's vocabulary as well as her attractive figure. He had read about the embroidered peach crepe de chine sheets on her bed and "was determined" to enjoy them. Arriving at one of her parties, he had pulled Cissy aside and showed her his silk pajamas underneath his pants. An amused Cissy promptly brought him to Senator Arthur Capper of Kansas and announced, "Mr. Palmer has come to sleep with me," and pulled up Palmer's trouser leg. Palmer came on another occasion and drank his fill. He managed to find Cissy's bedroom, saw a green negligee laid out on the bed, took off his clothes, put on the negligee and slipped under the sheets. On discovering him later, Cissy had him dressed and evicted, no longer amused.

This was not the kind of story Cissy wanted printed. She felt it made her a laughingstock. And she was outraged when Pearson classified her as one of the "middle-aged or aging ladies who dominate the Washington scene."

"Well, I've seen people mad in my life," said her secretary, Carolyn Shaw, "but I've never seen anyone like Cissy. I spent the whole trip trying to quiet her down. She started dictating one of her front-page editorials about Pearson and the book, and she was furious at me because I was purposely making mistakes in typing, trying to delay her until she saw Brisbane. Luckily, he was waiting for us at the house when we arrived." It took all of Brisbane's consummate tact to cool her and kill the editorial. She and Drew later were reconciled. They even became ardent admiring friends, but it was never again quite the same between them.

But Cissy soon had more important things to think about.

14

Learn to restrain your impetuous nature; you are quick-tempered and jump to conclusions hastily. Your judgment is good and usually right if you take time to give it due consideration. You are a jovial, fun-loving person and are popular among your acquaintances. Your love is apt to be tempestuous.
—Astrological Birthday Book entry for November 7, Cissy's birthday

The depression deepened in 1932. "No banks, no work, no nothing," remarked Will Rogers. There were 17,000 evictions a month in New York City. Respectable-looking men were selling well-polished apples on Manhattan streets. "At times, it seemed that half the city was selling objects of token value to the other half." A woman stepped out of a Rolls-Royce on Madison Avenue and sold it to the highest bidder for $150. The songs of the day were "Brother, Can You Spare a Dime?" and "I've Got My Love to Keep Me Warm." Many people were apathetic, numb. A jobless man had to be hospitalized after eating his first meal in seventeen days. A *New Yorker* cartoon showed a weeping debutante pleading with her parents: "Well, then can I come out *after* the revolution?" The sour joke was that even the banks didn't know where the money was.

"Create Work for Americans, Mr. Hoover," Hearst editorialized, and Cissy wired him: "You are the only leader the country has got."

Accusing Congress of doing nothing about the depression, Cissy editorially called for a national conference of concerned citizens to discuss the roots of the problem and possible solutions. Her friend Senator Burton Wheeler of Montana called the idea "admirable," and Senator Tom Connally of Texas said it would be "a great deed for the benefit of the country." The conference was never held, but so great and so mixed was the public reaction to her editorial that Cissy—still insecure—apologized to Brisbane for making herself a terrible nuisance "to you and Mr. Hearst." Then she added: "*I hate this*. . . . If I write any more editorials, they will be about birds and flowers, music and cherry blossoms."

Cissy was constantly looking for ways to present the effects of the depression in human terms, and Howey suggested that she "get the best literary name . . . going out penniless, hunting jobs . . . living for many days among the unemployed." Cissy impulsively decided to do this herself. "I think you have a lot of courage, and perhaps I ought not to let you do it," Hearst wrote her. But Cissy already had decided on her pseudonym— "Maude Martin." Felicia had used the name "Marion Martin" when she had made her own way in California, and some said that Cissy's choice showed that her rivalry with her daughter was still alive, that she wanted to prove that she could survive in a far harsher environment than Felicia had faced.

Cissy began her series with a description of an evening at an embassy dinner, chatting with a charming man and drinking cocktails from a small silver goblet. Returning to her Dupont Circle mansion, she found her bedroom with a bright fire burning in the grate, the gold-brocade spread folded at the foot of the bed, and the peach crepe de chine sheets turned down. Carefully laid out on two small Louis XVI chairs were her shabbiest clothes—a ten-year-old brown corduroy skirt, an old brown felt hat that had been rubbed in dirt, a pair of "historical" brown golf shoes, faded woolen stockings, and some moth-eaten woolen combination underwear that she had worn in Wyoming. After she had dressed, her limousine left her near the Salvation Army shelter. She had a comb, a toothbrush, and eleven cents in her purse, a drooping flower in her hat, and some grime on her face.

> "Through the glass of the door, you could see a small light in the little hallway. You ring a short timid ring. You wait. Nobody comes. You wait. Now you can't put your finger on the bell, and keep it there, as you usually do. You've got to wait a long time before ringing again. You're Maude Martin. It's 11:45 at night. You're frightened. You're asking for charity."

The Salvation Army people gave her an iron cot in a small room with four other women. "Play-acting for me," she wrote, "a good story—but a grim, terrible, earnest bad story for everyone else in the little room. Destitute, homeless, jobless, these women, or they wouldn't be there."

All night long she heard the women snore and moan in their sleep. In the morning she bathed with them in cold water, saw them cover their faces with crimson splashes of cosmetics, heard their hatred of the world and of the men who had destroyed them. "You better quit this rotten, dirty city," one of them told her. "Beat it. You'll never get nothing here." Another bitter woman, blaming President Hoover for everything, spat out, "I hope his ashes is scattered in hell."

At breakfast, Cissy started eating when a woman nudged her. "You gotta wait," the woman told her. "They say prayers first." Afterward, when they were scraping off their plates, a woman stared incredulously as Cissy threw away a small piece of bacon. "You put that in the *swill!* " she exclaimed. "I wanted to chew on that."

In the ten days she worked on the series, Cissy so immersed herself in Maude Martin that she found herself crying during her job interviews. She was offered two jobs: one as a cleaning woman at six dollars a week, another as a companion for an aged deaf couple at four dollars a week. The advantage of the second was that she could also baby-sit for neighbors at fifty cents a night.

"The Grand Canyon of Colorado yawns no more dizzily than the pit of gold between the lives of the rich and the poor. Rich people and very poor people spend their lives without ever coming into contact with each other—without being able to understand."

When it was all over, she remembered most the kindness of people. She remembered a Salvation Army woman saying, "We never refuse anybody; our front door is never locked." In the coming years, Cissy's unpublicized contributions to the Salvation Army would total more than $500,000.

Hearst papers everywhere reprinted Cissy's series. "You have the family genius for journalism," Hearst wired her. She soon had other causes, and "went to see for myself whether the children were cold and hungry" in some of the local schools. In this series, "Suffer Little Children," she demanded that the government establish a hot lunch program. "For four months, because of pedagogy, prejudice and red tape, nothing has been done," she told an official of the Emergency Relief Bureau. "On February 2nd you were finally forced into a little talk about crackers and milk. Four months. A long wait for hungry children." She kept after it almost a year until she won her fight. In the interim, money quietly came from her own pocket to feed the children. She demanded that "precautions [be] taken to avoid any appearance of pauperizing," that is, that the children would not know which of them were fed free.

Cissy poked her nose into all kinds of problems. An army of unemployed World War veterans came to Washington from all over the nation, demanding their promised bonus. The Government shunted them aside to Anacostia Flats, where they lived in tents and makeshift shacks. Cissy went to see the Bonus Marchers.

"There they were, sitting in the doorway . . . standing in small groups on the sidewalk, loitering here and there. Middle-aged women in their short sleeves. Pretty clean. Threadbare, shabby."

"We come here to get our bonus and we'll stay here until

1950 if we have to," a veteran with a battered face told Cissy. "All the money went to the bankers, didn't it? We can't borrow ten cents anywhere. . . . The banks keep right on grabbing up our homes, throwing us out and keeping the money. . . . We're acting decent. But we'll get the bonus. That's what we came for. . . . With this bonus we could get free and start again."

"Every man jack of them believe they've been gypped," wrote Cissy. "Right now they're being fed. But supposing these men get hungry?"

Evalyn Walsh McLean went with her and said, "Nothing in my life has touched me so deeply as what I have seen on the faces of those men of the Bonus Army." She went to the nearest restaurant and ordered a thousand sandwiches and a thousand cups of coffee (and later framed the receipt); afterward she sent clothes for the children and converted her home in Maryland into a temporary nursery for some of them. Cissy quietly helped too. Both were indignant when Hoover sent troops to burn the veterans' camp and turn them out. But Cissy found it hard to criticize General Douglas A. MacArthur, who led the troops. MacArthur had been her brother's commanding officer and his hero.

Although Cissy often said, "Joe is Joe and I am me," he had had an immense influence on her. Joe Patterson, who still held strongly populist views, was a Democrat, and so was she. National political conventions would be held in the summer of 1932, and Patterson was supporting the Democratic governor of New York, Franklin Delano Roosevelt. Uncertain which party Hearst would back, Cissy was finally delighted: "I'm so glad that Jesus loves me and that you came out today kerplunk for the Democratic party. It makes life simple, gay and a whole lot more interesting around the office."

Cissy was even happier when Hearst answered: "I hope you will be able to attend the conventions. I am sure you could contribute articles of unusual value. I don't suppose the convention melee is very agreeable, but if you could manage to put up with it, I think the papers would get much benefit from your articles."

Cissy's reporting was blunt and partisan. "Nobody is arguing, waving their arms, getting red in the face the way they used to," she wrote of the Republican convention, in Chicago. "Hoover is nobody's hero. I remember the 1920 Republican convention. You had to fight to make your way in or out of anywhere." The best thing about the current convention, she wrote, was the band. She reported that the Republican national committee chairman had roared, "I'm running this thing." She also described the keynote speaker as "still talking . . . [his speech] has lasted a long time—we have learned nothing." The convention was swept by a rumor that Alice Longworth would have a place on the national ticket. But, as Cissy reported, Alice declared, "I am *not* interested in the vice-presidency." Summing it all up, Cissy wrote: "The Republican convention . . . is an exhibition of the failure of a great political party." The headline read: "Mrs. Patterson finds much ado about nothing."

A week later, finding a different mood at the Democratic convention in Chicago, Cissy pointed out that politics was a business with the Republicans "while to the Democrats, it's a pleasure." Her first article was one of questions and answers:

> Where is the real business going on? The People we see around look sort of absent-minded.
> Real business is going on in stuffy little committee rooms and behind locked doors.
> What kind of real business?
> Barter and change.
> What are all those smartly-dressed ladies and gentlemen doing, sitting in those boxes?
> They are being prominent.
> Why do they all keep their mouths open?
> To let the talk in and let it out again.

Cissy saw some of her old friends in Chicago. Her mother, who continued to live at the Drake Hotel, was nearing her end. Freddie McLaughlin was still married to Irene Castle, but their marriage was rocked by frequent separations and threats of divorce. Cissy and Freddie now enjoyed "the only possible friendship between a man and a woman—the friendship of former lovers."

During the convention sessions Cissy sat next to Brisbane at the Chicago Stadium, and she gave this description of the nominating process:

> Temperature ninety degrees, clothes unchanged since morning; limp collars, crumpled suits, the damp and straggled hairline. . . . People without tickets squeezed in between seats and along the aisles like exhausted boxers. . . .
>
> The nominating speeches went on and on all night long . . . roars of bands and demonstrations. . . . It's human nature to seek the thrill of driving one's self to complete exhaustion. . . . The madness of keeping a convention going all night long . . . is based on the methods of the third degree . . . the psychology of exhaustion. . . . Take a bunch of delegates pledged to grim death for their own particular candidate. Keep them up all night. Noise, lights, bedlam, confusion. Let the old fatigue poisons get to work in full force and keep on working until the man's last resistance begins to fade out. Keep it up for a few days and nights and those unpredictable switches of votes begin. Many an innocent man has signed a confession just to rest his aching head.

Hearst supported Senator Jack Garner of Texas, an old friend from the years when they had both been congressmen. Hearst was against former Governor Al Smith because Smith had killed Hearst's chance to become a United States senator from New York in 1922 by refusing to run on the same ticket with the publisher. An isolationist, Hearst was against Newton Baker because of his internationalism. Hearst was leery of Roosevelt for the same reason until Roosevelt publicly ate crow, criticizing the League of Nations as "too often . . . a mere meeting place for political discussion of strictly European political and national difficulties." This prompted Heywood Broun's caustic comment, "The Governor is not one who opposes swapping horses while crossing a stream. He will change a horse for a mule, a mule for a goat, a goat for a shoat. If there is a mane or tail to which to cling, Franklin D. Roosevelt will not scorn to take hold, so long as the beast is travelling in his direction." Bernard Baruch found Roosevelt "too wishy-washy."

Though not present, Hearst was a power broker at this convention. Cissy was aware of his actions because she was close to his representatives in Chicago—his legal counsel John Francis Neylan and the columnist George Rothwell Brown, who wrote for her. Hearst knew that there was little chance that Garner, a southerner, would be nominated, but he was afraid that if Roosevelt did not win on an early ballot, his strength might begin to crumble, leaving the way open for the nomination of Smith or Baker. Jim Farley, who was running Roosevelt's campaign, finally—on the fourth ballot—called Neylan on behalf of FDR: Roosevelt needed California and Texas now! After consultation with Hearst, Neylan told Garner that "the Chief believes nothing can now save the country but for him to throw his delegates to Governor Roosevelt." Garner's consolation prize would be the vice-presidential nomination. Hearst proved persuasive, and the Texan announced his support of Roosevelt. Shortly afterward, FDR was nominated, and he chose Garner as his running mate. A veteran political leader commented, "It's a kangaroo ticket, stronger in the hindquarter than in the front."

But, in fact, the makeup of the ticket probably had little bearing on the outcome of the election. As Garner had told Roosevelt, "All you have to do is to stay alive until Election Day. The people are not going to vote for you. They are going to vote against the Depression."

Cissy had known Roosevelt long before polio had crippled him. As he stood before the convention accepting the nomination, she was caught once again by his easy charm—the lifted eyebrow when he made a sharp point, the slow grin when his audience laughed. She told Brisbane then that she wanted to interview all the Roosevelts.

At a lunch with Roosevelt soon afterward, Brisbane discussed Cissy and Joe. "Roosevelt spoke with a great deal of admiration about your brother," Brisbane wrote Cissy, and told her that Roosevelt suggested that she visit Hyde Park. Brisbane had earlier written Roosevelt about Cissy:

> She is, as I think you know, a very clever and intelligent woman, and an unusually brilliant writer. She wanted to buy Mr. Hearst's Washington *Herald,* offering him a great deal more than it was worth. Then she wanted to rent it for ten years. I urged him to let her rent it, as he has two newspapers in Washington. But he would do neither and said to me: "If she wants to go into the newspaper business in Washington, tell her I'll give her a job." So, at his suggestion, I hired Mrs. Patterson to run the Washington paper, and she has made a very great success of it. The "hiring" is rather a formality, since each trip to see Mr. Hearst in California in her private car costs her as much as she earns in a year.

At Hyde Park, Cissy toured the estate with Roosevelt's mother, who still owned it. "Oh yes," she said, "Franklin couldn't afford to run it by himself." Cissy looked down the lawn to the Hudson River and saw the Roosevelt children running on the grass "as free as young colts."

She lunched alone with Franklin, and he set the tone by reminding her "of the day about eighteen years ago when he cracked an old beau of mine on the shinbone at the Chevy Chase Club with one of those marvelous long balls he used to drive." Neither found it politic to mention that Cissy and her beau had been stretched out behind a stand of shrubs.

Roosevelt gave Cissy a hint of unorthodox things to come when they discussed the national budget and the future. "Plan ahead, way long ahead. . . . It isn't going to be just a question of will and hard work," he said. "We may have to experiment."

"I don't want to sound as though I were getting exalted or anything," Cissy wrote, "but there surely is a special radiance about this man which makes you feel better just to be around him. A 'bonny' frank manner. A high, free spirit. A natural warmth and subtle understanding." She said she felt "prouder of my country than I ever felt before, and convinced that this time we are going to have a real American of the finest type once more in the White House—Franklin Roosevelt."

Although Cissy tended to admire men far more than women, she was equally impressed by Eleanor Roosevelt.

> Mrs. Roosevelt has solved the problem of living better than any woman I have ever known. There is none of this business of self-destruction going on within her heart and soul, as with most of us. No longer any anger, envy, uncharitableness, remorse. . . . No longer any falling down just to pick yourself up, just to fall down again. Eleanor Roosevelt is the master of her soul. She makes me think of a beautiful, steady stream. A millstream, directed. Smooth and powerful it shines as it turns . . . the wheel which grinds the flour, which makes the bread, which goes out into the world.
>
> Now Mrs. Roosevelt's output of energy in itself is not the amazing thing. The amazing thing is that she conducts these crammed-crowded days of hers with a sure, serene and blithe spirit; with tenderness and sympathy and understanding.
>
> I don't believe anyone has ever known her to try to shift her responsibilities or her burdens. Here is one woman, at least, who doesn't push her hair back from her forehead at the end of the day and tell the world she is practically dead from exhaustion. . . ."

When she was interviewing Eleanor at Hyde Park, Cissy remarked, "There can't be any drain of sick vanity or wounded ego in you, as there is in most of us. That wastage that comes from forever wondering whether we're right or whether we're wrong. Whether we're being admired. What other people are thinking about." Eleanor chuckled and answered, "No, really, I have no time for all that, you see. There are too many other things to think about, besides myself. Too many other things I want to do."

In another article about her, Cissy wrote:

> This picture of Eleanor Roosevelt with her school books under her arm, self-righteous and somewhat bossy, is simply all

wrong. You have only to look once into her eyes, clever eyes, deep gray eyes, frank, laughing. You have only to hear her sweet, high voice, her funny little chuckle, to feel her charm and give right into it. And she is as warm and quick and responsive as Roosevelt himself. And so frank, and utterly natural that remembering the meanness and smallness and envy lying around loose in the world, you catch your breath, and feel just a tiny bit afraid for her and wonder.

I wish I knew Mrs. Roosevelt better. But as one very close to her said to me, "There are about ten sides to her, and it's pretty hard to catch up on all of them."

Cissy called Eleanor Roosevelt "the noblest woman I have ever known. I adore her above all women." In some ways, they were very much alike. Both were women of brains, drive, sensitivity. As girls, both had longed for a beauty they didn't have. Both now had moved into positions of real power. Cissy envied Eleanor's lack of vanity, constant sense of purpose, and unfailing serenity. None of her few women friends had been closer to Cissy than Rose Crabtree. But much as she loved and envied Rose, Cissy did not want to be Rose Crabtree; she wanted to be Eleanor Roosevelt.

In the interlude before inauguration, Cissy joined Roosevelt at Warm Springs, Georgia, his favorite vacation retreat. She went down in her private railroad car on which she lived while she was there. On most occasions, the more Cissy drank, the gayer she became. She sometimes slurred her words slightly, but she never became incoherent. And although she had been seen dancing alone in the kitchen, with extravagant gestures, nobody ever saw her pass out. But however merry Cissy might become, her temper was always quick.

Among her dinner guests from Warm Springs on the Ranger one evening were Senator Wheeler (without his wife), Senator James Byrnes of South Carolina, Roosevelt's new advisor Raymond Moley of Columbia University, and Louis Ruppel, who headed the Washington Bureau of the New York *Daily News*. Much champagne was drunk, and the conversation was lighthearted and laughing until Louis Ruppel made a critical comment about Joe Patterson. Cissy turned on him, saying, "I think, Mr. Ruppel, you are a very cheap type of man to criticize the man who happens to be your employer and my brother. I must ask you to leave." He left, and the party, briefly dampened, became again a warm, high-spirited gathering. But then Moley returned from the bathroom, holding a fitting he had worked loose to show the others: "No wonder people in the United States are so upset when the wealthy travel with gold-plated toilet handles." Moley's remark almost sobered Cissy. Using strong language, she hurried him on his way.

The incident became a national story. Hot as it was, her anger against Moley died as quickly as it had flared up, and she soon asked him to write a column for her. "I'm sorry I had too much champagne. . . . When I see you, I will tell you in detail why I am so truly anxious to get your 'stuff' and why I think it is important for Washington." But she would not forgive Ruppel for criticizing her brother. She called Joe and demanded that he fire Ruppel—and he did. Cissy had one basic demand of her staff: unquestioning loyalty.

March 4, 1933, was a cold gray day, but a large crowd had turned out for Roosevelt's inauguration. Cissy sat on a folding wooden chair in the stands, feeling chilled despite her sable coat. She watched the new President sworn in and listened, deeply moved, to his address. His statement that "the only thing we have to fear is fear itself" seemed to signal the beginning of a new era. Cissy watched Hoover's frozen face when Roosevelt talked of "the inaction of the past years." In her report, she wrote of Hoover: "I have seen people once or twice standing at the brink of an open grave with the same kind of despair."

The Roosevelts had a reception at the White House after the ceremony, and Cissy and the Meyers were among their guests. Agnes Meyer, whose husband had served in the Hoover Administration, felt the party was "undignified and shabby," particularly Eleanor Roosevelt's smiling announcement at the end: "Now your party is over." But all Cissy could remember was the new President, with his crippled legs, smiling warmly as he stood with difficulty at the door saying good-bye.

Roosevelt had asked Cissy to be chairman of the Patroness Committee for the Inaugural Ball. She was also asked to be associate chairman of the Democratic Central Committee, and Mrs. Roosevelt invited her to join her on the Committee on Human Needs. These appointments led some to overestimate her actual political power. Her friends, however, tended to be pleased and amused, rather than awed, by her new political prominence. "Your brother suggests that you probably will have a good deal of influence 'really,' " Brisbane wrote. "What are you going to tell the new President . . . to do about the debts, the Air Force etc. . . ?" And Raymond Moley reported that a friend had told him "that Mrs. Eleanor Patterson would probably be the person in Washington who would be closest to the new President . . . that it would only be necessary for me to send my card to Mrs. Patterson, and an appointment with the President could be arranged on three hours' notice. "

Although Cissy was not a member of Roosevelt's inner circle, she did have access to him. She was not like Evalyn Walsh McLean, who swept past the guard into the Oval Office, banged her purse on his desk, and said, "You better listen to Old Lady McLean." FDR roared with laughter at her. Cissy simply went to the White House, announced herself, and was usually ushered in quickly. But she did not do this often. She was an old acquaintance, and, more importantly, she and her brother controlled two of the few major papers that had wholeheartedly supported the President. In fact, the *Herald* was the only Washington newspaper that was pro-Roosevelt; FDR considered their support "worth more to us . . . than all the political meetings and speeches put together."

Cissy's influence reached out for many people. About this time, she received a letter from Mary Church Terrell, president of the National Association of Colored Women, which opened: "It does me good just to see you. . . . I am grateful to you for the courtesies you have shown me in the past." Terrell then proposed that a black woman be named to the Human Needs Committee. Cissy not only agreed but also immediately wrote Mrs. Roosevelt urging the selection of Mary Terrell. Cissy and

Mrs. Roosevelt had lunch and agreed on it. Cissy also asked Mrs. Roosevelt to go with her to some of Washington's homes for children, because "your visit would bring immediate action." In one of them, they found forty children "colored and white, ranging from eighteen months to seventeen years, caged together behind locked wire screens" because they had no place else to go. Conditions quickly improved.

Cissy also worked to obtain home rule for the residents of the District of Columbia—despite the opposition of some of her society friends who feared that the black majority in the District would dominate the municipal government. Cissy scandalized these same friends even further by printing stories and photographs of black citizens in Washington who were *not* criminals.

Cissy's concern for the poor and underprivileged was a constant thing. "Once she got sore and sent me to find out who had applied for relief and hadn't gotten any," said reporter Billy Flythe. "I found lots of them, some of them right out of Dickens—snowing outside, no heat, nothing to eat. Nobody knew about it, but she sent each family approximately six hundred dollars so that they could repair their homes and get food."

When she discovered that Washington's death rate from tuberculosis was the fourth highest of all American cities, Cissy ran articles demanding action until the Government built a TB hospital in the District.

The Hoover years had weighed on Washington like an oppressive bad dream. With the new Administration, the city suddenly awoke and exploded. More and more college graduates decided to go into government instead of going abroad or selling bonds, and Washington increasingly resembled a Harvard-Yale-Princeton reunion. Parties were less formal, more fun. The original social "cave dwellers" found themselves more and more cloistered unless someone like Cissy invited them to a party that mixed the old and the new Washington.

Cissy's invitations were eagerly sought. "Cissy was a power in this town, a goddamn powerful woman," said New Dealer Tom

Corcoran, "and when she gave a party, everybody wanted to come, because her parties were fun, really fun. . . . They were a ring-ding."

Two of her annual parties—one following the Gridiron Dinner and the other at Christmas—were highlights of the Washington social calendar. The Gridiron Dinner, an event known for irreverent political skits and commentary, is given each year by the Washington press corps. "Afterwards everybody there came to Cissy's party," said Mrs. William Randolph Hearst, Jr., "and I mean *everybody,* from the White House to the Supreme Court. When Cissy called them, they came."

At Christmas her Dupont Circle house was festive. In the foyer the busts of Scipio Africanus and Caesar Augustus wore wreaths of holly; there were masses of brilliant poinsettias everywhere; sprays of mistletoe hung from the glittering chandeliers; and always, an enormous tree.

Cissy's Christmas party began in the afternoon, when her friends brought their children, all of whom were given presents. She once gave gold compacts to the women and gold cigarette cases to the men. (Once when she ran short of cigarette cases, she gave the disappointed Eugene Meyer a box of cigars.) After the children were taken home, the adults stayed late into the night. Champagne flowed in magnums, and pheasants were dressed in their feathers after they were roasted. Mrs. Cornelius Vanderbilt once arrived at Cissy's Christmas gala wearing earrings, a satin dress, and nothing else: "I mean *nothing* else underneath."

Cissy was the ringmaster. Although it sometimes seemed that she had just opened the cages and let the animals out, she selected her guests carefully and moved them about like actors in a play. There always seemed to be several parties going on at once. A slightly tipsy Supreme Court Justice held forth in one corner; two *grandes dames* dueled with each other verbally to an appreciative audience; vaudevillians roamed the rooms doing magic tricks; a group crowded around the piano to listen to Duke Ellington. At one party Cissy found a newspaperman in the kitchen. He had discovered that he had gone to school with Cissy's footman and was helping him wash the glasses.

Agnes and Eugene Meyer were still regular guests at Cissy's parties. Privately, Agnes was critical of "the jawboning politicians" and "those queer Hearst people with good minds and unstable character. . . . Cissy is quite characteristic . . . they all amuse me." Cissy and Agnes now often disagreed politically, but they did agree they would rather be with each other than with "think-alike marshmallows."

This relationship changed dramatically soon after Cissy heard that the Washington *Post* was bankrupt and would be put on the auction block to pay its debtors. She was determined that the *Herald* acquire the *Post* and thus become the major morning daily in Washington. "This is our big chance," she told her advertising staff. She asked Hearst if he wanted her to bid "and if successful, combine with you. . . . If you would like to go into business with me, I would love to go into business with you." Hearst agreed.

Cissy then had a premonition. She called Eugene Meyer and asked if she could dine with him and Agnes that night. Meyer agreed without hesitation but warned that she would be the odd woman because it was too late "to go hunting for a man at this hour." In 1933 the bald, stocky, and scholarly Meyer was fifty-six years old. He had served under five Presidents, and Roosevelt had kept him on as head of the Federal Reserve Board. Meyer, however, had just resigned; he felt FDR "didn't know anything about finance, economics or law."

After dinner, Cissy cornered Meyer and asked him if he intended to buy the Washington *Post*. Meyer said he had no such intention, "no feeling about it at all." After Cissy left, he told Agnes about Cissy's question, and the subject was dropped. They planned to "grow old gracefully." But over the next days Agnes observed that her husband was growing restless and impatient. Noticing some dust on the banister, he told Agnes, "This house is not properly run." Agnes glared at him and said, "You'd better go buy the Washington *Post*. "

The day of the auction, June 1, was a pleasant summer day, and a large crowd gathered at the *Post* building on E Street. From an upstairs window Evalyn McLean, her hair tinted pink and the Hope diamond on her breast, watched the arrivals. She had committed her husband to a mental institution, but she wanted to keep the bankrupt paper for her two sons. Cissy was there, flanked by Hearst's general manager, Tom White, and a Hearst lawyer. Alice Roosevelt Longworth was there, and so was Mary Harriman Rumsey, among many others. Mary Rumsey was acting for her brother, W. Averell Harriman, and Vincent Astor, who wanted to put in Raymond Moley as editor.

The bidders were soon down to three: McLean, Hearst, and a lawyer who was acting for an unidentified client. When the lawyer bid $825,000, McLean dropped out. Cissy phoned Hearst, but he would go no higher. "I have nothing further to bid," said Cissy sadly when she returned. Even if Cissy could have bid higher, Hearst would not have been able to match the $2 million dollars the other lawyer had been directed to bid, if necessary.

"Sorry we did not get *The Post* but experience and evidence of your friendship and cooperation means more to me," Hearst wired Cissy. "I hope you are not disappointed."

Cissy was deeply disappointed. She had thought about bidding on her own, but she would not compete against Hearst and the *Herald*. She accurately guessed the *Post*'s new owner: "I think it's Eugene Meyer." She did not realize, however, that she had prompted his action.

"I am sure you are interested and pleased now that the cat is out of the bag, and that our friend Eugene Meyer appears as your morning rival in Washington," Brisbane wrote her. "As we could not have the *Post* for ourselves, I am glad that he has it, for he is an extremely fine young man, plenty of ambition, and he will give you a run for your money, which is important for *your* ambition. Mr. Hearst agrees with me." Brisbane added a postscript: "If you let Eugene Meyer beat you out in Washington, I shall disinherit you."

Brisbane was wrong in thinking that Cissy was "pleased." Cissy did not take competition lightly; she was a tough, energetic fighter. As friends, Agnes and Eugene Meyer were first class; as competitors, they were enemies.

Eugene Meyer looked like a mild man, but he once took a punch at a colleague who was ten inches taller than he. When

Cissy took over the contract from the bankrupt *Post* for its syndicated comic strips from the Chicago *Tribune*, and started printing them, Meyer sued for illegal use, claiming he had bought the Post *and* its comics. Cissy felt possessive about those comics because her brother had helped create many of them, including *Dick Tracy* and *Gasoline Alley.* Meyer didn't want to get into a court fight with Cissy and asked Brisbane to intervene. "Mrs. Patterson, I'm afraid would not welcome my meddling," answered Brisbane. Meyer then approached Cissy: "Cissy, why do we have to spend so much time suing each other?" Cissy gave a short, hard laugh and said that their lawyers needed the business.

The court fight lasted twenty months. The *Post* won. Meyer ran a six-column cartoon showing an imposing robed figure sternly saying to a group of comic strip characters: "To your Post!" "Never mind the Tribune features." Hearst wired Cissy, "I am perfectly satisfied not to have them and do not think Post will amount to anything, unless they get our Editor and Publisher."

Hearst didn't understand. Defeat galled Cissy. She hated to lose at anything. She hated even more to ask Meyer's permission to distribute the Sunday comics for the following Sunday, which had already been printed. Meyer agreed, asking Cissy to acknowledge the courtesy in a box on the front page of the news section. Meyer didn't understand Cissy either. His request enraged her, and at great expense, she replaced the disputed comics. That same day she sent her chauffeur with an elegantly wrapped box to the Meyer mansion.

Agnes accepted the package and took it to her husband at the *Post.* He opened it and found inside a smaller box, beautifully beribboned and surrounded by orchids. Cissy's card read, "So as not to disappoint you." When Meyer smilingly tore it open, he found a chunk of raw meat. For a moment they were puzzled. Then Agnes said icily, "It must be a pound of flesh [for] a dirty Jewish shylock." Eugene Meyer was appalled. Cissy, who almost never apologized, later told a friend, "I guess I made a mistake that time."

The war between them intensified. Meyer and Cissy viewed

their competition in very different ways: for Meyer, it was business; for Cissy, it was personal. Cissy gleefully twitted him when an enterprising *Herald* photographer got a picture of piles of *Post*s being dumped in the woods—a device that circulation men used to inflate their circulation figures. "You asked for it, Eugene," Cissy crowed in print. Meyer got back at her when the *Herald* printed an account of an execution before it had actually occurred.

In the small town of Washington, it was inevitable that Cissy and Eugene Meyer would soon meet. Their first encounter after the comic-strip controversy occurred at a Soroptimist Club luncheon, where Meyer was the guest of honor. Although they were seated next to each other, they did not speak. After the meal, it was customary for the guests to stand, link arms, and sing the club song. Cissy and Eugene looked at each other expectantly when the moment came; then Cissy smiled and took his arm and they sang together, "So now we get together as happy as can be." Soon afterward she saw him at a party given by Assistant Secretary of State Sumner Welles. This time, she rushed to him, embraced him, kissed him, and was irresistibly charming.

Cissy was more concerned about meeting Agnes Meyer again. The Meyers invited her to a big party, and she asked friends to accompany her. "I don't want to go there alone." Cissy wore a dramatic black and white dress. Agnes moved forward to greet her, and the two women stopped and stared at each other—both were wearing the same dress. They laughed, but not loudly.

Agnes might well have envied Cissy her job. Agnes's title at the *Post* was "vice president," but she had no real responsibilities. She was as competitive as Cissy, and their friendship never again flowered. A mutual acquaintance observed that they never again got close enough to stick a knife into each other.

The evening *Star* was then first in advertising, the *Herald* first in circulation, and the *Post* first in operating costs. (Meyer put more than a million dollars into the *Post* before it began showing a profit.) Meyer and Cissy had different journalistic philosophies. While he wanted to inform readers, she was more interested in entertaining them. Meyer concentrated on the government policymakers, courted the professionals. He told his reporters they represented the public and therefore had a right to see any government official. Cissy didn't care how reporters got their stories as long as they got them. While Meyer wanted his paper to be read by the Washington establishment, Cissy saw her audience as the whole community, particularly the government girl. She wanted complex issues presented in the simplest language possible, and she ordered her editors to study her brother's paper, the *News*.

She had a writer's sensitivity to words. Brisbane often reminded her of the need for brevity: "Eliminate, eliminate, eliminate. Cut out everything you can cut, and still you improve." While she agreed with this advice, she did not accept his dictum that the adjective was the enemy of the noun. She did not want her readers simply to gallop through a series of paragraphs written in telegraphic prose. She wanted the *Herald* stories to create a mood, to stimulate the readers' imagination.

One of her editors, Mason Peters, had long talks with Cissy into the early morning hours about language as a living thing, a musical thing. She urged him to keep copy spare but to add elegance with well-turned phrases and to strive for a distinctive rhythm.

Cissy was slowly realizing that she wanted the *Herald* to have the look, content, and quality of a magazine. She bought the best paper and the best ink (which did not come off on readers' hands). She wanted each page to be pleasing to the eye. She wanted a balance of type, pictures, and ads and was known to throw out an ad if it made a page unbalanced. Cissy was far ahead of other publishers in her lavish use of white space—extra lead between lines of type to give a more airy feeling.

"Use that beautiful type here that I like so much," she once said to a startled editor.

"Which beautiful type, Mrs. Patterson?"

"Well, it ran on the Woman's Page about six months ago, and I haven't seen it since."

Irving Belt was always able to locate the type faces that took her fancy. Belt was a former reporter who had fallen in love with typography. He had come from a family of cabinetmakers and was self-taught in Latin and Greek. He was a tall, slender man with an old-fashioned air. He and Cissy got along wonderfully well because he was completely unafraid of her. Belt built her a ship model, which she proudly displayed in a glass case over her office mantel.

Cissy liked legible type.

"I try to have a clean paper," she told an interviewer.

"Clean typography, do you mean, or in content also?"

Her eyes flashed, and she smiled. "Clean in typography only."

Hearst, in one of his moods, ordered his twenty-five newspapers to "go English." This meant adopting the format of a London newspaper that used pictures in octangular, triangular, and round cuts. Cissy looked at this layout and decided not to use it. Her judgment was intuitive: she thought that her readers would find the odd-shaped pictures disturbing. She believed that a newspaper should be easy to read, and this attitude shaped the design of the *Herald*. She wanted Page 1 stories to have no more than two jumps (that is, the articles would not be continued on more than two pages). This meant the reader would not have to keep on turning pages to finish reading a story.

I've always wanted every word to be perfect." she admitted. "I'm the sort of a bore who calls up the Composing Room to tell them to change a comma, and then calls them back again in a few minutes to say, 'Oh, put it in again.'"

She was also the sort of person who made sure she got what she wanted. When she visited the paper's stereotype foundry, the temperature was 130 degrees, "too damn hot for any human being." She ordered that a dozen more fans be put in. The next day she was down at the foundry again to see if the fans were installed. They were not. She was now the Red Queen ready to cut off heads. For Cissy the men in the foundry were as important to her paper as her best reporters. She called the electrical contractor herself and in her most regal voice demanded those fans *now*.

Cissy's normal speech was often so low that a listener might miss half her words, though still catching her meaning because she was exact in her diction and enunciation. Except for occasional rare words, she seldom used polysyllables. Generally, she picked the right word for the thought. This respect for words was matched by her feeling for pictures. She had frequent conferences with Bernie Harrison, who was then involved with picture layout. Harrison said:

> I would sit around my table with all the pictures submitted to the paper that day, and I would have my pile of those I had partially picked for the next day's paper, and she would join me for a couple hours each day, from about five to seven. She would sit right opposite me and pick out a picture and say, "What do you think of that?" I learned early in the game that you had to be honest with her, completely honest, because that was the only thing she respected. So I might tell her, "Well, that doesn't grab me . . ." or something like that, if I didn't like it. Lots of times, she would point out something I didn't notice. She really did have an eye for pictures. I remember once she picked out a picture of a newly selected Doughnut Queen, smiled, and said, "I know you boys like pictures like that but I want you to remember that we women also like to see pictures of a good-looking man." That stuck in my mind and once there was a Scottish festival with good-looking men in kilts and I picked one and played it big because I had remembered what she had said.

If a photograph reproduced badly, Cissy was immediately on the phone to the art department, engraving department, composing room, pressroom, to find out where the fault lay, warning all of them, "I want to know why these pictures aren't reproducing. If you can't tell me and can't improve them, you're all fired."

Cissy had a tell-tale look—her lips pursed and her head lowered to the right—that was a sure sign of her displeasure. If she accompanied this with a slight wave of the hand, her fingers held together, her employees knew a storm was brewing. Cissy hated excuses, and the only way to defuse her anger was to resolutely accept responsibility for the work she found unac-

ceptable. Brisbane had counseled her to work through department heads, never to bypass the person in charge. But she
could not do this. She was a born meddler; she had to know
everything about everybody; she had to be fully aware, fully
involved.

Nothing angered her more than the intimation that she was
not the active boss at the *Herald.* A Washington *Daily News*
columnist, George Abell, commenting on a trip she planned to
New York, remarked that she would be running her paper by
remote control, intimating that perhaps her presence wasn't
really necessary. Cissy bitterly resented any criticism of her
editorship. Riding whip in hand, Cissy stormed into the *News*
office yelling, "Where is that hairy ass George Abell? I'm going
to horsewhip him. Where *is* he?" The startled *News* editor
calmed her down, and the two were soon exchanging anecdotes
and laughing. That was typical Cissy—letting off steam, then
laughing. She later hired Abell to write a column for her and he
became her good friend.

"I was unnecessarily disagreeable to several people yesterday," Cissy wrote Brisbane, "but that was only because I hope
you would think me a smart girl." More to the point, she
enjoyed power, and frequently misused it. "She did it (her
work) with a combination of perfume and woodsmoke, with a
touch of sulphur—pungent, disturbing, and stinging to the
eyes." Her manner made most men weak in her presence. Her
thick glasses and steady gaze gave her a slightly menacing air at
times. Even tough, cynical Pat Frank, one of her best reporters,
would blush, shift his weight with embarrassment, and perspire
heavily when she called him into her office.

Cissy fired people often, but her staff knew there were two
kinds of discharges—temporary and permanent. Those who
were temporarily fired somehow knew it. They knew they were
not to work for another newspaper: if they did, they would
really be fired. She once fired an editor, got him a job with her
brother on the New York *Daily News,* and then called him
indignantly several months later to ask, "Well, when are you
coming back here?"

Herald reporters worked on the principle that they should

never raise their voices or throw a glue pot or threaten to quit if they could not get along with a particular editor. "Rise majestically from your desk, stroll out of the office and around the block, and when you return—presto—you will find the son of a bitch has been caught with his fist in the cookie jar and fired."

One employee Cissy fired repeatedly was Mike Flynn, her managing editor. Flynn had held this post when Cissy came to the paper, and she depended on him. Hearst had advised her early, "The *Herald* needs an able, stable, judicious, experienced managing editor. Mr. Flynn has a good deal of ability, but he is not stable, judicious . . . that you get along with him is a distinct tribute to your genius and generosity."

Flynn had two passions—racing and drinking. If he left the *Herald* early in the afternoon, everyone knew he was going to the racetrack. If he went to the men's room frequently, everyone knew he was going to take a drink from his flask. Cissy overlooked his eccentricities because he did his job well. She knew all of Mike Flynn's favorite speakeasies, and she was often the one who hunted him down, called him "you no-good sonofabitch," sobered him up, and took him home to his wife.

"Cissy loved Mike—always did," said editor Frank Waldrop. "He was like day and night to her." Mike was easygoing and unambitious and seldom raised his voice. But he was a professional. He knew his job and he knew Washington. He was a tall, good-looking man, about Cissy's age. Reporters knew that Cissy often called Mike in the early morning hours, asking him to drop by her house with a copy of the first edition. There were rumors about Cissy and Mike, as there were about her and almost every handsome man she knew. But Cissy rarely mixed romance with business, and she was especially circumspect with Mike because his wife was very jealous. Cissy courted Mike's wife with gifts and flowers and even sent the two of them on a trip to Europe. The Flynns had just sailed when Cissy discovered something Mike had forgotten to do and cabled him, "You're fired." Back from vacation, Mike returned to the office as usual, as if nothing had happened.

"Any dame that can't outsmart a man ought to have her head

examined," Mae West had told her. And Cissy had sent a humorous note to the women reporters for their *Guild Gazette*, "My sisters, I will give you a little advice. . . . Get the men to work for you. Get the men to do all your work for you. You will not have to work even to get the credit. It will come to you anyway and the men will never know the difference. Even if you are old and broken at the wheel as I am."

In a more serious mood Cissy stated that "women are the best reporters in the world. In regards to feature writing—by which I mean emotional writing—women from the very start have headed for first flight. I think men have shoved them out of many a position in which, to my mind, they could prove themselves superior."

Cissy had few illusions about herself and loved to poke fun at her own foibles. Once at an annual Women's Press Club party, Cissy satirized herself in a skit she wrote called "As a Woman Editor Sees Herself." One of the publicity pictures was a photograph of her on a hunting trip; the caption read: "Lion hunter Eleanor Patterson gets another goat." Asked what man in official life she most admired, she answered, "N' Gi is gone." (N' Gi had been a gorilla at the Washington Zoo. Cissy had started a campaign to save him when he contracted pneumonia; she had even asked Dr. Barach to bring his portable oxygen chamber to the zoo. But all efforts failed, and he had died.)

Mae West was also at the party, persuaded by Cissy to star in a skit. She played a Republican national chairman who was trying to put new life into the Grand Old Party with the slogan "Mae West or Bust." Eleanor Roosevelt lent her husband's lounging robe and long cigarette holder for a skit lampooning him.

Cissy's women reporters were the best dressed at the party because most of their clothes came from her. At least once a year, the word went out that the boss was having a "fire sale." They quickly gathered at Dupont Circle; there the clothes were laid out for their selection in the sitting room adjoining Cissy's fourth-floor bedroom. After the first such "sale," most of the women looked ready for a funeral—Cissy had given away the black mourning clothes she had bought after Elmer's death.

One of the women who had bought a small house confided, "I don't know what I would do if Cissy didn't give me all those clothes. . . . I don't have much money left over." Only one woman had feet as small as Cissy's, and she never had to buy any shoes. Besides throwing the "sales," Cissy impulsively gave Jackie Martin, her photographic editor, three fur coats. She gave her mink coat to a reporter she found shivering outside on a winter night. When the woman returned it the next day, Cissy said, "You should have kept it. I've got lots more." Cissy once admired a tailored suit worn by a reporter who had picked it up at one of her sales. The reporter jokingly offered to return it, and Cissy promptly accepted.

Despite all the fire sales, Cissy still had so many clothes that she drove her maid into a frenzy every evening when she asked for a particular gown. Jackie Martin finally decided to photograph all her clothes and put the pictures into an indexed loose-leaf binder. "I don't know how many pictures we took, but there must have been a couple hundred on the shoes alone. She even had some high-laced leather walking shoes. And some of her fur coats must have been twenty years old," said Betty Vitol, a picture retoucher in the art department. "Jackie even had me coloring the pictures, but Cissy said no, that was too much work." The catalog included some three hundred pairs of lounging pajamas and slacks, many made of satin, silk, or heavy velvet. She wore slacks a generation before they became widely worn.

Cissy was startled when she was named one of the Best Dressed Women of the World in the early 1930s. "How perfectly silly," she said, "I never spend more than twenty thousand a year on clothes." Her wardrobe was classically elegant. She never wore the more bizarre couturier designs favored by some of her friends.

She was five feet seven, kept her weight at 130 pounds, and never showed any bones. She wore little makeup and few jewels. At fifty-two she was a strinkingly handsome woman. And for all her amusement about being on the Best Dressed list, this recognition must have been especially warming to one who regarded herself as an ugly duckling.

Although so much in Cissy's life was going well, her relationship with her daughter remained strained. Felicia had returned to the United States in 1932 for the publication of her first novel, *The House of Violence*. She used the same surname—Gizycka—that her mother had published under. Her mother had written two novels, and so would she. Long afterward, without heat, Felicia would finally say, "I'm tired of being Cissy's daughter."

A reviewer said of Felicia's novel that it was "written with an understanding and perception surprising in so young a writer." She was twenty-seven years old, still restless and rootless. She had reluctantly accepted an allowance from her mother to maintain her frenetic Paris social life. There had been many men but no single love. Under her new arrangement with Drew, their daughter Ellen spent the summer months with her in Paris and stayed with him for the rest of the year.

The sadness was that Felicia was treating her own daughter as shabbily as she had been treated. Ellen had grown into a nervous child, too much indulged by her father, too little loved by her mother. "Ma was always after me for not loving Ellen enough," said Felicia, "and, at that time, I didn't." Felicia never remembered any family dinners, any real Christmas celebration, when she was a child. And now that she was grown, her mother begged her to come home for Christmas. But when she did, she found nothing had changed. There were tentative pecks on the cheeks but no warm affection. Then, soon, the tensions, caustic words, raucous arguments. "I won't be a witness to this violence," Felicia once said, walking out after a bitter fight.

"Whenever I saw her, I was always afraid of the next sentence, the next minute, because she was always finding fault with me," recalled Felicia. "We were always tearing at each other. When I got angry enough, and fought back, I could beat her down and she would retreat. Ma always laughed at her anger and her fights, but I hated it."

They both tried. Cissy had Felicia's picture—as a young girl—in her fourth-floor bedroom; she also had a large portrait of Felicia painted for downstairs and even had a party to celebrate its hanging. "Sometimes the two of us would eat alone together in her bedroom," added Felicia, "and she always encouraged my writing. I wrote some articles for her paper, one on the circus. We both loved the circus. She always gave me a byline."

Felicia had grown into a beautiful woman with exceptional talent. She had large gray eyes and honey-colored hair curled in page-boy fashion. She resembled her handsome father more than her mother. Her first short story—which her Uncle Joe had bought for *Liberty*—was reprinted in many anthologies. Brisbane wrote Cissy "how well she can write," and suggested, "how interesting it would be to have mother and daughter working on the same paper." But neither woman wanted to work with the other.

Felicia's room on the third floor at Dupont Circle was always ready for her. It had a large canopied bed, and Cissy often redecorated the large sunny room when she heard that Felicia was returning. But Felicia's visits were never long. The house, for her, had been a magic place in which to play as a child when her grandmother lived there, but she had never had any love here from her mother. "My mother found it easier to give me a sable coat than to give me any love."

Felicia spent much of her time in New York and told an interviewer: "You know, you can be quite lonely in New York during the day when everyone else is working. You begin to get terrible inferiority feelings. . . . Of all the girls I know, only one of them is successful at playing. Then there are the others, the ones who will work, no matter what. They are rare in any group of people. My mother is one of those."

Cissy's mother died at the age of seventy-eight in the fall of 1933. When her Aunt Kate had died the year before, she had said of her nurse, in her last words—"My God, what a bottom!" Cissy's mother's final words were: "Joe, Joe, where's Joe?" Cissy had no tears. There had been more hostility than love between them. Cissy had felt more affection for her Aunt Kate. When Rose Crabtree later visited the grave at Chicago's Graceland Cemetery with her, Cissy remarked coldly, "That's where she wanted to be buried." It was then, too, seeing the collected graves of her kin surrounding her grandfather, that she decided she would be buried there herself. She gave the gravesite next to Schlesinger to Felicia.

She had no longer any sense of family with Felicia.

One day after lunch Cissy went over to a small group of reporters in the *Herald's* city room. Smiling warmly, she said, "*You* are my children."

15

I know I have the body of a weak and feeble woman, but I have the heart and stomach of a King. . . .
—Queen Elizabeth I, speech to troops at Tilbury, on the approach of the Armada, 1588

Cissy had no gods. She would defy anyone. Although she loved her brother better than anyone else in the world, she defied him when she became publisher of the *Herald*. She defied him when she married Elmer Schlesinger. And when Joe took public issue with Hearst on a political matter, as he sometimes did, she sided with Hearst and blasted her brother.

Hearst was her hero. He had her complete respect and admiration. He had believed in her when her own family hadn't. Yet she often disregarded his orders, refusing to run some of the Hearst syndicate's editorials and features, and making her own decisions about the paper's format. When Tom White, Hearst's general manager, proposed a drastic cut in the *Herald*'s budget, she sent him a blistering letter (with a copy to Hearst): "I cannot understand why it occurred to you to hamstring a healthy, growing and increasingly popular property when you have so many corpses lying around to play with. If your program were carried out, the *Herald* would be just another corpse. I know you will believe me when I tell you that I will not attend the funeral."

"Now, sister, why get sarcastic just because Tom White is trying to temper the wind?" Hearst wired her. "Still think that one Mrs. Eleanor Patterson is responsible for the success of the *Herald* . . . As long as said Mrs. Patterson retains her health and brilliant editorial mind."

Having shown defiance, Cissy was charmingly conciliatory: "I love you next best in the world to Joe and for the same reason. You are two of the grandest men I ever knew. Don't forget I read every word you send me with a great magnifying glass, so please don't you get sarcastic either."

She was still relatively new to publishing, and Hearst thereafter was very solicitous of her feelings. "Hope you consulted Mrs. Patterson about my suggestions," he wrote Brisbane. "Please bear in mind that all my suggestions are naturally subject to her judgment and revision." He also urged her to "please always do what you think best. You generally know more than any of us."

Cissy wrote Hearst that her brother—despite their disagreement—had said that "you are the greatest newspaper genius the world has ever known." Hearst replied, "Tell the honorable Joseph that I highly appreciate his compliment, and at any rate the title lies among us three."

Despite her respect and affection for the Lord of San Simeon, Cissy later allowed her movie critic to review *Citizen Kane*, which was based on Hearst's career and personal life. This Orson Welles film had been ignored by the Hearst press because it presented the Chief in an unsympathetic light. "She not only let me review it," said Bernie Harrison, "but she let me say it was a great picture. That says a lot for her."

Her mind was her own, and she could always change it. During one of Joe's attacks on Hearst, Cissy commissioned Bob Considine, one of her former reporters, to write an article countering all her brother's arguments. She planned to print it under the headline "A Tribute to a Great American—William Randolph Hearst."

When the piece did not appear, Considine called her.

"Bob, I think it's the best piece I ever read on Mr. Hearst. . . . But I'm not going to run it."

"Why?"

Cissy sighed blissfully. "I made up with Joe."

She insisted, however, on paying Considine for the article.

"I don't want anything, Mrs. Patterson," Considine answered glacially.

Cissy insisted. "How much did you make on your last article in *Cosmopolitan* magazine?"

He hesitated. "I made seven hundred and fifty dollars, Mrs. Patterson."

A few days later, Considine received a check for $500, plus a note: "Dear Bob: I *called* Cosmo. Love, Cissy."

Ethel Barrymore, who thought Cissy and Joe were "absolutely dripping with charm," told her often, "Tell the truth. Truth is always more interesting." Sometimes Cissy's shortsighted eyes did not see the truth clearly, and in later years her judgment, her politics, and ever her patriotism would be questioned. But few who knew her well ever doubted her honesty. It was an honesty born out of humility and arrogance, out of the bitterness and disappointment of living. The only kind of truth she avoided was a truth that was not really important and would be hurtful to a dear friend. For example, Ethel Barrymore usually stayed with Cissy while she was performing in Washington, and when Cissy once saw her in a play Cissy thought was terrible, she could not bear to come home that night and face Ethel with the truth. (Felicia stayed up that night and heard the tipsy Barrymore relate her family's fascinating history in the theater.) If a truth, however, was *really* important, she would tell it—although it might tear up a friend. Her paper had few sacred cows. She even attacked FBI Director J. Edgar Hoover, a man she admired and had proposed for the post of attorney general. She let her paper flay prominent men, some of whom still had her love. She could denounce people in print, and embrace them in public, and feel no qualm of contradiction. She was both a street fighter and a great lady.

One of the men who admired both sides of her was Senator Huey Long of Lousiana. At the Democratic National Convention of 1932, Cissy had remarked that he made "the other so-called statesmen look like white mice." He wore fawn-colored suits with purple shirts and looked like a racetrack tout, but he was one of the most spellbinding orators of his generation. His revivalistic, and, indeed, demagogic, style was mesmerizing. His campaign slogan was "Every Man a King," and he gave the Depression downtrodden a scrap of hope.

Hearst regarded the short, stocky Long "with the fleshy pudding face" as "a very able gentleman, but he is another dictator. . . . I cannot support him." President Roosevelt was becoming alarmed by Long's growing national importance. Long had made no secret of his ambition: "If I am to fulfill my destiny, I will be President as I was born to be."

Cissy found Long magnetic rather than menacing. He rarely went to Washington parties, but he went to Cissy's. At her frequent small dinners, the keynote was quietly elegant opulence—tall silver candlesticks, masses of flowers, the finest crystal and linen, and absolutely superb gourmet food. One evening her guests included the Secretary of State in formal wear as well as several ambassadors with their ribbons and generals with their medals. Long arrived in a rumpled white suit and, looking at his elaborate setting of silver flatware, told a laughing Cissy, "I don't know what all these are for. Where I come from we use one knife and one fork to eat all our vittles with." After tasting the salad, he said, "My dear friend, you must let me come sometime and teach your cook to make salad dressing."

"My dear Senator," murmured Cissy, "why not now?"

Long went to work right in the dining room. "Hey you! What kind of dump is this—no Tabasco—get some quick! And bring some sugar!" he told a trembling footman. He talked about the history of salad from the pharaohs to Escoffier and then remarked, "We must dry this lettuce more thoroughly; improperly dried lettuce ruins more salads than careless cooks." The dressing done, he added it to the greens, gently tossing them.

He tasted a leaf, picked up another, and put it in Cissy's mouth, asking, "How about this, honey?"

"Another one of your miracles, Senator."

Long then took command of the dinner conversation; he overwhelmed the men, charmed the women, and conquered the cynics. Told the next day what a success he had had at the party, Long spit out bitterly, "A court jester, damn them."

While he damned others, he never damned Cissy. Friends heard Cissy say more and more often, "Let's call Huey. . . ." He became a Cissy "regular." An irritated Brisbane wrote her: "I could hardly expect you to come. To drag you away from Huey Long would be attempting the impossible. . . . I know you admire his terrific energy."

She also sympathized with his weakness. He told her that while he was governor of Louisiana, he got roaring drunk every night—"so I'd know I was the greatest man on earth." "All men are born to lusts," he told St. Johns. "Some for women, for power, for money—for likker. I had to lick my lust for likker, and I've done it. But sometimes I think I'm gonna die for it!" Then he picked up a bottle of gin, crashed it through a window, and started shaking and sobbing in her arms.

Harold LeClair Ickes, who was not one of Long's admirers, expressed his distaste frankly: "The trouble with Senator Long is that he is suffering from halitosis of the intellect, if the Emperor Long has any intellect." Ickes was FDR's Secretary of the Interior and head of the Public Works Administration, which had a budget of more than $5 billion. Besides setting up the PWA, Roosevelt had created a veritable alphabet soup of agencies, including the CWA (Civil Works Administration) and the WPA (Works Progress Administration), which financed more than 30,000 New Deal projects, from sewers to airports. There was also the CCC (Civilian Conservation Corps), the AAA (Agricultural Adjustment Administration), and the TVA (Tennessee Valley Authority), among others. In an effort to bring the country out of the depression, the President had closed the banks and reopened them with Federal Deposit Insurance, resolved the farm crisis, taken the country off the gold standard, proposed a Social Security Act. His innovative, and to some minds radical, policies gained him many powerful opponents. A *New Yorker* cartoon showed a group in top hats and evening dress, saying, "Let's go to the Trans-Lux and hiss Roosevelt." But one congressman compared him to Jesus Christ, and there were forty-one popular songs written about him. Walter Lippmann, who had dismissed him earlier as a lightweight, now stated that "the nation, which has lost confidence in everything and everybody, has regained confidence in the government and in itself."

Cissy's friendship with Ickes flowered in the early part of 1933. There were those close to the President who felt that FDR might well have asked Ickes to "keep an eye on Cissy." Hearst had become increasingly critical of the President, and Cissy's paper was the most widely read in Washington. Ickes was a peppery man of dry humor with a face that somewhat resembled that of a Pekinese. The press called him "Honest Harold" and "The Curmudgeon." He preferred the latter. Newspapers poked fun at his pencil policy: employees of the Interior Department were forbidden to discard pencils that were more than three inches long. And his wife joked about a speech prepared for her: "I have been able to be with my husband very little since he came to Washington. . . . I have never had such a good time in my life."

Cissy was attracted to this dour, practical man not only by his power but also by his past. The two had ties dating back to Hiram Johnson's campaign for the Presidency in 1920 on the Progressive party ticket. Ickes told Cissy he had loved her favorite cousin, Medill McCormick, "as Damon loved Pythias" and he had worked with Elmer Schlesinger on Johnson's campaign.

They began to see each other socially. Ickes spent a rainy evening on the terrace at Dower House. The conversation was so engrossing that they didn't want to move, despite the rain. "Finally she got a coat for herself and a coat and hat for me and we got along pretty well until it began to rain rather hard." Ickes thought Cissy was "a very interesting and very vivacious hostess. She is brilliant."

After Ickes' wife was killed in a car crash in 1935, he became a more frequent guest at Cissy's. Cissy sympathized with his loneliness, and she was impressed with his brisk, challenging mind. The two often had dinner alone at Dower House. "Cissy noticed that I was pretty tired after dinner and she took me down to the swimming pool where we sat and talked for some time," Ickes recorded. "She told me how foolish she thought I was to work so hard and allow things to worry me and I had to admit the force of everything she said." He was impressed again with her gentleness and friendly understanding. "I have come to be very fond of her. I have found in her the best friend I have made in Washington. She seems to be a very genuine person with broad sympathies."

An unsmiling man with skeptical eyes peering over rimless spectacles, Ickes was six years older than Cissy. He was not tall, and his head seemed a little too large for his compact body. Cissy liked his pungent directness and his hatred of sham. She was quick to criticize his radio speeches: "You talk too fast." Ickes noted that although Cissy was still loyal to Hearst, "she laughingly says to me that she does not care what I say in my speeches."

Hearst had grown increasingly disenchanted with Roosevelt's economic policies and was in search of a new candidate. He and Cissy and Brisbane traveled to Topeka in her railroad car to meet Alfred M. Landon, the governor of Kansas. The governor's mansion, with its lilac and snowball bushes, reminded Cissy of her grandfather Medill's house. Writing of the meeting, Cissy observed: "Everybody was taking stock of everybody else, saying one thing and thinking several times another." She raised the question: "Has this clean-living, simple man the power within him to guide our sorely troubled country out of its present wilderness? Has he?"

She liked Landon and told Hearst he was "simply grand." But she liked him less in later weeks when she heard his flat, dull speeches on the radio. And when Hearst's attacks on Roosevelt grew more rabid, she toned them down in the *Herald*. Ickes, who was a frequent weekend guest at Sands Point, found it amusing to polish up another attack on Hearst while he was staying at Cissy's house. One evening Cissy and Ickes went to a dinner at the Swopes's. The guests, among them Mr. and Mrs. Henry Luce and Mr. and Mrs. William Randolph Hearst, Jr., discussed the upcoming 1936 Presidential election. Luce and Hearst were for Landon, Swope and Ickes for Roosevelt, with Cissy keeping her own counsel. She had told Ickes earlier that she "was pulled both ways, by Hearst and my brother Joe."

When the *Herald* printed a syndicated Hearst column that called Ickes a Communist, Cissy pulled it out as soon as she saw it. She then called Ickes to apologize, saying that the piece was stupid and mean. "She said in a facetious vein that both of us might lose our jobs." Cissy also told Ickes that although her contract with the Hearst organization had expired, she had refused to sign a new one (which would have doubled her salary) and was therefore working for nothing. It was her way of maintaining her independence and her options. She confided that she was thinking of resigning as publisher unless Hearst changed some of his more rabid anti-Roosevelt policies. "I greeted this with loud applause," Ickes wrote.

Hearst was not alone in his animosity toward Ickes, who was regarded by many on the Right as being too Left. Bertie McCormick frequently attacked him in the Chicago *Tribune,* and a Washington newsman described Ickes as "the most personally unpopular person in the Roosevelt dynasty." The Kansas City *Journal* editorialized: "We do not like the weather we have been having, nor Harold Ickes." But Bill Bullitt told Cissy that Ickes was "the outstanding man in the Cabinet."

One evening at Dower House, Bullitt joined Cissy and Ickes for dinner. He was still slim and handsome, although he had lost much of his hair, and the ten-year difference in their ages, which had seemed so important on the Riviera in 1925, no longer mattered much. Bullitt, who as a young man had been described as "a planet all in the making, still largely in the incandescent state," was now the first United States Ambassador to the Soviet Union, and he arrived at dinner with a large package of caviar.

He and Ickes liked each other immediately. Both classified things as black or white, right or wrong, and both had similar political philosophies. There was a civil war in Spain, and both sympathized with the government in power. Bullitt had the greater brilliance and sophistication. He had written the book with Sigmund Freud about Woodrow Wilson (but had decided not to publish it during Wilson's widow's lifetime). He could speak wittily about his meetings with Lenin, Matisse, Clemenceau, Bernard Shaw, Picasso, and Einstein.

Bullitt and his second wife had been divorced in 1930, and he and Cissy were soon spending much time together. They often spoke French or German as they reminisced about Vienna and their young years. Their warm friendship did not escape notice, and *Vanity Fair* commented: "She is not beautiful, but has the most seductive figure, and it is a tribute to her charm that she is rumored to be engaged to marry Bill Bullitt, our Ambassador to Moscow." Brisbane reluctantly agreed to sanction "the union of May and December, if I must." At the same time, Harold Ickes confided to his diary the romantic news that he felt certain that Cissy wanted to marry Harold Ickes.

She soon had news of another friend. A call to her home came from the *Herald* on the night of September 8, 1935: Her friend Huey Long had been shot and killed in Louisiana. The Kingfish had run Louisiana like a fiefdom. He had controlled the judges, policemen, and tax collectors, and the state legislature had once shouted forty-four of his bills into law in twenty-two minutes. He left a heritage of gratitude and hatred. Just before his death, he had signed a contract for a book to be called *My First Days in The White House.*

Bullitt, meanwhile, returned to Moscow. Ickes was suddenly stirred by a much younger woman. Ray Helgeson, who was then Cissy's city editor, decided to marry Kitty Barrett, one of the youngest reporters at the *Herald*. "Cissy tried to talk me out of going with Ray," she said later. "I know Ray was a big part of her." Whatever her feelings, Cissy accepted an invitation to their wedding in Birmingham, Alabama.

Shortly before she went, she asked Harry Hopkins, then head of the WPA, to a small dinner party. He and Ickes were bitter rivals in the FDR power structure, their areas of responsibility occasionally overlapping. "Hunger is not debatable," Hopkins had said after distributing more than $5 million in his first two hours of office. "People don't eat in the long run—they eat every day."

The dinner discussion concerned the plight of the poor, and Hopkins' comments were blunt. "You've got to do one of two things: either poison 'em, or help them get on their feet." The lean, mournful-looking Hopkins pointed his finger dramatically at Cissy. "Goddammit, why don't you go look at 'em."

The table fell silent for a moment, and then Cissy said softly, "I will."

She and Jackie Martin, who came along to take pictures, went to the Helgeson-Barrett wedding and then rented an old Ford and headed for the east Tennessee hills. Cissy traveled through the hardscrabble country of the sharecroppers, the poor whites. "They had no beef cattle, and they had no cow, and could buy no meat and they could buy no milk—not even canned. Nor salt pork. No chicken and no eggs." She visited the one-room cabin where Willy Bertram, his wife, and their eight young children lived. A near invalid, Bertram could spend only an hour or two a day working the poor land of their small farm. "Never had no mule, ma'am," his wife told Cissy. "No vegetables this year 'cuz of the drought." They lived on dried beans cooked for hours with a "gravy" made of flour and water. They had beans for breakfast and again at noon. "An' coffee when we gits it. Supper? Oh, they's gen'ally some beans left over."

She saw hollow-eyed and listless children and their young mothers with leathery, careworn faces. "Now I know a little more about Pilgrim's Progress," she wrote. "For I have seen a hundred Hills Difficult and as many Sloughs of Despond, each with its quota of good Americans whose constitutional rights have somehow failed to put shoes on their feet and hope in their hearts."

She was angry. "After all, I'm a red-haired woman editor and I have something to say." This abysmal poverty was an "old and festering sore in the body of our nation," and she wanted Congress to heal it.

She wired Frank Waldrop, one of her editors who was then visiting Nashville:

Go to Rugby thirty miles from Harriman Tennessee and get photographs of Mrs. Bertram with her eight children and husband. Don't let them wash or dress up. Give Mrs. Bertram one hundred dollars. Contact her sister-in-law, also Mrs. Bertram, give her fifty dollars. Also give one hundred dollars to Mrs. Frogue same neighborhood. Get facts on real conditions Sequatchie Valley. How many poor etcetera. Get pictures of waitress at Gatlinburg Tourist Street restaurant who wears shorts, full length, preferably profile showing bare back. Get names of native craft industries and educational schools.

In one of six articles about this trip, Cissy recalled that her grandfather had traveled through that same Tennessee country on his way West. Had he stayed there, she wrote, "I cannot forget but for the grace of God it might have been Willy Bertram and his family taking a look at me in the midst of squalor instead of me calling on Willy and struck with wonder that he lives at all."

That series was a collaboration by Cissy and Frank Waldrop, a combination of Cissy's notes and conversation put into preliminary words by Waldrop and then edited, perhaps rewritten in part, by Cissy. Helgeson had brought Waldrop from the New York *Journal,* where the two had worked together. The two could hardly have been more different. Both were editors of enormous talent, but Helgeson was dash and flash, while Waldrop was a much more complex man. He was a broad-shouldered, handsome young man from Tennessee who had started out to be a soldier and had gone to West Point. But he had found his military studies uncompelling, and he was soon swept away by literature, public affairs, and history.

Waldrop's turn of mind was very close to Cissy's. When she searched for a way to express a complicated emotion or thought clearly and precisely, Waldrop almost invariably came up with the words that caught her exact meaning. Their mutual understanding, so quick and complete, was almost uncanny.

At one time or another Waldrop held almost every senior

editorial post at the *Herald*—from foreign affairs editor to managing editor—but most of his time was devoted to the paper's editorials. Cissy decided which of the Hearst syndicate's editorials the paper would carry. If Joe Patterson had a good editorial in his *News*, Cissy ran it in her *Herald*. At her direction, Waldrop studied Joe's editorials. "And I *never* got through learning from him," said Waldrop. "He was absolutely the best. He could do it in a sentence." Cissy would pinpoint an issue, and she and Waldrop would discuss it in great detail, perhaps even argue about it. Out of these rambling conversations, Waldrop would produce clean, hard editorials. Cissy soon realized that he expressed her ideas better than she did—and more quickly and with less pain. She then trusted him implicitly.

Anyone who wanted to stay with Cissy had to have not only exceptional talent but also an élan, an attractiveness, a spirit and style that stimulated and amused her. Waldrop had all these qualities, but even such a paragon as he could not completely escape the gusts of Cissy's temper. He and Cissy stood on the same side of most major issues, but they did have differences, some of them strong enough for Waldrop to have his share of "temporary firings" and resignations. His absences were always short because Cissy needed him, and she knew it. In a large sense, Waldrop replaced Drew Pearson as Cissy's alter ego.

She counted on Waldrop for advice, criticism, companionship. He saw himself as her "hired gun." If she wanted anything disagreeable done, he did it. When she wanted to shake up a department or fire somebody or start a law suit, Waldrop often acted as her agent. There were about Cissy and Frank, of course, the usual romantic rumors, but Cissy had adopted him and his family in a more complete way. Waldrop and his wife Eleanor were Felicia's age, and Cissy liked the warm ambience of their home. She gave more to the two Waldrop children than she ever gave to her own daughter. "Oh, she loved Andrew and she'd take him back in that little room and sit on the floor and read to him and they'd listen to *Peter and the Wolf* for hours and she didn't want to be disturbed," said Eleanor Waldrop. Cissy was not emotionally effusive with children; she never could be, even with her own grandchild, but she could always talk to them on their level, as she could talk with anyone.

Cissy had a much different relationship with her new managing editor, George Clinton (Ash) DeWitt (Mike Flynn had been shunted to other duties). A Howey import from Chicago (Howey still arrived periodically, filled with new ideas), DeWitt was a highly organized, highly competent editor who was serious about both eating and drinking. When he drank, he drank double martinis in rapid succession. Consequently he was often arrested for disturbing the peace, and the *Herald*'s police reporter was responsible for getting him out of jail and making the arrest records disappear. His wife spent a great deal of time buying and preparing his favorite foods, and when he was away from the office, Cissy would remark, "He's out in the country, digesting."

Cissy had him at Dupont Circle one night for a postmidnight chat about the day's paper. DeWitt was short and rotund with a rather brusque manner. Cissy asked, "You don't like working for a woman, do you?" and he replied, "I don't mind." Their editorial discussion continued, punctuated by frequent glasses of champagne. Suddenly DeWitt stood up and said, "Well, I certainly enjoy this, but you know I'm in love with my wife."

"Oh, you're in love with your wife, are you?" Cissy said, laughing. It was a remark she never let him forget.

Two weeks after he began working at the *Herald*, DeWitt was amazed and amused to see a piano wheeled into the city room. Cissy so much enjoyed listening to Duke Ellington that she wanted her staff to enjoy him too, and so she asked him to play in the city room that night. Somehow, the paper managed to get published. Cissy never lost the feeling that everyone who worked on her newspaper was a member of her family, although DeWitt kept trying to persuade her to work through her editors and department heads. Cissy's door was always open to anyone with a grievance or a suggestion.

"She *was* a genius," DeWitt stated. "She knew talent. She knew what to do about a news story. She knew more about

Women's Pages than anyone. She was a natural-born editor of pictures, writing, good reporting. And she was never satisfied. She always wanted improvements."

This appreciation did not save DeWitt from being periodically fired, like virtually everyone else.

"Look, Mrs. P., if you have no confidence in me, there's no point in my continuing here. You've talked about loyalty of employees; loyalty is a two-way street. Why don't you ask one of those boys to come down and do your editing, and I'll do the second guessing. I'm a pretty good Monday morning quarterback."

Cissy fired him, but the next day she sent him a baby picture of herself, with the message: "Still eighteen months old."

"You can't get mad at a woman like that," said DeWitt.

Joe once sat in on an editorial conference Cissy was having with DeWitt. As usual, she was blasting him for the mistakes she had found in that day's *Herald*.

"Why did you do that?" Joe asked after the meeting was over.

"Don't you?"

"No, never."

"But if you know he's wrong?"

"Well, he'll see it himself in the morning and be sorrier than you are."

Despite their differences in temperament, Joe Patterson was proud of his sister. Lunching with Brisbane, he praised her and added, "I might get a paper with Cissy." Brisbane advised Cissy to act on this idea. "You and he both know the newspaper business. You are both young, or at least you are and can drag him along. You are both engaged now in manufacturing profits, largely for others. You ought to have one good paper for yourselves and make it pay. . . . If I were thirty years younger, I should like to have one-third interest in such a paper."

But a partnership between Joe and Cissy would not have worked. A successful newspaper must be run by a single person, and Cissy and her brother were strong-minded individuals unwilling to take a position second to anyone. She might love him and imitate the best of him, but she would not follow him unquestioningly. The time had long passed when Cissy would allow herself to be ruled by another's decisions.

Speculating about Joe's serious interest in flying, *The New Yorker* discussed his rumored retirement from the *News*: "Some think Patterson's successor may be his brilliant, erratic sister. . . . There is a solid friendship between brother and sister, and Cissy gets more individual tutelage from Patterson than any of his own subordinates. He helps her out with many of her editorial problems."

If Joe had willed her the *News*, Cissy would have found it hard to tear herself away from the *Herald*. The *Herald* was hers just as the *News* was his. Taking over a successful, established newspaper would have offered little challenge to her.

If she had a single, overwhelming wish now, it was to *own* the *Herald,* to make it really hers. There was no longer any lingering hesitancy about her ability to handle it—as there might have been when she asked Hearst to join her in bidding for the *Post.* Now she knew she could run the *Herald* or any other paper in the world. But Hearst still would not sell.

"What a pity you are not poor and compelled to show what a woman can do," Brisbane wrote her. "You'd enjoy REAL DESERVED fame. . . . Nobody works except by compulsion, except yourself, and you only work a little, relying on genius for the rest."

Brisbane, as always, was her constant critic: "Don't try to WRITE WELL, and don't *think* about it. Never cultivate a style. If you try to write in some particular clear or limpid way, you won't be natural. And without naturalness, nothing is worth a penny. . . . Make it bare and direct, less conventional and Cissie-esque. What I mean for elimination in serious editorial writing are such colloquial phrases as 'feeling sort of bewildered' when 'bewildered' alone would have done the trick better."

Cissy called him "my old-fashioned darling" but listened respectfully when he told her that cigarette smoking "makes the face sallow, spoils the shape of the mouth, makes the eyes heavy, fills the hair with permanently unpleasant nicotine suggestions, develops a mustache." She soon proudly replied,

"I've sworn off smoking again, as always—in moments of great emotional uppity."

Brisbane was most persistent in urging her to concentrate on increasing the amount of advertising carried by the *Herald.* "Get out those blacksmith diamond bracelets, get out that smile that would melt the Rock of Gibraltar, and CULTIVATE THE ADVERTISERS. You can't get the business any other way; and GO GET IT!"

In the first nine months of 1935, the *Herald* posted the largest gain in advertising of any Washington paper. "The most important news of all," Cissy wrote Brisbane, was the first substantial advertising order from Washington's largest department store, Woodward and Lothrop. She also asked Brisbane's help in persuading General Leonard Wood, then chairman of Sears Roebuck and Company, to channel some of his company's advertising to the *Herald* instead of the *Post.* "I know of no outside consideration, not even the intellectual charm of such a young person as Mrs. Patterson, that would influence your advertising." Brisbane wrote Wood. "But I do know that you advertise to reach PEOPLE, and I think you will be interested in the fact, which I guarantee, and which you might like to confirm through your people in Washington, that the circulation of the Washington *Herald,* in which you do not advertise, averages 96,000 against the Washington *Post,* in which you do advertise, which averages 59,000 gross print."

Cissy soon got her first order for advertising from Sears Roebuck.

Politically, Cissy had become unenthusiastic about Landon's candidacy, and she told Ickes she felt that Roosevelt's reelection was inevitable. She was not, however, wholly happy with Roosevelt, and she was especially disturbed by his Court-packing plan. The Supreme Court had invalidated eleven New Deal laws, crippling FDR's social and economic programs. Before that, in its 140-year history, the Court had nullified only sixty laws. The President attacked the Court, calling it a group of "nine old men," and presented a plan to enlarge it. This proposal caused a congressional fury, and Cissy's friend Senator Wheeler led the fight to defeat it. In this, he had Cissy's support.

Her political quarrels with the President did not affect her friendliness toward Eleanor Roosevelt. The picture retoucher at the *Herald* still had instructions to make Mrs. Roosevelt's pictures as attractive as possible. Cissy gave a party at Dower House for Mrs. Roosevelt and the local women's press corps. It was an informal summer buffet at the swimming pool with entertainment by a group of black spiritual singers Cissy had brought from New York. When Cissy was about to dive in the pool, someone reminded her she was still wearing her pearls. "Oh, I forgot to take them off, but water is good for them." Just before she dove in, she was overheard to say, "Get in there, you indulgent old coot."

She was fifty-four years old then, her body still firm and limber. Eleanor Roosevelt remarked on how youthful she looked in her wide-skirted Indian print dress and garden hat.

The two women were at ease with each other, full of warmth and small jokes, but Cissy knew, better than most, the real Roosevelt story. She knew that Roosevelt had provided an unmarked car at his inauguration for Lucy Mercer, an old love from his days as Assistant Secretary of the Navy. Alice had told her how often she saw Franklin and Lucy together when Eleanor was away from Washington. Cissy also knew about FDR's intimacy with his secretary Missy LeHand. The President told the writer Fulton Oursler that he had thought about writing a mystery story about a rich man who wanted to disappear into a new life: "He's tired, fed up with his surroundings and habits. Perhaps his wife, to whom he's been married for twenty years, now definitely bores him." And Eleanor Roosevelt later told Arthur Schlesinger, Jr., that she once considered writing a novel, to be titled *All Passion Spent,* about a disillusioned wife. Cissy long ago had heard that Roosevelt had asked his wife for a divorce in 1917 in order to marry Lucy. Thinking of their five children, Eleanor reportedly had asked him to wait a year. If he still wanted a divorce then, she would give it to him. In the interim, however, Lucy married.

Eleanor Roosevelt had a White House party for women reporters to which Cissy went. Mrs. Roosevelt acted in a skit in which, dressed as a man, she did a gavotte. Afterward there was a showing of Nancy Cook's "Indiscreet Movies," her home movies of the Roosevelts at play. Nancy Cook was a close friend and Hyde Park neighbor. One film that Cissy knew about, which dated from the time FDR was governor and which was not shown, showed Eleanor Roosevelt horseback riding with a handsome State Trooper escort. The trooper helped Mrs. Roosevelt off her horse, holding her close as she moved slowly into his arms. Cissy was delighted to hear that there had been a romance between the two, that Eleanor had given him the money to buy a house in upstate New York.

"I am always sorry we do not see more of each other," Eleanor wrote Cissy after the White House party.

Cissy's feud with Alice Longworth was almost revived when she heard that Alice had loudly remarked in a fashionable restaurant, "I don't care what they say, I simply *cannot* believe that Eleanor Roosevelt is a lesbian."

Something that whipped up Cissy even more was the battle for custody of the young heiress Gloria Vanderbilt. Adela Rogers St. Johns got copies of the court transcripts from Gloria's mother and brought her to Cissy's house on Dupont Circle. To keep her scoop secret, Cissy converted a whole floor of her house into a makeshift city room with a small staff, complete with copy desk and wire service. No one was allowed to leave the house for the three days it took to write the articles about this case. "Cissy was a riot," said St. Johns. "She was dressed in some kind of flowing robe and looked like some high priestess, floating around giving orders." When the story broke, Cissy struck hard in a front-page editorial:

> With that amazing chameleon-like gift of the American snob, the Vanderbilt clan took unto themselves the distinguishing characteristics of Old World aristocracy. They acquired a sense of special privilege. They became saturated with a thoroughgoing belief in the supremacy of their own particular class and

kind. Now Mrs. Gloria Vanderbilt Whitney, great granddaughter of Ferryman Vanderbilt, is convinced that it is not only her duty but her right to take little Gloria unto herself and away from her mother. For, you see, little Gloria is a Vanderbilt child. To cut short: the odd thing about the whole affair is that Mrs. Whitney and her clan appear to have lost sight of the fact that Gloria Morgan Vanderbilt is the mother of this child. Flesh of her flesh, blood of her blood, bone of her bone. Born of her loins in anguish and fear. If old Ferryman Vanderbilt were alive today, would he not feel pretty disgusted over the whole sorry spectacle? Don't you think he would say, along with the rest of the plain, honest-to-God men and women, "A child belongs to its mother!"

Gloria Vanderbilt was made a ward of the court, custody given to her aunt, Mrs. Harry Payne Whitney. Her mother was given visiting rights. For Cissy, the affair was a reliving of her own fight for her own child, and it made her guilt even greater.

Felicia had not lingered long before going abroad again to work on another novel. She stayed in Sicily for some months before returning to Paris. During a trip to London, she renewed her friendship with Dudley de Lavigne, an Englishman she had met some time before in Washington. He was an insurance broker, the brother-in-law of Viscount Castlerosse, who wrote a gossip column for the London *Sunday Express.* Castlerosse was a member of the social set clustered around the Prince of Wales. Lavigne, whose purse did not match his tastes, was described as "tall, slim and not very energetic." Felicia wrote few letters, and Cissy had mused to Rose, "Has she a new love affair?" When Joe Patterson visited London, he met Dudley. He saw that Felicia did indeed have a serious suitor. Dining alone with her, he warned her, "Now Cissy's bad-tempered and red-headed and a strange genius and she'll cut you off without a red cent if you marry Dudley."

Soon after, Cissy received a cable announcing the marriage in April 1934. She had not been invited to the wedding, and she commented bitterly to Brisbane, "I have never heard this gentleman's name before," adding that she didn't know if he was young or old.

Cissy did go to England to meet Dudley, and the three visited Hearst's estate in Wales for a few days. Cissy was not pleased by the marriage, but she did not cut Felicia's allowance—which was then $40,000 a year, tax free.

Felicia's daughter had a new stepmother in 1935. Drew Pearson had married Luvie Moore Abell, the former wife of his best friend, George Abell. Luvie was tall and elegant with a young son named Tyler. Incensed by her remarriage, Abell took his five-year-old son to the Isle of Sark in Great Britain. Drew and Luvie had traced them and had succeeded in finding the boy and returning him to the United States. After a lengthy legal battle, Luvie and Drew were awarded custody of the child.

Cissy relived her past in all this, and she was drawn to Luvie. The two became fast friends, and Cissy gave her a part-time job as a movie critic. (For one of her first pieces, Luvie faced the viewers instead of the screen and wrote a story about their reactions.) Luvie soon was closer to Cissy than Felicia had ever been. They saw each other almost every day. Cissy visited the Pearsons frequently, and they spent an extended period with her at Dupont Circle while their own house was being renovated.

Drew was still Cissy's unpaid unofficial editorial advisor. By this time, he was also a successful syndicated columnist. He and Robert Allen had capitalized on the popularity of their two *Washington Merry-Go-Round* books by starting a column of the same name. In her gratitude for Drew's help, Cissy featured his column on the *Herald's* editorial page and she hired his brother Leon as a reporter.

For her tenth birthday, Cissy gave her granddaughter, Ellen, a 285-acre farm near Potomac, Maryland, and made Drew the custodian. This became yet another family home for Cissy. She loved little Tyler Abell, and he was one of the few children she kissed and hugged. "She listened to me tell my dumb riddles over and over again," said Tyler, "and she would play with me for hours."

Cissy once gave him a Christmas check for $200 (to which

Luvie vigorously objected). She took him on a tour of her paper. At Dower House she showed him the secret tunnel used as an escape passage during the Civil War.

Cissy wrote Joe that this was her real family. "It's a sand family," he predicted. "It will dissolve in the first storm."

Ellen was a quiet girl, sometimes so withdrawn she almost seemed invisible. Ludwell Denny, a family friend, once saw her on a ship bound for Europe. Accompanied by her governess, she was going to Paris to spend the summer with her mother. She was standing alone at the rail, "the most forlorn girl I ever saw."

Felicia's marriage lasted less than a year. When she cabled Cissy that they had decided on a divorce, Cissy promptly sent her own lawyer to London to handle Felicia's case. "She has behaved very badly and probably will behave worse," Cissy wrote Hearst. "Felicia is, as you know, very devoted to Marion. If Marion were to cable Felicia, just a little word, and something short, about all meeting up in California, I know it would delight her."

"Marion and I are very sorry about Felicia," Hearst replied. "Marion will send message immediately. Of course, be more than delighted to have Felicia here as soon and as long as possible. Personally I don't think it any calamity to be free of that British heel. If Felicia would consult with her Ma and her Step-Pop (that's me), we would choose her a good one."

"Felicia telephoned me from London," Cissy later answered. "My only criticism is that you were too indulgent, and how I loved it." She added that she once again had redecorated Felicia's room for her arrival.

Cissy looked forward to their cross-country trip to California; alone together in the Ranger for several days, she and Felicia would have to talk to each other. But just before leaving, Cissy invited Count Alfred Potocki to join them. It seems likely that she could not face a lengthy confrontation with her daughter, sure to be marked by tension and fury. She had known the Count when she was a bride in Poland and he was a young boy. He was now forty years old, the bachelor heir of Lancut Castle near Warsaw, with its hundred thousand acres. Potocki's presence in the railroad car changed the tone of the trip. There was a feeling of rivalry between the beautiful young daughter and her charming, powerful mother, and some heated arguments ensued. "I felt sorry for Alfred," said Felicia.

The Count courted Felicia for the next few months, and there were many printed rumors about a forthcoming engagement. After the romance cooled, it was said that Cissy had refused to give Felicia a dowry of a million dollars, the sum requested by Potocki. Felicia went to New York, and Brisbane reported: "I had the pleasure of seeing your daughter for a few moments the other day. Howey brought her in and I believe she's going to work for Howey on the *Mirror,* writing about fashions. I think she could do very well." But Felicia was eager to return to Europe. Cissy asked Tom White, Hearst's general manager, to help Felicia get a job on *Harper's Bazaar* in Paris. White did, and Felicia never knew of her mother's involvement.

Before she left for Paris, Felicia joined Cissy and Drew at a family dinner. She left the table before the meal was over, and for once her mother sympathized with her. "Drew sat there like a pouter pigeon," Cissy said. "He had his present and former wives, and each wife's child—not to mention me, his mother-in-law—all looking up to him, the cock of the walk, the goddamned boss of the barnyard."

About this time, Cissy also left a party before the dinner was done. Brisbane was her escort, and her only excuse was that she was "vaguely hurt." He had his own explanation: "It is because you are a lioness without any 'kill' just at this moment, no striped zebra, no nice fat prongbuck, so, in despair, you have to make conversation even with the jackals that follow you around."

Cissy soon found new game to stalk—Thomas Justin White, Hearst's general manager. "I do not know Mr. White very well, although I have met him off and on," she wrote Brisbane. Soon, however, she reported, "If Mr. White calls me Cissy, I shall call him Tom. He is rather pontifical at times, you know."

It was White's job to restore health to the Hearst empire of now twenty-seven newspapers, ten magazines, assorted radio stations and real estate holdings, and a vast art collection. Its staff of 27,000 had an annual payroll of $50 million. Hearst's total debt was now $126 million, and he was seventy-four years old.

Hearst had never fully recovered from his losses in the stock market crash in 1929. But he continued to borrow millions to buy more and more—everything from buildings to armor—and he refused to sell anything. Then the bankers began closing in to collect on their loans.

With the Hearst empire close to bankruptcy, White had to cut budgets, consolidate papers, and eliminate losers. In the process, he and Cissy had crossed swords often and earned each other's respect. White had a round face with strong features; one of his eyes had a slight cast. He was slightly older than Cissy, self-possessed, energetic, and charming with "the loveliest dearest brogue." His mother had come from Dublin to the Chicago World's Fair to exhibit Irish lace. She had brought fourteen-year-old Tom along, and they stayed after the Fair closed. Tom went to a Chicago business college and held a variety of jobs before he became a newsprint salesman for Hearst. His rise in this organization was meteoric. "Mr. White is as fine as they make them," Hearst told Cissy.

"I'm glad that you really like White, and that he likes you," Brisbane wrote Cissy, "because as general manager, his friendly attitude can make it easier for you. . . . I have written to Mr. White, assuring him of your undying etc. etc., and I can do so sincerely from your very friendly remarks concerning him. What I said was, 'I am quite sure that the fair young publisher has no place for you in her black books. In fact, in spite of her highly suspicious nature, I really believe she is a good friend of yours.'"

Hearst invited Cissy and Brisbane to San Simeon, and Cissy answered, "About the trip West, AB will never go with me. But everybody says that Mr. White has great personal charm, and I think he's very dignified." Hearst replied that he had wired White to come West, "and I hope he will meet you in Chicago."

White joined Cissy in her railroad car. "If I had to make a picture illustrating that trip," Brisbane wrote Cissy, "I think I would show a very nice little boa constrictor traveling with a white mouse. If I were a passenger, it would be a gray mouse."

White was no mouse, and he later described the trip as "delightful."

"You will arrive, gaze upward in tender, girlish suppliance into the face of the big bad wolf," Brisbane wrote, describing their arrival at Hearst's Enchanted Hill, "then turn around and walk right out again, hop on the private car, give Tom a big drink of Elmer's rye whiskey that would knock the hind wheel off a Ford car, and settle down to the trip home. . . . I *know* you, but only Dorothy Parker could *describe* you, and I am going to tell her to do it."

This was an affectionate, teasing letter from a man in his seventies, but woven through it was a thread of jealousy. He had spiritually adopted Cissy, and once again she was being pulled out of his orbit. As he predicted, Cissy and White seemed in a hurry to get back to the privacy of their railroad car. They cut their visit short, and Brisbane—who was also a guest—said he had explained their early departure to Hearst. "I thoughtlessly blurted out the truth, namely that you run because you fear my fascinating personality will break down your maidenly reserve." Then he added, "My kindest regards to your little playmate."

"There is only one unhappy thing about your visits to the Hill," Hearst wrote her, "and that is we miss you so much when you go away." Hearst also mentioned that he had heard White had headed East on a train with an "unknown woman." In a short note to Cissy after the trip, White wrote, "Again and again, thanks, thanks, thanks, and a long restful sleep to you."

"For a large man, he is very quick on his feet and I don't know whether I can catch him," Cissy confided to Brisbane. To shorten the race, Cissy leased a suite in the Hearst-owned Ritz Tower in New York. Brisbane wrote that he had told Hearst's son Bill that she had taken this apartment.

Imagine my horror when I saw a strange light come into his eyes, and he remarked, "That's fine. I live there. Tom White lives there, and Jack Neylan always stays there when he comes to

New York. . . ." I said to myself, "Great Heavens, I've thrown my ewe-lamb into a den of tigers, lions and wolves." . . . I heard in my mind a pitiful cry . . . savage woof-woofs at the door of the apartment . . . behind which you cowered. It was all very terrible. Then the scene changed, the door was flung open, a lady with flashing eyes came forth, exclaiming dramatically . . . "Who are you that presume to woof-woof at the door of a great lady editor?" Three minutes later, from the tip-top of the Ritz Tower, there came hurtling through space one tiger—White, one lion—Neylan, one wolf—Bill.

And the lady at her super-grand piano playing Beethoven's soft strains, "When Johnny Comes Marching Home Again, Harrah! Harrah!"

P.S. I am lunching with White next Wednesday. Why don't you lunch with us?

Cissy now found reasons to come to New York more often. When she and Tom found the Ritz Tower too public a meeting place, Cissy rented a house on Gramercy Park. "I am glad you have a house to which you can 'invite your soul,'" Brisbane wrote. "You know what I mean." Then he added, "I do not approve. . . . That is not what I told you." It was Brisbane's way of saying he was jealous of White's sharing Cissy's "love nest."

Brisbane reminded Cissy of the realities of her situation. He and Hearst, and everyone else, would wink at a casual affair with Tom White, but a serious romance would be regarded with grave disapproval. White had a wife and five children, and he was a distinguished Catholic layman, firmly opposed to divorce.

Cissy knew all this and did not care. She even smiled wryly when Brisbane invited her to "supply the intellectual brilliancy, youth, verve, savoir faire and PEP" by joining him and Tom White and Mrs. White for lunch at the Colony. He enclosed some sketches of Cissy looking at Tom, Tom looking at Cissy, Mrs. Tom warily watching the two of them, and Brisbane looking neglected.

During a summer visit to Long Island, Cissy and a friend

were dining in a restaurant when her friend identified a plump, pleasant-looking woman as Mrs. White. Cissy stopped eating. "She was fascinated. She just sat there watching her."

Describing herself to Washington society editor Hope Ridings Miller, Cissy said that she had no intermediate gear: "I'm either in high or I'm in low." When she was in high, when she and Tom were alone together, Cissy entertained him with devastating takeoffs of their friends. A talented mimic, she missed no nuance of a person's behavior or appearance. With the rest of the world, Cissy was often autocratic; with Tom, she was more often a laughing, giggling girl. And Tom kept her laughing. He could cope with both the queen and the girl because his mind was as sharp as hers, his wit as quick. He soon learned her mercurial moods, her quick tears and laughter. She found him wonderfully interesting and amusing.

"You looked better, healthier, more defiant than at any time since I first saw you walking across the field in Chicago when Von Bernstorff was the Apollo Belvedere," Brisbane wrote her. Proposing a dinner in Washington for the three of them, Brisbane promised to "chaperone you both with an efficiency born of desperate jealousy." He wondered, though, about the advisability of sitting between them. "I suppose that both my ankles will be terribly bruised, but what do I care?"

In a moving note, he wrote her, "Take my advice and don't get old." In reply, she sent him a new biography of Benjamin Franklin and pointed out that when Franklin was eighty, "an unfortunate. lady fell passionately in love with him. But he broke her heart with his philanderings."

Although White had a family to look after and the Hearst empire to manage, he played an increasingly important role in Cissy's life. He advised her on the rental of her Sands Point home, her income tax, her newspaper business problems. He sent her books to read and said, "[I am] happy that you do not waste your time on novels, like the very wise person you are." He did think she might dip into *Anthony Adverse* "for fun." He became her representative within the Hearst organization. "I think that, really, Mrs. Patterson will have to select, with Mr. Hearst's approval, her own personnel and handle them in her own way," White wrote Brisbane. "She is perfectly competent to do this, having the talents you so aptly describe for handling men."

Within a short time, White's monogrammed pajamas were neatly folded in the bedroom bureaus at Gramercy Park, Sands Point, Dupont Circle, Dower House, and even Lyford Cay in Nassau, which Cissy rented on a regular basis. Cissy took Tom to Nassau with Walter Howey and Happy Robinson. It was a wicked whim of hers to invite this trio of remarkable men, each of whom was strongly attached to her. It took a lot of liquor to loosen up any spontaneity.

Happy left the group and went to town. "I couldn't sleep because of those goddam waves going back and forth," he said. "The Lady traced me down and asked me why I left the house, and I told her. Then I told her about the Holy Ghosters—you give them some money and they go through all these weird dances—so she went with me to see them. She was out of this world."

Hearst invited her and Tom for another visit. Her railroad car was being serviced, so Hearst sent a plane and pilot for them. Brisbane pictured them flying together over the Rocky Mountains, "he, stern and thoughtful, you with your neck twisted round, looking up in 'simple, touching, girlish diffidence.' On these occasions, he little knows what is in the back of that Cissy head. Sometimes, as my friend says, 'You could be put in jail for what you are thinking.'"

The small plane hit bad weather near the mountains and was forced to crash-land. They were badly shaken but not hurt. "Can you remember the horror of some of your childish nightmares?" Cissy wrote to Brisbane. "Thank God for the deliverance and for the safety of all of you," Hearst wired her. "Please stop flying across the continent. The trip is too long and too tiresome and too damn dangerous. The new trains will cross in two-and-a-half days, comfortably and safely." But after their stay at San Simeon, Cissy insisted on flying back to New York.

Cissy had a birthday party—her fifty-fourth—and Tom sat on her right, in the place of honor, as he always did now. He made the most moving and wittiest toast of the evening. He also read Hearst's birthday greeting. "There is no way I can describe to you how grandly Tom read your beautiful message last night, or how deeply moved we all were." It was a dinner for fifty. Cissy wore ruby velvet lounging pajamas and a brocade jacket with all the warm, rich tones of an old church window—midnight blue, emerald green, bits of gold, and dashes of scarlet. The large cake was trimmed with dozens of ribbons to pull, each enclosing a capsule with a verse about Cissy. When she was a young woman in Paris, a noted photographer had told her, "I *must* take your picture. You know you are not beautiful, but you have *something*." That night, her "something" was in sparkling evidence, heightened by champagne. "The most hypnotically enchanting woman," someone said. That night, as her friends remember, she was particularly sensual and sultry. It was as if she were publicly announcing, "I have finally found a man who wants nothing from me, who loves me for myself alone."

She and Tom decided to go to Europe together in the early fall of 1936. While they planned this trip primarily as a romantic holiday, White did have some business to attend to, and Cissy wanted to write about the Parisian fashions. Brisbane's first response was cool. "I hope you will have a good time and arrange to keep your competitor Eugene Jr. from making any progress while you are gone." Then he became more fatherly: "Have a good trip and let it really do you some good. Don't sit, worrying and chewing the mental rag, and wondering why you are not a combination of Horace Greeley, Northcliffe, Hearst and Tom White all rolled into one. Walk up and down the deck with your shoulders back and get some fresh air. Stay up on the deck ten hours a day. And please see that Tom White does the same, and does not attend to any business on the boat."

The ship was more roomy than a railroad car, and they still had their honeymoon privacy. Felicia then was traveling elsewhere in Europe. In Paris, Tom introduced Cissy to his sister, Carmel Snow, who edited *Harper's Bazaar*. "You will surely fall in love with my brother," Snow said to Cissy.

"Everybody falls in love with my brother Tom." Cissy's rejoinder was quick: "Well, you should meet my brother, Joe."

Bill Bullitt was also in Paris, having been named ambassador to France. His Russian experience had made him bitterly anti-Soviet. Italy had attacked Ethiopia the year before, a rearmed Germany had reoccupied the Rhineland, and Hitler and Mussolini had formed a Rome-Berlin axis. Bullitt, however, was more concerned with the threat of communism than that of fascism. France was home to Bullitt. Ickes had described him as "more French than the French themselves." Cissy and Tom joined him at his chateau in Chantilly, where he had a superb chef and a wine cellar that held 18,000 bottles. While White traveled on business, Bullitt took Cissy to elaborate balls and entertainments. He revived Cissy's memories of their Riviera romance, and then he wooed her again.

Bullitt was in his element, and White was not. Bullitt was the more brilliant and White the warmer of the two. Compared with the sophisticated Bullitt, White seemed like an old shoe. Whenever she compared them, Cissy realized that she far preferred White. But in one important area Bullitt had an edge: while White was married, he was not.

Both White and Bullitt resented Cissy's attempts to play one against the other, like a belle at a prom. White was especially indignant; after all, Cissy had come to Europe with him. Out of all this came a heated argument between Cissy and Tom, so full of fury that she left and went by herself to the country for a few days. When she returned, Tom was gone. "Compared to you, Puck in the Midsummer's Night Dream was an old-fashioned, one-cylinder Cadillac," Brisbane wrote her after hearing of these difficulties.

Bullitt did ask her to marry him. But she knew that if she accepted, she would have to become an ambassador's wife, a sophisticated shadow who would go where he went. And she would have to give up control of the *Herald*. She was not yet ready to do that, for any man. She was flattered, found it difficult to refuse, but had no lingering regrets.

With all her emotional turmoil, Cissy still had a job to do. She threw herself into covering the fashion shows, and her articles were "so far as I know, the first fashion news cabled out of Paris."

She described the taffeta bows looking "like airplane propellers," and the outrageous plaids "smart as the dickens, if you can wear them." She also passed on Chanel's account of the creation of her famous "wraparound." Chanel had a date for the races and no time to sew any buttons on her newly designed coat, so "she had the genius to wrap the coat tightly about her charming figure and hold it in place by the simple process of pressing her little hand upon her tummy."

Cissy and White were back on their old footing soon after her return from Europe. He gave her a malachite sculpture as a peace offering, and she put it in a place of honor, warning her maid, "Don't let anyone break that." But there were still fights. Frank Waldrop once received an emergency call to come to Dupont Circle. He found Cissy and Tom in opposite corners of the room, not talking to each other. "Frank," said Cissy curtly, "will you please tell Mr. White that . . ." and she gave him her message. "You can tell your publisher . . ." answered Tom. And so it went all evening.

Roosevelt was reelected in a landslide in 1936; Landon got the electoral votes of only Maine and Vermont. Despite her reservations, Cissy had supported Roosevelt. She still agreed with most of FDR's domestic policies, and was surely influenced by her brother's still-ardent support of Roosevelt. The end of the Depression was still not in sight. At his second inaugural, Cissy heard FDR state that one third of the nation was "ill-housed, ill-clad, ill-nourished." Frank Waldrop was surprised to find Cissy reading a well-thumbed copy of a new book on economics by J. M. Keynes.

Germany's Max Schmeling that year defeated Joe Louis for the world's heavyweight boxing championship, but the black American Jesse Owens evened the score at the Olympic Games in Berlin by winning four gold medals. A popular song was "Pennies From Heaven," and a hit Broadway play was *You Can't Take It With You.*

Thrown out of a nightclub for being drunk and noisy, Cissy and Tom conceived an elaborate plan to stage a fake police raid at the club. Brisbane vetoed it because "it occurred to me that you might get excited and kill somebody."

Back at the paper, she was the one threatened with death. Ray Helgeson had separated from his young wife, Kitty. Cissy was incensed and offered to take in her and their baby. "Cissy even offered to adopt us," said Kitty. Helgeson had been drinking more heavily, and he was becoming more erratic and violent. When a girl reporter refused to date him, he drove his car onto the sidewalk in an attempt to run her down. A compulsive gambler, he was so deeply in debt to other gamblers, and so afraid of them, that he carried a gun.

Cissy was furious at Helgeson, almost fired him, and finally transferred him to the sports department. It was as if she had drained the life out of him. Now he almost slunk through the hallways. One day, after drinking heavily, he barged into Cissy's office, pointing his gun at her and saying, "I'm going to kill you."

Cissy stared at him. "You haven't the nerve," she said quietly. "Now get out." He wavered, then left. But Cissy was wrong about his nerve. He did use the gun years later—to kill himself.

Despite his growing debt, Hearst had added two floors to the Times-Herald building, so that each paper could have separate quarters. Cissy now had a more sumptuous office suite, which included a private bathroom. She occasionally came to work directly from a horseback ride and would then shower while her maid laid out fresh clothes. When she wanted absolute privacy, Cissy would lock herself in the bathroom; her secretary would slip important messages under the door.

Hearst was always urging her to visit him. "You are such a wonderful businesswoman that I feel sure you will have cleaned up your desk and be ready to take a rest. At any rate, we want to see you out here even if the darn old paper goes to rack and ruin." When she made changes in the paper's layout or content, she always informed Hearst, saying, "I am entirely responsible for these changes. If you don't like them, please don't scold anyone but me." He seldom scolded. "As a matter of fact," he wrote her, "I nearly always agree with you, which must mean that we both have very good judgment on newspaper matters."

Earlier that year, she and Brisbane had given Hearst a Rolls-Royce for his birthday. "You are very bad, both of you, after the prudent way I brought you up, to go and get your grandfather such a magnificent car. It is a marvel. . . . Everything on the ranch now is going to be geared up to match the car. . . . If I go busted, it will be trying to live up to my new and beautiful possession."

Tom and Brisbane told Cissy how close to being busted Hearst was in 1936. She tried to help in unobtrusive ways. She made her railroad car always available to him: "The windows have been washed and the carpets have been cleaned, and the beds, which were always too short, have been made longer."

Brisbane still pouted when Cissy went to New York to see Tom without seeing him too. "You were in New York; you saw TOM." But Cissy still saw much of Brisbane. They went to a prizefight together, and he was delighted when she stood on a wooden chair and yelled. She drew a sketch of him which he criticized: ". . . too much forehead, not enough chin . . . we always want what we haven't got." He was always sensitive to her moods. "You sounded cross and a little tired last night on the telephone. Has something come up to worry you?" He was still an unsparing editor. She was hurt when he suggested cutting a paragraph out of a story she had written, "but I must confess it makes a better story." He was most grateful when she gave a formal party for his young son at Dupont Circle. Sixty-five young people were invited, and Cissy sat on the balcony, peering down at them through the potted palms.

Brisbane went abroad with Hearst and Marion Davies in the winter of 1936. Hearst was irritated because Cissy would not accompany them, but she did not want to leave either the *Herald* or Tom. On December 12, Brisbane wrote Cissy that he was seventy-two years old that day "and am trying to think of something I can do that will be worthwhile, assuming as I do that I shall last sometime longer. Success after seventy-two is not impossible and it would set a good example. . . . There is no old age except when you lose your independence."

Cissy went to New York to greet Hearst, Davies, and

374

Brisbane on their return from Europe. As always, Marion had many stories to tell. In London, "everybody was talking about Wally Simpson, Wally Simpson, everything was Wally Simpson." She had met the new King, Edward VIII, at a party: "Charming. I have to say that; he really was." One of his close friends had told her about the King and Wally: "He's madly in love with her—he'll never be in love with anybody else—very soon they're going to be married." Marion had rushed back to the hotel and told "Pops" her news, and he had called New York immediately to tell them to prepare for the marriage story. "I was a little previous," Marion said now. Then, on December 11, 1936, the abdication speech. "I must say, I did cry," said Marion. "I couldn't help it. I almost made a river. 'The woman I love.' . . . It was so wonderful." The Duke of Windsor married Wallis Simpson six months later.

Cissy remembered Wallis Simpson as a sleek woman who had stayed with her aunt in Washington in the spring of 1934. She had gone to the parties at the F Street Club—a very chic, very private club—and Cissy regarded her as an "adventuress." Cissy felt sorry for the former king, whom she had met when he was the Prince of Wales.

Marion told of going to Germany to see Hitler. Hearst had asked him why the German Government had adopted an anti-Semitic policy. Hitler answered that there was no persecution of any sort in Germany. But Marion told Cissy of the signs forbidding Jews from entering shops: "Juden Verboten"; they reminded her of the notices she had seen when she was a little girl: "No Irish Need Apply."

Marion and Hearst had visited Winston Churchill, and he had showed her his pond with his swans, white and black. Two of them started fighting, which was "horrifying because one grabs the other by the throat." Trying to get them to stop, Churchill threw stones at them, cursing them. But the fight did not end until one had killed the other.

Cissy and Marion traded all kinds of stories that night, with some sentiment and much champagne since it was Christmas Eve. Hearst was with his advisors, getting critically bad financial news about his empire. Early next morning, Cissy telephoned Marion, her voice hoarse with grief. "A.B. just died," she said. "About four o'clock."

"Good Lord, Cissy, aren't we in enough trouble. Better not say anything to W.R."

But Hearst had picked up an extension and had heard the news. "He's crying like a baby," Marion whispered over the phone. She persuaded Hearst that there was nothing he could do, that she and Cissy would go directly to the Brisbane home.

Brisbane's wife greeted Cissy and Marion, asking, "Would you have some sherry?" Then, "Would you like to see Arthur?"

"So we went in," Marion said afterward, "and here he was, just the way he died, with an encyclopedia right in front of him. He'd been reading the encyclopedia. He's just lying there, dead, and he's got the book right there. And they're sitting around and drinking. Irish wake, practically."

Once out of the house, Marion said to Cissy, "Let's go down to '21' and get plastered." And they did.

Cissy had lost more than a father. He had been her cheering squad, her hard critic, her anchor, her "old-fashioned darling." He had worried about her drinking, her love life, her moods, her happiness. He had been a loving friend who wanted nothing from her and everything for her, and no one would ever take his place.

She and Marion both felt the funeral was "revolting." The church filled with a sea of celebrities, dozens of photographers taking pictures while the service was going on. "I'm getting a little sick," Marion whispered, "I think I have to go home." Cissy's voice was grim and firm, "No. Wait until it's all over." The two took a long walk afterward. "This is like a fantastic story you read but didn't believe," said Marion. They decided they didn't want to get drunk again; they wanted to go home.

At the funeral, Hearst had looked like a beaten man. Brisbane once had said of him, "I can't stand being around him very much. . . . He is too exciting." Now he was an old man faced with financial ruin, caught in the midst of a complicated power play by his closest executives. Tom told Cissy that some of the banks had joined forces with several Hearst employees—whom he and Hearst had long regarded as trusted friends—and were maneuvering to force Hearst into bankruptcy. They then intended to take control as trustees.

Hearst and Marion returned to California, and during the next months he was forced toward bankruptcy. But his opponents had not taken Marion's loyalty and feistiness into account.

"They knew they had him all sewn up as far as his bank account was concerned," Marion later confided to Cissy. "They didn't figure on me. They said they needed an immediate million dollars to stave off bankruptcy. The old story of me running around with a sable coat over a nightgown in the middle of the night—that was no joke."

She called up her business manager, "Get me a million dollars right away. . . . I want to sell everything I've got— everything."

That afternoon at five, her agent came to Marion's studio with a certified check for a million dollars. She gave the check to Tom White. He stared at it and said gruffly: "God bless you."

But the bankers were not finished. After a round of meetings, they insisted another million was needed. Marion called Cissy, and she immediately dispatched a check for this amount. "I admit I must be one of the grandest men in the world to have such a grand friend," Hearst wrote her. Cissy wanted no interest on the money she had advanced, but Hearst insisted on paying 5 percent.

Tom told Cissy how indecisive Hearst had become, that he had almost sold his magazines to Joe Kennedy but that Marion had stopped him. Hearst's disastrous experience had a traumatic effect on Cissy. This man, whose power had seemed beyond her imagination, was being pushed aside. His treasures were being auctioned, and he had, in effect, been put on an allowance. She suddenly wanted out of it all. "I have grown too old and tired to work anymore," she wrote Hearst, "so will you please accept my resignation effective immediately." But when she reread what she had written, she crossed it all out; she never sent this letter, but she kept it with her personal papers.

Hearst wrote Cissy a short note: "She [Marion] just loves you, and I do, too—whisper." The words "I do, too" were written smaller than the opening of the sentence, and the word "whisper" was tinier still. The word "love" was one he rarely used.

The $2 million raised by Cissy and Marion simply staved off immediate disaster. The only cure for the crisis was liquidation and consolidation on a massive scale. While White was administering this radical remedy, he and Cissy talked seriously about her buying the *Herald*. She wanted it badly now. Tom knew that Hearst had to dispose of both the *Herald* and the *Times*. Cissy was not interested in the *Times*, but she told Tom what he already knew: she felt more and more that the *Herald* belonged to her, and she wanted him to help make it truly hers.

Tom White woke Cissy in the middle of the night early in 1937 with a phone call. Hearst's financial situation was again so desperate that he was considering Eugene Meyer's offer of some $600,000 for the *Herald*.

Meyer's offer was not solicited, and Hearst had not yet discussed it with Cissy. Cissy telephoned Hearst at three o'clock in the morning, crying, "Mr. Hearst, please don't sell it to Eugene."

"What do you want me to do?"

"Let me have it. I'll even take both papers. Let me lease them."

"O.K., Cissy. Tell my lawyers what you want them to do, and I will tell them to do it."

She wrote Hearst:

I love you—I love you because you have given me the happiest and most interesting time of my life. I love you because you have had the patience and the care and the kindness to uphold me always—from the very beginning when I didn't know which way to take the next step.

Joe Patterson says you are the greatest newspaper genius the world has ever known. So, of course, I would love you for this reason, if for no other. But, aside from this reason, and aside from that, I think I would love you anyhow. I love you.

When you don't use the owner's money, you are obliged to use your brains. Brains, not money, make a paper.

—Arthur Brisbane to Cissy

"Sometimes, at the end of a long, drawn-out and difficult struggle, when you suddenly win your point, you feel sort of flat and let down. Maybe I should, but I don't feel that, way down," Cissy wrote to Hearst in an open letter on the *Herald* front page on July 21, 1937. "You have contended for a long time that the responsibility of the management of your two papers . . . would prove too heavy a burden for me. But I have stubbornly believed that I could prove to you that I was right and you were wrong. . . . Well, these past seven years have passed like a dream—the grandest and most brilliant adventure of my life. But these last seven years, I hope, will pale before the next five."

At Tom White's direction, Cissy had been offered and had signed a five-year lease on both the *Herald* and the *Times,* with an option to buy both papers. The *Times* offered another challenge when she decided to make it an even more personal paper than the *Herald,* with many more columnists. (She had asked Ickes to find a New Deal supporter to take the *Times* from her, but he had had no success in this search.)

Cissy did not believe that money was something to be thrown off the back of trains. She didn't like to gamble, because she didn't like to lose. While she could spend vast sums impulsively, she also saved old envelopes to use as scratch paper.

"I must admit I have learned the difference between the gay and delightful editorial side and the grim business side," she told an interviewer. "It was all delightful before. All I had to do was build up circulation, and anything I wanted was at Mr. Hearst's expense. I must say he was always very generous. But now things are paid for out of my own dollars and cents. It is an eternal struggle to make income balance expenditures."

On the problem of being a woman publisher, she said, "Men are not at all sensitive about taking a woman's money, but they don't like to work for her. Sometimes one can overcome this by persuasion, sometimes it takes violent methods, but the woman must not let herself be licked."

Cissy went on to state that American women had learned that laws passed in Washington could change the tenor of their lives—the taste of the things they ate, the texture of the things they wore. Women had become especially interested in legislation banning child labor and laws protecting the consumer, "including adequate food, drug and cosmetic laws." Cissy wanted to arouse all her women readers by showing them how national and international events affected their homes and families. Someday, she said, women might get aroused enough to elect a woman President.

Cissy's relationship with the reelected Roosevelt was still good but no longer glowing. He had sent a gracious message to be read at her annual dinner for her 1,200 newsboys. "When your picture was thrown on the screen, a great big yell went up which shook the walls and dropped bits of plaster from the ceiling," Cissy wrote him. "But when your message appeared, the roof flew off—and so far as we know hasn't been located since." As a postscript, she added: "You remember the Dower House, don't you, Mr. President? It's as lovely as ever it was. Maybe in the Spring, would you drive out some day?" The President replied that he would like to go out to the Dower House "when the nice weather starts."

Hearst had not only urged Landon to run against Roosevelt, but he had also stated publicly that "the race will not be close at all. Landon will be overwhelmingly elected and I'll stake my reputation as a prophet on it." With the idea of healing wounds, Cissy arranged a meeting between Roosevelt and Hearst. Hearst was invited for a White House weekend. Marion Davies was not invited and planned to stay with Cissy. Cissy had a party for them the night before the weekend, a dinner for 50 with 200 more invited for dancing and a midnight supper. "By one o'clock, the ribbon clerks were all out of it, and things really got going." After drinking so much "she almost fell down the stairs," Marion finally went to bed at eight in the morning. "Of course I had an awful hangover," she remembered. Hearst later told Cissy that the White House was drafty and he had slept poorly there. He said the President was charming, but they had disagreed on some issues.

Roosevelt showed his old ebullience at the annual Gridiron dinner. He said he had read the newspapers avidly during the past campaign.

In a great serial which ran for several months in the papers, one of the characters bore the name of Franklin D. Roosevelt. Whether this character was to be a hero or a villain I could not at first make out. But as that magnificent work of imagination developed, I decided that this character Roosevelt was a villain. He combined the worst features of Ivan the Terrible, Machiavelli, Judas Iscariot, Henry VIII, Charlotte Corday and Jesse James. . . .

He was reelected and the great 1936 campaign serial turned out to have a most surprising ending. On the morning of November fourth the editors decided that this villain was, after all, a reasonable person. He was deluged with editorial advice— suave advice, friendly advice, advice based on the apparent assumption that this man was really a reincarnation of a cross between Little Eva and Simple Simon.

Cissy laughed heartily at the President's sardonic comments about the press. Months afterward, she had a long private meeting with him at the White House. Roosevelt again complained about inaccuracy in news stories, and she asked him for a specific example. "Look," he said, picking up a copy of the *Herald,* "Pearson and Allen say I like Danish pastry. I don't! I *never eat it!*" They then discussed what measures were necessary to put business back on its feet.

After Cissy remarked that she thought the country was still caught in the grip of fear, Roosevelt told her, "Write out exactly what you think I could say that would banish fear. I dare you."

She took him at his word, and in an Open Letter published on the front page of the *Herald,* she wrote:

> You said once with eternal truth, that the only thing to fear is fear itself. Fear is depressing industry. With due respect, you should concede the obvious. The fear is the fear of you. . . . It is the fear that, if you work out a conservative plan, you won't stay put. It is the fear that if a plan of yours is proved bad, you will stick to it stubbornly because you are unwilling to admit that, like the rest of us, you make mistakes.
>
> You should inform the American people that proud—as you should be proud—of the great moral and social advances which have been made under your leadership, you are willing now to consolidate these and attempt no more until your Cabinet, your Congressional leaders and you agree that the nation can foot the bill.
>
> You should announce that your only effort will be to raise the national income without devaluation. . . . You should explain that, in order to do this, you and your administrative circle will refrain from favoritism toward any economic groups, disturbing speeches, sudden and new proposals to Congress and attacks on groups and individuals who happen to disagree with or criticize you. You should set a high example by clearing your mind of private hates. . . . You should let administrative silence "like a

poultice come to heal the blows of sound" and permit industry to go to work in an atmosphere of peace and security. . . .

But the chief thing is to eliminate fear and thus restore confidence. You alone can do that. But you must do it thoroughly, forsaking hate and vanity, and resuming that patience with which you so nobly and courageously conquered an illness that would have broken the spirit of most of us.

This Open Letter was widely reprinted throughout the United States, particularly in the Hearst press. When she was interviewed by *Editor & Publisher,* a smiling Cissy said, "I suppose it was very fresh of me to write it. Do you think he'll be mad at me?"

A mutual friend later told Cissy that the President had said, "It's a good letter, but you know she didn't write it." This infuriated Cissy.

Cissy, then, still generally agreed with Roosevelt on major policies. So did Joe. He had enthusiastically supported FDR's reelection in 1936 and even approved Roosevelt's efforts to enlarge the Supreme Court. In the summer of 1937, the *News* ran a ballot asking its readers if they wanted a third term for Roosevelt; the paper happily reported a 2-TO-1 vote in the President's favor. While Joe remained a staunch isolationist, he had no quarrel as yet with the President on this issue. Like Roosevelt, he believed that the country must have a powerful navy and a strong defense system. Joe foresaw the war with Japan and urged the Administration to prepare for it.

Bertie McCormick had broken early with Roosevelt. While he praised FDR for his handling of the banking crisis in 1933, he soon viewed the New Deal as a domestic disaster. The *Tribune* grew increasingly critical, and even vituperative, calling Roosevelt a "dictator." In the 1936 election, McCormick warned that a Landon defeat meant "doomsday." The *Tribune* headline on election morning read: "Last Day to Save Your Country."

To his secretary, FDR was a kind, gentle man; to the American people, he was a calm man at the fireside who radiated hope; but to his enemies, he was a formidable and ruthless foe. Cissy knew his darker side, but she was not afraid of his anger. When she felt strongly about something, she acted. And, determined to prevail, she would take on any opponent.

Early in Roosevelt's second term, Cissy became embroiled in a heated dispute with the President about Washington's cherry trees. President Taft's wife had directed the planting of the first hundred cherry trees near the Tidal Basin. When they died, a noted Japanese chemist replaced them with three thousand trees as a gift from Japan. Cissy loved these trees, and she was incensed to learn that FDR had picked the Tidal Basin for the site of the Jefferson Memorial. This construction would mean the destruction of several hundred cherry trees, and she accused the President of "the worst desecration of the beauty of our capital since the burning of the White House by the British." She alerted all the community groups from the Chamber of Commerce to assorted women's clubs, and she headed a delegation of three dozen that intended to make a direct plea to the President to save the trees.

Unable to see Roosevelt, they sang a chorus of "Trees" to the Presidential secretary, marched to the Tidal Basin, and physically overpowered the workmen who had started digging. They then refilled some of the excavations and chained themselves to the threatened trees.

FDR laughingly told his morning press conference that a hoisting device might be used to lift the trees (and the ladies chained to them) and move them to new holes elsewhere "all to be done in a strictly humane manner." No longer smiling, he bitingly accused a local publisher—without naming names—of "flimflamming" the public just to raise circulation. Only 88 trees were involved, he said, not hundreds. Answering in her usual front-page editorial, Cissy quoted an Interior Department report listing the total as 585 trees. An adjoining cartoon labeled "Flimflam policies" showed a disreputable figure representing Roosevelt saying: "All right, so we *lied* to you—so what? And we're cutting down your damn cherry trees."

As her final emissary, Cissy sent Evie Robert to plead with FDR. The wife of Lawrence "Chip" Robert, the Assistant Secretary of the Treasury, Evie was the darling of the Democrats, the glamour girl of the New Deal, and a Roosevelt favorite. When FDR saw Evie, he said, "Oh, Evie, I'm so glad you came. All day people have been calling about those trees, and I'm delighted you're here for a social visit."

When Evie tried to bring up the threatened cherry trees, FDR skillfully turned the conversation to other subjects. As she left, Roosevelt smiled and said, "Have you seen my dearest friend lately?" (Since Cissy's "Fear" editorial, the President had referred to her as "my dearest friend.") Evie reported all this to Cissy, and Cissy smiled ruefully. "He always was smart," she said.

Roosevelt won the battle, and the trees came down. But he paid a price; Cissy did not forget her defeats easily.

Cissy most enjoyed people who were both unorthodox and unpredictable, and she and Evie became inseparable. If Cissy envied Evie's youthful beauty and brass, Evie was genuinely fond of Cissy and admired her power.

A *Herald* story described Evie as the most beautiful blonde in Washington, "tall, slender, with smooth shining hair, the color of ripe corn. Her eyes are large and blue, with black lashes and brows. Her features are Grecian in their perfection." Cissy delightedly informed everyone that Evie had "the morals of a mink" and would bed with any man. It was said that Evie had once been called to testify as a character witness. She was told that the opposition lawyer had a list of 165 men with whom she had supposedly had affairs. "Why, if that were true," said Evie, "I would never have had time to train my dog Coco."

One of Evie's most publicized parties was given for her horse, John the Baptist. The horse's stall was done up in flowers and ribbons, and a band played "Happy Birthday." Guests were invited to bring children and pets. Alice Longworth was there, and so was Cissy with her granddaughter and her white poodle, Lily Langtry—which Felicia had given her. Everybody brought presents.

If Evie was beautiful and hard, with an unending supply of unprintable stories, Ann Smith was beautiful and soft—and a listener. Ann was a neighbor of Cissy's in Upper Marlboro, where she had been born and bred. Her mother had died when she was very young, and Ann regarded Cissy not only as a mother figure but also as the woman she most admired. She even named one of her daughters Eleanor "Cissy" Patterson Smith. Both Evie and Ann were younger than Felicia. Ann was the adoring daughter Cissy had always wanted, while Evie symbolized the young version of another side of Cissy. Cissy was careful to keep the two young women apart. Evie and Ann became essential to Cissy. They were more than friends. They were confessors, they were stabilizers, they recharged her emotional batteries.

Most of the several dozen women who worked for Cissy were attractive as well as talented. Cissy knew their backgrounds, their habits, their problems. "It was like living under a monarchy," said Jackie Martin. "She looked after you and took good care of you. But in return you were expected to give not only a hundred percent loyalty, but not to have any rights of your own, to exist apart from her in any real sense. It was almost like owning someone."

Cissy didn't believe adults should have their tonsils removed. When a young woman reporter told her that her doctor had recommended this procedure for her, Cissy was indignant and refused to let her do it. The young woman's brother finally appeared in Cissy's office and banged his fist on her desk. "My sister *is* going to have her tonsils out and you're *not* going to stop her!"

Knowing that a young woman writer was in desperate need of diversion, she assigned her to cover the nightclubs. "Betty, now we'll see you with a Bird of Paradise in your hair." When that didn't help, Cissy offered to finance a trip to Vienna to a psychiatrist she knew. When another female reporter had an alcohol problem, Cissy paid for her cure, finally putting her on a pension. She called her women employees "my ravishing little characters" and invited many of them to her parties. But Cissy never forgot who was boss. "You could get close to her sometimes, but not too close because then you were on treacherous ground," said a woman who worked for her.

Time magazine took notice of the growing number of women on Cissy's papers and headlined an article "Cissy's Henhouse."

Cissy was enraged. The only woman on *Time*'s Washington Staff was Mary Johnson, and Cissy decided that she must have written the piece. She found a picture of Johnson in a scanty costume singing "My Heart Belongs to Daddy" at a National Press Club dinner. She printed the picture with the caption "Her Heart Belongs to Daddy" and the headline "Henry Luce's Poulette." Cissy wrote: "Mary doesn't stop at being a cute little trick. She is a wise little guy besides and knows her onions. So when she turned in a story, which even her good friend Arthur Krock now regrets as false, malicious and untrue, she knew what she was doing. But let us not censure this charming child too severely for dishonest reporting. If Her Heart Belongs to Daddy, so does her typewriter. And if she doesn't write as she is told, she loses her job. . . . You know how it is."

Frank Waldrop told Cissy that in using her power to ruin a defenseless girl, she had been like an eagle going for a butterfly. In fact, Mary Johnson had nothing to do with the article. She had been away skiing when it was written by a male colleague. Luce sent a note to Johnson that he was flattered by Cissy's estimation of his charm and power. And half a dozen lawyers, who had been battered by Cissy at one time or another, eagerly approached Mary about a libel suit. Mary, however, followed Krock's advice and let the scandal die quietly. Realizing that she had been wrong, Cissy felt guilty about her actions for years.

What had enraged Cissy about the story was that some of her friends felt it implied that she was a lesbian and the *Herald* was her harem.

Her staff was not surprised; rumors about Cissy and romantic involvements with women had been circulating for years. Pointed comments had been made about her relationship with her picture editor, Jackie Martin. Jackie made no secret of her own feelings. "Well, men don't ask me out so I go out with women. They're just more available." She and Cissy went together to the theater, concerts, and dinners and spent weekends at Lyford Cay, Dower House, and Sands Point. Jackie was one of the few regularly invited to Cissy's small dinners and parties. The staff knew that Cissy gave Jackie lavish gifts, including several fur coats and even a Cadillac. Jackie confided to a reporter that Cissy had offered to build her a house near hers on Dupont Circle. Everyone on the paper knew that Jackie and Cissy often dined together alone in her Dupont Circle bedroom.

One of Jackie's assistants delivered a copy of the morning paper to Cissy's house late one night. The next morning he reported to some of the staff that he had walked quietly into the room and found Cissy and Jackie in an ardent embrace. Two days later, he was fired.

Jackie and Cissy did have their open fights, and Jackie often threatened to quit. Cissy once stormed into the art office and demanded to know who had picked out the pictures she was holding. Told that Jackie was responsible, Cissy blurted, "Well, sometimes she picks pictures like she picks her nose." In leaving, Jackie said, "I couldn't take it any longer. . . . I guess it just didn't work. I carry away no grievances." One of the more cynical staff members said, "Why should she care about Jackie when she's got Evie."

Given Cissy's curiosity and loneliness, it is not unlikely that she did experiment with lesbianism. She had the *Herald* sponsor a teenage beauty contest, and it was remarked that Cissy was always there to help the young girls dress and undress.

"We talked about it openly among us," said one of the women reporters, discussing Cissy's possible lesbianism. "It was a kind of common knowledge and we all had the feeling that it was true, but how do you know about things like that?"

Cissy did have a preoccupation with beauty. She ordered a series of articles, "Beauty and the Past," about the beautiful women in history. She also began a series called "The Eternal Triangle." "I wrote that for years," said Betty Brennan, "and on every kind of combination of love. Before I was finished, I was down to rabbits."

Cissy later assigned Brennan to another series; she gave her a copy of her novel *Fall Flight* and told her to use it as a pattern for articles about the private life of a Washington girl. She also gave Bob Considine a volume of Maupassant's tales and told him to write fictional stories about government girls, using the French author's plots.

Many of these articles were for the *Times*. Cissy dressed up the *Times* in a new format; she assigned her best writers, many of them women, to the paper and ran a number of her pet features in it. She started a column of housekeeping hints, and although it carried the byline of her housekeeper, Mrs. Sibilla Campbell, many of the articles were dictated by Cissy herself while she was in the bathtub. Her Ranger steward, Alonzo, was called on to provide a recipe column. His specialty was boned chicken under glass, but the first column featured fried bananas, a favorite with Cissy. (She liked to make fried bananas and chicken, flamed with brandy, for special friends.) She fired Alonzo when she discovered him lavishly entertaining his friends on the Ranger with her caviar and champagne, and his cooking column was replaced by one signed by her black cook Rebecca. When Rebecca left, Cissy hired a French chef but fired him when she discovered he had filled the kitchen shelves with canned soups.

Cissy never lost the gnawing fear that everybody wanted something from her. When she found someone who didn't, she would hold him or her close. "If I woke up one morning and found I had nothing left," she told her neighbor Rhoda Christmas, "you would be the first person I would call." Rhoda had first impressed Cissy by curing Cissy's horse of a kidney disease. When Cissy asked for a bill, Rhoda replied, "You don't send bills to neighbors." Cissy afterward persuaded Rhoda to write a column on horses. Cissy issued strict orders about Rhoda's column: it was never to be dropped from the paper, for any reason. One editor who disobeyed this rule was fired.

Someone else who wanted nothing from Cissy but her friendship—and whom Cissy also hired to write a column—was Evalyn Walsh McLean. McLean was a Washington institution, known for her kind heart, Hope diamond, and extravagant parties.

"What will I do?" she once asked Alice Longworth. "I simply can't get my budget below $250,000 a year. Flowers, $40,000; household, $100,000; travel, $35,000. . . ." Alice considered

Evalyn's carefully itemized expenses and replied, as it was expected of her: "Evalyn, you are quite right. You simply can't shave it one cent."

Evalyn's house, Friendship, was a large yellow *palazzo* in northwest Washington. Her dining room seated a hundred, and a thousand guests could dance in her ballroom. Attendance at her regular Sunday night parties averaged over three hundred. Evalyn entertained in a lavish style; she once had five thousand yellow roses flown from England for a party. Her guests included everybody from Calvin Coolidge to Walter Winchell. One British ambassador, Lord Halifax, said, "I shall always be indebted to Mrs. McLean; in her house I have met half the persons of influence who have become my friends in Washington."

McLean kept all her seating plans and menus on file so that she could avoid duplication. Cissy was always invited, always seated between the most interesting men. Among her dinner partners were movie producer D. W. Griffith, Supreme Court Justice William Douglas, Senator Robert Taft, FBI Director J. Edgar Hoover, Father Edmund Walsh, Alfred DuPont, heavyweight champion Gene Tunney, ambassador to Russia Joseph Davies, General Omar Bradley, and Senator Alvin Barkley. Cissy preferred sitting next to her old friends such as Senator Hiram Johnson and Senator Burton K. Wheeler.

Many Washingtonians were amused when Cissy hired Evalyn McLean to write a column. Evalyn herself thought it "an awful waste of white paper. . . . It seems a bit fantastic that Cissy, who has accomplished so much good and done such wonderful things with her newspaper should be willing to allow such waste." But Cissy knew exactly what she was doing. The skinny, overdressed, unbeautiful Evalyn soon had a large readership. Everybody always wanted to know about the Hope diamond, and she wrote:

It is not a white diamond, but a very dark blue, almost black. The peculiar thing about the Hope diamond is that it doesn't require different lights. If you put it directly under any light, and keep it there, you can see it change, sometimes getting darker and sometimes getting a greenish color. I personally am not afraid of the Hope diamond, but I always warn my friends not to touch it. It is a strange and fearful thing how many people who have touched it have had unnatural and a great many times horrible deaths soon afterwards. . . . I am sitting back on the sidelines letting the curse and the blessing fight it out together.

The curse often won, even with Evalyn: her husband died in an insane asylum; a young son was killed by a car; a daughter committed suicide.

Evalyn was younger than Cissy but looked older. She had large, bulging, dark-gray eyes, which were almost always covered by blue glasses. She had a harsh, croaking voice, and she talked loudly. She said what she wanted when she wanted to. At a dinner at her home, the famed Father Walsh sat on her right. He was the head of Georgetown University, the developer of the Foreign Service Academy, the author of many books. Evalyn suddenly pulled off the wig she was wearing, scratched her short, thin, dyed hair, and said in her loud voice, "Father Walsh, goddammit, you lied to me." The long table fell quiet; Father Walsh calmed her down, and nobody ever learned what the "lie" was.

Evalyn drank excessively and took drugs. In one of her columns, she quoted an entry from her diary, written when she was fourteen: "I feel utterly and hopelessly alone. I am too desperate to go on. Where can I turn for help?" She had lost none of this desperation, and Cissy introduced her to Dr. Barach. "She drank so much she would weave instead of walk," said Barach. "Cissy told her I would help her stop drinking, and I did, for a time. As part of the therapy, we would drive in her chauffeured limousine to several saloons, and I admired her courage. There she would sit in a tough waterfront saloon wearing her Hope diamond. She and Cissy had that same courage—it was a bond between them."

A greater bond was their mutual dependency. They were friends, they were peers, they trusted each other, they wanted only each other's love. They knew each other's secrets, shared each other's heartaches. They both had hot tempers, but they both knew how to laugh at themselves after a fight, Evalyn calling herself "an old Irish woman" and Cissy referring to herself as "a shanty-Irish bitch." Cissy was smarter, more aggressive; Evalyn was softer, more trusting.

Evalyn took off the Hope diamond only when she went to bed, and it rested on her night table while she slept. She kept a fortune in jewels in a suitcase under her bed and pulled it out to show special guests. "All those emeralds and diamonds . . . emeralds like sparrow eggs." When Cissy chided her about carelessness, Evalyn opened a drawer and showed her a gun.

Cissy once had remarked how typical it was of Evalyn to have a $3,000 bedspread and an unpainted toilet seat. It was also typical of Evalyn later during the war to stop her weekly society parties and invite only enlisted men and women from the armed services.

Evalyn thrived on drama and excitement. When the Lindbergh baby was kidnapped, she attempted to contact the abductors. She met in her home with a man who fraudulently claimed to know where the baby was. She paid him $100,000 as the ransom. The money was never recovered. Before the transaction, she had stationed the Poe sisters, two reporters for the *Post*, behind the draperies with guns.

Elizabeth and Vyella Poe, who were proud of being direct descendants of Edgar Allen Poe, looked like staid maiden aunts, and they carried stickpins and vials of pepper to forestall rapists. They were two of the best reporters in Washington, and Cissy offered them each a thousand-dollar bonus to leave the *Post* for the *Herald*. They didn't take her offer seriously until they returned home one evening to find two packages on the hall table, each containing a thousand dollars in small bills. They switched to Cissy.

If a man had been murdered on the steps of the Washington *Post*, many Washingtonians believed that the crime would have been reported first in the *Herald*. Cissy had created a competitive, aggressive atmosphere in her city room. "It was ridiculous but wonderful," said Mason Peters, one of her editors. "It was filled with more bustle than any news could possibly justify. . . . Everybody milling around with the hub-bub going."

Part of the excitement came from the feeling of living under the gun. When Cissy said, "Jump," everybody asked, "How high?" She would say, "I think I'll go downstairs and raise hell. I don't know what about, but I'm going to raise hell anyway." And she did. She still hired and fired at whim. She met an actress named Hedda Hopper at Hearst's ranch. After listening to Hopper's stories about Hollywood stars, Cissy said, "Why don't you write a gossip column?"

"Write?" said Hopper. "I can't even spell."

"You don't have to spell," answered Cissy. "When you go home, dictate a letter to me. If I like it, I'll pay you for it."

Cissy liked it, and Hedda Hopper was soon a nationally known columnist.

"Fire her! Her eyes are too close together," she once said of a reporter. Then she explained, "You know, I have horses; and I've found that when a horse's eyes are too close together, that's a horse you can't trust!" On the elevator one day she met a *Herald* employee who was unshaven and unwashed, and she ordered that he be fired. City Editor Mason Peters wanted to keep the man because he was an expert at page makeup. He then developed a signal system. When the elevator operator spotted Cissy arriving at the main door, he would rush up and tell Peters. The offending employee would hide under a desk in the art department while Cissy was in the area. This ruse worked for several months, until Cissy accidentally discovered him. She called in Peters, ready to fire him for not obeying orders. Peters explained how vital the man was and Cissy gradually relaxed.

"But how did you hide him all this time?" she wondered.

Peters explained, and Cissy gave her funny little laugh and dropped the subject. There is no record that the man either shaved or bathed more often, but he was not fired.

"She enjoyed power. She misused it frequently," said one of Cissy's reporters, "but I will say, in the way she misused it, you could get mad, but somehow you enjoyed it, whether you were the brunt of it or not. There was a liveliness to it. Oh, I miss that in Washington, I really do. Cissy was a publisher who dared to be daring."

393

Cissy kept her executives always on edge. They became sensitive to the smallest subtleties in her behavior. Often, the threat of her anger, rather than the anger itself, was enough to get something done. The whole staff watched as an executive entered her office. They watched to see how long he stayed, whether the door was open or closed, whether he came out happy or troubled, alone or with her. An executive was in great favor if Cissy, smiling and with her hand on his arm, showed him out of her office.

While she could not bear stupidity, she was compassionate toward weakness. She would forgive a reporter on a two-week drunk if he had a good excuse. She was tolerant of romantic scandals as long as the employee involved told her all the details. One Christmas, Cissy arrived for a staff party and said, "Merry Christmas" to a rewrite man, Matt Tighe. "Merry Christmas, goddamn you," the drunken Tighe answered.

"Why did you say that?" she asked.

"Do you realize you've got a girl here in the library who is the sole support of her mother, and you're paying her a lousy fourteen dollars a week?"

The girl was home having a bleak Christmas dinner with her mother when the doorbell rang. It was Cissy's chauffeur with an envelope. Cissy's note read, "I'm so sorry. I didn't realize the circumstances. Enclosed is a check which may help." The check was for a thousand dollars, and the librarian promptly used some of it to buy a piano.

Cissy was adept at the grand gesture. When her city editor reported that he was sick, Cissy first sent her chauffeur to confirm that he was *really* sick. "I believe her entire kitchen staff then arrived in two limousines," said Mason Peters. "Butlers, footmen, cooks, scullery maid—at least six staff people from Dupont Circle—all in livery—showed up at my crummy, hideous little rooming house with all kinds of jellied aspics, marvelous foods, consommes, nourishing broths, pâtés, a tremendous amount of food, which presumably was my reward for being truly sick and not drunk."

A high point for Cissy Patterson, editor and publisher, occurred in November 1937. She called in her executives, placed a ledger on the table, and began to turn its pages. The men stood there, puzzled, as Cissy ran a finger down the red-inked columns, one red-inked column after another. Her finger stopped at the last column on the last page; then she turned to the men and smiled her greatest smile. The last figure in the last column was written in black instead of red.

That week, for the first time in its history, the Washington *Herald* had showed a profit. It was only $350, but to Cissy it represented a financial miracle. Her brother had told her she would never be a successful publisher until her paper showed a profit. Not only had she made money but she had more than doubled the original circulation of 61,000—part of which had been throwaway. Her circulation was 30 percent greater than that of the *Post*.

Cissy celebrated with a staff party at her home, and the $350 profit didn't even pay for the champagne.

The next year saw Cissy more energetic than ever. "Let's start a travel page tomorrow," she said. Her staff gulped and did it. "How about a men's page with a column on men's fashions?" Advertisers rushed to get in it. She even introduced a column called "The Male Animal," which gave advice to the lovelorn men and which carried the first letter on homosexual problems ever printed in an American newspaper. She came up with fresh ideas for the real estate section: "I am going to tear into it . . . just to see what I can do with a photographer and with solid news along the lines of the food section. . . . I want first to make people LOOK at it. Then I want to create an appetite in the mind of the readers for owning a home, planting a garden, getting those window boxes, changing those front steps. I want to put life, action, DESIRE into the thing. I believe we can sell these ideas to the advertisers." And she did.

She encouraged reporters to think up their own assignments. One reporter did an article on the life of a butler; another went on an archaeological expedition in Virginia. When a reporter complained he couldn't get a decent mint julep in Washington, she said, "Write a story about it." When she discovered that another reporter was interested in cemeteries, she suggested, "Poke around the old ones and write about it."

Occasionally she still felt an urge, "what the psychiatrists call a compulsion," to write her own stories. She interviewed the forbidding, bushy-browed John L. Lewis, then head of the 4-million-member Congress of Industrial Organizations. He was a close friend of Evalyn McLean. She was there to comfort him when his wife died. Lewis and the CIO had strongly supported Roosevelt, but now they were critical of the President. Cissy invited him to her home for a buffet lunch and got a front-page story. Lewis told her, "I want to point out that the greatest tragedy of the New Deal is . . . the lack of competent and coordinated manpower." Since the policies of the Roosevelt Administration were proving ineffective, he said, it was now up to labor and capital to cooperate in pulling the country out of its troubles. "I am a critic of Roosevelt's Administration, but I shall always be an admirer of his aims and ideals."

Although Cissy and Joe both opposed Bertie's intense diatribes against Roosevelt's domestic policies, they often disagreed about supporting some specific New Deal policies. Cissy, after all, still felt some kind of editorial tie, however loose, with Hearst. If she had been on her own, her support for Roosevelt would have been stronger. This became another sticking point in her growing determination to make the final break and buy the *Herald*. But on international policy, Cissy, Joe, and Bertie were in complete agreement: they wanted the United States to stay out of any foreign war. They were disturbed by a new tone in some of Roosevelt's speeches. In his "Quarantine the Aggressor" speech in June 1938, he noted: "When an epidemic of physical disease starts to spread, the community approves and joins in a quarantine of the patients in order to protect the health of the community against the spread of the disease. . . . It has now reached a stage where the very foundations of civilization are seriously threatened. . . ."

Unsettled by Roosevelt's deviation from an isolationist stance, Joe Patterson editorialized: "We wish the President could clarify his foreign policy before any more of us commit ourselves on the question of a third term." Cissy was even more persistent in her demands that Roosevelt make his position clear.

Harold Ickes, Cissy's closest friend in the Roosevelt Administration, remarried suddenly in 1938. Cissy had the news early, but the bride-to-be tearfully pleaded with her not to print the story until they were ready to announce it. She promised "with all my heart" that Cissy would have an exclusive release on the wedding. When Cissy saw the story printed in a rival paper, she told her managing editor, "We deserved it. You see what happens when you don't print the news?" She still cabled the couple, offering them the use of Dower House when they returned from their honeymoon.

Perhaps, in marrying, Ickes had done what Cissy would have liked to do. She and Tom White still met often, but she now felt an increased yearning for a permanent, public relationship. She had once told an admirer, "I'll give you my heart always, but never my newspaper." But now she was ready to share everything with Tom. No longer did she joke that the only thing that ruins a love match is marriage. When she took her hairpins out at night, her long hair falling almost to her waist, she wanted someone there to watch and admire. She felt so lonely as she took the elevator up to her empty fourth-floor bedroom every night.

Cissy arranged a meeting with Virginia White, Tom's wife, at the Carleton House in New York. She later told Ellie Waldrop how she "got all gussied up" for the confrontation; she rehearsed all the clichés: that Tom needed his freedom, that "it's bigger than all of us." As she sat waiting nervously, the doorbell rang, and the butler showed in Mrs. White. Cissy's plan flew out of her mind: "I forgot all of the speeches, and I just said, 'But you see, I *love* him.'" Mrs. White stared at her and said, "So do I."

It was rumored that Cissy later offered Mrs. White a million dollars to consent to a divorce, but her offer was firmly refused.

Cissy heard that Irene Castle, the dancer, was suing Freddie McLaughlin for divorce. She called her secretary to get the Ranger ready, and they were off for Chicago. Freddie was still an impressive man, a tall, dark-eyed, commanding figure. Long after their romance had ended, long after he had married, he and Cissy had seen each other in a restaurant. They were with other people, but as he passed her, Freddie whispered, "I love you." And she whispered back, "I love you too." He and Cissy were perhaps too much alike to make a success of marriage, but their affection never faded.

Cissy arrived in Chicago with a proposal for Freddie—not of marriage, but of business. She wanted him to come to Washington and run one of her papers. She told him, "Nobody thought I could do it, and I didn't know anything about the newspaper business. You don't know anything about it either, but you know how to run things. Two amateurs like us—we'll show them all how we can do it." But Freddie had a thriving coffee business, and he was too independent to work for anyone, especially Cissy.

In this time of restlessness, Cissy spent a weekend with her brother.

Joe was happier than he had ever been. He always wanted power, and the *News* had given it to him. The President of the United States was his friend. Joe regarded Roosevelt as a fellow aristocrat, a kindred spirit who wanted to better the lives of people so that they would not take to the barricades. Accused by a wealthy friend of arousing the masses, Joe answered caustically, "You've got me wrong. I just keep them contented while you fellows milk them." Roosevelt's New Deal was Joe's New Deal. Joe told Cissy that Roosevelt had offered him the post of Secretary of the Navy, but he had turned it down. He did not want to leave the *News,* the base of his power. The paper was still on a skyrocket and had the largest circulation of any newspaper in the country. Even Joe's personal life was peaceful; he had finally got his divorce and had married Mary King, then women's editor of the *News.*

Cissy told Joe that she wanted to exercise her option and buy the *Herald* and the *Times.* She told him that being a publisher had been the most fulfilling experience in her life and that she would never be completely content until they really belonged to her. Joe was adamantly opposed to her decision. He repeated his litany of all the hazards and headaches faced by a newspaper owner. He reminded her that the *Herald* had never shown a big profit and probably never would. If she owned these papers, she would lose millions of dollars from her own fortune. He urged her to let Hearst have the papers back: she would have the fun, and let him pay the bills.

Cissy listened attentively to her brother, as she always did. But she already had made up her mind. She told Tom White her decision. Hearst now agreed to let her buy the papers. His empire was still afloat, thanks in part to her, and his affection for her was real and deep. It was not easy for him, however, to give up these papers. It still meant much to him to dictate memos to his scattered editors that always began: "The Chief says. . . ." He still relished his front-page editorials, in which he made his personal pronouncements on national affairs. It had hurt, though, to see his private life exposed in a *Time* magazine cover story several months earlier. "No other press lord ever wielded his power with less sense of responsibility; no other press ever matched the Hearst press for flamboyance, perversity and incitement of mass hysteria. Hearst never believed in anything much, not even Hearst, and his appeal was not to men's minds, but to those infantile emotions which he never conquered in himself: arrogance, hatred, frustration, fear." In response to which, Hearst shrugged and said, "Nobody likes us but the people."

Cissy saw a different Hearst, an old lion in a new jungle, struggling to survive. She was proud that she had won his respect.

On January 31, 1939, Cissy printed this front-page announcement:

> I would like to make a statement to end all statements concerning the lease and sale of the Washington *Herald* (morning) and the Washington *Times* (evening).
>
> On August 7, 1937, I *leased* both properties from Mr. William Randolph Hearst with an option to buy. On January 28, 1939, I exercised my option and *purchased* both properties and all their physical assets, with the intention of merging the two unnaturally divided papers into one.
>
> I use this word "unnaturally" after considerable reflection and some years of intensive experience. It has been an experience of

waste of time and talent, worry and ceaseless effort to keep these twin newspapers as separate entities and apart.

There has been, contrary to public opinion, a limited duplication of circulation between the *Times* and *Herald*—only 17.3% of the whole. That is, 183,009 people are reading today either the *Herald* or the *Times,* and the reason for that is simple. Some of our readers want their paper with their morning coffee, while others prefer theirs around noon, or when they get home at night.

So, for sound editorial as well as business reasons, we have finally decided to pull up the sluice-gates, which artificially divided these properties, and let the two papers merge into one.

I will close without the usual quota of pompous promises and merely say I hope you will like the new *Times-Herald,* Washington's only around-the-clock newspaper. . . .

The *Times-Herald* was the first round-the-clock newspaper ever published in a large city. Features and comics remained constant all day, but the news changed. Cissy said that the *Times-Herald* had been born because "I loved the morning paper and wouldn't let it go."

Publishing the *Times* and the *Herald* as separate papers had proved to be impractical and unprofitable. Arthur Newmyer was one of those who urged the twenty-four hour operation. Starting as a copyboy on the *Times,* he had become its publisher, and under his management the paper had made money. He later worked for Tom White as assistant general manager of Hearst enterprises and helped negotiate the final sale of the papers to Cissy. She then hired him as her associate publisher to handle the business side of the papers. Newmyer incorrectly assumed that he had the power to hire and fire. He soon crossed swords with Cissy on this issue and found himself relegated to a quiet corner for the next several years.

When the papers merged, Cissy had the difficult task of firing thirty-seven people whose jobs would be eliminated. An employee said: "Everyone who wasn't fired got the word of a meeting. She gave an awfully nice speech and said some people would have to be let go because we couldn't use two sports editors or two society editors, etc. It was a very nice speech and everybody applauded her. I remember one lady from the Society Department who realized she wasn't being fired and said, 'Oh goody!' and then was embarrassed by the silence that followed. It was quite a drinking night at the Herald Square Inn for the thirty-seven who were fired."

The Newspaper Guild called a meeting to discuss a strike to protest the firings. Cissy, who was trying to find jobs elsewhere for the discharged workers, went to the meeting. Those who expected her to give a fiery defiant speech were disappointed. She quietly told the guild members that she had been urged by astute businessmen to shut down the *Herald;* had she chosen to follow this advice, hundreds would have been out of work instead of a few dozen. But she had stood firm: "I want to save this paper for you and myself because I think you love it as I do." She told them that if the *Times-Herald* kept all the employees of both papers on the payroll, the new venture would fail. Then her voice broke. "If there is a strike . . . I will lock the doors and they will never be opened."

There was silence, some tears, but no strike. Her staff knew she meant what she said.

The *Times-Herald* had ten editions. The first edition was on the street about eight o'clock at night, the last at five the next afternoon. In the city room the hubbub of phones, voices, and typewriters never ceased. "Well, I wasn't quite satisfied with the first edition this morning," Cissy commented on the first day the *Times-Herald* was published. "It was still a bit fresh—maybe a little disorderly in spots. But just watch us go." Asked about her editorial policy, she smiled. "A steady, middle-of-the-road policy is the best way to be popular and prosperous, but what fun is there in that?"

The *Times-Herald* was a hybrid that made sense and soon made money. For Cissy the paper's early years of evolution and growth were probably the happiest time of her adult life. Every day there was a new challenge, something new to try.

Toward the end of 1937, a newsboy asked to see Cissy one day. He was "the scrawniest, most sullen and forlorn little newsie I ever saw. . . . He fairly tottered under a great load of papers." He claimed the business office had refused to give him a refund of ninety-nine cents for the papers he hadn't been able to sell. Cissy gave him a dollar, and he bolted. She glanced at the top paper and saw the headline *"Happy Birthday To You!"*

The front-page story read: "And so Happy said, 'T'ro out the Pally-Royal ad' and the editors said, 'Kill page one' and Irving Belt said, 'Toss the eight column line in the hell-box—we're making over the paper.' . . . There's a helluva lot of news popping around this world today . . . but we decided the only news that's worth a hoot is the fact today is The Boss' Birthday."

It was signed by every employee of the paper.

Cissy was fifty-six years old. If her paper failed now, she knew there would be many, including her brother, who would say, "I told you so." But she also knew, deep within her, that it would not fail. She had proved herself. She had paid her dues.

17

The way to fight a woman is with your hat—grab it and run.

—John Barrymore

In September 1939, Germany and Russia invaded Poland. Hitler already had taken over Austria and Czechoslovakia. Great Britain and France declared war on Germany, England sending an expeditionary force to France. President Roosevelt declared the United States neutral.

For Cissy, Poland was a land of youthful gaiety and warm friends. She lamented the slain Poles and the burning cities, but her main concern was to keep the United States out of war. "This must be done—at any cost."

Cissy had been bred on isolationism. The Chicago *Tribune* of her grandfather, father, and brother had preached a strongly isolationist gospel. Her brother had returned from World War I a hero, but an embittered one, convinced his country could gain nothing from participation in a foreign war. Her cousin

Bertie was even more cynical about international affairs, more determined to have the United States steer a neutral course. Senator Borah, Cissy's long-time intimate, had always been a strict isolationist, and so were her close friends Senators Hiram Johnson and Burton Wheeler. Hearst was an "America First" isolationist. Her new friend John L. Lewis was bitterly opposed to war: "Because if there is a war, labor has to do most of the dying."

Cissy's isolationism did not mean that she did not have a true hatred of Hitler. Frank Waldrop's editorials in the *Times-Herald* called him "a lunatic on a ledge" and stated that "the structure of urban civilization on the continent hinges on the depravity of a dictator." But if Cissy's editorial sympathy for the European nations attacked or threatened by Hitler was consistent, so was her isolationist stance: "Fight in France again, or in the South Seas, 12,000 miles away? Never. Never."

Waldrop wrote in depth about the Polish tragedy, probably with more detail than any other paper in the country. His indignation was Cissy's indignation. "The Poles were just brave fools. They were sure their friends would not let them down." Poland's ambassador to the United States, Jerzy Potocki, commented to Cissy before the invasion, "We envoys of countries about to be invaded ought to organize a bridge club. We now have precisely enough for three tables, and the fates are dusting off chairs for a fourth."

Potocki was the youngest son of the Count and Countess Potocki, who had been close friends of Cissy's. The ambassador had been a child when she was a bride, and his brother had courted Felicia. With Poland lost, the dark, dashing diplomat moved into Dower House while his wife went home to Peru. When he was preparing to join her some months later, Cissy and her friends gave a series of farewell parties for him, and Waldrop wrote a full-page article, beginning: "Poland is not yet lost."

Cissy never succeeded in totally separating her emotions and her political beliefs. Several months before the invasion of Poland, King George VI and Queen Elizabeth of England visited the United States. Cissy met them at a picnic the

404

Roosevelts gave for them at Hyde Park, and she wrote movingly of the Queen:

> How many daughters of the very rich and very powerful remain through life as sound and sane as this sturdy little Queen? How many are as unselfish in any line of duty? How many are as physically sound? As mentally clear and clean? . . .
>
> Listen girls, weren't you struck by the admiration for Elizabeth of all our men-folk, young and old. Even the toughest of all reporters smiled and surrendered as she passed by. . . . Stocky, sturdy little Queen. Sound of body and sound of mind. Unfaltering. Serene. She has taken away with her the admiration of millions of our people.

Asked whether she thought Americans should curtsy to the royal couple, Cissy said, "I think we should politely shake hands. The King and Queen are coming here to see Americans, and if we act like American ladies and gentlemen, I think we'll be all right."

Felicia was another visitor. She had returned home for the publication of her second novel, *Flower and Smoke*. Like her first novel, it was autobiographical: in a vain search for contentment, the heroine returns to Vienna—as Felicia had—to find her childhood world gone.

One of the novel's characters, a self-centered, shallow, and unlikable woman, appears to have been based on Cissy. At one point, the heroine says to her, "You're vile." And many of Drew Pearson's traits appear in a character named Lion, an arrogant and unsatisfactory lover.

"Now that you've written two books [about yourself]," prodded Cissy, "hadn't you better try something else?" The critics were kinder. One reviewer wrote: "The writer's imagery is sharp, her characterizations clever, gently sardonic, illumined with the powers of observation some quiet women own. . . . It is a novel of modern times, of trivial people, and starred with promise." Another saw "a strange wild savagery" in the book.

Felicia told an interviewer that when she was a little girl, her mother had told her repeatedly that if she didn't stand up straight, she would never get married. Finally, her mother had given up and said, "All right, then, be round-shouldered and someday you'll write a great book."

"The world of action doesn't seem glamorous to our youngsters," Felicia continued. "They've seen their mothers engage in business, writing, painting and otherwise be generally undomestic, and they want to marry and settle down. I know my twelve-year-old daughter Ellen and her friends certainly have this opinion."

Felicia had worked hard on her novel, but she also had played hard. "Felicia has spent the greater part of her life abroad, and she is one of those glamorous young cosmopolites who is equally at home in London, Paris, Cannes, Biarritz, Deauville or Palm Beach. . . . Her entire thirty years of life have been spent doing whatever popped into her head. [She is] a blithe young spirit full of energy and ideas." This description appeared in a New York society column, which also noted that Felicia reviewed restaurants in Paris for *Harper's Bazaar*.

There was no longer any one man in Felicia's life; there were many. Burned by her second marriage, she was reluctant to try again. Shortly after her return to the United States, Felicia saw her cousin Alicia, who had divorced Joe Brooks and married the middle-aged mining millionaire Harry Guggenheim several months before. Her father was bitter about her action because Brooks, who had been an All-American football star, had been his wartime friend. Joe Patterson had promoted Alicia's marriage to Brooks, just as Cissy had encouraged Drew Pearson's courtship of Felicia. Joe lunched with Felicia about this time and began the conversation with a caustic question. "Now, why do you girls keep getting divorces?" He was so tense and constrained that Felicia found it hard to talk to him.

Felicia and Alicia saw the similarities in their lives. Both were willful and intelligent; both had failed to escape from the domination of their parents. But while Alicia loved and admired her father, Felicia had little affection for her mother. As she later said, "I spent so much time hating my mother. How could I ever really love anyone else?"

In 1939, Cissy was fifty-eight and Felicia thirty-four, but their meetings still ended in heated arguments. Cissy accused Felicia of giving her daughter, Ellen, too little time and attention, and this criticism was true. And the quarrels between Cissy and Felicia remained full of bitterness and guilt. After one argument Cissy's eye fell on Felicia's portrait. She started throwing things at it, shouting, "You're a terrible girl . . . you're a terrible girl." The next morning, looking at her damaged painting, she burst into tears. Cissy once asked a friend, who had a loving relationship with her grown children, "How did you do it?"

Bertie McCormick had no children. His wife Amie died that year and left him more lonely, more arrogant, more embittered than ever. He gave her a military funeral, complete with the firing of salvos by a detachment of troops. Behind her casket, he had a horse led with its stirrups crossed and eyes hooded in black "as if she were a fallen general."

Polish refugees began arriving in Washington, some of whom Cissy called "cousin" because they were distantly related to Count Gizycki. She never forgot anyone who befriended her. Cissy supported a number of these refugees until they were resettled, and she found jobs for others. One woman, the daughter of an old friend, remembered that when she was a little girl in Warsaw, Cissy had neighed like a horse to make her laugh. Cissy now gave her a job on the *Times-Herald*—in the classified section "because you'll meet more people there."

Cissy hired a Polish cook and would often call up her newfound Polish friends, saying, "Come on over tonight. We're having a Polish dinner." She also hired a Polish maid. When the maid was found to be suffering from cancer, Cissy paid for her prolonged hospitalization. Later she found a Polish priest to give the maid the last rites and provided a proper funeral. Walking her poodles with Luvie Pearson, Cissy often mused that perhaps she should have stayed with the Count, had a lot of children, and lived the life of a Polish countess. "After all," she said, "he was the only man I ever really loved."

A surprise arrival in Washington was Cissy's girlhood friend Marguerite Cassini. "This is the famous Marguerite Cassini who used to have all Washington on its ear," commented Cissy, in introducing her to some of her editors. "I used to envy her terribly."

"There was a mocking note in her voice," Marguerite recalled. "We were about the same age, but I looked and felt much older. Cissy, now rich and powerful, was still slender, red-haired, smartly dressed, still rode horseback every morning though she may not have gone to bed until dawn, still gave off a kind of electric zest. While I, living in Europe, had assumed the habits of Florentine women, who do not resist age. I was tired, I had let myself go, put on weight, my hair was gray, I dressed always in black."

In Italy, Marguerite had been known as "La Lupa," the she-wolf fighting for her two sons. She now asked Cissy to give her son Igor a job on her newspaper. Cissy agreed but in return asked for permission to publish Maggie's memoirs—which one of her reporters would write. Maggie reluctantly agreed, and the series was called "I Lived for Love."

Igor went to work at the *Times-Herald* writing obituaries, but his big chance came when he ran into Mussolini's son, who was making a private visit to Washington. They chatted casually in Italian, and Igor wrote a story about this encounter. Cissy was so pleased that she soon gave him his own gossip column, called "These Charming People." Cissy had earlier hired Martha Blair, a young divorced socialite, to write this column. She took Blair and her children into her home for a short time and helped send the children through school. Blair moved out when she married *New York Times* columnist Arthur Krock. Soon afterward, Cissy told one of her editors, "Kill the Blair column. It bores me."

Cassini became one of her young protégés, and he and his mother and brother Oleg, who became a noted fashion designer, were frequent guests at Dupont Circle. Although Oleg angered Cissy by drawing an unflattering cartoon of Ambassador Jerzy Potocki to illustrate his brother's column, she later gave a dinner for a hundred people to celebrate his marriage to the actress Gene Tierney in 1941.

Igor's gossip column got him into serious trouble when he reported an indiscreet item about a society girl in nearby

Warrenton, Virginia. Several of her friends kidnapped him, beat him, stripped him, and threatened to emasculate him. They finally let him go after covering him with tar and feathers. Igor called in his story from a hospital, and Cissy put it on the front page. She was outraged by this attack on one of her reporters. She promptly filed a complaint against the men, and they were brought to trial and found guilty. They were given small fines and suspended sentences.

Years before, several of Cissy's reporters covered a lynching of three blacks in nearby Maryland. When the mob burned the reporters' cars and set fire to their hotel, Cissy asked a friend, the Secretary of War, to send a plane and get them out, but it proved unnecessary.

Only the unwise or the unwitting ever tried to intimidate Cissy or her staff. The chairman of the House Committee on Military Affairs visited the *Times-Herald* and forbade its editors from publishing any stories about the activities of his committee. If they defied him, he said, he would subpoena their reporters and force them to disclose their sources. Cissy ordered Waldrop to continue his series of critical pieces, intensifying his research and his charges. When he was subpoenaed to testify, Cissy instructed him to refuse to answer any questions. The committee chairman retreated in disarray.

Representative Maury Maverick of Texas rued the day he took issue with Cissy's crusade for home rule for the District of Columbia. He rashly said, "Hell! We got to have slaves somewhere. It might as well be in Washington." Waldrop's editorials never let him forget this statement, and the ridicule heaped on him by the *Times-Herald* hastened his departure from the Congress. Cissy's policy was plain: "The people of Washington pay taxes. They die in war. They are subjected to the Constitution and the laws that stem from it. And they are oppressed, for they have no voice in their government."

Cissy felt strong enough to take on anyone. When the local movie houses complained that their printed handouts were not published as written, she wrote a memo to her movie reviewer: "You are *forbidden* to print handouts or any free publicity plugs." She fired a reviewer who disobeyed.

Secretary of the Navy Frank Knox, concerned about the need for military secrecy, warned her, "If you publish a picture of a British ship in an American port, I'll put you in jail." When the British ship *Malaya* arrived in New York, Cissy ran a picture of it on the front page. Knox did nothing.

The *Times-Herald* published a scoop about security leaks at the Civil Service Commission: confidential documents about the Panama Canal had been passed to two German agents. Cissy had started a system of paying five dollars for any tip that resulted in a news story, and this was one of the payoffs.

Rival papers stepped warily with her. When an afternoon paper proudly broke a story about marijuana traffic in Washington, Cissy reprinted this story alongside one on the same subject that the *Times-Herald* had published two months earlier. The headline was a wry comment: "Well, well, just two months late."

She could be personally vindictive, too. When a particularly smug and snobbish socialite made news, Cissy personally selected a photograph of her to run with the story. "Why that's a terrible picture of her," a subordinate ventured to say. "I know," said Cissy, laughing, "we'll use it big."

With rare exceptions, a story was a story to Cissy, no matter whom it hurt; she spared no one's feelings, not even her own. She once noted the arrival of a distinguished-looking Polish countess and sent a reporter to interview her. Only much later did the reporter learn that the countess was an illegitimate daughter of Count Gizycki.

One of the few stories she killed for personal reasons concerned a robbery. Two women wearing men's clothes jumped on a senator in the street and robbed him of his wallet. The senator was William Borah, and she would not run a story that made him look ridiculous. Borah, her "western tiger," died in 1940. She had seen little of him in his later years, when he had stayed close to his books and his papers. His blond wife, "Little Borah," who loved socializing, but rarely went out because of her unsocial husband, later went to parties without him and brought back to him all the gossip. On the Senate floor, Borah was regarded as an anachronism. Cissy was saddened by the decline of his power, because she had known him and loved him in his glory.

John "Black Jack" Bouvier and Joseph Kennedy, the ambassador to Great Britain, were among Cissy's new friends. Both appealed to Cissy because they were open and aggressive. She and Kennedy were politically close; both were strong isolationists. (Bouvier's daugher Jacqueline and Kennedy's son John would later meet and marry.)

Kennedy's daughter Kathleen ("Kick") began to work at the *Times-Herald* in 1940 and later wrote her own column, "Did you happen to see . . . ?" She was "a sweater-and-skirt girl with a child's shy smile." Her father lunched occasionally with Waldrop to check on her.

By early 1940 the French and British armed forces had established their positions behind the Maginot Line—Cissy said they were waging a "sitz-krieg"—and were waiting for the Germans to make the first move. The German army, in a blitzkrieg attack, burst through this line with incredible speed, and Paris fell in June 1940. The British evacuated what troops they could at Dunkirk, and the Battle of Britain began.

Bullitt had returned from Europe and had told Cissy about his recent visit to Warsaw and the horrors of the occupation. He had pulled down the shades in his railway car as it passed through Germany so he would not have to look at the Nazis he now hated. He had believed that appeasement would forestall the destruction of Europe by war, but he now believed that the United States had to join the struggle against Germany. The British newspaper publisher Lord Beaverbrook came to the United States to plead Britain's cause. He spent an evening with his friend Joe Patterson but could not shake the latter's isolationist convictions. And neither Bullitt nor Beaverbrook could convince Cissy that the United States must enter the war.

"We must, if necessary, stop our ears and bind our arms, as Ulysses did, until we are past the sirens," stated a Hearst editorial that Cissy reprinted in 1940. "The way of peace and neutrality will be hard and the costs great [but] not one American boy shall die fighting on foreign soil in this or any war."

In September 1940 the *Times-Herald* ran an editorial that showed Cissy was not unmoved by the arguments for intervention:

Germany, Italy and Japan are now publicly combined against us, two years to the day after Munich.

France is in the dust. The Ambassador of Great Britain to the United States cries, "Send us more of everything, and quickly."

We must realize that we are pretty much alone in the world at this moment, with England in the tide of war up to her neck, France gone, and Russia—inscrutable.

We have all followed the career of Hitler with the greatest passion, and missed no opportunity to tell him that we think he is a rat.

Indignation against Mussolini when he decided to swing on Addis Ababa was hotter here than in Paris.

We wanted to see justice triumph and right prevail. We wanted to have the honorable men manage the affairs of the world.

As we roll toward our destiny, we are hearing more and more from the advocates of a fight for democracy, and from people with proposals to save democracy by keeping us out of war.

But the question remains: Now that we have followed these men of good will and honor to the present corner, can we make them turn? How are we to endure the years ahead?

The springtime of American life is over. We are up against the hard reality now.

Cissy had gone as far as she could go. She had shown a recognition of the danger the war posed to the United States, and she had expressed an understanding of those who urged intervention. But she long ago had drawn a line and she would not cross it: No American soldiers would fight in a war outside the United States.

President Roosevelt had repeated that same phrase about not fighting in any foreign war, which was why Cissy and Joe Patterson continued to support him. "The third term issue would be important in normal times," Cissy stated in an editorial. "[But] in times like these, it seems to us that the big thing is to elect the best President we can. Certainly Roosevelt is the best presidential candidate the Democrats could put up."

Cissy had an alternate Democratic candidate, if Roosevelt decided not to run—her friend Senator Burton K. Wheeler. The Republicans selected their candidate—Wendell Willkie, a businessman whom Ickes called "the barefoot boy from Wall Street." Cissy wrote: "We'd vote for Roosevelt on the theory that, having lived with the problems of the Chief Executive for seven years, he knows more about them than Willkie or any other New Dealer such as Hull, Farley, Hopkins, Ickes or Wheeler."

In September 1940 the British desperately needed destroyers: their shipping losses in five weeks had been more than 400,000 tons. Roosevelt proposed sending them fifty "over-age" U.S. destroyers, relics of World War I. Joe and Cissy saw this as a one-way deal and editorially insisted that the United States should keep the destroyers "to defend [itself]." At a Hyde Park dinner, Roosevelt confided to Joe that the deal was reciprocal, that the United States would get certain British outlying bases for defense. "I'll kill you if you reveal this," the President said smilingly. Grudgingly, then, the *News* editorially approved the destroyer deal, and afterward endorsed Roosevelt in the November election. Cissy also urged Roosevelt's reelection to a third term.

As the publisher of the only Washington newspaper to support FDR's bid for reelection, Cissy had impressive political clout. But, remarkably, she often refused to use this power. This reluctance was evident in her dealings with the Associated Press. The AP was a publishers' cooperative whose members shared the cost of maintaining a worldwide news-gathering organization. Both the Washington *Star* and the Washington *Post* were members and boasted about their direct access to foreign news, and Cissy wanted in. According to the rules, applicants could be kept out by members who considered them too competitive. Cissy's application for membership was rejected, and she turned for help to Assistant Attorney General Thurman Arnold, who was in charge of the antitrust division of the Justice Department. Cissy liked Arnold. A Wyoming native, he had once advised Cal Carrington on a legal problem, and Cal afterward referred to him as "my lawyer in Washington." Arnold was often a guest at Cissy's home, and his son later married Cissy's granddaughter. When Cissy described the AP's monopolistic practices, Arnold suggested she sign a complaint. Taken aback, she replied that she had thought the Government initiated antitrust actions. Arnold then decided that since Cissy had been such a strong Roosevelt supporter, a simple letter from her might be enough to get things started. She still demurred. As she later explained, "Thurman Arnold said, 'If you want an AP membership, I can get it for you. I won't start it myself, but if you will send a member of your staff around the country and get some complaints from newspapers in your situation . . . I guarantee to break the monopoly and get you that membership.'"

"I come from four generations of newspaper people," Cissy said, "and I didn't like the smell of it. I went home and thought it over and I refused to act." She didn't want any political favors. She wanted Arnold to act out of principle, on his own initiative.

Arnold retained his own memory: "Cissy Patterson got me to feeling I was yellow." The AP membership rules were later changed.

Roosevelt's reelection prompted an editorial suggestion from Cissy: "Mr. President, in this critical hour of the country's history . . . how would it be to offer Wendell Willkie a place in your Cabinet?" While FDR did not do this, he did use Willkie as a personal emissary abroad.

Cissy, Joe, and Bertie did not need to hold secret meetings to discuss long-term isolationist strategy. Their philosophies were remarkably similar, because all three had sprung from the same soil—and all had retained most of the attitudes they had acquired in childhood. In addition, Joe and Cissy often talked to each other on the phone. A month after Roosevelt's reelection, they both agreed, editorially: "We're issuing Britain a blank check. . . . Very few of our war party people expect to do any fighting, but they yearn to see our brave boys go out and fight other peoples' boys."

Cissy, Bertie, and Joe made sure that Roosevelt knew exactly where they stood. The President, however, remained unmoved by their calls for American neutrality. He knew the Nazis were a threat to free nations throughout the world, and he was determined to help America's allies as much as he could, short of actually going to war. This attitude was evident in the Lend-Lease program that he proposed in January 1941. This bill would give the President the authority to sell or transfer any defense article to any government "whose defense the President deems vital to the defense of the United States." For example, under the Lend-Lease program the United States would send munitions to Great Britain, now sorely tried, and would accept a delayed payment for these goods—not in dollars, but in kind—after the conclusion of the war. In a press conference the previous month Roosevelt had said that "quite aside from our historic and current interest in the survival of democracy in the world as a whole, it is equally important from a selfish point of view and of American defense that we should do everything possible to help the British Empire to defend itself." FDR then used the analogy of lending a neighbor a garden hose to help him put out a fire. Churchill's appeal to the American public was "Give us the tools and we will finish the job."

Roosevelt's opponents were quick to denounce his proposal. The Chicago *Tribune* said that Lend-Lease would mean the "destruction of the American republic." Senator Wheeler said, "It will plow under every fourth American boy." Joe Patterson's editorial, which Cissy reprinted, was headlined "President of the World—Maybe?" It discussed the dangers of bringing the four freedoms to the world by means of a bloody war and asked, "What the hell is going on anyhow?"

Joe Patterson felt that Roosevelt had betrayed him. "He lied to me," he told Senator Henrik Shipstead, and, bursting into tears, he repeated, "He lied to me." Roosevelt had been his friend, and no publisher in America had supported the

President as long and as loyally as he had. If there was a power elite in this country, Joe Patterson felt that he was a member of it. Now, suddenly, everything was gone: the power, the friendship, the trust. Joe felt despair and hate. He had been taken in like a schoolboy, and he wanted revenge.

Cissy shared Joe's outrage. By the middle of 1941, they both had pinned the label of "dictator" on their former friend, even suggesting that he might try to cancel the congressional elections in 1942. Cissy's isolationist stand soured many of her friends. A strong Roosevelt supporter, Ernest Cuneo—who occasionally gave Cissy legal advice—reminded her that Hitler's fascism threatened democracy everywhere, but Cissy was haunted by a tragic vision of young American men dying in battle on foreign soil. "How the hell can you go on like this?" she once yelled at him. "*I* wake up screaming!"

Another one of Cissy's young protégés was Dick Hollander, whom she had hired as city editor. Cissy invited him and his wife to her dinners and parties, "and was very very open and kind to me. She seemed to respect what I was doing." Hollander decided to enlist in the war against fascism by joining the Office of Strategic Services, an agency involved in undercover activities. Cissy did her best to dissuade him and offered him a generous raise. When he persisted, she gave him a farewell dinner. At the end of the evening she held out her hand. "If you keep quicksilver in the palm of your hand, it will stay. But if you try to squeeze it, it runs out between your fingers. I've obviously used the wrong technique in trying to keep you." Several days later, Cissy ran a front-page editorial titled "Letter to a Young Man." Without mentioning Hollander's name, she told his story, calling him misguided and stating that he was obsessed by a romantic notion of personal sacrifice.

Cissy and Joe saw each other more often that year, as if they needed each other's support. During this difficult time Cissy had a small dinner party at Sands Point. Bernard Baruch was there, and so were the Swopes and Ernest Cuneo. Cissy held up the dinner because Joe was late. Her formally dressed guests passed the time with cocktails and conversation. Joe finally arrived, without a tie, his collar open.

He had been to West Point, where his son James was a cadet. James was on parade, and Joe did not ask to have him called away. He had simply watched him from a distance. Joe told Baruch about Beaverbrook's visit. "They want us to go over there, and we're not going. My mind is made up." Watching his son in uniform had given him a more personal stake in peace.

Roosevelt had come to regard the entry of the United States into the war as inevitable. He tried to assess the nation's mood. As he told his confidant Harry Hopkins, he would rather follow than lead the American people into war. He felt that though the country was girding for battle, many still had to be convinced that America must take up arms. Then, on December 7, 1941, came the Japanese attack on the American forces at Pearl Harbor.

Charles Duffy had had a hunch. Duffy was the night managing editor of the *Times-Herald*. On December 6 he had asked a photo editor to put together a page comparing American and Japanese military strength. "I know we have some good sharp pictures of those big coastal guns at Pearl Harbor. Work one of those into the page. This will be a war page. Just lock it up and have it ready."

Frank Waldrop also had had a premonition. On Sunday, December 7, Waldrop did not have to work, but something pulled him to the office. When the news of the Japanese attack on Pearl Harbor flashed across the news wires, Waldrop was in instant command. He knew that most of the circulation men were at a football game, and he had an announcement made on the stadium's public address system, telling them to return to the office. The *Times-Herald* was probably the first major newspaper in the country out on the street—hours ahead of any other paper in Washington—with the most detailed news available.

Sunday Editor Chalmers Roberts sat on the floor with Cissy in her office listening to the radio. Roberts had angered her in earlier months by trying to get some of his interventionist ideas onto the Op Ed page. "I think you are a nice young man, but pretty fresh," she had told him then. Now, as the news of the disaster kept coming in, Cissy bitterly asked Roberts about Roosevelt, "Do you suppose *he* arranged this?" Later when she learned that American cryptographers had broken the Japanese codes before Pearl Harbor, she was convinced that Roosevelt had known in advance that the Japanese intended to attack.

Henry and Clare Booth Luce had guests in Greenwich, Connecticut, on that Sunday. The Luce rule was that meals must not be interrupted by messages. A butler broke this rule at dessert time by handing Mrs. Luce a note on a silver tray. She tapped a spoon on her glass to get her guests' attention.

"All isolationists and appeasers, please listen. The Japanese have bombed Pearl Harbor."

Luce publications had labeled Cissy, Joe, and Bertie "The Three Furies of Isolationism" who "increased their howls [and] ground out their daily gripes at the risks involved in the administration's policy of trying to stop Hitler." Joe Patterson had answered in two editorials called "Family Portrait." In these he described the Scotch-Irish heritage of the Pattersons "whose great ambition was to get as far away from England and English aristocratic ideas as they could possibly get." "It is also natural for us, with our midwestern background, to think first of America in times like these, and to hate to see Americans kidded and cajoled into impossible crusades to remake the world. . . . We were pushed into World War I, however, and by some of the same forces as are now pushing us into World War II."

Clare Booth Luce impulsively sent Cissy a mammoth bouquet of roses with a card: ". . . How do you like everything now?"

"How do I like it?" Cissy replied. "I hate it. How do you and Henry like it? The terrible thing about you two is that you neither hate nor like very much. You just go on having a wonderful time."

Cissy reprinted the editorial Joe had written after hearing of Pearl Harbor. It spoke for both of them: "Well, we're in it.

God knows Americans didn't want it. But let's get behind our President and fight for America first."

Almost immediately, Joe went to see the President. "It took balls for Joe to go to the White House to see Roosevelt—after he had called Roosevelt a dictator," said Washington editor Walter Trohan. But Joe had been a wounded hero in World War I, and now his country had been attacked. Besides, he had been one of FDR's most loyal supporters for three terms. Joe arrived early at the White House and was ushered into the Oval Office. Roosevelt was busy signing papers, and Patterson stood waiting for five minutes. Finally the President looked up, and the two men shook hands.

"Well, Joe," asked Roosevelt, "what can I do for you?"

"I am here, Mr. President, to see what aid I can be in the war effort."

He was sixty-two but still straight and strong, and he had written a friend of his hopes to serve with the Army in the field. Roosevelt stared at him for a moment and then said in a hard voice, "There is one thing you can do, Joe, and that is to go back and read your editorials for the past six months. Read every one of them and think what you've done."

"I remained standing for fifteen minutes," Joe recalled afterward, "while he gave me a pretty severe criticism for the way the *News* conducted itself during the year. . . . He likewise said that as a result of our conduct we had delayed the effort by from sixty to ninety days." FDR told him how Congress had been influenced by the editorials in the *News* and the *Times-Herald.* "At the end, he told me to pass on the word to Cissy to behave herself."

Joe stayed with Cissy that night, and his fury became hers. Walter Trohan, who was there that evening, said he had never seen anyone as angry as Joe was. He heard him say, "That man did things to me that no man should ever do to *any* man. . . . All I want to do now is outlive that bastard."

From that day forward, Cissy's hatred of Roosevelt became an obsession. She forgave attacks on herself, but she could not and would not ever forgive this humiliation of her brother.

Roosevelt could easily have converted both Pattersons to his cause. Instead, he created two bitter and powerful enemies.

Cissy needed a more distant retreat than Dower House or Sands Point, and she found what she wanted in Sarasota, Florida. Lyford Cay in Nassau offered her all the privacy she wanted, but the fourteen-mile-long Siesta Key in Sarasota had the attraction of old friends from Chicago. Led by the Potter Palmers, the Chicago rich had discovered this small Gulf town and had made it their winter retreat. The Palmers had bought 26,000 acres with a hunting preserve and private bayou. Their son Honoré had inherited this property. His tall, slender wife was a friend of Cissy's; not a friend who shared secrets, but a friend who loved the same things she did—a fast ride, a good swim, a handsome man. She had her own sorrows. Two sons had died within two years of each other, and her cold, but charming husband was in love with her sister.

Cissy bought a house that suited her mood. Small, private, and luxurious. It was set on a seventeen-acre estate and faced a long, empty, beautiful beach. Her mood then was reflective, with a need for that privacy. In the large, high-ceilinged living room, a wall of windows looked out on the water. Opposite these windows was a mirrored wall that reflected the seascape.

The house had a Hollywood modern look (although the chandelier had come from the movie set of *Gone With the Wind*). Cissy brought down her own painters and decorators from Washington to make her Sarasota house more personal. It had only two porches, two bedrooms, two bathrooms. It was her private house.

"We had a house right near her," said Mrs. Clifford Rodman. "My husband would go for a morning walk on the beach each day and he'd stop by Cissy's house to pick her up and the two would take a long walk together. I would see the two of them laughing their heads off. Cissy was lots of fun, with a terrific sense of humor, always saying what came into her mind, always gay."

But Cissy was not always gay. She was a brooder. She was an expert on second thoughts. She would call the paper to give an order; shortly after, she would call again and reverse herself.

She still suspected most of her friends of self-interest and trusted very few. The older she got, the fewer people she liked. "And those I do like, I find I do not like very much." She found herself objecting too much, consulting too long, adventuring too little, and repenting too soon. Evalyn McLean bought a house near Cissy's. Cissy would walk over to find her reading in bed, her wig off, wearing a green eyeshade and white gloves over her carefully creamed hands. The two usually went on the town together, often getting drunk but almost never disorderly. In a column on drinking, McLean had written that most people drink to escape worry, "because they are not sure of tomorrow."

Sarasota's social world was a small one. Grace Palmer was often accompanied by a handsome young escort, an actor who had known her son. He had gone hunting with Grace and told Cissy how it sickened him to smash the head of a wounded dove with the butt of his gun. After Cissy told him that he looked like a Greek god, he expected her to make a pass at him, but she didn't. She did probe for details about his relationship with Grace. Evie Robert, who was often one of Cissy's houseguests, advised the actor, "Don't talk of your sexual adventures with Cissy because Cissy is like all the McCormick-Patterson clan—if there's any fucking to be done, they want to do it." Cissy described Evie to her friends as being "loose as a goose." Evie herself, sitting on the dais of a national Democratic dinner, pointed to one man after another at nearby tables saying, "I slept with him . . . I slept with him . . . I slept with him." Cissy laughed fondly when she told stories about Evie. But when a young man in Florida told her that he had slept with Evie the night before—"and I didn't even have to tell her I loved her"—Cissy slapped his face hard.

Cissy's dinner conversation was usually anti-Roosevelt, but she would not allow any criticism of Eleanor Roosevelt in her home. "Oh, no!" she would say, and make a spirited defense. Eleanor visited Cissy in Sarasota, and Cissy had a small dinner party for her. One of the guests used some strong language and then apologized, but Mrs. Roosevelt smiled and said, "Please, don't let that trouble you; I've heard much worse in my time."

Cissy herself used four-letter words fluently, a trait that endeared her to some of her younger guests. They admired her for many reasons: she never flaunted her power or her money, she always talked to them on their level, and she seemed genuinely interested in what they had to say. One young man, a friend of Felicia's, told Cissy about a disagreeable discussion he had just had with a visiting magazine publisher. Cissy put her arms around him and said, "Who the hell cares about him. He's full of shit. The only reason I have him here is because I like his wife." Then she added sympathetically, "I can understand why you had ulcers."

Cissy treated all of her daughter's friends royally. "Cissy was very good about second-hand loving," Felicia later commented. Cal Carrington acted as an intermediary in arranging Felicia's visit to Sarasota to try at a reconciliation in 1941. The three rented a cruiser and went to the island of Spanish Wells. A peasant woman there gave Cissy a small doll, and Cissy, moved by this gesture, burst into tears. Felicia thought, "Why hasn't she ever cried for me?"

The reconciliation didn't work. After too many drinks, Cissy said all the ugly things again—that Felicia was wasting her life and ruining her child. Cal later told Felicia what he had told her before: "You know, honey, she took a de-spite to your Dad, and I think that's what it's all about."

One reason Cal liked to visit Cissy in Sarasota was that he had found a new admirer, a trapeze artist with the Ringling Brothers circus. Ringling had reopened its winter headquarters in Sarasota several years before. The mansion of John Ringling North was patterned on the Doges' palace in Venice and had eight gondolas moored off the terrace. The living room, sixty-five feet long and fifty feet wide, was three stories high and had a pipe organ. North had an excellent French chef, and Cissy seldom missed his private parties. And twice a week he took her to the nearby hotel he owned where she could see his new circus acts. The show never started until they arrived.

Cissy loved originals and invited many of the circus people to her home. Among her favorites were a transvestite trapeze artist and a snake charmer called Texas Jim. She kept these new acquaintances apart from her more staid friends. When one of her Chicago friends arrived unexpectedly, Cissy met him at the door and laughed. "Don't come in," she said. "The place is full of bums."

Cissy had lost none of her impulsiveness. She once ordered one of her editors who looked like "a blond Byron" to come to Sarasota. His job was to distract John Ringling North's girl friend so that North could get away. Cissy later took a reporter with her on a whimsical trip in the Ranger to see Edgar Allen Poe's room at the University of Virginia. She spent five minutes looking at it, then returned to the train. She told the station-master that she had decided to go on to Williamsburg, Virginia. She wanted to see "Jack's restorations." ("Jack" was John D. Rockefeller, Jr.)

"You're in luck, Mrs. Patterson," said the stationmaster. "We have one train a day to Williamsburg, and it's due in an hour and a half. We'll attach Ranger to it and down you'll go."

"I don't want to wait that long," said Cissy. "Bring around an engine."

Walter Howey returned to Washington in 1942 for one of his occasional visits. He still supervised the Hearst papers in Boston and had offered Felicia a reporting job, which Cissy had persuaded her to turn down—by raising her allowance. "She didn't want to let me get out of her control, I guess," said Felicia.

Howey was giving more time to his inventions. He had devised an automatic photoelectric engraving machine and a system of transmitting pictures by sound waves. His latest was a mechanical device to squeeze and strain the contents of an entire case of oranges at one time. He told Cissy he had designed it to spare himself the effort of making mixed drinks by hand. He held a press conference in Washington to demonstrate it. But he had already sampled a great many drinks, and the machine blew up. Also blown up were any remnants of a Cissy-Howey romance. He had found himself a wife.

Despite the increasing number of reporters and editors who were going into the military service, the *Times-Herald* had been kept on an even keel. For Cissy, though, much of the challenge was gone. Her bitterness about the war had begun to sour her. But she was still concerned enough about the paper to kill features she disliked and to restrict advertising to specific pages and columns. She declared, "We should not scrimp on news content." And when her business manager proposed a budget cut, she scribbled a memo: "But why save the dough now?"

Cissy felt strongly that a newspaper would operate better if its employees had a share in its profits. Her ideas often baffled her business manager, Bill Shelton. He came from a rural area of Virginia where men were men and women were glad of it. Shelton was honest and knowledgeable, but Cissy made him feel inarticulate. The more she sensed this the more she tore into him. "You couldn't show fear of her, or she'd eat you," he said. She deliberately intimidated Shelton even though she regarded him as invaluable. When she discovered that he had managed to squirrel away a considerable profit for the paper, she was indignant rather than pleased. The profit, she said, belonged to her newspaper executives, and she distributed handsome bonuses. More quietly, she continued to pay for the schooling of children of some of her editors who had gone to war.

Her granddaughter, Ellen, had started going to boarding school, the exclusive Miss Gill's in New Jersey. Just before Pearl Harbor, Drew had a family birthday party for Cissy. She was sixty years old, and Joe made a comment that cut her deeply: "You have reached an age when nobody will ever love you for yourself alone." It was the last family dinner they would all have together.

Drew had become extraordinarily successful. "Washington Merry-Go-Round," the column he wrote with Robert Allen, was syndicated in almost 600 papers with a total circulation of 40 million. Drew still had his radio program and it had an audience of many more millions. He liked to say nobody owned him. He wrote of himself: "Because of his independence he is either loved or hated; there is no middle ground of affection where Pearson is concerned."

Cissy's relationship with Drew deteriorated quickly after the entry of the United States into the war. They had disagreed

424

violently about American intervention before Pearl Harbor. They also argued bitterly about FDR, and his policies. But she still hedged her feelings, telling a friend, "Drew may be the bastard of the world, but he's been like a father and mother to Ellen." She continued to edit his columns heavily, and relegated it to the back pages, finally putting it on the comic page.

One of Cissy's heroes was a man she had first met at her cousin Medill's wedding, General Douglas A. MacArthur. She and Joe both wanted Roosevelt to bring MacArthur back from the Philippines and put him in charge of all the American armed forces. When the General was beseiged in Corregidor, Cissy muttered to a friend, "That's where they want him— where he'll be out of the way." When her friend disagreed, Cissy refused to listen.

In their column Pearson and Allen often praised MacArthur for his military accomplishments, but they leavened this praise with frequent references to his egotistical arrogance. Their attacks on him dated from their Merry-Go-Round books, in which they blasted MacArthur, then chief of staff, for routing the Bonus Marchers from Anacostia Flats. They quoted a letter to the General in which the unnamed writer suggested MacArthur be awarded another medal with "a ribbon on it, down the middle of which will be a long streak of yellow, with a piece of bologna on the end." They also charged that MacArthur had been promoted to major general because of his wealthy father-in-law's friendship with the Secretary of War.

Cissy ordered one of their anti-MacArthur columns killed. "Pull it out. The hell with it. If I have to print opinions opposed to my own to stay in business, I'll get out."

Realizing that their differences were irreconcilable, Drew wrote to her in February 1942 protesting her censorship and asking that their contract for the column be voided. "You are perfectly right, dear Drew," she answered, "both from your point of view and my own. Long disgusted with your column."

Before replying, however, she had asked her circulation manager, Happy Robinson, how much the paper would be hurt by the loss of Drew's column. He told her not to worry about it but to explain her action in a front-page box. She did. "We dropped the Washington Merry-Go-Round because of the poisonous attempts Pearson and Allen have made—are still making—to smear the reputation of a great soldier and, in our opinion, one of the greatest Americans of all time, General Douglas MacArthur."

Pearson and Allen tried to buy a full-page ad in the Washington *Post* to state that they had not been fired by Cissy, that they had quit. In fact, Allen insisted that he had started negotiations earlier to switch their column to the *Post*. But Eugene Meyer had had his fill of fights with Cissy, and he refused to accept their advertisement. He did agree, however, to their request that he run their column on the comic page—because they felt it was the most widely read page of the paper and made their column all the more distinctive.

From this time on, whenever Pearson and Allen were mentioned in the Washington *Times-Herald,* they were called "The Headache Boys." Cissy then vindictively fired Drew's brother Leon, the *Times-Herald*'s Latin American correspondent, and hired George Abell, Luvie's former husband, to write a column that would replace "Washington Merry-Go-Round." Distressed by these vengeful intrigues, Luvie Pearson resigned as Cissy's movie critic.

To this point, Cissy's actions were distasteful, but her subsequent behavior was unforgivable. She began a series called "Having A Wonderful Time," attacking all those that she felt had wanted the war and were still happily in Washington. She persuaded her brother to let George Dixon, an employee of his Washington bureau who had a gift for the editorial hatchet, to write for the *Times-Herald* under the byline Georgiana X. Preston—to keep him anonymous. And she collaborated with him. Their first victim was Drew, and they headlined the article "QUAKER OAT TURNED INTO SOUR MASH," commenting on his former Quaker pacifism now converted to a fiery interventionism.

She called Drew "one of the weirdest specimens of humanity since Nemo, the Turtle Boy." She said he had two faces, each with poison sacs. "For years now we have had to keep our pet gila monster away from him because in a battle of fangs, it wouldn't be a fair fight." She intimated that he might be a superspy, that he was "America's outstanding journalistic heel," and she longed "to play chopsticks on his baldish head with a meat cleaver."

She told a friend that if they were in Chicago, she "would have him rubbed out." And she shocked Luvie Pearson by saying that she wished she could break up Luvie's marriage to Drew.

Drew was tempted to sue for libel, but his daughter said, "That's exactly what Grandmother wants. Don't give her that satisfaction."

The rupture between Pearson and Cissy was absolute. Cissy had rarely broken so completely with anyone. She had differed strongly with Bill Bullitt and had argued with him constantly; yet she had traveled to Philadelphia to hear him speak, offered him the use of her Dupont Circle house, and never let politics interfere with their warm friendship. *Times-Herald* articles on Bullitt were critical but never rancorous. The Swopes were in complete disagreement with her on the war, but this never impaired their relationship. Baruch's opinions were also in opposition to hers, but the two never stopped flirting.

Diagnosing the Cissy break with Drew, mutual friends blamed it on love, drink, and Dr. de Savitsch. The love was real. Whether Cissy took on Drew as a son or a lover, or both, the general feeling was that "he could have had it all," the whole of her fortune, the paper, everything. Instead, he had made his own success, his own fortune, and he had taken his leave of her. This rejection turned her love into hatred and rage, and her increased drinking fueled her fury. Dr. Eugene de Savitsch added the final fillip by introducing her to drugs to get her out of depressions and give her highs.

Dr. de Savitsch lived on a street near Dupont Circle. He was unmarried and urbane and was delighted to fill in as an extra man at Cissy's dinners. De Savitsch was a Russian emigré, reared in a world of tutors, maids, and religious instructors. His father had been a prominent Russian prosecutor and judge. In his autobiography, De Savitsch claims to have performed with Anna Pavlova in a ballet—he danced the part of a eunuch in a Turkish harem.

A *Times-Herald* article on De Savitsch described him as "one of the wittiest tongues in town." He was twenty years younger than Cissy, and older women found him attractive and "safe." De Savitsch once invited one of Cissy's friends, a young matron, to his apartment for a drink. Knowing his reputation, she accepted, then was startled when he made a pass at her. "I went because I wasn't worried; I thought he was as queer as a three-dollar bill."

De Savitsch was a brilliant conversationalist who could talk knowledgeably and wittily about St. Petersburg, Denver, Japan, Paris, and the Belgian Congo. He was a society doctor whose patients included Alice Roosevelt Longworth and Evalyn Walsh McLean. Some questions had been raised about his medical skill. There were rumors of bizarre errors in diagnosis and wildly improper use of medication. His repeated applications for a license to practice surgery in the District of Columbia had been turned down on the ground that he was unqualified. But many patients swore that he had saved their lives. He was a strong advocate of vitamin B_{12} injections and gave them to most of his patients. To a small, select group of patients, he gave cocaine. Evalyn McLean became so addicted to cocaine that she sometimes needed the constant supervision of a nurse. She still managed, however, to hide drugs around her house. Cissy probably started to take cocaine out of curiosity, but she soon was taking it more and more often. "If I could only find you another vice," a friend told her, "you'd leave me a million dollars." Cocaine made the unpredictable Cissy even more unstable.

Cissy had met De Savitsch at the home of the Wylies, a couple who were frequent guests at her more intimate dinners. John Wylie worked in the intelligence section of the state department. He was tall, heavy, almost ugly, and a heavy drinker. Cissy and he had been young together in Europe, and their friends said that she was in love with him. Despite his looks, or because of them, he had a way with women. Cissy remembered how he and Wallis Warfield Simpson had slipped away together from a small dinner at the F Street Club. Wylie's wife, Irena, was an extraordinarily talented artist. A Polish Jew, she had escaped from the Warsaw ghetto just before the Nazis had come. She did a portrait of Ellen for Cissy, and a sketch of an opal eye which Cissy hung in her fourth-floor bedroom. Cissy was devoted to her. The Wylie home was always filled with writers and artists and diplomats, and Cissy often went there when she was lonely.

During these years, Cissy spoke frequently on the phone with her brother, Tom White, Rose Crabtree, and Marion Davies. At the start of the war, Hearst and Marion had moved from San Simeon to another of his estates, Wyntoon (which Marion called "Spittoon"). They had left San Simeon because it was in clear view of the Pacific Ocean, and the Chief felt a Japanese submarine might attack his castle because of his strong anti-Japan stand before the war. Wyntoon was in the wilderness, 250 miles north of San Francisco; a stone and timber castle and several smaller castles had been built on the 67,000-acre property. Marion told Cissy she was bored with too much backgammon and bridge and not enough merry people. Hearst was close to eighty, but he still played tennis. The Lindberghs had been there, and Cary Grant and Joe Kennedy and his sons. Although she liked all of them, she missed Cissy, merry, merry, Cissy. But Cissy was not at this time so merry.

Her quarrel with Pearson coincided with her war on Walter Winchell. Winchell was the nation's leading gossip columnist, and Cissy had always featured him in her paper. Like Pearson, he had a popular radio show. "Whenever Cissy came to town," recalled Winchell, "she romanced me to take her riding in the car along the crime beat and tell her anecdotes and tales of the beautiful people and not-so-beautiful gangsters who populate Broadway." He had a car radio equipped to receive police signals, and the one that fascinated Cissy most was Police Signal 1030: "Crime in progress! Use caution! They are armed!" If they heard a 1030, she and Winchell would rush to the scene.

"She liked me so much," Winchell remembered, "that when I brought my daughter to Washington, Cissy insisted we not return to Manhattan in 'a silly little old regular chair car' but in her private pullman."

Cissy and Winchell later broke over the war. He had come to one of Evalyn McLean's parties early in 1942 with his friend J. Edgar Hoover. They were sitting with Cissy and Evalyn when Cissy suddenly said to Winchell, "Why don't you quit looking under your bed for Nazis?"

"You mean, and finding them?"

"I mean, your column, which is read by only servants down here, is becoming a bore the way you keep after Nazis."

"Mrs. Patterson, why don't you get another boy."

Cissy left the table and the party, and Winchell soon felt her anger. His column, which was frequently shortened, was now, as Drew's had been, relegated to the back pages. At the same time, Cissy described him in print as a middle-aged ex-chorus boy suffering "from a chronic state of wild excitement, venom, and perpetual motion of the jaw." She called him "a popgun patriot," "a grimy clown," "one of those whispery, furtive characters who used to pop up from nowhere to ask if we'd care to buy some spicy French postcards." She referred to that "chamber of horrors he calls a brain." When she heard him on the radio, she yelled, "Turn the bastard off." And in one headline almost an inch high, she called him a "cockroach." She told friends, "There isn't a night goes by that I don't get down on my knees and pray that they take the sonofabitch off shore duty and put him on a destroyer that will sink."

Winchell counterattacked, describing her in his column as "the craziest woman in Washington, D.C."

Cissy called Waldrop. "I want to sue Winchell, and I want you to sue him TODAY!"

"Do you want to talk about it?" asked Waldrop.

"No, because if I do, you'll talk me out of it."

It was Cissy's way of saying, "Look, I know damn well I'm making a fool out of myself, but I want to do it." She did sue him but later dropped the suit because his contract made him immune to damages.

"He is forever boasting that he is the American [whom]

Hitler would most like to hang," Cissy noted. "In what respect does that make Hitler different from anybody else?"

This vitriolic attack was probably triggered by liquor and drugs, but its source might have lain deeper. The isolationist gospel she preached had been loudly rejected by most Americans, her readers among them. She was exhausted and embittered by her long battle to change public opinion. She realized that she was engaged in a losing fight, and she did not like to lose. Her defeat was doubly galling because it represented a victory for Roosevelt. Cissy might well have turned some of her rage toward FDR's supporters. Perhaps it was this emotion that gave the hysterical tone to her attacks on Winchell and Pearson.

The war was going badly in the summer of 1942. The Germans were sweeping through North Africa, and the Japanese were scoring one success after another. The only good news came from Midway, where American ships overwhelmingly defeated those of the Japanese navy. The Chicago *Tribune,* the *Times-Herald,* and two dozen other papers later printed an article by a *Tribune* war correspondent which indicated that the United States had prevailed because the Japanese codes had been broken.

Four days before Pearl Harbor, the *Tribune* and the *Times-Herald* had published some American secret war plans. "That's the worst thing we ever did," said Waldrop. The leak supposedly had come from the Air Force, since the plans favored the other services. "It showed that we planned to put our military weight in Europe, rather than in the Pacific, with an expeditionary force of five million."

Within days after the article was printed, the German general staff recommended that to prepare for this inevitable attack from the United States, troops should be transferred from the Russian to the western front. Hitler refused.

After the war plans were published, it was rumored that both papers would be charged with treason, but no action was taken. Now, however, in the Midway case, the Department of Justice decided to file charges that the *Tribune* and the *Times-Herald* had betrayed U.S. military secrets. Since none of the two dozen other papers printing the article had been charged, it looked like a Government vendetta against the two newspapers.

The American cryptographers had sworn never to reveal that the Japanese codes had been broken. Attorney General Francis Biddle felt the disclosure of this breakthrough had been tantamount to treason because it gave the Japanese the chance to change their codes.

Waldrop was called to Chicago to testify before a grand jury. Cissy went with him. "She just came as my friend," said Waldrop. "I never felt closer to anybody." In the middle of the testimony, the Navy disclosed that a Navy censor had passed the *Tribune* article. Forced to drop the case, Biddle said he "felt like a fool." The full truth about the case was never publicly revealed.

In contrast to this serious crisis, Colonel McCormick created a small wave of national laughter by a widely published letter: "You do not know it, but the fact is that I introduced the ROTC into the schools; that I introduced machine guns into the Army; that I introduced mechanization; I introduced automatic rifles; I was the first ground officer to go up in the air and observe artillery fire. . . . I forced the acquiring of the bases in the Atlantic Ocean." A cartoon referred to it as "Col. McCosmic's letter," and it was published in the *News* with the caption "Whatta man!"

Soon after this, in August 1942, a Pennsylvania congressman, Elmer Holland, demanded that the FBI investigate "America's No. 1 and No. 2 exponents of the Nazi propaganda line—Cissy and Joe Patterson."

Speaking from the floor of the House, Holland said, "I hate to think, Mr. Speaker, that the hatred of any American family is so great toward our President that they would welcome a victory by Hitler in preference to a democratic government in this country headed by Franklin D. Roosevelt."

"You're a liar, Congressman Holland," Joe Patterson editorialized in the *News*. "What Holland said about me and my sister is a lie. We are not 'Hitler-followers.' . . . We do not seek to bring about a fascist victory hoping to be rewarded afterwards. . . . This country has treated us well—superlatively well. What could we gain by having it fall?" Cissy reprinted her brother's editorial, adding: "To the above statement, I heartily subscribe. You are a liar, Congressman Holland, and you know it."

But Holland continued his attack: "Daily these publishers rub at the morale of the American people. Daily they sow suspicion. Daily they preach that we are a nation of fools, led by rascals into a hopeless struggle. Daily they wear at the moral fiber of the people, softening it, rotting it, preparing us for defeat."

Fighting back, Cissy printed "The Duty of Newspapers," an editorial her grandfather had written during the Civil War.

The country is engaged in a war upon which hang momentous consequences, not alone to our government . . . but to every man, woman and child living beneath our country's flag. It is a war for national existence, and for individual freedom and prosperity and happiness. . . .

. . . Leading and influential journals like our own are in some sort regarded as watchmen on the walls, to look for approach of danger toward what their readers hold dear. They have had thrust upon them the duty, not always pleasant, of acting as conservators of the public good, often at the expense of their private interests. Men look to them not only for facts but for opinions. They do not often create, but they shape and give direction to public sentiment. They are the narrators of facts, the exponents of policy, the enemies of wrong. . . .

. . . We are not of those who believe that, because the country is in danger and all private interests are threatened, or because military power overrides the civil law, it is the province of journalism of the better sort to keep silence when incompetency overtakes the management of public affairs, or hold its peace when unblushing rascality under the guise of patriotism is doing its deadly work.

. . . We know what the peril is which attaches to plain speaking. We know that our personal interests would be better served oftentimes by silence than by honest speech. . . . We make no claim to infallibility. . . . We go our own way at our own time, in our own manner, in company of our own choosing, knowing as we do that vindication will be sure to follow. We can afford to be honest, and fearless, and to wait. . . .

It did not help Cissy's cause when rabble-rouser preacher Gerald L. K. Smith nominated her to his personal hall of fame. With her, he named Bertie and Joe, as well as several leaders of anti-Catholic, anti-Semitic groups.

Joe, Cissy, and Bertie were widely denounced as pro-German, and they faced attacks from all sides. In December 1942, Roosevelt sent a German Iron Cross to New York *Daily News* columnist John O'Donnell—whose articles Cissy also published. The Philadelphia *Record* had accused O'Donnell of being "a Naziphile" who favored the "destruction of the British Empire and liquidation of Jews." O'Donnell later sued for libel and won.

Cissy had fired Managing Editor DeWitt for the third and last time, and Waldrop was running the paper. With most of the earlier staff now gone to war, copygirls had replaced copyboys, and amateurs were everywhere. When Cissy demanded Waldrop's time and attention, he refused, explaining that he had to run the paper. "Frank, you're throwing gold away for silver," Tom White told him, indicating that it was more important for him to be with Cissy whenever needed. Waldrop detailed how rough it was to try to run a paper with a skeleton staff. "What about her?" asked Tom. "Don't you think it's rough on her?" The public pressure on Cissy had intensified enormously.

Cissy was getting an increasing amount of hate mail. A bomb was thrown into her newspaper building. Then, one day, unobtrusively set in the middle of an ad for a house on the want-ad page in the *Times-Herald,* was the line SHIT ON ELEANOR JEW PATTERSON.

She had stood undaunted against the President of the United States, the Attorney General, the American public, but this—in her own paper—this almost crushed her. "Maybe if I were not so old, I would go and tear the building down."

The culprit was never found, despite investigations by the FBI and private detectives and the use of lie detector tests. The irony was that she was under simultaneous attack by some of Washington's Jewish advertisers. A speaker at the Advertising Club said, "I accuse the Patterson family of trying to divide the American people. . . . I accuse the Pattersons of resorting to the oldest, most cowardly and bestial device—anti-Semitism, which is anti-Christian and anti-American. . . . You don't have to spend your money with people who say they don't like you, and who want to destroy you."

Cissy's attitude toward Jews was confused and complex. She had married a Jew; her former son-in-law was part-Jewish and so was her granddaughter; several of her lovers had been Jewish or part-Jewish. Dr. Barach, who had helped her know herself, was Jewish; Herbert Swope, who had made her part of his family, was Jewish; Bernard Baruch, whom she admired so extravagantly, was Jewish; and Happy Robinson, whom she trusted more than anyone else, was Jewish. Yet her conversation was studded with all the derogatory clichés about Jews that she had picked up at so many parties from so many peers. She laughed delightedly at anti-Semitic jokes. And now her new concern that Jews were the strongest backers of the war.

Waldrop talked with the Jewish advertisers. He understood their emotions and told them, "You're people just like me, and if you step on my feet, I'm going to step on yours. But not *because* you're a Jew but just because you stepped on my *feet*." He was able to persuade them to continue advertising in the *Times-Herald*. And, as usual, Happy Robinson saw the heart of Cissy's problems. He told her flatly that she would continue to be attacked so long as her readers were for Roosevelt and she wasn't.

While she was defending herself against charges of anti-Semitism, Cissy was busy promoting a new social hostess for Washington, Gwendolyn Detre de Surany Cafritz, the wife of one of her major Jewish advertisers, Morris Cafritz. Some said Cissy liked Morris, a fiercely independent real estate man, more than she liked Gwendolyn. Many of Cissy's horrified friends asked why she was promoting a Hungarian Jewess as the capital's leading social hostess. Why not? asked Cissy. Wasn't Elsa Maxwell once a pianist in a nickelodeon? For Cissy this was part of the fun of power. She laughingly repeated Mrs. Cafritz's remark: "I *always* invite senators, but I seldom play around with the Lower House."

During this period Cissy encountered Harold Ickes at a Washington party. They had not met for several years, but she had attacked him in print as "Dishonest Harold . . . the one man in Washington who could get a black, gold, and chromium-tipped bathtub when chromium was going to war; the one man who got a government car to deliver his eggs when gas was rationed; the one man who wrote a book about himself to tell the world what a great guy he was." She had run a photograph of his new iron fence, citing it as a fine example of the national drive to save metal. She had also zeroed in on him in a radio talk entitled "The Jawbone of an Acidulous Man." In it, she had charged him with besmirching the American press. "You have proved yourself cheaper and trickier in your own reporting than anything your bilious fancy has conjured up against the press." But, at this party, she and Ickes greeted each other warmly—"Why, Harold . . ." and "Cissy dear . . ." —kissed demonstratively, and embraced each other.

At another party soon afterward, their meeting was something less than cordial, and they exchanged bitter words about the war. "I punched Harold Ickes right in the jaw," Cissy told Frank Waldrop the next day. Cissy was delighted when Evie Robert said she was calling her puppy Ickes, "until it was housebroken."

Nor were her other friends safe from her barbed attacks. One of the men who had moved in and out of her life since Schlesinger's death was Bernard Baruch. He was a self-made millionaire who radiated power and advised political leaders from a Washington park bench. Baruch had been as staunch an isolationist as Cissy, but he had moved closer to Roosevelt, particularly after Lindbergh sprinkled the anti-war speeches he made with references that some interpreted as anti-Semitic.

Baruch was six feet three, with ice-blue eyes that twinkled, and a soft, deep, southern-accented voice. "He was an indefatigable ladies' man—and the ladies succumbed in droves to one of the handsomest men of his time." Cissy was no exception.

She made her Sands Point house available to him, and he fondly wrote her that "our habitual desire has been to promote the welfare and happiness of each other." Yet when Baruch gave an opulent dinner for Harry Hopkins early in 1943 and Igor Cassini wrote a blistering, mocking account of it—he observed that the dinner cost the equivalent of 88,200 bullets—Cissy smilingly approved the column for publication.

Although Cissy's power had diminished, she could still destroy almost anyone who crossed her. Few had the courage to confront her. She was too unpredictable, too unstable, too strong.

Bill Bullitt once brought a young State Department friend to a party at Cissy's. This hapless youth described the *Times-Herald* as "fascist" within her earshot. Cissy soon ran a front-page editorial: "If the Army really needs ALL the able-bodied young men it can get, it can find in Secretary Hull's fold an assortment of rich, able-bodied and unmarried boys of no particular use to anyone. . . . There are plenty of intelligent girls available to more than adequately fill the jobs of these young men. . . ." With the editorial, she ran the pictures and short biographies of twenty State Department career men "who do not choose to fight."

Republican leader Thomas E. Dewey charged that an "American Cliveden set in Washington" was scheming to use the Republican party to get a negotiated peace. President Roosevelt bluntly called this group "The Dower House Set." In a letter to a friend, FDR complained: "Honestly, the real trouble is not in the people or the leaders but in a gang which unfortunately survives—made up mostly of those who were isolationists before December seventh and who are actuated today by various motives in their effort to instill disunity in the country. Some are publishers like Bertie McCormick and the Pattersons. . . ."

Cissy countered by attacking the "Yellow Potomac Set," who, she said, were more concerned with keeping their jobs than with winning the war.

Despite her public show of indignation at Dewey's and Roosevelt's remarks, Cissy would have happily accepted a negotiated peace. She simply wanted the killing to stop. So did Joe. "Father hated war so much that it made him a different man," Alicia said of Joe. "I think it was because of what he went through in the first war. He was gassed twice, you know."

By 1943, Joe was no longer the scrappy, energetic man of a few years before. The war weighed heavily on him. And the attack by Representative Holland had filled him with rancor. His daughter's pro-Roosevelt stand during the war had so angered him that he had rewritten his will. Alicia was no longer one of those named to run the *News* after his death—even though the growing success of her Long Island tabloid, *Newsday*, attested to her ability. All his life, he had wanted love. He thought he had found it in his readers, but now everywhere he saw only a growing hate. Others' hostility hit him harder than it did Bertie because Bertie was less sensitive. Opposition seemed to make Bertie more bristling and bombastic than ever. Even Bertie, however, had a gnawing malaise deep inside him. Whenever he stayed at Cissy's house in Washington, she had his bedroom cleared of valuable things. During the night, while the house slept, Bertie would rant and roar and break things. In the morning he would be his usual aloof self. There was never any mention of what had happened the night before, but he would tip the servants heavily.

For Cissy, too, the fun was gone, the dreams were bad.

18

The excitement of life is a wonderful thing, but when the beauty of youth has went, there's no more excitement in it.

—Cal Carrington

Cissy was sixty-two in 1943 and fighting against fat. She told Waldrop she didn't care much anymore. She slept more poorly than ever, the lights in her bedroom burning all night long. The interaction of drink and drugs added violence to her temper. She more and more frequently had second thoughts in the middle of the night and automatically reached for the phone.

She ate alone more often now. She favored a small Italian restaurant near the corner of 14th and L called Mama Ceresa. She and Mama had developed a rapport. Cissy always took the same booth, the farthest one back against the wall, where she could see everything. As soon as she sat down, Mama would bring her a tall water glass filled with champagne. A copyboy, Sidney Epstein, who later became a Washington editor, delivered newspaper proofs to her booth about seven-thirty every night. Whenever he came, she was always alone. She seldom talked to him. She simply took the proofs, swiftly started reading, crossing out paragraphs, making notations, often muttering to herself, occasionally cursing quietly. The boy stood there waiting, then hurried away with the finished proofs.

Cissy knew what was going on at the paper, but she no longer cared with the same intensity. She no longer looked around the elevator and asked, "How are you all doin'? Anybody having any trouble?" She no longer insisted that a page be replated—as many as five times—until she was satisfied with it. But she still wanted every error she found corrected. Told that an edition was almost at the end of its press run, with less than 5,000 copies still to be printed, Cissy answered, "I'd want it corrected even if there was only one copy left." Waldrop also never forgot what she told him about editing: "You're so damn intellectual. . . . Why don't you just *feel* it?"

One of her young editors was with her on the balcony overlooking her ballroom at Dupont Circle. Two dozen finalists of "The Golden Mirror Contest"—her newspaper's teenage beauty contest—were there for an afternoon tea dance. "I was standing next to Cissy," he said, "and we were watching these lovely young girls dancing. I looked at Cissy and I saw this look of terrible sadness on her face. And then a tear came. Then it hit me. She didn't want to get old. She hated the idea of getting old."

Cissy was too powerful to be completely lonely. She could always pick up and phone, and people came. But now there were more new faces. A great many friends found it politically prudent to avoid her. "I cannot keep friends more than six months," she complained.

Two friends that stayed faithful through the later years of her life were Evie Robert and Ann Smith. Wherever she went, she always seemed to have one or the other with her. Cissy told Evie that she was leaving her the black pearls—the piece of jewelry she wore most often. Whenever Evie got angry or contrary, Cissy would dramatically finger her black pearls and say, "Now, now, Evie." Evie usually calmed down quickly. They had a minor falling out on a point of principle: Evie claimed she had shot and killed a bear when Cissy sent her to Jackson Hole. Cissy later learned that Evie had bought the bear skin, and blew up at her.

Evie wrote a column for Cissy called "Eve's Rib," and Cissy fed her a variety of items for it. Evie was not immune to being temporarily fired. Yet when Cissy drank too much and passed out somewhere, it was often Evie who came to get her and put her to bed. She enjoyed Evie's gossip about her many love affairs. "Did you sleep with him?" Cissy always asked.

Ann Smith was the quiet one, the soft, sweet one, the mother of six children who looked unbelievably young. "One of the most beautiful young women I have ever seen came [to a party] with Cissy Patterson," a society writer noted. "She has enormous blue eyes—the pure Greek type—and looks like the Flying Victory of Samothrace would have looked had she a head. She was a combination of Princess Martha of Norway, Ingrid Bergman and Zorina." "Your little friend Mrs. Smith is a perfect beauty," Evalyn McLean wrote Cissy, "and she was the sensation of the party. More people asked me who that beautiful child was than I can remember. . . . I really love to look at a woman as beautiful as Mrs. Smith. It makes me feel sort of good inside."

This was exactly Cissy's feeling, and when Ann Smith became seriously ill, Cissy insisted that she stay at Dupont Circle. Cissy cared for her more than she ever cared for her own child. It had been a long time since Cissy had felt she was really needed by another human being.

One of her new friends, who had moved into her house for a while, was the pilot Eddie Rickenbacker, who once told her, "You may be Cissy to millions, but you'll always be 'Mumsy' to me."

Another new young friend for Cissy was Austine "Bootsie" McDonnell, who married Igor Cassini and later became Mrs. William Randolph Hearst, Jr. The dark-haired Bootsie was beautiful and very bright. When Igor went to war, Cissy let Bootsie write his column, and it became more popular than ever. Cissy fed Bootsie many of her items, including one about Dorothy Schiff Thackery, the publisher of the New York *Post*. Since Mrs. Thackery was married, and since the item told of her involvement with another man, she sued and got an apology. Mrs. Thackery was not then a working publisher; she had bought the *Post* for her husband.

Kathleen Kennedy, of whom Cissy had been very fond, left the *Times-Herald* in 1943 to go to England. She was defying her father to marry the son of the non-Catholic Duke of Devonshire. She was later to die in a plane crash.

Kathleen's brother Joe was killed in the war, but her brother John returned from the Pacific a hero and visited Cissy at the *Times-Herald*. He wanted to be a newspaperman, and Cissy printed his reportage on the United Nations conference in San Francisco.

Cissy still gave parties, but they were smaller and less frequent. Occasionally she would go to bed before the party was over, and one of her young subhostesses, such as Ellie Waldrop or Evie Robert, would see her guests to the door. She once wired Ellie and Evie from Sarasota, "Let's have a party when I get home," and they had one waiting for her when she arrived. At one of her parties, she made a more dramatic entrance than usual: several of her miniature poodles were taking a free ride on her long, trailing dress. Her evening clothes were still eccentric but dazzling. One evening she wore black silk pants, a Chinese brocade coat, and Japanese sandals. At another party one of her guests asked, "Is that really a kimono?" "My dear," replied her husband, "that is not what matters. What does matter is that it looks like one and that only our Cissy would dare to wear such a thing."

Cissy enjoyed twitting her guests. She once pinched Lord Halifax on his backside, and when he turned, she said, "Pardon me, I thought you were Mr. Justice Frankfurter." (Halifax was extremely tall, Frankfurter extremely short.) Evalyn McLean arrived at a party without her Hope diamond but wearing a giant jeweled cross on a chain. "Evalyn, I gave you that to hang on the foot of your bed," Cissy remarked.

"Migawd, Cissy," Evalyn yelled, "I couldn't lug my bed here, could I?"

Cissy discontinued her Gridiron parties because she said she was "too tired and busy to bother." She was also too tired with fighting with newsmen about the war. But her annual Christmas party was a tradition she still maintained. "I'd like to cut that list," she confided. "There are a lot of names on it that I don't like. But if I cut some of them off, then their children will miss the party. No, I'll just have to put up with them all!" But on another occasion she had commented cynically, "You see those sonsofbitches dining in my home. As long as I can feed them, serve champagne, and have a larger bank account than theirs, I can buy and sell even their souls."

Cissy didn't feel that way about dogs. "We are alone, absolutely alone on this chance planet, and amid all the forms of life that surround us, not one, excepting the dog, has made an alliance with us," wrote Maurice Maeterlinck. Cissy certainly shared his feelings. Her dogs went everywhere with her. When Toto swallowed a stone, she brought in a leading New York surgeon (who later operated on President Eisenhower). While driving her dogs from one house to another, her chauffeur hit a pole, wrecked the car, and gashed his head. The frightened dogs escaped into the woods, and the chauffeur refused to go to the hospital until the dogs were found. Cissy wouldn't care about the car, but if the dogs were lost, so was his job. He took the dogs home by train.

On Cissy's orders the Washington *Times-Herald* Animal Rescue League Ambulance roamed the city, picking up homeless animals. When she saw a sad mongrel on her way to the office, she tucked it under her mink and brought it with her. She would then run its picture and find it a home. No newspaper in the country printed more editorials against vivisection than the *Times-Herald,* and yet she fully reported congressional committee hearings opposed to her antivivisection crusade. No newspaper printed more animal pictures—but they had to be *good* animal pictures.

Cissy's dogs had all died except her gray poodle Butch. She

had a sketch made of her and Butch for a Christmas card, with a Latin motto that translated: "Gentle when stroked, fierce when provoked." It applied to both of them. Evie always brought her own dog, Coco, with her when she visited Cissy. Butch and Coco had a tug-of-war over a beautiful chiffon handkerchief, which split right down the middle. Evie started to scold Coco, but Cissy said, "Hush, Evie. Let them have it. There are so many more chiffon handkerchiefs like that, but where did you ever see two poodles having such a good time?" When Coco jumped on Cissy's lap, spilling her mint julep, Cissy commented, "She's done me a great favor. It's been so hot. It was time for me to change clothes anyway." She walked out of the room, taking Coco with her.

Butch slept in her room with her, listened appreciatively to her monologues, loved her for herself as no man now ever would. Yet she never confused dogs with people, never humanized them. When she found a guest playing with her dog, she asked if the dog had bitten him yet. "You can't trust the damn things," she said. "He bites me every once in a while."

But she loved animals. She now regretted the killing she had done and tried to give away her animal heads. She was in New York once with a friend and they were going to a small party for the Duchess of Windsor, when Cissy suddenly said, "Let's go to the zoo instead." And they did.

She did not like snakes. Evie playfully put a snake in Cissy's refrigerator and Cissy did not find that funny. She called the *Times-Herald* and had someone come "to snake-proof my house."

Marion Davies called to talk about the death of their two dachshunds, her Ghandi and Hearst's Helen. "When Helen died [he] just had her in his arms. He cried and cried." "Pops" was still the same; he still slipped a note under her door every morning and wouldn't let anyone wake her up. They were moving back to San Simeon, she said, and she was delighted. Hearst wouldn't even let her go to San Francisco to buy clothes—he had the stores send clothes to her for her selection. Marion said Hearst still had his own teeth, used glasses only for reading, and had a good appetite. Despite all her gay chatter, Cissy sensed that Marion was almost as lonely as she.

Cissy had six homes with ninety rooms, and 1,300 employees to worry about. Yet she told Waldrop, "I'm lonely." And she told Mike Flynn's wife, "I don't want to die alone."

As always, in her loneliness, Cissy reached out to Rose Crabtree:

> If I could telegraph myself out to Flat Creek . . . and if the whole place were sweet and clean, and if the whole of Jackson Hole hadn't slept in my beds for the past several years, and if I had a cook, and if there weren't mosquitoes and trout flies, and if I weren't too old and decrepit to sit on a horse—far less ride up and snaggle down Sheep Mountain—I'd come out to see you all. But it really is too far and I'm too old and weary.

She had been having what she called "spells"—pains in the chest and a feeling of faintness. Doctors diagnosed heart problems and warned her that from then on she would have to "travel in second gear." Cissy didn't know how to live in second gear, and she wrote to Rose:

> I don't know whether to believe them or not. Maybe if I didn't live in this outrageous house with cupids stringing marble wreaths and flowers all over the G.D. place (excepting for the back side—plain brick garbage cans and old rubbish cans out there), they wouldn't try to keep me an invalid. . . . I don't believe the doctors will let me go into a high altitude. But I'll tell you this much, and *sincerely*. Rather than be a sick old lady with nurses and doctors around me for the rest of my life, I'll *come anyway*.

One day in 1943, she suddenly became ill. Her servants called in Dr. de Savitsch. When Frank Waldrop came to visit, De Savitsch solemnly told him, "You'll never see your boss alive again." And Cissy did feel as if she were dying. Tom White arrived and she asked, "Tom, come here and make the sign of

445

the cross over me." De Savitsch then put Cissy under sedation, giving strict orders that she have no visitors. After many days, Evie Robert stormed in and "raised hell and told Cissy to get rid of De Savitsch and get another doctor." Cissy seemed too weak or too drugged to care. Frank Waldrop then slipped in to see her when De Savitsch was away. Her secretary had called and told him that Cissy had been kept semicomatose for weeks. When Waldrop saw her, Cissy seemed almost floating. She grabbed his arm and stared at him and said, "Get me a doctor. . . . I've got to have some help. This man is trying to kill me." Waldrop did rescue her. She was later examined by the noted cardiologist Dr. Paul Dudley White, who said, "Why, you've got a nice little heart!" Cissy repeated White's phrase over and over again in telling the story.

Cissy ran a full, detailed exposé of De Savitsch, literally calling him a quack. He sued but thought better of it, and the case never came to court. Before long, the black-haired, pasty-faced doctor was facing an FBI inquiry about his use of drugs, and he fled the country.

While recuperating, Cissy wrote to a friend: "The bedpan *burns* me up! I don't mind anything much but that!"

Cissy reached again for Rose: "I don't know why you find so many excuses not to visit me anymore as you used to. . . . I don't believe you realize how old I am. Really, Ma Reed was a beauty compared to me now—and what's more, she hasn't got a doggone thing on me today for unadulterated meanness."

Cissy never lost her power to destroy. One of the seamier stories that summer of 1943 was the one she circulated about Sumner Welles, the distinguished-looking Undersecretary of State. Bill Bullitt wanted his job. Bullitt had been sidetracked to the Department of the Navy as a special assistant. The "blazing comet in the sky" was not blazing anymore. "Bullitt is one of those 'he's up, he's down' guys." He was then down. He was so down that he told Cissy that Welles had made a homosexual overture to a black railroad porter, and had been caught, but the indictment was quashed. Bullitt had accumulated a large file of court documents about the incident. Word reached Roosevelt, and his press secretary Steve Early asked Bullitt to "answer the allegation that I had turned over the documents to Cissy Patterson . . . at a dinner." Bullitt admitted that he and Cissy had been friends "for over thirty years . . . always disputing on political matters but remaining friends." As for the specific charge, he called it "a complete lie." Welles resigned. Bullitt edged quickly into eclipse. He decided to run for mayor of Philadelphia—his grandfather had written the city's charter—but he was defeated after a disastrous campaign.

The war was going well. By 1944 the Germans and Japanese had been beaten back on all fronts and victory was in sight. Cissy's feelings about Roosevelt were unchanged. When she blasted FDR's friend Archibald MacLeish, the noted poet who was then Librarian of Congress, FDR wrote him: "I welcome you to the Society of Immortals. Bertie McCormick started it many years ago, even before we entered the First World War; and he incorporated it in 1919 when he broke Woodrow Wilson's heart and made him the first of the Immortals. The only trouble is that Bertie, Joe Patterson and Cissy deserve neither hate nor praise—only pity for their unbalanced mentalities."

When Harry Hopkins, FDR's closest advisor, became ill, the President ordered him to rest and warned him, "Cissy Patterson . . . wants to kill you off as soon as possible—just as she does me."

Many of Cissy's close friends felt she had lost her sense of proportion. When her anti-FDR campaign became more and more hateful, Happy went to see her. "Lady, what are you doing?" he asked.

"But, Hap," she said, "he wants to run for a *fourth* term!"

Her brother Joe's editorial headline was "NO FOURTH TERM FOR CAESAR." And Cissy reprinted it. She wrote Baruch: "Dear Bernie, I've been living in this house since 1903, and I've seen 'em come and seen 'em go—and this crowd's *goin'!*" She was wrong. When everyone said how old and tired he was, FDR took a long ride in an open car in the rain while campaigning in New York. When some said he had lost his touch, he made his famous Fala speech, which must have made even Cissy smile:

447

These Republican leaders have not been content with attacks—on me, or my wife, or on my sons. No, not content with that, they now include my little dog Fala. Well, of course, I don't resent attacks, and my family doesn't resent attacks, but Fala *does* resent them.

You know—you know—Fala's Scotch, and being a Scottie, as soon as he learned that the Republican fiction writers in Congress and out had concocted a story that I had left him behind on an Aleutian Island and had sent a destroyer back to find him—at a cost to the taxpayers of two or three or eight or twenty million dollars—his Scotch soul was furious. He has not been the same dog since.

In the fall of 1944, Cissy and Evalyn McLean had dinner with Dr. Alvan Barach in New York. In a fit of temper years before, Cissy had told Barach, "You Jews are trying to get us into the war." But, later, she had let him write an article for the *Times-Herald* which opposed her own views on the war. She now asked Barach whom he was voting for. He answered that he was voting for Roosevelt. "I remember distinctly how Cissy and McLean put down their forks, and did not finish their steaks, and sat there in absolute silence. I finished my steak, said good-bye, left, and not another word was spoken. And we never saw each other again."

Cissy lost another friend when Freddie McLaughlin died that year. He had come to visit her once in Washington with his daughter, still as vital and dogmatic as ever.

Bertie McCormick remarried in 1944; his new bride was a lovely divorcée, Maryland Hooper. Cissy didn't go to the wedding. "Cissy's still upset over Roosevelt's reelection," a friend explained. She did give a big party for the newlyweds when they stayed with her in Washington. Bertie went to bed early, after a long talk with John L. Lewis and a short one with Cal Carrington. "Where did she pick him up?" he asked his wife. Shortly after midnight, the Colonel appeared on the small balcony in the ballroom wearing red-and-white pajama pants and a green jacket. Frank Waldrop was the first to see him, and Bertie called out to him, "Don't these people know when to go home?" Then, in a louder voice, to the two hundred guests, he said, "Why don't you all go home? You're keeping me awake!" And then, "Maryland, when are you coming to bed?"

Everybody laughed but no one left.

Cissy called Bertie and his wife "The Royal Family." They always stayed with her when they were in Washington. Once, as Bertie was leaving to give a radio speech, he said, "I hope you will listen to it, Cissy."

"Well, of course, Bertie, of course I will."

After dinner, two green-liveried servants brought in a radio that was set in a Louis XV cabinet; they fiddled with the knobs until the Colonel's voice came through. He was giving a speech about the American Revolution, and in his accented monotone droned on and on. Cissy fidgeted and groaned and finally yelled, "Take the damn thing out of here! Take the goddamn thing out of here!" As the servants hurried it out, they forgot to unplug it, and the Colonel's voice continued to blare. In a now-controlled voice, Cissy turned to Bertie's wife. "Maryland, forgive me, but I am just not feeling well. Will you excuse me?" Cissy left the room and then summoned one of her guests, George Abell. "George, you really must take care of this for me. Give them any excuse you want, but I can't go back there. I can't face the Colonel."

Later in the evening, the Colonel returned. "Where's Cissy? Where's Cissy?" Abell told him she wasn't feeling well and had gone to bed. "Well, too bad that she missed my speech," said the Colonel. Abell said she had heard the speech and found it fascinating.

Cissy was outraged by Roosevelt's election to a fourth term. When Cissy hit hard, she looked for the belt—and hit below it. She collected a page of pictures of the worst of the war hell, the dead and the mangled and the dying. The only words she used on the page were Roosevelt's campaign promise: "I have said this before, but I shall say it again and again: Your boys are not going to be sent into any foreign wars."

It was raw and shocking, and some regarded it as treasonous. Cissy's advertising manager said he couldn't take it anymore, and left. His only son had been killed in New Guinea. Tom White had talked to him: "You feel your son's death and what goes on here have got a connection, don't you?" Yes, said the man, he did. He felt that if he continued to work for someone who cursed the President and the Government, he would be desecrating his son's memory. "I don't blame you," said White. "I don't think you should stay. You don't have to, and you shouldn't."

Tom White was a man big enough to see both sides. Hearst was his boss and Cissy was his love, but his mind was his own. He knew the war was a closed subject for Cissy.

In counterpoint, Waldrop showed her the first photographs taken of the Nazi concentration camps. Cissy had refused to believe that they existed. She classified reports of huge death camps with the World War I propaganda about Germans raping nuns and cutting off their breasts. It seemed absolutely incredible to her that the Germans would deliberately and systematically kill millions of Jews. Then she saw the pictures of the naked dead piled like cordwood, the mindless men standing almost naked behind barbed wire, the children's shoes piled high in front of the giant gas ovens. "Look at that face," she told Waldrop, "that could be Christ on the cross." Then she burst into tears, the first time Waldrop had ever seen her cry.

Increasingly now, Cissy drank more, smoked more, used more drugs. Friends felt that she was becoming more unpredictable, more unstable. Frank Waldrop was then closer to her on a daily basis than almost anyone else. He was flabbergasted one day when she suddenly slapped his face and then rushed from the room after they had a slight disagreement about a picture of a dog. Frank thereafter felt increasingly protective toward "Mrs. P."

She no longer appeared daily at the *Times-Herald,* but she still insisted that Waldrop send her proofs of any editorials he wrote, before they were printed. She did not want to be twitted by friends at dinner if they discovered that she didn't know what her paper was saying.

A reporter who was asked to go to her home found her having her hair brushed. Her eyes were closed. He announced himself hesitatingly and asked, "You wished to see me, Mrs. Patterson?" "No," she answered, her eyes still closed, "you're fired."

Her paper was no longer the fun it once had been. It was making money and operating smoothly—thanks to Frank Waldrop—but the challenge was gone. She even talked to her brother about letting his daughter Alicia take over the *Times-Herald*. But Joe warned her, "Stay away from Alicia. You'll only hurt her the way you've hurt everyone else." Coming from him, the cut was especially deep.

It was a cruel thing to say, but Joe was privy to Cissy's war with her daughter. He knew how quickly Cissy turned on people, more quickly now than ever before. He knew the intensity of his sister's hatred. And he did not want it turned on his daughter.

Cissy's degeneration was becoming more tragically obvious. She became much heavier and drank more often to excess. But no matter how drunk she was, she always managed to maintain her poise. "Even though I do not behave like a lady," she said, "I can walk like a lady."

When she complained to her dentist of not feeling well, he bluntly told her, "Mrs. Patterson, you have a hangover." She thought this was one of the funniest remarks she ever heard; she said nobody had ever spoken to her like that.

"I have to drink," she once explained, "because I have to forget all the mean things which I have done."

She still had her favorite enemies and seldom let them rest. She called Clare Booth Luce "a lovely asp" and Henry Wallace "a crystal-gazing crackpot." She and Waldrop started one story in their "Having a Wonderful Time" series with the sentence "The train to Washington stopped with a jerk, and the jerk got off."

Cissy never stopped attacking Drew Pearson in print. She had remarked his resemblance to Robespierre, and when she visited St. Elizabeth's Hospital for the Insane, she saw an inmate who shared this likeness to the notorious revolutionary. The doctor described the patient as obsessed by flowers, canaries, little children, and blood. Cissy later found a profile of

Robespierre and matched it with a facing picture of Pearson "without wig" to point up the similarity. In a bylined full-page story, called "Crazy, Like Foxes," Cissy wrote:

Ah, Drew, rose-sniffing, child-loving, child-cheater, sentimental Drew. Vicious and perverted Drew—as like as two peas in a pod to that poor creature who beckoned to us from the ward of the criminally insane. Incidentally, you GI Joes, when you happen to listen to the phony Quaker Pearson of a Sunday night— Bleeding Heart Drew—never forget that although in perfect health in 1917, he managed to "thee" and "thou" himself out of service in World War I. Then, as now, Drew was a yellow-bellied slacker.

Drew, "who was no glass of milk," counterattacked. In one of his Sunday night radio broadcasts, he said, "The British have organized a society for protection against mothers-in-law, but what we really need in this country is an organization for protection against ex-mothers-in-law. I would like to be a charter member."

Cissy was deteriorating in many ways and cared less what people thought about her. At a baseball game, watching a friend's son play, Cissy wore a green velvet housecoat, a sable stole, and bedroom slippers. Fortified by hot green turtle soup heavily laced with sherry, Cissy decided to get closer to the game and approached the first baseman with the idea of testing his beard to see if it was real. Seeing this red-haired apparition coming for him, the young first baseman took off for right field. Only after considerable persuasion did Cissy return to her seat.

Rumors circulated about Cissy and her handsome chauffeur. Someone had also seen the columnist Westbrook Pegler escorting her on a tour of Washington bordellos for "queers." Dower House, it was said, was the scene of bizarre sexual orgies, which Cissy liked to watch. Some servants later swore that this was true, adding details about drugs.

But when Cissy's mind was sharp, it was very, very sharp. Someone who regarded her as the devil incarnate met her at a party, argued violently with her. At the end, when both were bloody and unbowed, the man was smiling, and he confided to a friend, "Do you know, I kind of like the old witch."

Cissy often caused discord and havoc, but she also did much good. She heard about a black girl in Virginia who had killed her father when he had attacked her. Cissy got Eleanor Roosevelt interested in the case, and the two checked out the facts and asked for further investigation. The girl was ultimately released, and Cissy wrote Mrs. Roosevelt: "Some day I hope it will be possible to tell her what she owes to you. . . . If she needs help, she will know where to come."

Franklin D. Roosevelt died in April 1945. He was in Warm Springs, Georgia, working on a speech. The last paragraph read: "The only limit to our realization of tomorrow will be our doubts of today. Let us move forward with strong and active faith." Oliver Wendell Holmes had called him a second-rate intellect but a first-rate temperament. But to most Americans, he had been a happy warrior of great courage, "a crippled man who had taught a crippled nation how to walk again."

Evie Robert was with Cissy at Dupont Circle when Waldrop called to say that he was putting a large picture of Roosevelt on the front page and starting his obituary there. "Frank, hold everything," said Cissy. "All that's necessary on the front page is a picture of Roosevelt. You don't need his name. Everybody knows who he is. Just the dates of his birth and death. Nothing else on page one."

She was the instinctive editor, and absolutely right. Toward the end of Roosevelt's life, her acrimony toward him had begun to fade; at his death, she gave him the dramatic dignity he deserved. She told Waldrop the next day, "Fill up the paper with Truman—he's the story now."

The war was over. It was estimated that 35 million had died in the war, with 10 million more dead in Nazi concentration camps. A popular novel was George Orwell's *Animal Farm,* and the movie of the year was *The Lost Weekend.* The new music was something called "Bebop."

And 1945 was also the year that Felicia said, "I divorced my

453

mother." On her annual allowance of $40,000, tax-free, Felicia had lived well. She had a house in New York City on East End Avenue and another house in Towners, New York, near Pawling, where she kept her two horses.

She was forty years old, and she had decided to strike her blow of psychological liberty. A complete break with her mother took courage. Her only other income—$3,500 a year—came from a trust fund set up by her grandmother. Felicia gave up both her houses (her mother agreed to keep her horses at Dower House) and set out to make her living by writing. Besides publishing her two books, she had written short stories, some of which appeared in anthologies.

Joe's wife, Mary, who was still women's editor at the *News*, bought several of Felicia's stories. Mary was one of those who kept after Felicia to go back to her mother. "There are evil people around her trying to manipulate her," Mary said, "and you should be with her." Cissy offered Felicia a whole floor to herself at Dupont Circle and said, "We wouldn't even have to see each other." Felicia refused.

Before the final break, Felicia had once taken her mother to a meeting of Alcoholics Anonymous. Cissy was impressed and said she would discuss it with Joe. "Joe says I'm too old to join," she told Felicia.

Joe died in May 1946 at the age of sixty-seven. He had done his own share of serious drinking and died of cirrhosis of the liver after several months of illness. He was a modest man who had told his architect to design a house in Ossining, New York, that didn't look too expensive. He cared little about the show of power but relished the feel of it. One of his concerns was to prove he was "a regular guy," and he did, and often wore informal clothes at formal places, preferred movies to parties, and made friends with cabdrivers and Bowery bums.

He had earned his phenomenal success as publisher of the newspaper with the greatest circulation in the country. He had proved his courage in war. He had kept close to his principles. He had tried to dominate his children just as Cissy had tried to dominate Felicia, and he had failed, just as Cissy had failed. That hurt him. But what had crushed him, what had made him bitter and vengeful, was the path of his President in the recent war. At the end he had converted to Catholicism, the faith of his wife. But he had not died with the pride and the happiness that he had hoped to have.

Cissy was desolate. She felt that the greater part of herself had died. The two had stood together against the great strength of the American majority. They were bound by more than blood and bone. They were of a single mind on the issues of the world. They had both lacked love as children, both found it difficult to give as adults. She adored him and he was proud of her. Their closeness was one of the heart, spirit, and mind.

Joe's body rested in Cissy's home in Dupont Circle, and Cissy acted more like his widow than his sister. Those who had never seen Cissy cry saw her cry then.

She had sent Walter Trohan to select a burial plot for his boss in Arlington Cemetery. The family had wanted to bury him in his Army uniform, but it didn't fit, so he wore the uniform of a war correspondent. Cissy had ordered a blanket of roses but was told that the coffin should be covered with the American flag. Trohan was in the house with her afterward, and she showed him Joe's letters—she had kept all of them. Her great pride were his letters of approval. "It was the only time I've seen her cry," said Trohan. "She should have married her brother. He was the only one she ever really loved."

When Felicia came to the funeral, Cissy embraced her with an almost desperate affection she had never shown before. "I could just feel love," said Felicia. "It frightened me." Cissy said she didn't want to be alone that night, and Felicia returned with her to Dower House. Cissy had been drinking heavily, but for once, there was no fight, no anger, no hate. Evie Robert arrived unexpectedly, and Felicia noticed a strange look on her mother's face, "a tight, almost senile smile as if she was hypnotized, as if she had been subjugated by Evie. I had never seen that look on her face before. . . . I left her with Evie."

Evie and Ann Smith were both Catholics. Cissy and Count Gizycki had been married in a Catholic ceremony. Her brother's conversion to Catholicism just before his death had had a great impact on her. She had met Father Edmund Walsh at Evalyn McLean's house, and now she sought him out again. Father Walsh was regarded as "one of the world's great authorities on war, revolution, and the manipulation of power." He was almost a match for Cissy. For the next two years, even though she did not convert, Cissy saw him often. Father Walsh did help her to decrease her drinking for a time.

Colonel McCormick asked Cissy to become chairman of the News Syndicate Company, replacing her brother, soon after his death. She and Bertie were also board members of the parent organization, the Tribune Company. She replied:

> Now, listen, Bert, you and I have all the money—and then some—that we either want or need. We have all the "power and the glory" that either of us care to be bothered with. I don't know how you feel about it, but I have more than I want. I don't like it. . . . Now, Bert, as you may well understand, all of these exaggerated reports of my rise to power are bad for the *News*. They are pure joy for our competitors. . . . It is bad for the *News* to have the idea get across that a tired and already overworked old woman like myself is either head of the *News*, or figurehead of the *News*.

She did serve reluctantly for a time, insisting that the *News* operate completely independent of her.

Cissy wanted Joe's daughter Alicia to join the trustees of the *News* and *Tribune,* and Alicia wanted it, too. She told Bertie, "Alicia is a smart little cookie. She has a lot to offer." But he regarded Alicia as a Roosevelt liberal and a dominating woman, and he didn't want another woman on the board. Cissy insisted, noting that he wouldn't dare refuse if Joe were alive. Later, in a letter, she reminded him how he had reacted: "You were possessed by a queer kind of rage. . . . I won't forget your lunging across the dark verandah at me, gripping the arms of my chair, baring your lower teeth (very odd indeed) and bellowing in my face—'Joe's dead.'"

Cissy always considered the Colonel stuffy and dull and had called him "the greatest mind of the thirteenth century." "All the McCormicks are crazy except me," the Colonel once said, then pointed to Walter Trohan, Washington bureau head of the Chicago *Tribune*, "and Walter sometimes isn't sure about me."

Cissy carried the fight for Alicia to the *Tribune* board meeting. Bertie and Cissy were seriously concerned about who would succeed them in the family. Bertie had no children. His brother Medill had had three children; the son had been killed in an accident, the older daughter was a strong liberal who regarded any profits made by the Tribune Company as "blood money," and the younger daughter was not yet considered old enough.

Cissy asked Trohan what to do. "I don't like my will," she said. "I want your advice. What would you do with my paper?"

"Leave it to your daughter," Trohan advised her. "Blood is thicker than water."

Cissy shook her head. Felicia had "divorced" her, and she had "divorced" Felicia.

Cissy's nineteen-year-old granddaughter, Ellen, was married in the fall of 1946. When she had gone to New York University, George Arnold came courting. He was the son of Drew Pearson's close friend Thurman Arnold, a former federal judge and assistant attorney general—whom Cissy also knew well. Cissy was then in Florida. She later claimed that the wedding invitation arrived at the last minute, almost as an afterthought. She believed that she had been snubbed. "I'll just be a poor old thing up in the church somewhere." And she had not forgiven Ellen for an earlier breach. She had given Ellen an expensive necklace at a time when Cissy and Drew were at the most vituperative stage of their fight. Some said Ellen had returned her gift, which cut Cissy deeply. Ellen later insisted she had put the necklace in a safe. But the safe had jammed, and she could not get the necklace for Cissy's next big party. She wore a pin instead, and Cissy was offended by what she mistakenly regarded as a deliberate affront. Ellen openly sided with her father against her grandmother, and she and Cissy seldom saw each other after that.

Cissy's real break with Ellen came when Ellen sold the farm

Cissy had given her—to Drew. Cissy had offered to buy the farm back at a much greater price, but Ellen had refused. An embittered Cissy sued Drew, but to no avail.

Cissy did not go to the wedding. Perhaps she did not want to see either Drew or Felicia.

Cissy still hoped that her niece Alicia would take over the *Times-Herald*. In many ways, Joe's daughter was much like Cissy: she had a "crazy instinct," flair, and energy. She had made a considerable success of *Newsday*. "Does that little lady in the tweed suit really run that big, noisy Long Island newspaper?" a disbelieving banker asked one of her editors. "Run it?" he replied. "Hell, she drives it!" Asked what she wanted in her paper, Alicia gave the Cissy-Joe formula: "Dogs! Cats! Murders!" Her old admirer, Adlai Stevenson, remarked, "I've always thought of Alicia as a man." A handsome woman with a good figure, and a healthy outdoors look, Alicia had some of her aunt's shyness and insecurity, but she was not suspicious of people. Like Cissy, Alicia wanted power. "I not only want to be as good as Cissy," she told friends, "I want to be better."

Her mind distorted by alcohol and drugs, Cissy decided that she would be acting on one of Joe's warmest wishes if she could get Alicia to divorce Harry Guggenheim and remarry Joe's friend, Joe Brooks. She made an offer to Alicia: If Alicia would do this, "I will leave you the paper." Told of this, Colonel McCormick's wife, Maryland, was indignant. "Cissy," she said, "how *could* you interfere with her life?"

Interfering with other people's lives was Cissy's pastime. On the paper, she helped arrange marriages as well as break them. Although Alicia turned down her offer, Cissy was still determined to further her niece's career. She again approached Bertie about putting Alicia on the parent board of the *News*.

Bertie again vehemently refused, even though Cissy intimated she had done some research in their family wills and found facts that might prove embarrassing to Bertie. "I made up my mind that if you got tough with me, I'd get tough with you—but good!"

This statement was part of an eight-page letter Cissy had

Waldrop deliver to the Colonel at his estate outside Chicago. In her rambling letter, she also mentioned a number of offers she had refused for the *Times-Herald,* including the most recent one of $5 million. "You should realize that you have never, and can never, *stampede* me off my chosen ground. Neither could Joe. Joe could appeal to my reason, sentiment, or affection easily enough, but he could not bully me into doing anything I did not care to do.

"In the name of God, Bert, why did you pull that 'ham' act at the last director's meeting in Chicago. . . . There you stood, putting on the six-foot-four business, waving your arms about, glaring like a maniac shouting your denunciations of Alicia. Why?"

After reconsideration, Bertie finally agreed to name Alicia to the board if Cissy would resign. Cissy promptly did this and told Trohan, "I won, I won!" What she won was a further release from her responsibilities.

One of the few men of Cissy's age who still courted her was an elegant old-fashioned Marylander named Dunn. A wealthy Baltimore judge, he was a widower and wanted to marry her. Cissy was most fond of him; he was a delightful man. But then he made a remark that cost him her hand: "Now, Cissy, you understand I would never interfere in the operation of the newspaper." Cissy was tired and depressed and *wanted* someone "to interfere."

Walter Trohan went to Dupont Circle to visit and noticed a photograph of a young woman, which was displayed on a side table. "That's a beautiful gal," he said. "That's me," said Cissy softly. She paused and smiled. "You're the only one who hasn't told me that I haven't changed." Cissy wanted Trohan to become one of her editors and promised to build him a house and put a considerable sum of money in escrow for him. But he had seen one of her editors at a party playfully put her foot on his neck, saying, "I'm your slave." He had also heard Cissy bawl out another editor over the phone, "Get off your fat ass, you sonofabitch." Then Trohan told her, "That, Mrs. Patterson, is why I wouldn't work for you."

With all her desire to let go, Cissy still found herself pulled by her paper; she made unexpected visits, presenting ideas that had little of the sense or interest that had made her a respected editor. She once explained apologetically to her editors, "Don't you see, it's all I have left. If I let you alone, what am I to do?"

Her self-portrayal was always pitiless. She once drew a self-portrait, not quite a caricature, but it was more cruel than honest.

Writing of the horror of a drunken woman in a *Times-Herald* editorial, Cissy said: "Her eyes are bleared, her dress is below one shoulder and above both knees, her makeup is all over, and she is weeping. . . . The whole world is full of them now. Go to the little cocktail lounges in the late afternoon and see the old crows sniggling to themselves and making eyes at the men. Go to the parties and see them make absolute fools of themselves."

Evalyn Walsh McLean was dying in 1947. Cissy was there, the Waldrops, Thurman Arnold and his wife, and Supreme Court Justice Frank Murphy. Father Walsh gave extreme unction to Evalyn in her oxygen tent, in her own bed at home, while Cissy went down on her knees to pray.

Immediately after the sixty-year-old Evalyn died, Cissy went back to the paper, her emotions under tight control. She wanted personally to supervise Evalyn's obituary. Thurman Arnold was Evalyn's executor, and he took Frank Waldrop with him to collect the jewels that were scattered around her room in drawers, vases, slippers. They put them in a shoebox, tied with a string. The banks were closed, so they took the box to J. Edgar Hoover, who gave them a receipt: "Received, one shoebox, said to contain . . ."

At the *Times-Herald,* Cissy was faced with the problem of finding a picture that flattered her friend. Those available were too realistic. Then she remembered a portrait of Evalyn in her home that gave her a glamour she had never had. She ran a copy of this with her obituary.

The two women had been queens of Washington, Evalyn more transparently open, Cissy a complex of convex and concave mirrors full of shadows and hidden depths. "In all the years I've known Cissy, I've never felt I really knew her,"

Evalyn once told Maggie Cassini. Yet there were few women with whom Cissy shared more laughter.

"Evalyn Walsh McLean is one of the few people in the world with as much money as I have," Cissy once told her secretary. "I can trust her. She doesn't want anything from me."

Neither did Marion Davies. She had called to say that Hearst, now eighty-three, had had a severe heart attack. His doctors had insisted they leave San Simeon and move into the city, where he could be more carefully watched. She had found a place in Beverly Hills, but he had wept when they left San Simeon. It was as if he knew he would never move back.

Evalyn McLean's death shattered whatever peace Cissy had found after her brother's death. She slept less and less, drank more and more. She now started drinking at nine in the morning, her butler usually bringing her a magnum of champagne. She was frequently late for her own dinner parties, and she would often say to her guests, "Let's not eat; let's just drink all night."

She sometimes invited a group of guests for dinner, came down drunk, argued with them, and sent them home before dinner had been served. When she was going to a party, she often told her chauffeur, "I don't think I'll stay through dinner. I can't stand this crowd." And, indeed, she would be back at the car within the hour.

Her servants complained that she was always watching them. "You couldn't hear her sneaking up behind you. You had to be careful." She kept guns by her bedside, in her car, in her purse. *Time* magazine had called her "the most hated woman in America," and she felt that her life was in danger.

In her loneliness, Cissy thought more and more of the past. She wanted to make one more trip to Jackson Hole in the summer of 1948. She had not been there for almost fifteen years. She also wanted to see Marion and Hearst. She had sold the Ranger, but she planned to rent a private Pullman and take Frank and Ellie Waldrop with her. She wrote Rose, telling her to hire a cook and have Forney Cole clean up the place. She said she would try not to think of the mosquitoes and the trout flies. She wanted to enjoy the peace of Flat Creek again, even if she

461

couldn't ride anymore. She wanted to camp and cook in the open, putting eggshells in the coffee grounds the way she used to.

"You know, darling," she had written Rose, "years may come and years may go, but you know how much I have always loved you."

Cal Carrington had come for his annual visit to Washington, but Cissy's nerves were on edge, and she called the Waldrops, asking them to hurry over and divert Cal "because I can't stand the clicking of his false teeth."

Her granddaughter, Ellen, was living in Chicago, where her husband, George, was finishing law school. In the spring of 1948 they traveled to Washington with Cissy's great grandchild. There had been no real reconciliation, but a grandmother was still a grandmother. The baby was a redheaded boy, but Cissy was not pleased that they had named him Drew. Cissy looked at this baby in her lap and smiled and said, "It looks like a fat sausage tied with strings."

She started to play the parlor game of the rich, the changing of wills. In her first wills she had left everything to Felicia and Ellen. She told Trohan that she was leaving Dower House to Ann Smith because Ann had so many children. But in one will, she left it to her neighbor and friend, Rhoda Christmas, because Rhoda's family once had lived there.

"Hap, what do you do with your money?" she once asked. After Robinson said his wife took care of it, she told him to tell her that "one day you're going to be a wealthy man." Cissy had decided to leave her paper to her top executives. "You fellas put up with me, and I'm gonna leave you the paper," she had told them.

Cissy's butler once encountered Felicia by chance. "Why don't you come and see your mother?" he asked. "She's changing her will, and I think she might really want to see you."

"I don't have the time," Felicia answered.

Since their "divorce" the two women had seen each other only twice—once at Joe's funeral and again when Evalyn Walsh McLean was dying.

462

Obsessed by her mortality and torn by loneliness, Cissy went to seances. She had always remembered the vivid vision of Count Gizycki she had had on the day of his death. She also spent more time with Father Walsh.

She always knew what her paper was saying. The Inquiring Photographer once visited St. Ann's Orphanage in Washington, asking the children what they wanted from Santa Claus. Cissy was struck by a little girl's request for "a redheaded doll" and promptly ordered the advertising department to provide all the requested presents. Cissy herself approved the color of the doll's red hair.

She was also busy making further arrangements for her trip to Jackson Hole with the Waldrops. They would take a month and go on to California to see Hearst and Marion, then return through Canada. She was elated by the prospect of this trip. At a party, she felt high enough to do an imitation of Alicia Patterson Guggenheim during her first board of directors meeting at the *News*.

Tom White died of a heart attack in July 1948. His death crushed Cissy. He had come to see her less frequently in the last years, but he was even more welcome when he was unexpected. They had been so much at ease with each other, with the quiet consideration and affection of "old marrieds." His picture was next to her bed. They had talked often on the phone. They were part of each other. And his was a funeral she would not be able to attend. She would cry alone in her bed. "People my age don't grieve deeply anymore," she told Felicia. But her Marlboro friend Emily Stafford said, "After Tom died, I don't think she wanted to live."

Agnes Meyer once wrote: "Do anything to me but do not let me die." Cissy, too, had searched for immortality in religion and with the psychics. But now she was overwhelmed by weariness, and death had become far less dreadful. Some fears, however, still lingered. She asked a friend to pray for her, that when her time came, someone would be with her. "I don't want to die alone."

A Polish priest she knew in Washington had composed a

prayer for Cissy: "My God, I doubt your presence and even your existence. I wish to be happy as I was being a child. Nobody really and truly loves me. Help me."

Cissy had always delighted in her rich resources of imagination and memory. But now her memories gave her great pain. Gone were the days when she woke up excited about going to work. Gone were the days when she woke up with a loving man in her bed. Gone were the days when she looked forward to an exhilarating morning ride on her horse. She no longer got a kick from champagne, and it took more drugs to give her a high. She confided to a young woman reporter that she didn't trust anyone anymore, and she told another, "I guess I'm bored."

George Abell persuaded her to come to a small dinner. Father Walsh was there. He and Cissy had become friends, but she found it as difficult to surrender to Catholicism as she had found it difficult, all through her life, to give herself to anything or anyone—except her paper. Her independence was her life blood. George walked her out to her car after the dinner, and a man rushed out of the shadows to hand her a subpoena. She had refused to pay for a rug she thought overpriced, and the merchant was suing her. Cissy took the subpoena, tore it up, and said, "Shit." That was the last word George ever heard her say.

She telephoned Rose Crabtree to tell her of the change in her plans. "I can't ride anymore. I'm too old for the rough trip by that road. I'm old, and I'm very sick. I'm going to die. Rent me a nice place at the foot of Teton Pass, where I can look at Sheep Mountain."

"Shut up that talk about dying," said Rose. "Come on out here and you'll get well."

One night at Dower House, when she couldn't sleep, she had a bottle of beer with her night watchman. She had fired the previous man because she had found him asleep on the job—and she had startled her guests that night by coming in waving a loaded pistol. "Nobody ever knew what to expect next."

Some neighbors arrived one night for dinner, a quiet dinner

on a hot night. Emily Stafford remembered that Cissy's face that night was as red as her hair. The Staffords left early, and Cissy was in bed by eleven with some books and the latest edition of the *Times-Herald*. Her gray poodle Butch was with her. She was still reading at 1 A.M. when the night watchman came to take Butch for his walk.

The next day was Saturday, July 24, 1948. Cissy's stepdaughter, Halle Schlesinger, arrived with her husband, Julian Bach, to have lunch with Cissy. They rang the doorbell, and the maid answered. Her eyes were "absolutely glassy," and she seemed to be looking straight through them when she said, "Mrs. Patterson isn't here anymore." Halle said, "*What!*" and the maid continued, "Mrs. Patterson is dead."

She had not rung the bellpull at eight that morning; it was her signal to the servants to take Butch out again and have her breakfast ready in fifteen minutes. The servants waited several hours before Cissy's personal maid ventured into her bedroom. She was sitting in bed, her right hand holding *The Golden Violet*, her head on the book, her lipstick pressed on the pages. The lights were still on. Cissy had died alone, just as she had worried she would.

Waldrop was soon there, calling everyone. When he told Felicia, she asked, "Should I come down?" She could not pretend a deep grief, any more than Cissy could when her mother had died.

The house was soon filled with stunned friends. Ann Smith would not go in to see her dead friend; she wanted to remember her the way she was when she was alive. Rhoda Christmas felt that someone who loved her should be in her room. Her pajamas were undone, her legs bare, and Rhoda asked the doctor if it was necessary for her to be so exposed with all the police going in and out of the room. He said she could be covered, and Rhoda covered her. She asked the doctor about the purple splotches on Cissy's face, and he said that they were usual when a person had died while sitting up. Rhoda saw no pills on the floor, although one servant claimed she had seen some.

In Jackson Hole, Rose cried. Cal said, "If only we could have had one more trip together." Cousin Bertie got the news in Paris, and started whistling loudly. His wife heard him sing in the bathroom, "I'm the last leaf on the tree. . . ."

The funeral was held in the same Dupont Circle ballroom where she and Gizy had been married. The casket was covered with yellow roses, her favorite flower; there were enough flowers in the house to fill four freight cars. Their scent was so strong on the hot day that two people fainted. Alicia persuaded Felicia to get black mourning clothes. Father Walsh approached them about the possibility of a Catholic service and burial, but Alicia said abruptly, "No, we're Presbyterians." "Ma wanted to be cremated and buried in Chicago," Felicia later added.

The Reverend Dr. Dudley E. Stark, pastor of St. Chrysostom's Episcopal Church in Chicago, conducted a ten-minute service. Cissy might have applauded its brevity but would have squirmed to hear the Reverend describe her as "that saintly woman."

There were many sad faces, but the only man weeping openly was Happy Robinson. Her old adversary Drew Pearson caused a stir when he arrived for the service. He would write movingly of her: "A great lady died the other day—a lady who had caused me much happiness—and much pain." The *Times-Herald* staff had come to say good-bye. There was no obituary for her in the files, and they had used the one from the *News*, which began: "How do you say good-bye . . ." Felicia took the ashes to Graceland Cemetery in Chicago. A private railroad car carried the immediate family and some close friends such as Jackie Martin and Happy Robinson.

Happy Robinson had said, "She didn't die a bad death." Life was a short run, and she had milked it. She had lived the way she wanted to live, and as long as she wanted to. She had had all the power and the glory, but she had missed much of the love. She had earned her pride. Mike Flynn said, "She was a hell of a sight better newspaperman than I am." Her world was the world of *The Front Page* and the luxury liner, and they were both going, or gone. Money had been her pleasure and her curse, and perhaps Felicia was right about her—perhaps she might have been an even greater woman had she been born a washerwoman in a mining camp. "There is a price to hate," Barach had told her, "and you can't take it out on anyone else. You must take it out on yourself." And she did, oh, how she did. She had taken wrong roads, but she cared, she gave a damn, she *wanted* to do the right things.

She had great courage. She was not a phony, and she was never boring. "Don't forget what Bertie said," she wrote a friend, "that in me the world has lost its greatest ham actress." No one could laugh more loudly at her than she could. There was never a dull moment or a predictable one with Cissy. Only at the end did she want peace without loneliness. And, now, she had finally found it.

Epilogue

Just before dawn on September 15, 1948, seven men waited at the Washington National airport. They were the *Times-Herald* executives to whom Cissy had willed her paper, and they were waiting for a young rewriteman who was flying from Clarksburg, West Virginia, with three suitcases. The suitcases belonged to Charles Bell Porter, who, the afternoon before, jumped, fell, or was pushed to his death from his hotel room. He had been the treasurer of the *Times-Herald* and Cissy's financial confidant for almost fifteen years; he knew as much about her as anyone else. He had been named with the others to inherit the newspaper; he would have been the eighth man. But four months before, Cissy had fired him and had written him out of her will. Porter had agreed to testify for Felicia, who was fighting to have the will declared invalid. In her suit she claimed that Cissy had been of "unsound mind" when the will had been drawn up and that the document had been obtained "through fraud, duress, coercion and undue influence." Porter had said he was writing a book about Cissy. Everyone knew he was a meticulous man who took careful notes. The seven men knew that one of the suitcases was filled with papers. Their concern was that it might contain a later will with new inheritors, or it might have strong evidence to help invalidate the current will.

"It was a three-paragraph item from the AP wire," Sidney Epstein, who was then a rewriteman, remembered. "I took one look at it and I stood up . . . and yelled, 'Jesus Christ, C. B. Porter just killed himself!'" Three feet away sat Assistant Managing Editor Mason Peters, one of the seven who inherited the *Times-Herald*. He grabbed the AP dispatch and read it. "Get on the phone and get an airplane," he snapped to Epstein. "You're going to Clarksburg." Epstein first called the Clarksburg police for more details. After learning that they were holding Porter's three suitcases, Epstein asked Peters for instructions. "Get those damn suitcases and bring them back. I don't care how you get them, but get them.!"

It was 7:30 P.M. The Clarksburg airport was closed, and the nearest landing strip was at Pittsburgh. Epstein was joined by the acting treasurer, John Barber. The AP story had stated that Porter's handwritten will, naming Sibella Campbell as his executrix, had been found on his body. Barber had raced to Campbell to get a signed authorization allowing them to bring back Porter's suitcases. Campbell was Cissy's blunt German housekeeper.

After arriving in Pittsburgh, Epstein and Barber boarded a twenty-one-passenger DC-3 that had been chartered to take them to Clarksburg. Epstein had called the West Virginia state police and asked them to light the runway at Clarksburg by training the headlights of police cars on it. They agreed. "Well, it's never been done before [landing at night] at Clarksburg, but we'll try it," said the pilot.

Epstein and Barber arrived at the Clarksburg police station

about 1:30 A.M. The police were reluctant to release the suitcases. Drew Pearson had called them, warning them to safeguard the cases. Drew was financing Felicia's fight to break the will because their daughter Ellen had been disinherited. He was concerned that the seven men might find some important evidence—or a later will—and destroy it. Barber produced his note from Campbell, and the police chief called the district attorney for advice. After this conversation he told them, "You can't take them, because they're not sealed."

"Well," said Epstein, "do you have any Scotch tape?"

Some tape was found, and the suitcases were "sealed." Barber stayed behind to arrange for the transfer of Porter's body. Epstein took the three suitcases to the waiting chartered plane, returning to Pittsburgh. Before taking off for Washington, Epstein called Peters, telling him when he would arrive. It was almost 5 A.M. when Epstein landed at the Washington airport.

The seven men had a hurried discussion. Where should they go to look at the suitcases? Not to their homes, certainly. But where? Epstein said that his girl friend lived nearby, and they decided to go there.

"I rang the bell," Epstein recalled, "and my girl's mother answered the door. It was still dark outside. I don't know what she thought when she saw me with these seven guys, and I gave her some crazy explanation. I guess she thought that all reporters were a little whacky anyhow. But she said, 'Sure, Sid, come on in.'"

"So we went in, and the eight of us sat on the floor, and I opened the suitcases. We must have made quite a sight. They all got busy rummaging through this stuff. I don't think they found a damn thing they felt was important. Anyway, they all went home, and I took the suitcases to the housekeeper."

Drew Pearson publicly berated the Clarksburg police for releasing the suitcases. Pearson earlier had publicly declared that Cissy did not die a natural death. He suggested she had been murdered by one or more of the seven men who had inherited her paper, because they were afraid she was about to change her will. He now intimated that Porter had also met his death through foul play. "Apparently some people believed he knew too much. . . . The circumstances surrounding Porter's death are strange indeed, including the fact that he jumped or was pushed through a window screen."

Sibella Campbell revealed that Porter had made the 140-mile trip to West Virginia by cab. He had gone to see a priest who was a friend of his. The priest was away on a trip, and Porter spent four days in the hotel, waiting for him. Porter was a bald, pink-faced, wispy man of fifty-two who walked with fast, small steps like a wind-up toy. He was a homosexual. Cissy knew this "and laughed about it." He was a British subject, a graduate of Edinburgh University with a doctorate in philosophy with a concentration in criminology and law. He talked with a strong Scotch burr. He had booked passage back to Scotland but had canceled it to testify at the hearing on Cissy's will.

Porter's closest friend, a swarthy young seminary student, told the press, "We were sure Porter was murdered when we read of his death. He was sure he was being shadowed by private detectives, and he was in deadly fear of being killed. He told me, 'They're out to get me.' He said they wanted his private papers. Besides, he never would have killed himself. He cared too much about life. He collected Chinese porcelains and rare books; he was a fastidious aesthete. If ever he did want to kill himself, he would have taken pills. Such a messy end would have horrified him."

The police insisted Porter had committed suicide. On the bureau in his room, he had left his glasses and watch. An almost empty bottle of sherry had also been found in his room. A boy claimed he had seen him on the ledge before he jumped.

That same week, police found Betty Hynes dead in her bathroom in Washington. Betty Hynes had been Cissy's social secretary and society editor. Cissy had promised to leave Betty enough money in her will "to clean up [her] mortgage." She had not done this. Betty had been despondent, and a bottle of sleeping pills was found near her bed, almost empty. She was an alcoholic, but her friends insisted she was not suicidal. Her brother revealed that there had been a robbery—the window screen forced and some of Betty's papers were missing. Pearson again implied that perhaps Betty "knew too much," and her evidence might have helped break the will. A doctor, however, ruled that she had died from heart failure.

Felicia's New York apartment also had been ransacked, and a detective discovered that her telephone was tapped. After this break-in, she left a piece of paper in her suitcase, placed so that it would fall out if the case were opened. It fell out. She also knew she was being followed. Her cousin Alicia warned her, "They'll be after you like a pack of vultures." She was referring to the seven men at the *Times-Herald* and their representatives.

One of the first of this latter group to approach her was Alicia's former husband, Joe Brooks, a lawyer who represented the seven. He wanted Felicia to sign a document stating that she accepted the will and would not contest it. She refused. Calls came from various people at the *Times-Herald* pleading with her to sign the document; they told her that if she didn't "We can't pay our employees. . . . We don't have any cash."

Cissy's estate was set at $16,586,571. Felicia had been left $25,000 a year, "to keep her off the streets," Cissy had remarked. She also got the Sands Point home, some North Dakota property, and Cissy's personal effects. Cissy left Dower House to Ann Smith; the Dupont Circle mansion to the American Red Cross; her ranch at Flat Creek to her niece, Josephine Patterson Reese; some Washington real estate, a sable coat, and her black pearls to Evie Robert. "The Seven Dwarfs"—as they had been dubbed—who inherited the *Times-Herald* were Frank Waldrop and William Shelton (who were also her executors), Happy Robinson, Michael Flynn, Irving Belt, Mason Peters, and Frank Jewell. Jewell was head of the advertising department and the most recent arrival of them all. Cissy left her horse, War Chief, and her dog, Butch, to Rhoda Christmas, but left no money for their care and insisted they never be sold. "She gave me what she loved most," said Rhoda. She left $5,000 to Henry Lefort's son, Jerry. Lefort had been her chauffeur, but she had fired him "because he slammed the door on me." She left $10,000 to her secretary, Margaret Barney, but only $3,000 to Rose Crabtree. She wanted pensions continued to seventeen people, among them Polish refugees, former employees, and Cal Carrington. She also wanted contributions continued to a long list of charities, most of which helped children, with a further provision for an organization "aiding Polish refugee children of Catholic origin." She gave her granddaughter, Ellen, nothing, "inasmuch as I have made a substantial gift to her during my lifetime." Ellen did not contest the will.

Felicia's attorneys felt she should challenge the will because after the bequests and taxes were paid, the estate might not have enough capital to ensure that Felicia would receive her annual income for the rest of her life. Her attorneys were Randolph Paul and Lloyd Garrison in New York and Harold Kertz in Washington. They agreed to ask for $200,000, half of which Felicia planned to give to the St. Phillips Inter-Racial Church, where she worked. Her lawyers began to collect evidence proving that Cissy was in "unsound mind." Depositions from her servants and friends contained lurid stories of drugs, drink, sexual orgies, lesbianism, perversions. A safe deposit box was found to contain seven previous wills. In the early ones, Felicia had been given everything. By checking the various wills, friends could tell when they had dropped out of favor. Nobody could understand why she had left so little money to her best friend, Rose Crabtree. Was it because she felt money had hurt her and might ruin Rose?

There was much talk of "missing wills." Jackie Martin claimed that Cissy had recently talked of a new will that left the *Times-Herald* to her, Happy Robinson, and Mike Flynn. Others insisted she had finally decided to leave the paper to her niece Alicia. No such wills were found.

One of Cissy's friends, with whom she had discussed wills, was the lawyer Ernest Cuneo. He saw her shortly before her death. Commenting on her mental soundness at the time, he later said, "Not only was she in her *right* mind, but one of the brightest I ever encountered."

After much deliberation, Felicia changed her mind and decided not to contest the will because she did not want her mother's reputation destroyed in a bitter court hearing. And she knew that the opposition lawyers would tear into her own

473

relationship with her mother, attack her own personal life. It would be too ugly and too wrong. She had never really wanted any of her mother's money alive, and she did not want it now.

Harold Kertz persuaded her to give him two more weeks to arrange a settlement. If not, they would voluntarily withdraw the case before it came to trial. Felicia agreed. Kertz arranged a final $400,000 flat sum for Felicia—twice the original figure discussed—and the case was over.

Before she died, Cissy was heard to say, "They'll have a damned good fight when I've gone. I've fixed that!"

The story of her death and her will was Cissy's kind of story. She would have played it big all over her front page, day after day. When the *Times-Herald* published her will, Mason Peters admitted, "I played it the way The Lady would have wanted it. I put the headlines in two lines of 96 [point]. I smashed the hell out of it. That was the eight star edition. But tonight it's a dead duck. We've got a good shooting here in town, so the hell with the will. I'll put the line on the shooting and play the will down in the left-hand columns."

Cissy would have understood, and approved.

She would *not* have approved of the sale of the *Times-Herald* within a year to Bertie McCormick. Some of the seven were over sixty and anxious to retire, and Bertie bought the paper for $4 million. While they were not "instant millionaires," each of the seven got about $650,000.

Bertie decided to make the paper "a little bit stuffy." He killed Cissy's Page 3, "the rape and murder page," and swiftly made the paper "as dull as a year-old want ad." After several years of heavy losses, in 1954, the seventy-three-year-old McCormick sold the *Times-Herald* to Eugene Meyer of the Washington *Post* for $8,500,000. The *Post* absorbed some of the *Times-Herald* features and used its building as a warehouse. Cissy was dead and so was her paper.

Cissy's horse and her dog died soon after she did. When Cal died in 1959, Felicia put a plaque on his grave, a cowboy on a horse, the horse's head bowed. Cissy would have liked that. But somebody stole the plaque. Cal and Rose had argued after

Cissy's death about her angora chaps; Felicia finally gave them to a local museum.

Cissy's Dupont Circle house was jammed with women when her clothes were put on the auction block. "Why, Cissy wore that at a party I gave for her ten years ago. I've GOT to have it! . . ." "She bought that riding habit when I gave her my gray mare. . . ." There were 300 pairs of lounging pajamas and slacks, over a hundred pairs of shoes, including high-buttoned ones, 20 pairs of riding boots, and more than 150 evening dresses, some dating back to the 1920s. The sale lasted five hours.

The Red Cross sold the Dupont Circle house to the Washington Club, a women's organization. Most of the house's furnishings were sold: the Louis XVI chairs, the Gobelin tapestries, the Chippendale sofas, the Chinese and the Aubusson rugs, the Tiffany silver, the Spode china, the Hepplewhite tables, the Sheraton bookcases, the Queen Anne chairs, the crystal chandeliers. Nobody remembered what happened to the plates Evalyn Walsh McLean had given her, plates with paintings of her favorite dogs. Cissy never used them. "I couldn't eat my food and see my dogs."

> She was gay and she was witty
> She was wise and she was pretty
> Now she's dead, let's not flout her
> Let's not say dull things about her.

This verse appeared in the New York Daily *News* editorial about Cissy. Other obituaries called her "the greatest editor in America" and "the most powerful woman in the country." But Evelyn Peyton Gordon, society editor of the Washington *Daily News,* wrote, ". . . most of all I'll remember her as shy."

Cissy's grave at Graceland Cemetery was next to her mother's, and they had never before been so close. Her father and brother were buried at Arlington National Cemetery. In the cluster of family graves under the Medill monument were those of her grandfather and her beloved cousin Medill. Her grave

475

was unmarked for a long time, and when a monument was finally erected, the birth date on it was wrong: she had been made three years younger. That would have made her smile.

But she, who had admired fresh flowers, especially yellow roses, would have been infuriated by the single plastic red rose on her grave many years later.

Twenty years after Cissy's death, Drew Pearson had a large dinner for his family and friends. Table talk turned to Cissy. A guest recalled "that a great many people at that dinner had considerable cause for bitterness, and even hate for Cissy. It was quite a testimonial that everyone not only spoke kindly of her, but admiringly. I guess she stood the test of time."

What Cissy would have liked even more were Felicia's remarks almost thirty years after her death. "Please put in the book that Cissy's great-grandchildren have broken out of the cycle of hate, that they are normal, loving children." Of Cissy, Felicia said softly, "I am at peace with her. I have made friends with my mother." She told of several strange incidents. When a reporter was interviewing her about her mother some years after her death, they were startled by a heavy thud of a falling box in a nearby airless closet. There was no explanation for the fall and the reporter was so shaken he had to leave. And once, when Felicia was talking about Cissy with a friend, the two women saw a book seem to push itself out of the bookcase and fall to the floor. It was Kipling's *Kim,* a book Cissy had often read to Felicia.

If anyone could find a way, Cissy would.

Chapter Notes
and
Critical Bibliography

CHAPTER ONE

At the time of this writing, there were, fortunately, a great many people who knew Cissy Patterson well at different stages of her life. To supplement this source, there are, of course, a number of important collections of pertinent letters and papers and other documents. In this first chapter, the reference weight is on books and papers. A prime source is the Chicago Historical Society. It offers a vast amount of material, including letters, memoirs (some privately printed), newspaper and magazine clippings, and photographs. The Chicago *Tribune* archive has an excellent library of material on the McCormick family, a well-researched genealogy as well as letters, papers, and photographs. The files of the *Tribune,* as well as those of the other newspapers of the time—the Chicago *Daily Inter-Ocean,* the Chicago *Daily News,* the Chicago *Chronicle,* and the Chicago *Daily Examiner*—are all invaluable sources concerning the daily history and flavor of the times. Of special importance concerning the social life of the time, while also detailing some of the travel movements of the Patterson-McCormick families, are the files of *Elite* magazine.

Fascinating social comment is contained in "The Chicago Society Directory and Ladies' Visiting and Shopping Guide" (Ensign, McClure, Chicago, 1876). "The Story of Society in Chicago" *(Chicago* magazine, Sept. 1911) is also worth examining. Even more important are Mrs. A. A. Glessner's unpublished journals of the 1880s, at the Chicago Historical Society. They preserve much of the intimate flavor of the times.

The best material about Joseph Medill comes from his own writings, mostly newspaper articles for his own paper, such as his account of the Chicago fire. There is also an excellent autobiographical sketch he wrote for the Massillon (Ohio) *Independent* (undated clipping at the Historical Society) and an intimate reminiscence about his friend Abraham Lincoln, printed in *The Saturday Evening Post* (Aug. 5, 1899).

Philip Kinsley's three-volume *The Chicago Tribune—Its First Hundred Years* (The Chicago Tribune Co., Chicago, 1946) is a basic source book. Other volumes of interest on early Chicago include *Chicago—The History of Its Reputation* by Lloyd Lewis and Henry Justin Smith (Harcourt Brace, New York, 1929); *Prairie Avenue* by Arthur Meeker (Knopf, New York, 1929); *Old Chicago Houses* by John Drury (University of Chicago Press, Chicago, 1941); and *Chicago* by Stephen Longstreet (McKay, New York, 1973). Two most interesting books on Chicago from the British point of view are *Through America,* by W. G. Marshall (1881) and *Through Cities and Prairie Lands* by Lady 'Duffus Hardy (1881). Of interest is an article in *Harper's* magazine: "Chicago: Illustrated and Descriptive" (Nov. 1882). *Harper's* articles of this period are generally most informative.

Aside from the *Tribune* archive, my main source of genealogy was the Genealogical Room at the New York Public Library. The State Historical Society of Wisconsin also has some family historical material, mainly in the Nettie Fowler McCormick Papers and the Anita McCormick Blaine Papers.

On Lake Forest, a book of some interest is *Lake Forest, Illinois: History and Reminiscences* by Edward Arpee (Lake Forest, Ill., 1953). There is also a good historical sketch by John J. Halsey of Lake Forest University and another by Russell V. Kohr, who concentrates on the Presbyterian Church.

Cissy Patterson by Alice Albright Hoge (Random House, New York, 1966) is especially good on Cissy's early years.

Of some, but lesser, interest, there is *The Battle for Chicago* by Wayne Andrews (Harcourt Brace, New York, 1946) and *The Legendary Eighties* by Herman Clark (McClurg, Chicago, 1941).

Stately Homes in America by Harry W. Desmond and Herbert Croly

(Appleton, New York, 1903) furnishes a good look at the Newport of the time. The Harvard University library provided the background on Miss Hersey's School in Boston, as well as details on Blair Fairchild. Lloyd Lewis, in *Postscript to Yesterday* (Random House, New York, 1947), catches much of the flavor of the period. So does "A Lawyer Looks at the Past," the unpublished reminiscences of Frances Ernest Matthew in Chicago.

Cissy's description of Clark Street comes from her autobiographical novel, *Fall Flight*.

CHAPTER TWO

The European Division of the Library of Congress is the invaluable source of information not only on Austria and Poland at the time of Count Gizycki but on the genealogy and background of the Count himself. More specifically, there are such detailed references as Volume IV of *Herbarz Polski,* by Kaspra Niesieckiego, S. J. (1839), and the even more valuable Volume VI, by Adam Boniecki (Warsaw, 1903). The Library of Congress is also a treasure trove of documents, maps, pictures, and references of other kinds concerning this area of Europe at this time. It was even able to provide detailed descriptions of Nowosielica and its environs, where Cissy and Gizy lived. On this, it was indeed even more valuable than the library and other facilities in Warsaw. Janina Hoskins, at the Library of Congress, not only pinpointed this material, but enriched it with her own background in the area.

The Osterreiches Staatsarchiv Kriegsarchiv and the Osterreiches National-bibliothek in Vienna, on the other hand, provided a large amount of relevant material, much of it with illustrations, illuminating the social life and bringing alive the prominent people in Vienna at the time. By far the most important specifics and stories that made this period live for me came from my interviews with the Countess Wurmbrand in Monaco. A marvelous woman with an incredible memory, she was not only part of this milieu, but she had introduced Gizycki and Cissy to each other and knew them intimately. Her help, and her letters, were of crucial importance. She even provided a rare excellent photograph of the Count.

Beyond this, and equally indispensable, Cissy's autobiographical novel, *Fall Flight* (Minton, Balch, New York, 1928), gives us Cissy's most personal insight into this place and period, and details most explicitly her relations with Count Gizycki.

A number of books about Vienna are of varying value, some of them most interesting but none of them vital. They include *Vienna* by Ilsa Barea (Knopf, New York, 1966); *The Fall of the House of Hapsburg* by Edward Crankshaw (Viking, New York, 1963); *Vienna, Yesterday and Today,* by J. Alexander Mahan (Brentano's, New York, 1928); *The Eagles Die* by George R. Marek (Harper & Row, New York, 1974); *Vienna* by Martin Hurlimann (Viking, New York, 1970); and a novel, *The Countess,* by Hans Habe (Harcourt Brace, New York, 1962), which provides some good perspective. A highly worthwhile book on Poland is *History of Poland* by O. Halecki (Roy Publishers, New York, 1943).

Aside from *Tribune* archive material on the McCormicks, there are Colonel Robert McCormick's own memoirs and autobiographical radio talks. The single best biography of Colonel McCormick is *McCormick of Chicago* by Frank Waldrop (Prentice-Hall, Englewood Cliffs, N.J., 1966).

Material on Mark Hanna, and his daughter Ruth, comes from the Hanna papers in the Manuscript Room of the Library of Congress. *Hanna* by Thomas Beer (Knopf, New York, 1928) is an excellent study. There is also material in my own book, *The Bosses* (Putnam's, New York, 1964). Two volumes of *Our Times—The Nineties* and *The Turn of the Century*—by Mark Sullivan (Scribner's, New York, 1926) give a good sense of the American scene at the time. An excellent article about this period appeared in the Westminster *Gazette* (Feb. 18, 1905).

CHAPTER THREE

Some of the most vivid description of this era in Washington will be found in *Never a Dull Moment* by Countess Marguerite Cassini (Harper, New York, 1956). Alice Roosevelt Longworth's autobiography, *Crowded Hours* (Scribner's, New York, 1933), is better in other areas. *Princess Alice* by James Brough (Little, Brown, Boston, 1975) is also helpful. But Ethel Barrymore's memoirs, *Memories* (Harper, New York, 1955), is meager.

Alice Roosevelt Longworth, who was there, provided a personal account of Cissy's wedding in an interview, but the newspapers and magazines in Washington, as well as in New York, were all thorough in their coverage of it, particularly *The New York Times,* the Washington *Evening Star,* and the Washington *Times. Elite* magazine was similarly good. *Town Topics,* whose "facts" were often highly suspect, was highly accurate in its intimate descriptions of the wedding and its aftermath. But the best stories of the wedding and the honeymoon came from Cissy herself, in her accounts to some of her close friends such as the Waldrops and Ann Smith. She also referred to these events in various interviews over the years.

A general book on this period, on the mores of the time, is *1900* by Edward Tannenbaum (Anchor Press, New York, 1976). *Washington Life* by Ellen Maury Slayden (Harper & Row, New York, 1962) gives a good view of Washington in this period. The files of the magazine *The 400* are also worth researching for this period.

CHAPTER FOUR

Cissy's sworn testimony at her divorce trial in Chicago, as recorded by the Circuit Court of Cook County, January 13, 1917, offers the most comprehensive look at her life with Count Gizycki. It's both detailed and graphic.

Countess Wurmbrand's letters from Count Gizycki, again, are invaluable here. The material on Warsaw comes from interviews with people who were there at the time, particularly Rafal J. Lepkowski, a former diplomat of the Polish embassy. Of considerable value, too, is *My Life Here and There* by Princess Catacuzene (Scribner's, New York, 1921). A good book of background is *The Blaze: Reminiscences of Volhynia* by Sophie Kossak (Allen & Unwin, London, 1927).

Again, Cissy's *Fall Flight* provides the most personal descriptions of this time of her life. *A Matter of Life and Death* by Virgilia Peterson (Atheneum, New York, 1961) gives another view of an American woman married to a Polish prince and living with him in Poland.

The report of Alice Roosevelt's wedding comes largely from her own memoirs and highly detailed newspaper reports of the time, especially from *The New York Times*.

CHAPTER FIVE

The intimate details of Cissy's relationship with Count Gizycki again come from her own courtroom testimony. The dramatic byplay in the chase and negotiations for the child was explicitly reported in the American press on a continuing basis. Probably the single best source on this are the files of the New York *World*. Cissy recounted many of these stories to some of her closest friends, and their memories generally jibe on this. The letter from Robert Patterson to President Taft is on file at the National Archives in Washington. So is the letter from President Taft to the Czar of Russia.

The references to McCormick come from the files of the Chicago

Inter-Ocean and the Chicago *American* as well as the *Tribune*. An interesting article on him appeared in *The Spectator* (May 6, 1905).

Princess Catacuzene's memoirs served as good background for this chapter, as did the files of *Elite* magazine.

CHAPTER SIX

Of particular importance for this chapter are the files of the Chicago *Tribune* and the New York *World*. Cissy's divorce court testimony was also pivotal.

A good insight into Chicago social life at this time, however partisan, can be found in several of Joseph Patterson's novels, particularly *A Little Brother of the Rich* (Grosset & Dunlap, New York, 1908). *The Fortnightly of Chicago* by Muriel Beadle (Regnery, Chicago, 1973) was also valuable. Another fine source is *Many Lives, One Love* by Fanny Butcher (Harper & Row, New York, 1972).

Count Johann Heinrich von Bernstorff wrote two books, *My Three Years in America* (Scribner's, New York, 1920) and *Memoirs of Count Bernstorff* (Random, New York, 1936), but, unfortunately, both are too diplomatic to be revealing. A good insight into the Count is contained in *The Zimmerman Telegram* by Barbara Tuchman (Macmillan, New York, 1958). *Latest Contemporary Portraits* by Frank Harris (Macauley, New York, 1927) also has an interesting evaluation. The files of *The New York Times* are rich in their coverage of Von Bernstorff. There is also some worthwhile material on him in *Mr. Wilson's War* by John Dos Passos (Doubleday, New York, 1962).

Charles Dewey acted with Cissy in the Aldis Theatre, and my interviews with him were especially valuable, and so were his privately printed memoirs, *As I Recall It* (lithographed by William & Hintz, Washington, D.C.). A lesser source on the Aldis Theatre , but worthwhile, is *My Chicago* by Anna Morgan (Seymour, Chicago, 1918). The Aldis plays were well reviewed in all the Chicago papers, and even in the Boston *Evening Transcript*. The Chicago Historical Society has an extensive file on the subject.

George Seldes in *Lords of the Press* (Blue Ribbon Books, New York, 1941) wrote a pertinent assessment of Colonel McCormick. *Editorials of Henry Watterson* compiled by Arthur Krock (Doran, New York, 1923) has some interesting newspaper comment on this period. Some of the 1912 Progressive party convention material comes from my book *Ballots & Bandwagons* (Rand McNally, Chicago, 1964).

My interviews with Cissy's daughter, Felicia Magruder, as well as Felicia's magazine articles on this period, were very valuable. The letter from Count Gizycki to Countess Wurmbrand, which was most revealing, was dated November 24, 1911.

CHAPTER SEVEN

Rose Crabtree's letters from Cissy, as well as her own recollections and those of her son, Hank—and their photographs—provide the intimate core of this chapter. Felicia's memories add a vital supplement, and so do her own articles on the subject in *Teton* magazine (Vol. 10, 1977) and *Vogue* (Apr. 1, 1965). There is also a good article about Rose Crabtree in *Delineator* magazine (Sept. 1922).

Some of the best materials are Cissy's own writings on the area in her novel *Glass Houses* (Minton Balch, New York, 1926) and in her articles for *Field and Stream* magazine (June and Sept. 1923) and *Liberty* (Oct. 24, 1925). In addition, Cissy wrote articles for the Chicago *Herald-Examiner*.

A fine source of material on this area at this time is the Archive of Contemporary History at the University of Wyoming, which also has some of Cal Carrington's letters. Ricks College supplied an interesting recorded interview, on tape, with Cal Carrington.

The Jackson Hole Library has an excellent section of reference books on the area, the best of which are: *Wyoming* (Oxford University Press, New York, 1941); *The Diary of a Dude Wrangler* by Struthers Burt (Scribner's, New York, 1924); *Homesteading With the Elk* by Bertha Chambers Gillette (Utah Printing Co., Salt Lake City, 1967); *Utah* (American Guide Series, Hastings House, New York, 1941). Struthers Burt also wrote a good article on Cal Carrington for the *Reader's Digest* (Oct. 1948). The files of the Jackson Hole *Guide* and the Jackson Hole *News* are excellent background sources. Again, the best are the interviews with Jackson Hole residents, many of whom knew Cissy, and some of whom worked for her.

Books of lesser value, but worth examining, include: *Jackson Hole* by Frank Calkins (Knopf, New York, 1973); *The Cocktail Hour in Jackson Hole* by Donald Hough (Norton, New York, 1951); and *Snow Above Town* by Donald Hough (Norton, New York, 1943).

CHAPTER EIGHT

There is a large library of good books on Chicago newspapers. *Madhouse on Madison Street* by George Murray (Follett, Chicago, 1965); *Before I Forget* by Burton Rascoe (Literary Guild, New York, 1937); *A Child of the Century* by Ben Hecht (Simon & Schuster, New York, 1954); and *Chicago: The Second City* by A. J. Liebling (Knopf, New York, 1952) are especially good. *The Front Page,* the play by Ben Hecht and Charles MacArthur, captures much of the mood.

For general Chicago background at this time, besides the newspapers and magazines, there is *Chicago With Love* by Arthur Meeker (Knopf, New York, 1955) and Meeker's previously mentioned book, *Prairie Avenue,* as well as the other aforementioned Chicago books by Fanny Butcher and Lloyd Lewis and Henry Justin Smith. John Tebbel's *American Dynasty* (Doubleday, New York, 1947) and Robert Casey's *Chicago, Medium Rare* (Bobbs Merrill, New York, 1949) both contain some excellent material.

Rascoe's book, *Before I Forget,* is also a great source on Walter Howey and Joseph Patterson. Two other very good sources on Patterson are *Tell It to Sweeney* by John Chapman (Doubleday, New York, 1961) and *Deadlines and Monkeyshines* by J. J. McPhaul (Prentice-Hall, Englewood Cliffs, N.J., 1962).

The best single source I found on Walter Howey was Adela Rogers St. Johns, both in her interviews with me and in her books, particularly *The Honeycomb* (Doubleday, New York, 1969).

Descriptions of Borah come from Cissy's book *Glass Houses,* as well as from the Chicago and New York newspapers. The Harding material was in my book *Ballots & Bandwagons* and some of it is from *Only Yesterday* by Frederick Lewis Allen (Harper, New York, 1931). A more comprehensive source is *The Shadow of Blooming Grove* by Francis Russell (McGraw-Hill, New York, 1968). *Borah* by Claudius O. Johnson (Longmans, New York, 1936) is of some value for information on both Borah and Harding, but then so is *Chip off My Shoulder* by Thomas L. Stokes (Princeton University Press, Princeton, N.J., 1940), and it is a more interesting book. Of lesser importance, but worth checking: *The Mirrors of Washington,* Anonymous (Putnam's, New York, 1921) and *The Puppet Show of the Potomac* by Rufus Dart II (McBride, New York, 1934).

The article on Joliet prison by Cissy Patterson was in *New Republic* (Jan. 27, 1917).

A book of interest on the *Tribune* was *James Keeley* by James Weber Linn (Bobbs Merrill, New York, 1937). Charles Dewey's memoirs are also pertinent to this chapter.

Cissy's article on the Salmon River trip was in *Field and Stream* (June, 1923).

CHAPTER NINE

Interviews with Felicia and her letters to Rose Crabtree and my interviews in Jackson Hole were all basic for this chapter. The Agnes Meyer papers in the

Manuscript Room of the Library of Congress offer key research. The William Bullitt papers at Yale University are less valuable, except for more general background.

Drew Pearson's papers, now at the University of Texas, have much to offer. Even more so are interviews with his widow and his close friends. Oliver Pilat has written an excellent book, *Drew Pearson* (Harper & Row, New York, 1973).

Some good books on this period in Paris include: *The Best Times* by John Dos Passos (New American Library, New York, 1966); *The Left Bank Revisited* (selections from the Paris *Tribune)* edited by Hugh Ford (Pennsylvania State University Press, University Park, 1972); *Shakespeare & Co.* by Sylvia Beach (Harcourt Brace, New York, 1956); *The Amateur Publisher* by Hugh Ford (Macmillan, New York, 1975); and *Paris Was Yesterday* by Janet Flanner (Viking, New York, 1972).

The files of *The New Yorker* magazine of this period, especially the Letters From Paris by Janet Flanner, are also excellent background.

The record of the land sale is in the Teton County Court, in Jackson Hole.

Nan Britton's book, *The President's Daughter* (Guild, New York, 1927), is barely of passing interest. *The Inside Story of the Harding Tragedy* by Harry M. Daugherty (Churchill, New York, 1932) is much more important.

Most relevant is Cissy Patterson's article in *Harper's Bazaar,* "A Sentimental Journey From Fifth Avenue to Warsaw." Her hunting articles in *Field and Stream* are also necessary here.

CHAPTER TEN

Interviews with Dr. Alvan Barach, and access to his papers and articles, were very valuable to assessment of Cissy in this chapter. Some of his more interesting articles include: "A Doctor's Humanity: An Obsessive Response to a Childhood Experience," (Bulletin of the New York Academy of Medicine, February 1971), "Promethean Anxieties," (Columbia University Forum, Fall, 1966), "A Physiologic Psychologic Function in Man," (Perspectives in Biology and Medicine, Summer 1974), and "The Impulse to Yield," (Journal of the American Geriatrics Society, March, 1963).

The Evalyn Walsh McLean papers at the Library of Congress and the Herbert Bayard Swope papers at the Special Collections Library at Boston University all have key bearing on this chapter. So do the Pearson papers and the Agnes Meyer papers.

The best material on Elmer Schlesinger comes from members of his family, his son and other relatives, and friends. The files of *The New York Times* have considerable background on him. Similarly, the best material on Swope also comes from his son and daughter and friends, particularly Robert Moses. E. J. Kahn has written an excellent book, *The World of Swope* (Simon & Schuster, New York, 1965).

Among the most interesting sources on the Algonquin Round Table and its social set are *The Twenties* by Edmund Wilson (Farrar, Straus, Giroux, New York, 1975); *Blessed Are the Debonair* by Margaret Case Harriman (Rinehart, New York, 1956); *Do Not Disturb* by Frank Case (Stokes, New York, 1940); *The Vicious Circle* by Margaret Case Harriman (Rinehart, New York, 1951); *George S. Kaufman* by Howard Teichman (Atheneum, New York, 1972); *The Algonquin Wits* by Robert E. Dresnan (Citadel, New York, 1968); *New York City Folklore* by Benjamin A. Botkin (Random, New York, 1956); *The 20's* by Frederick J. Hoffman (Macmillan, New York, 1949).

There are also several fine books for more general background of the period: *The Aspirin Age,* edited by Isabel Leighton (Simon & Schuster, 1949); *Mrs. Astor's Horse* by Stanley Walker (Stokes, New York, 1935); and a splendid collection of articles from the New York *World, The Best in the World,* edited by John K. Hutchens and George Oppenheimer (Viking, New York, 1973).

Background for the Coolidge material comes from various interviews as well as several good books: *A Puritan in Babylon* by William Allen White (Macmillan, New York, 1958); *Meet Calvin Coolidge* edited by Edward Connery Latham (Stephen Greene Press, Brattleboro, Vt., 1960); *Calvin Coolidge, The Quiet President* by Donald R. McCoy (Macmillan, New York, 1960); and *Grace Coolidge and Her Era* by Ishbel Ross (Dodd Mead, New York, 1962). H. L. Mencken wrote an excellent piece on Coolidge which may be found in *The Vintage Mencken,* edited by Alistair Cooke (Knopf, New York, 1955).

The files of the New York *Daily News* are a virtual barometer of Joe Patterson's editorial evolution. They also contain Cissy Patterson's article on the Ruth Snyder murder trial.

Waldrop's book on McCormick again is indispensable.

Background on the depression comes from Mark Sullivan's *Our Times, The Twenties* (Scribner's, New York, 1935). Many of Cissy Patterson's letters are scattered among her family and friends, and they are revealing of this period.

CHAPTER ELEVEN

Absolutely vital for this chapter and for the book is the extensive material in the Brisbane-Hearst-Patterson collection at the George Arents Research Library at Syracuse University. Aside from the Crabtree letters, no correspondence is more intimate, or more important.

Important also are the taped interviews with Marion Davies that form the basis of the book by Pamela Pfau and Kenneth S. Marx, *The Times We Had* (Bobbs Merrill, Indianapolis, 1975). *Citizen Hearst* by W. A. Swanberg (Scribner's, New York, 1961) is a comprehensive work on its subject. *Hearst, Lord of San Simeon* by Oliver Carlson and Ernest Sutherland Bates (Viking, New York, 1936) also offers some provocative facts. Of lesser interest is *Marion Davies* by Fred Lawrence Guiles (McGraw-Hill, New York, 1972). Ilka Chase in *Past Imperfect* (Doubleday, New York, 1942) offers some interesting anecdotes about Hearst, and so does Louella Parsons in *The Gay Illiterate* (Doubleday, New York, 1944) and in *Tell It to Louella* (Putnam's, New York, 1961).

Interviews with Felicia on this period were again most important.

Burton Rascoe's book, particularly in reference to Joe Patterson at this time, was also valuable.

CHAPTER TWELVE

Frank Waldrop said that the best and only way to research the newspaper career of Cissy Patterson properly was to read the product, the Washington *Herald,* and later the Washington *Times-Herald.* He was, of course, absolutely right. Her newspapers are the sure index to Cissy's evolution as an editor, the offbeat ideas, and the high imagination. The papers' files are an absolute gold mine for Cissy research.

Much of the Hearst material, the Marion Davies tapes, the Drew Pearson papers, and, most of all, the Brisbane letters, are of real meaning here. The core, however, is still the interviews with so many of the *Herald* staff who remember so much. The best, for this section, were Adela Rogers St. Johns and Mason Peters.

The books by and about Alice Roosevelt Longworth add some material, as does, in particular, an article from *The Saturday Evening Post* (Sept. 19, 1931). For Nicholas Longworth, *The New York Times* gave him extensive coverage, as did the Washington *Post* and the Washington *Star* and, of course, the Washington *Herald.*

CHAPTER THIRTEEN

The Maryland Historical Society has a good file on Dower House. The British Psychical Society in London, however, had little to offer on its research of Dower House ghosts.

The key interviews for this chapter were with Charles Dewey, Happy Robinson, Carolyn Shaw, and, again, Adela Rogers St. Johns—among many others. Frank Waldrop, with his superb memory, was absolutely vital.

The Brisbane letters form a backbone for this period.

Of interest in books are *Washington Merry-Go-Round* by Drew Pearson and Robert S. Allen (Liveright, New York, 1931) and *More Washington Merry-Go-Round* by the same authors (Liveright, New York, 1932); *The Aspirin Age* by Isable Leighton (Touchstone / Simon and Schuster, New York, 1968), which furnishes an excellent survey; *Look Back With Joy,* by Beatrice B. Fahnestock (Andromeda, Washington, D.C., 1975), a personal reminiscence of the era and its social life; *Five Million Words Later* by Bruce Bliven (John Day, New York, 1970); *There's No Place Like Washington* by Vera Bloom (Putnam's, New York, 1944); *High Low Washington,* Anonymous (Lippincott, Philadelphia, 1932); and *Dateline Washington* edited by Cabell Phillips (Doubleday, New York, 1949).

CHAPTER FOURTEEN

The Franklin D. Roosevelt Library at Hyde Park, New York, is a vast, endless reservoir of information. The basic reference work is the multivolume collection *The Public Papers and Addresses of Franklin D. Roosevelt* compiled by Samuel I. Rosenman (Random, New York, 1938). Of the biographies of FDR, the best are Arthur Schlesinger, Jr.'s *The Coming of the New Deal* (Houghton Mifflin, Boston, 1958); James MacGregor Burns's *Roosevelt: The Lion and the Fox* (Harcourt Brace, New York, 1956); and Frank Friedel's *Franklin D. Roosevelt: The Triumph* (Little, Brown, Boston, 1956). Eleanor Roosevelt's autobiography, *This I Remember* (Harper, New York, 1949), and Joseph P. Lash's *Eleanor and Franklin* (Norton, New York, 1971) are also important. I also made use of my own notes and materials on the Roosevelts from *The Human Side of FDR*, which I wrote with Richard Harrity (Duell, Sloan & Pearce, New York, 1960) and our *Eleanor Roosevelt* (Duell, Sloan & Pearce, New York, 1958).

The FDR Library also has some correspondence between the Roosevelts and Cissy and some photographs.

The Agnes Meyer papers were also good at this time, and so were the Evalyn Walsh McLean papers. Of some interest is Evalyn Walsh McLean's autobiography, *Father Struck It Rich* (Little, Brown, Boston, 1935).

The Oral History Library at Columbia University has the tape of the account of Eugene Meyer of how Cissy Patterson unknowingly stirred in him the idea of buying the Washington *Post*. A definitive book on the *Post* is *The Washington Post* by Chalmers M. Roberts (Houghton Mifflin, Boston, 1977).

The best single book I have found to catch the facts and feeling of the Bonus March is *Another Such Victory* by John D. Weaver (Viking, New York, 1948). The best single book I have found to catch the facts and feeling of the thirties is *Just Around The Corner* by Robert Bendiner (Dutton, New York, 1968). For some supplemental facts there is *The Bonus March* by Rogers Daniels (Greenwood, Westport, Conn. 1971).

For the 1932 Democratic convention, I used my book *Ballots & Bandwagons*.

The Brisbane letters and the *Herald* files were as indispensable as the interviews.

Also, the Women's Press Club of Washington has a library of its skits and of clippings, which were highly useful.

CHAPTER FIFTEEN

Most valuable here were the Harold Ickes papers at the Library of Congress, Manuscript Division, as well as his three-volume autobiography, *The Secret Life of Harold L. Ickes: The First Thousand Days, The Inside Struggle,* and *The Lowering Clouds* (Simon and Schuster, New York, 1954). Also of interest is *Autobiography of a Curmudgeon* (Reynal & Hitchcock, New York, 1943).

Interviews with Waldrop, St. Johns, and Felicia were of particular importance for this chapter. So were Luvie Pearson and the Pearson papers and books. The Bullitt papers at Yale were of lesser importance. Several books did offer some interesting sidelights on Bullitt: *The Diplomats* edited by Gordon Craig and Felix Gilbert (Princeton University Press, Princeton, N.J., 1953); *William C. Bullitt and the Soviet Union* by Beatrice Farnsworth (Indiana University Press, Bloomington, 1967); and *Architects of Illusion* by Lloyd C. Gardner (Quadrangle Books, Chicago, 1970). There was also an interesting reference to Cissy in a letter from Bullitt to Roosevelt in *For the President,*

Personal and Secret; Correspondence Between Franklin D. Roosevelt and William C. Bullitt (Houghton Mifflin, Boston, 1972).

Paul F. Healy's interview with Ash DeWitt was very valuable. His book *Cissy* (Doubleday, New York, 1966) is particularly important for the newspaper years. Bob Considine's newspaper and magazine articles about Cissy and his interviews with me were also illuminating.

The New Yorker profile on Joseph Patterson (Aug. 6, 13, and 20, 1938) provided good insight. Felicia provided even more, and so did Patterson's son James.

CHAPTER SIXTEEN

Cissy's personal letters to friends and family were of great interest here, but the stories she told to friends, who retold them to me, were of equal importance.

Interviews with Waldrop, Barach, Peters, and McLaughlin's daughter Barbara Kreutz were significant here, and so were Paul Healy's interviews with Jackie Martin and Evie Robert—who were no longer alive when I began this book.

An interesting reference book was *The President Speaks off the Record* by Harold Brayman (Dow Jones, Princeton, 1976). On the social side: *Embassy Row* by Hope Ridings Miller (Holt, Rinehart & Winston, New York, 1969). Others of value: *Washington By-line* by Bess Furman (Knopf, New York, 1949); *Let Them Eat Caviar,* by George Abell and Evelyn Gordon (Dodge, New York, 1936); *Leaning on a Column,* by George Dixon (Lippincott, Philadelphia, 1961); and *Washington Quadrille* by Jonathan Daniels (Doubleday, New York, 1968). An excellent social survey of this period is *The Washington Game* by William Wright (Saturday Review Press, New York, 1974).

A basic book on Washington, D.C., is the one done by the Federal Writers' Project, *Washington—City and Capital,* (American Guide Series, Washington, D.C., 1937).

The incident of the cherry trees was documented in great detail in the Washington press, but there are also references in the records of FDR's press conferences and in his correspondence in the Hyde Park Library.

Ladies of the Press by Ishbel Ross (Harper, New York, 1936) is highly informative.

CHAPTER SEVENTEEN

Frank Waldrop wrote a number of excellent articles on Poland and the Potockis for the Washington *Times-Herald,* and Ann Smith supplemented this information for me with her own very complete file of letters and papers.

Igor Cassini was detailed in his interviews about his participation at this time, and, similarly, in his book *I'd Do It All Over Again,* written with Jeanne Molli (Putnam's, New York, 1977). Cassini's *Times-Herald* columns are particularly pertinent and ,interesting, and so are those of his former wife, Austine, now Mrs. William Randolph Hearst. Interviews with Mrs. Hearst were highly revealing.

Flower and Smoke by Felicia Gizycka (Scribner's, New York, 1939) should be read in this context, and so should her *The House of Violence* (Scribner's, New York, 1932).

A number of books on Henry Luce and his wife should be read for their relevance here, particularly, *Luce and His Empire* by W. A. Swanberg (Scribner's, New York, 1972) and *Time Inc.* by Robert T. Elson (Atheneum, New York, 1968). The files of *Time* magazine during this period are also essential reading.

Another book backgrounding Joseph Patterson is *The News* by Leo E. McGivena and others. The files of the New York *Daily News* are also necessary reading for this time, particularly the editorial pages.

Political Animals by Walter Trohan (Doubleday, New York, 1975) has much to say about both Cissy and Washington at this time. So do Oliver Pilat in his Pearson book and T. Harry Williams in *Huey Long* (Knopf, New York, 1969). Agnes Meyer's autobiography, *Out of These Roots* (Little, Brown, Boston, 1953), contains added reflections.

The material on Sarasota came primarily from interviews there, as did the material on the circus.

American Journalism by Frank Luther Mott (Macmillan, New York, 1950) is a comprehensive book, well worth reading. So is *First Rough Draft* by Chalmers M. Roberts (Praeger, New York, 1973).

Of little value is *In Search of Complications* by Eugene de Savitsch, M.D. (Simon & Schuster, New York, 1940). He tells little of what we need to know.

For general quotations, I found Allen Andrews' *Quotations for Speakers and Writers* (Newnes Books, London, 1969) a valuable book.

CHAPTER EIGHTEEN

The *Times-Herald* files are the backbone of this chapter, especially the coverage of the war and the politics, the columns, and the society news.

The papers of FDR, Marion Davies, Bullitt, Ann Smith, and Rose Crabtree are all of import here.

Interviews with Walter Trohan in Ireland supplied many pieces of the mosaic of the Cissy story. So did the interviews with Mrs. Robert McCormick, Felicia Magruder, and Dr. Alvan Barach. George Abell and Mrs. Emily Stafford furnished good sidelights. So did Mrs. John Bolling and Happy Robinson. But the key interviews were those with Frank Waldrop and his wife Eleanor. Their memories were vital in fleshing out this story.

EPILOGUE

Sidney Epstein, a prime figure in this epilogue, supplied the full details for this section. Court records supplied the actual details and the inventory of possessions. Newspapers in Washington and New York were exhaustive on reporting the story of the will.

Acknowledgments

The birth of this book took three years, with research that ranged from Wyoming to Warsaw, Poland, including interviews with hundreds of people and the checking of many collections of private letters and papers. To all those people who contributed time or materials, I acknowledge my deep gratitude.

Frank Waldrop, Cissy's editor, closest daily associate, and friend—and, finally, the executor of her will—unstintingly gave me the benefit of his time, his wisdom, and his remarkable memory, as well as of his files and photographs. His wife, Eleanor, had her own personal contribution. Few knew Cissy as intimately as they did.

Countess May Wurmbrand in Monte Carlo, with a marvelously rich memory, recaptured the world of her dear friend, Count Gizycki, and made him come alive for me. She also provided me with a very revealing letter from the Count at the time of his divorce, as well as a rare photograph, and she detailed the courtship of Cissy and the Count in Vienna. Countess Wurmbrand's nephew in Vienna amplified her recollections.

Alice Roosevelt Longworth was vivid in recalling the Washington days of the young Cissy whom she loved, and the later Cissy with whom she feuded and whom she afterward admired. Rose Crabtree, whom Cissy loved more deeply than any other friend, was most moving in reconstructing their lives and adventures in Wyoming. I am appreciative for her permission to reprint from their correspondence and use some photographs. I am also grateful to her son, Hank, for his help.

Dr. Alvan Barach, Cissy's analyst and friend for many years, provided insight into her years in New York and the troubles of her soul. James Patterson was kind in making available some letters about his father, Joseph Patterson.

Paul F. Healy was generous in providing me with his notes and papers from his own book on Cissy. Particularly important were his interviews with some people who had died before I had begun my book. Oliver Pilat was equally kind in sending me his notes and records from the biography he wrote on Drew Pearson. I also appreciate the file of clippings, papers, letters, and photographs—as well as a painting of Cal Carrington—provided by Cissy's friend, Mrs. Ann Smith. Charles Dewey gave me access to his privately printed memoirs, which described his days as an amateur actor in Chicago with Cissy, as well as his time in Poland. I also thank Mrs. Katherine Graham for permission to see the papers of her mother, Mrs. Agnes Meyer. Cissy's grandniece, Mrs. Alice Arlen, who also wrote a book about Cissy, was good enough to share her memories with me.

I am indebted to my dear old friend, Paul S. Green, who followed up so superbly on many interviews in Washington. He also checked out all kinds of information for me. Paul was invaluable. Shirley Green, the best source of picture information in Washington, helped find some key photographs.

Joseph Borkin, who knows more about Washington than almost anyone else, was a prime source of information—not only about his friend and client Drew Pearson but about many other key people in my book. I am especially thankful to Borkin for introducing me to his friend and coauthor, Frank Waldrop.

Janina Hoskins, specialist on Poland and East Europe at the Reference Department of the Library of Congress, provided help above and beyond the call of professional duty. She not only found genealogical records, histories, and old maps of the Gizycki estate area, but she introduced me to former

Polish officials who knew both Cissy and the Gizyckis and their world of Austria and Poland. Particularly helpful was Rafal J. Lepkowski, a former diplomat of the Polish embassy. Miss Hoskins gave me the benefit of her memories and experiences in that world and provided translators for many documents.

Joan Gold Lufrano, a good friend and researcher in Chicago, made my book a personal cause in searching for documents, articles, books, and photographs and following up on my leads and interviews.

Larry Hall did some of the preliminary research in Jackson Hole, Wyoming, like the fine reporter he once was, and provided many leads for me to explore. Orin Nisenson became a private detective in rooting out facts about Cissy's early Harvard beau and about Miss Hersey's School in Boston.

My dear friend Guyo Tajiri, still a superb reporter and editor, checked on a variety of things for me in the California area and interviewed Elmer Schlesinger's son, Peter. Mrs. Ann Ebner in London was once again available to follow up on some of my research there.

My nephew Robert Pastel had his research initiation at the George Arents Research Library at Syracuse University on the Brisbane papers collection. He did an excellent job, and I am grateful to Manuscript Librarian Carolyn A. Davis and her staff—especially Ed Lyons—for assisting him. I also express my thanks to Mrs. Chase Mellon, and her son Seward, for permission to quote from the Brisbane letters.

The staff of the Osterreiches Staatsarchiv Kriegsarchiv and the Osterreiches Nationalbibliothek in Vienna were helpful and very patient with my attempt to reconstruct Cissy's life in Vienna. I must give special thanks to Leopold Moser, Dr. R. Steininger, Helge-Franz Hanauska, and Robert Kittler. My thanks, too, to Maci Borski in the Polish embassy in Vienna and Sylwester Kruppa in Warsaw.

For their help at the Chicago Historical Society, I am grateful to Archie Motley, Larry Viscochil, and their staff. At the Chicago *Tribune* archive, my special thanks to Mrs. Lee Major and Harold Hutchings. My thanks, also, to Gene M. Gressley, director of the Contemporary History Archive at the University of Wyoming, for making available Cal Carrington's letters. And my appreciation to Dr. Rulon S. McCarrey of Ricks College in Idaho for an oral history tape made by Cal Carrington shortly before his death.

The New York State Library Staff was cooperative, particularly Mrs. Jean F. Hargrave. I am indebted to the staff of the Westport Public Library, in Westport, Connecticut, especially Diane Flynn and Ruth Adams, and to Donald Gustafson of the Connecticut State Library. My thanks also to Jean Kirol of the Teton County Library in Jackson Hole, Wyoming, and Arthur C.

495

Tannenbaum of the Elmer Holmes Bobst Library at New York University for making available to me the files and photographs of the defunct New York *Herald Tribune.*

I am also grateful to the Humanities Research Center of the University of Texas and its director, F. W. Roberts; the staff of the Oral History Library at Columbia University; the staff of the Arthur and Elizabeth Schlesinger Library on the History of Women in America at Radcliffe College; the Hoover Institution on War, Revolution, and Peace at Stamford University; the patient staff of the Reading Room at the British Museum in London and also at the Public Records Office in London; the friendly people at the Sarasota Historical Museum in Sarasota, Florida; and to Timothy Beard at the Genealogical Room of the New York Public Library.

Once again I am indebted to Christine Lane and the staff of the Oyster Bay, Long Island, Public Library, including J. Peter Johnson, Ken Weil, Marianna Hof, Annette Macedonio, Gene McGrath, Gloria Hanrahan, Evelyn McNamara, Martha Layton, Ellen Coschignano, Fran Mancini, and Lori McNamara Ranaldo.

Most welcome was the contribution of Barbara McLaughlin Kreutz of material on her father, Frederick McLaughlin; and of William Friedman, on his uncle, Elmer Schlesinger. Earl Pruce researched the picture file at the Baltimore *News-American,* and Jane Freundel in Washington; Harold Kertz, Washington attorney for Felicia Magruder, opened his files on their fight to break Cissy's will; Mrs. Robert McCormick availed me of her letters and photographs; Ben Bradlee permitted me to reprint pictures from the Washington *Post* files; Luvie Pearson gave me access to the Drew Pearson papers, now at the University of Texas; Herbert Bayard Swope, Jr., allowed me to examine his father's files at Boston University's Mugar Memorial Library—and my special thanks to its Director of Special Collections, Dr. Howard B. Gotlieb. Hy Turner opened to me his splendid collection of books on newspaper history; Kenneth S. Marx sent me the original transcript of his taped interviews with Marion Davies; and Michael Myers found the transcript of the court trial of Cissy's divorce from Count Gizycki.

In France: my thanks to Aline Mosby and Louise Spicehandler for checking information for me. And, to my friend John Byrne, for his patient detective work on the Riviera.

In Ireland: my thanks to Walter Trohan for his hospitality and his great help.

In Jackson Hole, Wyoming: I appreciate the help of Ellen and Jack Dornan, Mildred Buchenroth (who also made available to me a valuable clipping), Dr. Don MacLeod, Mrs. Albert Feuz, Fern Nelson, Eddie Schultz, Slim Lawrence, Herbert Wall, Roger LaVake, and Almer Nelson. I am particularly grateful to the working staff of the Flat Creek Ranch and the Bar B C. I also appreciate the letters of Mrs. Thurman Arnold. And I am grateful to Herbert F. Wall for enabling me to visit Flat Creek Ranch and to Rex Ross for all his help. My added thanks to Gene Downer of *Teton* magazine.

In Florida: I am indebted to Peter Pollack, Mrs. Rose Palmer, Ida North, Mr. and Mrs. Reginald McVitty, Pat Buck, Sally Glendenning, Rudy Bundy, Helen Griffiths, William Lawson, Mrs. Rose Boyer, Mrs. Alden Hatch, Art Clark, Mrs. Mary Sanford, Lois Wilson, Kitty and John Denson, Charles Van Rennselaer, Sara and Irving Larner. I am also obliged to Ed A. St. Philip for his detailed tour of Cissy's home, now the Gulf and Bay Club.

In Chicago: among the many who were so helpful, I must list Mrs. John McCutcheon, Mr. and Mrs. Edward Arpee, Mr. and Mrs. Rosecrans Baldwin, Mrs. Clive Runnels, Max Hart, Willard King, Frank D. Mayer, Jr., Mrs. R. Wintherbotham Shaw, Frank Taussig, Mr. and Mrs. Arthur Veysey, Judge Abraham Marovitz, Mrs. Nancy Schlesinger Leboldt, Judge Julius Hoffman, Arthur Schultz, Paul Welling, Mrs. Clifford Rodman, David Weil, Robert Rosenman, Athlyn Deshais Faulkner, and Mrs. Sidney Haskins. My thanks also to the managers of the Onwentsia Club and the Saddle and Cycle Club in Chicago for making their files available, and to Mrs. Jane Dick.

In Washington: there are too many names to mention, and I ask understanding from those whose names are not here. Among those, however, who helped so much to recreate Cissy's Polish background, aside from Miss Hoskins and Mr. Lepkowski, I must also add Ann Gorski, whose family Cissy befriended and supported; George Lasocki, who served as Cissy's funnel for her financial aid to so many Polish friends; John de Rosen, who knew many family stories in Poland about Cissy and the Count. Gladys McEeney Werlich, whose husband served with the American embassy in Poland at the time Cissy was there, was also Cissy's neighbor and friend in Washington, and her contribution was vivid.

Those who worked in Washington on the *Herald* or, later, the *Times-Herald,* and who helped me in graphically detailing their working years with Cissy, include: Adela Rogers St. Johns, whose memory was prodigious and invaluable; Mason Peters, Harry A. (Happy) Robinson, Mrs. W. R. Hearst, Jr., Bob Considine, Sidney Epstein, Betty Brennan, Dick Hollander, Igor Cassini, Sam Shaeffer, George Abell, Betty Vitol, and Page Wilson. Among others I must list: Bob Addie, Robert Allen, Dick Borwick, Katherine Brooks, Billy Flythe, Edward Folliard, Myron Glasser, Leo Hochstetter, Frank Holeman, Dolph Holling, Edward Hotze, Russell Jones, Mrs. Arthur Krock, Veda Ward Marcatonio, Kay McCarter, Marie McNair, Jim McNamara, Inga Runwald Hook, Arthur Scott, Lee Wade, and Kitty Wiley. I am also indebted to Carolyn Shaw, who served as Cissy's secretary and who remembered so much, and to Cissy's butler, Archie Lye, who let me have some of his home movies of Cissy; and to the family of Mike Flynn, who let me use their clippings and photographs.

Others in Washington whose help was of so much value include Hope Ridings Miller, former society editor of the Washington *Post;* Arthur Newmyer, Jr., whose father was once Cissy's publisher; Kay Halle, whose knowledge of Washington is unique; Chuck Roberts, Mrs. Mary Sanford, Esther Tufty, Grace Tully, George Livingston Williams, Dr. William Chase, Ernest Cuneo, Tyler Abell, Yvonne de Augustin, Julius Duscha, Paul Kaplen, Arthur Godfrey, and Beatrice B. Fahnestock.

Elsewhere, I am indebted to Arthur Gelb, Robert Moses, Ann Landers, Mr. and Mrs. Arnold Gingrich, Julian Bach, Jr., Richard Clurman, Countess di Grassio, James A. Farley, Morris L. Ernst, Dorothy Schiff, Mrs. Walter Hirsch, Mrs. Robert Peck, Jane Swope Bryant, Louis D. Pecora, Mary Johnson Tweedy, Mrs. Lorraine Mintz, Katherine Pastel Daneshgar, Mrs. June Kelley, Dr. George Crile, Jr., Carl Larsen, Mrs. C. C. Kernke, Betty Copithorne, Diana Vreeland, Dorothy Denny, Peggy and Howard Katzander, Harvey Storch, Gene Rachlis, Jack Ryan, Ed Wergeles, Paul Saffron, Ed Plaut, Lloyd Garrison, Lady Benson, Ruth Montgomery, Etta Wanger, Tim Seldes, David Karr. My added thanks to Emily Stafford, Cissy's good friend, John Coit for his interview with Mason Peters, Susan Kismaric for her special help, and to Joseph Willen.

For their ever ready help on this, as on other books, I thank Joyce and Allan Andrews, Marvin Sleeper, Ed Cunningham, Richard Paul, Stanley Swinton and Naomi Van Clair.

For helping me translate necessary documents, I owe thanks to Doris Cramer, Dr. Arnold Price, and Ursula Sternberg. For her own considerable help, I thank my dear friend Olga Barbi, senior editor at *Newsweek.* For his wise psychological analysis of my cast of characters, I am also grateful to noted psychologist Dr. Murray Krim.

To Harriett and John Weaver, my dear friends, my deep gratitude, once again, for making my projects their own, and sending me a steady stream of clippings, research, memoranda, and excellent suggestions.

To Ruth and Larry Hall, my tried and true friends, who have not only corrected my galleys—as they have so often before—but whose comments have enriched my book: To them, my thanks and my love.

Without Mari Walker, my faithful friend and secretary, who has typed all my taped interviews and illegible notes and manuscripts—and who also gets so personally invoved in each of my projects—without her, this book might have been so much longer in the making.

My thanks, too, to Sophie Sorkin and her copy editing staff, particularly Kathleen Howard and James Daly.

My most personal thanks to my dear friend and former editor, Phyllis Grann, who first suggested that I write this book; my superb editors, Michael Korda and Nan Talese, who kept close in all stages of this book and did so much to shape it into what it is; to Peter Schwed for his personal encouragement; to Eve Metz, who designed the book; to my children Betsy and Tina, who helped so enormously in the research, and who are now expert researchers, and to my son Maury, who made his own contribution; but, most of all, to my wife, Marjorie Jean, who was the first to read my manuscript and edit it, and whose criticism was so valuable and encouragement so constant.

Index

506